Motivational Des

John M. Keller

Motivational Design for Learning and Performance

The ARCS Model Approach

 Springer

John M. Keller
Instructional Systems Program
Florida State University
3204G Stone Building
Tallahassee, FL 32306-4453
USA
jkeller@fsu.edu

ISBN 978-1-4419-1249-7   (hardcover)   e-ISBN 978-1-4419-1250-3
ISBN 978-1-4419-6579-0   (softcover)
DOI 10.1007/978-1-4419-1250-3
Springer New York Dordrecht Heidelberg London

Library of Congress Control Number: 2009938709

Printed on acid-free paper

Springer is part of Springer Science+Business Media (www.springer.com)

This book is dedicated to
Cecilia

Preface

- What are the critical components of learner motivation?
- What is the responsibility of a designer, instructor, counselor, coach, or parent for learner motivation?
- How can you determine what motivational tactics to use and when to use them?

It is customary to begin a book or major article about motivation by pointing out that it is a powerful influence on performance and that it is a complex aspect of human behavior. This book is no exception in that regard. Both of these generalizations are quite true, but it is also the case that having knowledge about motivational concepts and theories is seldom sufficient for a person who is trying to design learning environments that will stimulate and sustain their students' motivation. This book has been written for people who are involved in designing or delivering instruction. This includes instructional designers, performance technologists, trainers, teachers, curriculum developers, and anyone else who is responsible for stimulating and sustaining peoples' motivation to learn. The principles and methods in this book can be used by any of these people in school settings as well as private, public, and military sector training design and delivery. Furthermore, the approaches described in this book have been used in many international settings. One final point is that there are no prerequisites for students or professionals who use this book. It assumes no background in psychological or pedagogical theory.

Purpose

The aim of this book is to provide an introduction to the concept of motivational design and to then support it with knowledge of motivational concepts and theories, a systematic motivational design process, and tools to support motivational design activities. Motivational researchers have produced numerous strategies for stimulating or changing one or more specific components of learner motivation and all of them are useful within their specific area of application. However, the goal of this book is to present a generalized, systematic approach that is holistic in nature with regard to the various aspects of learner motivation. The book aims at being "self-sufficient" in that it provides a sufficient understanding of motivational concepts and theories to support the motivational design process and a thorough explanation of the design process itself.

Another goal of this book is to assist the reader in understanding motivational concepts within a framework that is broader than formal psychological research. Any reflection or research into the "why" questions concerning why people do what they do are motivational questions, and efforts to answer these questions are not restricted to any particular area of human inquiry. Scholars, philosophers, poets, novelists, and others have contributed much to our understandings of these questions. Science leads toward demonstrable principles but the other sources of knowledge can make valuable contributions to insight, understanding, and empathy. Clinicians, in the broad sense of the concept to include designers, teachers, and others, benefit from being able to interpret people's behaviors within the context of their values and experiences. I am convinced from long experience that it is helpful in understanding the richness of psychological concepts to see how they have been articulated by people with different perspectives and in different eras. Thus, there is a small amount of this type of cultural and intellectual background in the chapters where the foundational psychological concepts are described (Chapters 4 – 7), but the primary focus is on validated psychological constructs that are most relevant to creating motivating learning environments and motivated learners.

Background

My purpose in writing this book is to provide a validated, theoretically based, procedural approach to analyzing motivational problems and designing solutions. As illustrated by the various sections of this book, this approach has a long history of development, it has been implemented and validated in many different contexts, and it is already familiar to a large number of educators and educational researchers in many parts of the world. Some parts of the book contain material that I have developed and revised over many years and other parts describe recent developments. A fundamental assumption of my approach is that motivational design is a problem-solving process that proceeds from a rational analysis of the problems to the development of motivational strategies that are appropriate for those problems. This approach is not grounded in a particular psychological school of thought. Rather, it integrates virtually all of them by using systems theory and certain superordinate concepts to give each theory a place in the overall process where it provides the best explanations for relationships in that context. This organizational and conceptual structure is described in the first three chapters.

Organization

There are four parts to this book. The first part, Chapters 1, 2, and 3, contains descriptions of what is meant by motivation, especially in the context of learning, and to provide an in-depth explanation of what is meant by motivational design. This is followed by an explanation of the ARCS model which is the motivational theory and design process that provides the primary frame of reference in this book. "ARCS" is an acronym for Attention, Relevance, Confidence, and Satisfaction. Each of these concepts represents a cluster of related motivational concepts and theories. The ARCS model consists of this integration of research and best practices for motivation and a systematic approach to applying this knowledge to motivational problem solving.

In the second major part of the book (Chapters 4, 5, 6, and 7) there is a chapter for each of the four major components of the ARCS model. Together, these chapters provide a comprehensive summary of current and historically important motivational concepts and theories. Each chapter has a psychological foundations component that includes motivational concepts and theories that are relevant to that section. Each of these chapters also has a section containing a set of subcategories based on the major concepts in the chapter and examples of motivational strategies and tactics.

The third part of the book (Chapters 8, 9, and 10) describes the systematic motivational design process. This process is explained in detail and illustrated with procedural guides in the form of worksheets. The first two of these chapters include two embedded examples that illustrate how to use the templates and one of these examples extends into Chapter 10.

The final part of the book (Chapters 11 and 12) contains auxiliary information including alternative approaches to motivational design depending on the setting in which it is being used; tools such as checklists and measurement instruments to assist in application and research; ways of using the design process in a variety of delivery systems including online instructor-led and self-directed settings. Several recent areas of research that have promise for stimulating additional research are also included.

Acknowledgments

I am grateful to numerous people who have contributed to the development of my ideas during the past 30 years since I published my first paper on this topic which eventually resulted in what is now called the ARCS model. It is difficult to identify everyone and as always when compiling a list such as this it is all too easy to omit someone who should be included. Before I even present my list, I will apologize for that! Some of the people whose influence has been strongest due to their contributions to my ideas, their work with me as collaborators, and their research which led to confirmation of various aspects of the ARCS model are, in no particular order, Katsuaki Suzuki, Chan Min Kim, Markus Deimann, Hermann Astleitner, Seung-Yoon Oh, Tom Kopp, Sang Ho Song, Ruth Small, Bonnie Armstrong, Sanghoon Park, Bernie Dodge, and Tim Kane. I also want to express my deep appreciation to my wife, Cecilia, for her careful review of the text, her help with preparation of the final manuscript, and for enabling me to spend enormous amounts of my time on this manuscript.

Contents

Tables

Figures

1

Chapter 1 – The Study of Motivation

Forethought

Overheard in a coffee shop (Figure 1.1):

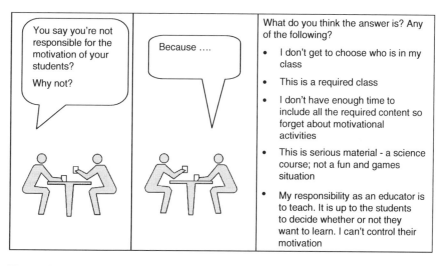

Figure 1.1. Coffee Shop Conversation.

When I work with teachers, trainers, and even professors and ask them about student motivation, I find that many of them do not want to be held responsible for learner motivation and the reasons they give are illustrated in Figure 1.1. Do you agree with any of these? Are they real reasons or just excuses for not accepting the motivational challenge? These attitudes are not uncommon among educators and in some ways they are right. It is true that you cannot control another person's motivation. People do things for their reasons, not yours. But it is also true that an educator or other person of authority influences the motivation of others. You can stimulate your students to learn, or you can kill their motivation. Your influence will not likely be neutral.

J.M. Keller, *Motivational Design for Learning and Performance,*
DOI 10.1007/978-1-4419-1250-3_1, © Springer Science+Business Media, LLC 2010

Introduction

Motivational design, the central topic of this book, provides a bridge between the study of motivation and the practice of enhancing or modifying people's motivation. On one side of the bridge are concepts, theories, and principles resulting from the study of human motivation, and on the other side are procedures, successful practices, and design processes that have resulted from the work of designers and practitioners whose aim is to improve learner motivation. Frequently, this bridge is represented as being one way as in the expression, "from theory to practice," which suggests that scientists discover basic principles and practitioners apply them. However, the process is not nearly so linear; that is, it is not possible to prescribe a direct application to practice for every motivational principle that has been empirically supported, and not every successful practice can be explained by a particular motivational concept. Why? One reason is that research-based motivational principles are normally derived from bounded settings and application settings are not bounded. Researchers manipulate some conditions in their studies while holding other conditions constant, as in experimental or quasi-experimental studies, or they make generalizations based on a limited number of observations in contextualized environments as in qualitative studies. As a general rule, in neither case can the results be directly applicable in an unqualified way to contexts of practice. Again, we can ask, "Why?" It is because a designer is not able to control environments in the same way as the researcher and there is too much variation in situations to be able to generalize from qualitative studies. The designer must endeavor to anticipate all of the actual and potential influences in specific, not generalized, situations and then determine which motivational factors can be addressed and to what degree. The designer then has to decide which tactics to use to modify the motivational characteristics of the learner's environment, or what direct interventions to use to help bring about desired changes in the learners. Thus, the bridge is two-way. Designers and practitioners learn from the work of researchers and create ways of incorporating that knowledge in practice, and researchers can learn from observing relationships in contexts of application which then provide a basis for theorizing and testing.

With respect to knowledge derived from practice, there are many talented people who are excellent motivators due to their experiences, personalities, knowledge, and intuition. But, a limitation of this knowledge is that like the researcher's knowledge it also tends to be bounded, but the boundaries refer to the individuals who possess the knowledge and talent rather than to the conditions that are established for research. In this case, it can be difficult to isolate the specific attributes of successful practices from the overall personality and actions of the individuals which limits the transferability of these skills and knowledge to other people. As a result of these two sets of conditions, learner motivation continues to be a leading challenge to educators. Even though there are many individuals who have specific motivational talents and there is an enormous amount of research on human motivation, there has been little systematic guidance for those who are trying to learn how to be more predictably effective in motivating their learners. A primary purpose of this book is to provide such guidance in the form of a motivational design process; that is, it consists of a general model of design that is grounded in motivational theory but also incorporates systematic audience analysis based on the primary components of human motivation to diagnose specific motivational problems that exist in a given situation. Then, the results of this analysis lead to the design and/or selection of motivational strategies that are compatible with the learners, instructors, and learning environment.

To summarize, the differences between motivational design and motivational theory are comparable to the differences between instructional design and theories of learning and instruction. In fact, this distinction occurs in almost every profession with regard to the relationship between clinical practices versus basic research. The assumption of this author is that a designer must be a problem solver who diagnoses situations and then employs all concepts and strategies that are appropriate, not a technician who selects and implements strategies from a list of prescriptions or a theoretician who restricts his perspectives to a single conceptual perspective. It is possible to work from a restricted conceptual foundation as, for example, the applied behavioral analyst, humanist, or constructivist, but this approach tends to impose limits on the way problems are defined and solutions are produced. It is assumed here that it is more fruitful and effective to use multidimensional approaches based on systematic problem solving. These and other issues are discussed in the remainder of this chapter which addresses the question of what is motivation and describes two of the conceptual issues that pervade the study of motivation.

What is Motivation?

Motivation refers broadly to what people *desire*, what they *choose* to do, and what they *commit* to do. In other words, investigations of motivation attempt to explain the deeply held concern among people as to *why* we do the things we do. Attempts to answer this question are found in virtually all areas of human inquiry and expression including literature, music, philosophy, and science. In Nikos Kazantzakas' *Zorba the Greek*, Zorba asks, "Why do the young die, why does anybody die?" Certainly the pathos in this scene following the cruel death of a widow when she violated village mores reflects times in people's lives when they are most desperate to answer the *why* question, but we also seek answers during good times. Writers, artists, and philosophers explore these issues and may have deep personal insights into these dynamics of life, but in psychology the goal is to gain scientific knowledge that can be used to predictably explain and improve human experience.

Motivation is generally defined as that which explains the *direction* and *magnitude* of behavior, or in other words, it explains what *goals* people choose to pursue and how actively or intensely they pursue them. This includes all goal -directed behavior ranging from the effort of an infant to attract its mother's attention to an anthropologist trying to discover the meanings embedded in the knotted string arrays that have survived from ancient Peruvian cultures. This definition describes the elements of motivation (magnitude and direction) but does not explain how or why people identify and choose their desired goals.

There are many theories and concepts that attempt to explain the dynamics and attributes of motivation and, generally speaking, these motivational theories can be grouped into four categories based on their presuppositions and domains of inquiry. The first group is grounded in human physiology and neurology and includes studies of genetics, physiological processes of arousal, and physiological processes of regulation. Another group consists of the behavioral approaches which include the well-known principles of positive reinforcement (operant conditioning), classical conditioning, incentive motivation, and environmental influences on sensory stimulation. The third group, which is the one that has been receiving the most attention in recent years, consists of cognitive theories including expectancy-value theories, social-motivation, attributional theories, and competence theories. The fourth group, which has been growing rapidly in popularity (yes, there are fads even in scientific research), includes studies of emotion and affect.

Categorizations such as this are useful for organizing existing areas of research, but they are limited in their utility for clinical applications and for generating new lines of research. Designers and clinicians require a holistic understanding of their area of specialization to support problem-solving approaches that include diagnosis and prescription. But, each established area of basic research and theory tends to have one or more dominant paradigms for inquiry and researchers tend not to cross over from one domain to another. For example, research on the effects of rewards on peoples' behaviors is based on observable consequences of implementing specific contingencies of reinforcement. People working in this tradition do not generally use self-report measures based on inferences about internal psychological characteristics of people.

This makes it difficult to develop a comprehensive theory that would generate new lines of inquiry and support holistic design or clinical diagnosis. In fact, if one works within the established approaches to research and development, it might not even be possible to develop a comprehensive theory. This is because the dominant epistemological perspective within a given theory is based on the quest for a single set of premises or principles to serve as its basis, and this assumption underlies both *hypothetico-deductive* and *empirical* theory development. In the hypothetico-deductive approach hypotheses are formulated based on the underlying theory and then tested by means of controlled research. In the empirical approach, studies are conducted, data are collected, and generalizations are formed which lead to the formulation of general principles or premises which then lead full circle to a hypothetico-deductive process of generating and testing hypotheses in an effort to validate the theory. Regardless of which starting point is adopted it may not be possible to develop a comprehensive theory based on a single theoretical perspective in the tradition of hypothetical-deductive theory development. Why? Because, as one moves from one theoretical area to another, one's presuppositions and domains of inquiry change. For example, a fundamental tenet of behavioral psychology is that one can develop an adequate theory of human behavior by examining people's reactions to environmental stimuli. Cognitive psychologists are opposed to this in principle. They believe it is not possible to adequately explain human behavior without considering internal activities of information processing. How then, one might ask, is it possible to have a holistic theory if at least two of the necessary components have incompatible assumptions?

The position taken in this book is that of a *perspectivalist* (Wheelwright, 1962). This is a philosophical position which posits that truth tends to be contextualized and relative. Each theory has certain presuppositions, methods for conducting research, and a domain within which investigations are conducted (Kuhn, 1970). Explanations of phenomena are true within the given context provided the research has a high level of internal validity, but the theory is generally not able to provide adequate explanations outside the given domain. Thus, behavioral psychologists are not able to provide explanations of internal information processing activities of people. Of course, they do not even try to do this because of their assumption that adequate explanations could be found in the relationships between observable environmental stimuli and human behaviors. But, even in principle they are not able to explain these presumably internal processes. However, it is possible to aggregate these theories into a higher level model that increases the totality of their explanatory power.

Such a theory has provided a foundation and frame of reference (Keller, 1979, 1983b) for the component parts of the ARCS model. Called the *Macro Model of Motivation and Performance*, it uses system theory to illustrate the relationships among the parts in terms of inputs, processes, and outputs (Figure 1.2). There are three rows in the model with the middle row representing major, measureable outputs of motivation and performance; the top row representing psychological characteristics that influence motivation, learning, performance, and attitudes; and the bottom row representing environmental influences on these behaviors.

The first three components of the ARCS model (attention, relevance, and confidence) are located in the upper left part of the diagram. The labels include the primary areas of psychological foundations for each part together with the ARCS model labels. They are separated into two

Personal Characteristics

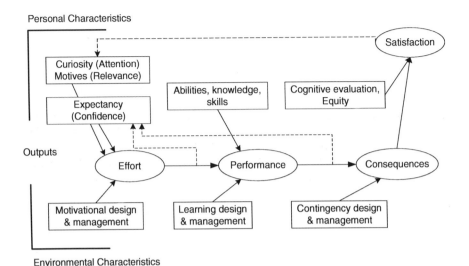

Environmental Characteristics

Figure 1.2. Keller's Macro Model of Motivation and Performance (Adapted from Keller, 1979, 1983b).

boxes in keeping with the expectancy-value theory of motivation, and the "value" box is further divided into curiosity (Attention) and motives (Relevance) in keeping with the primary conceptual foundation of each (see Chapter 3). The satisfaction category of the ARCS model is represented in the upper right of the diagram as a consequence of the integration of the actual consequences of performance with respect to the intrinsic and extrinsic outcomes that occur and the learner's cognitive evaluation of them. In other words, the learners will experience positive or negative feelings and attitudes when they compare the actual consequences of their performance to what they expected and what other people have received.

The Macro Model of Motivation and Performance also illustrates how motivation, which influences the amount of effort that a person will exert toward achieving a goal, combines with their knowledge and skills to influence their overall performance. The final part of the model acknowledges the role of the environment in motivation, learning, and performance. Motivation is influenced by the degree to which a teacher and the instructional materials provide a curiosity arousing and personally relevant set of stimuli together with challenge levels that encourage feelings of confidence and whether there is an absence of the kinds of stressors that would inhibit effort. Similarly, the instructional characteristics of the learning materials such as clear objectives and explanations combined with examples and learning activities will influence performance.

This system diagram also includes feedback loops. For example, there are dotted lines from two places on the output line back into expectancies. This illustrates that the degree to which the learner success-fully accomplishes the task and that success leads to the expected outcome will have an effect on one's expectancies for success in the future. There is also a feedback loop from Satisfaction to Attention and Relevance, which illustrates that one's actual experiences with the outcomes of a goal-oriented set of behaviors will influence the value one attaches to that goal in the future. In other words, if you work extremely hard to learn some gambling strategies and earn the money to pay for a trip to Las Vegas, and if you have an exciting and successful experience there, it may increase the value you attach to pursuing this type of activity in the future, but if it does not fulfill your expectations, it will probably decrease this desire.

ARCS-V: An Expansion of the Traditional ARCS Model

If a person's motivation to achieve a goal is strong enough there is little that will deter the person from persisting until the goal is accom-plished. This relationship is reflected in traditional expectancy-value theory which postulates that behavior potential is the product of the strength of a person's expectancy for success and the personal value of the desired goal as illustrated in Figure 1.2. This model also assumes automaticity between behavior potential and action; that is, a person will pursue the goal with the highest product of expectancy and value. However, this assumption is not always met. People have multiple goals and the strength of one goal can vary depending on the saliency of other goals. A boy named Markus has a strong desire to achieve a high grade in his introductory psychology course because he wants to major in psychology and have a career as a clinical therapist. Thus, his immediate goal of excelling in his introductory course has a high value because it is instrumentally connected to future goals. However, on a Saturday 1 week before his literature review paper is due, his friends want him to spend the afternoon playing soccer with them. He values his friend-ships and enjoys playing soccer, but he also knows that he still has to devote many hours to library research and summarizing research reports. What will he do? Will he tell his friends he can't do it because realistically he knows how much work he has to do, or will he rationalize his situation and play soccer because he still has 1 week before the deadline? The answer to this question will depend not only on the strength of his original intention but also, because of the goal conflict, on the strength of his *volitional* skills, otherwise known as *self-regulatory* behaviors.

Motivation generally refers to that which explains people's desires and choices, as reflected in expectancy -value theory, while volition refers to the actions people take to achieve a goal. Furthermore, volition can be viewed as having two phases. The first is commitment, or pre-action plan-ning, and the second is self-regulation, or action control. Pre-action plan-ning, according to Gollwitzer (1993), is characterized by initial attraction to the goal, formation of intentions to commitment to the goal, and intentions for action which refers to planning for action. Managing one's intentions is critical to preserving one's goal orientation and commitment. People frequently discount statements of intention because they are not highly predictive of whether a person will actually do what he or she said she was going to do. But, Gollwitzer would refer to these as weak intentions because they lack certain characteristics of what he would call strong intentions. A strong intention is one in which a person not only indicates a commitment to a goal but also formulates a concrete plan as to when and how to accomplish the goal. For example, in a study of this concept, just before they left for winter break, Gollwitzer and Brandstätter (1997) asked a group of college students in Germany to write an essay describing their Christmas Day experience and to turn it in when they returned. During the class, they were asked to write a note to their professor describing their intentions to do this task. The researchers analyzed the notes and rated them according to whether they were concrete as to when and how the essay was to be written or whether they were simply vague commitments to write the essay. After the students returned they found a positive correlation between strong commitment and completion of the task. Students who said something such as, "after breakfast on the morning after Christmas, I will sit at my desk in my room and write my essay," were far more likely to complete the task than students who simply said, "I will write my paper soon after Christmas and before I return to college."

The other aspect of volition, which Kuhl (1984) calls *action control theory*, consists of a list of six principles, or strategies, describing self-regulatory attitudes and behaviors that help protect one's intentions; that is, they help a person stay on task and avoid distractions after having made a commitment to achieving a given goal. The six action control strategies are (Kuhl, 1984, p. 125):

1. Selective attention: also called the "protective function of volition": it shields the current intention by inhibiting the processing of information about competing action tendencies.
2. Encoding control: facilitates the protective function of volition by selectively encoding those features of incoming stimuli that are related to the current intention and ignoring irrelevant features.
3. Emotion control: managing emotional states to allow those that support the current intention and suppress those, such as sadness or attraction, in regard to a competing intention that might undermine it.
4. Motivation control: maintaining and reestablishing saliency of the current intention, especially when the strength of the original tendency was not strong ("I must do this even though I don't really want to.").
5. Environment control: creating an environment that is free of uncontrollable distractions and making social commitments, such

as telling people what you plan to do, that help you protect the current intention.

6. Parsimonious information processing: knowing when to stop, making judgments about how much information is enough, and to make decisions that maintain active behaviors to support the current intentions.

Kuhl assumes that processes of action control underlie virtually any kind of activity and may be called into play to protect a current intention when one's ability to perform the intended actions is weakened due to the strength of competing tendencies or a weakening of the original intention (Kuhl, 1985). The effectiveness of employing action control strategies has been confirmed in many studies in a variety of behavior change settings (Kuhl, 1987) as well as in educational settings (Corno, 2001; Zimmerman & Schunk, 2001).

These concepts of pre-action planning based on intentions and commitment, and action control over self-regulation as a means of managing one's behavior in such a way as to remain on task have led to an expansion of the macro model that provides the conceptual foundation for the ARCS model. The original macro model is illustrated in the upper half of Figure 1.3. The left-hand side of that figure contains the components of expectancy and value that underlie the three concepts of attention, relevance, and confidence. These contribute to the amount of effort a person will exert to achieve the goal. In the expanded model, two additional outputs have been added. The concept of effort from the original model has been modified to more specifically refer to the selection of a given goal and is called effort direction. A second behavioral outcome which reflects intentions and commitment is called effort initiation, and the third, which is the outcome of action control, is called effort persistence. This model does not imply that one must always employ metacognitive strategies related to intention commitment and self-regulation because they might not be necessary if one's desire to accomplish the goal is strong enough. Thus, these additional components of the model illustrate how self-regulatory components are under learner control and can be incorporated when appropriate. The model also illustrates how environmental influences in the form of encouragement, scaffolding, intermediate goal setting, and so forth can assist a person whose self-regulatory skills are not well developed. The fully expanded version of this model is called the Motivation, Volition, and Performance (MVP) theory and incorporates other modifications than those listed in this brief presentation concerning the motivational elements of the model (Keller, 2008b).

Both the Macro Model and the MVP Model have several uses. First, they allow you to conceptually array various concepts and theories of human behavior according to which aspects of behavior they are most effective in explaining. For example, many concepts and theories of motivation are

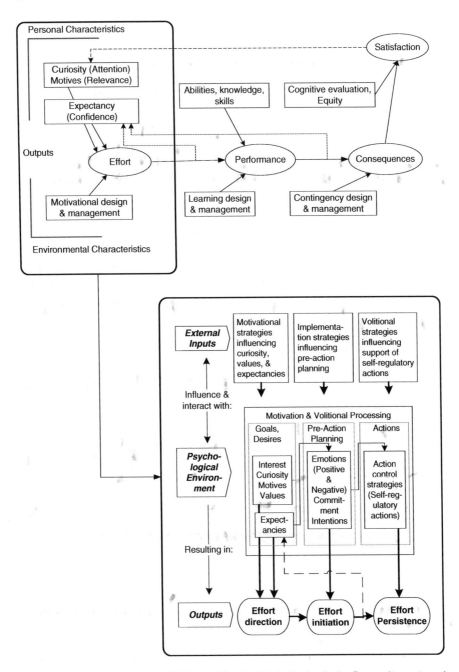

Figure 1.3. Modification of Keller's Macro Model to Include Commitment and Volition.

subsumed under the category of *motivational and volitional processing*. As can be seen in the output line (Figure 1.3), their primary influence is on the degree to which people undertake to achieve a certain goal and persist in their efforts to be successful. They help explain what people want to do and theories of learning help explain what they are able to do. In other words, theories of learning help explain the degree to which people have capabilities, prior knowledge, and information processing skills to achieve certain goals, given that they want to accomplish those goals. The model illustrates how principles of learning, which are subsumed under the *information and psychomotor processing* category, combine with motivational influences to affect learning and performance. And, to incorporate one more example, theories of instruction would be represented by learning strategies that are introduced as external inputs into the learning environment.

Actual research projects would normally incorporate specific concepts and variables contained within these categories as there is no one overall variable representing an entire category. The model provides a frame of reference within which to locate the type of research that is being conducted. However, it would not be expected that the research would consist of a study of the effects of expectancies and practice on learning and performance, which are three of the boxes within the model. Instead, the study might investigate the effects of self-efficacy (Bandura, 1997) and deliberate practice (Ericsson, 2006) on the development of expertise (Ericsson, 2006) in shooting free throws in basketball, which are specific concepts and variables within those three boxes. Similarly, the model can be useful as a means of organizing specific research studies and identifying areas in which there are research opportunities because of the existence of little or no research in a given area. For example, we have very limited knowledge about the interactions of motivational processing and information processing as represented in the box in the center of the diagram.

Another major use of the model is for clinical practices. It provides a basis for diagnosing performance environments, especially when the learners' attitudes and performance are below expectations, to determine whether the problems are more likely due to motivational, volitional, or learning problems. And, more specifically, if it appears that there are motivational problems then the next step is to become much more precise in determining what the problems are, which is one of the major purposes of this book. This diagnostic information is then used as a basis for creating motivational strategies that are targeted to solving specific problems. This systematic motivational design process is not unlike the systematic instructional design process that is used for identifying learning requirements and strategies for designing learning environments in which students can master the desired goals.

Conceptual Challenges in the Study of Motivation

The study of motivation is complex because of the sheer number of motivational concepts, constructs, and theories that have been formulated to explain aspects of motivation and because of the complexity of environmental, cultural, and personal factors that interact to influence a person's motivation at any given point in time. Chapters 2 and 3 of this book contain a categorization scheme and model that assist in organizing all of these motivational concepts and factors that influence motivation, but there are several meta-level characteristics that help clarify some of the conceptual challenges of one's motivation and misunderstandings regarding the study of motivation. The first concerns the relationship of motivation to the affective versus cognitive domains. The second pertains to the concept of trait versus state. Even though the old school of trait psychology is no longer current, these concepts prevail in regard to characterizing motivational conditions. Finally, there are the concepts of intrinsic versus extrinsic motivation which have been the subject of much research and theory and add to the understanding of the initiation as well as to the consequences of one's actions and subsequent motivation. Following is an overview of each of these concepts. They will be discussed further in various parts of this book.

Affective vs. Cognitive Domain

Does motivation belong to only the *affective domain*, or does it relate to the *cognitive domain*? Are these domains even meaningful in regard to motivation? The distinctions between the cognitive (Bloom, 1956), affective (Krathwohl, Bloom, & Masia, 1964), and psychomotor (Harrow, 1972; Simpson, 1972) domains were introduced in the 1950s, 1960s, and 1970s as a means of classifying educational objectives. Motivation has often been associated with the affective domain (Martin & Briggs, 1986; Tennyson, 1992) or as part of what are called *non-cognitive variables* (Messick, 1979). In contrast, Briggs (1984) discusses motivation as an independent area from the affective domain, an area to be intensively studied.

However, considering that motivation refers to internal conditions that result in the pursuit of specific goals, it is not meaningful to attempt to classify this broad component of human behavior as being contained within the affective, or non-cognitive, domain because it also has cognitive elements. Motivation incorporates emotionally based characteristics including such things as fear and attraction, psychomotor components such as frustration and aggression, physiological components such as hunger and arousal, and cognitive components such as expectancies for success. For example, the attributional theories of motivation (Rotter, 1966; Weiner, 1974) are primarily cognitive. They focus on people's interpretations of the causes of outcomes and their predictions of future success.

Thus, it is not meaningful to attempt to assign motivation exclusively to the affective or cognitive domains. Specific motivational concepts can belong to one domain or another, but they can also have attributes belonging to more than one domain. The concept of need for achievement includes deliberate choices about goals and acceptable levels of risk of success versus failure, determinations of what obstacles and facilitating forces will affect the likelihood of success, and anticipated feelings that one will have following success or failure.

Trait vs. State

A concept that permeates discussions of motivation is that of trait versus state. A personality trait is a predictable tendency to behave in the same way in a variety of situations. For example, a person with a high need for achievement will tend to behave competitively in the workplace, on the highway, while playing board games, and in conversations or arguments with friends and family. The concept of traits originated in the study of genetics but was also applied in the development of personality theory where there have been varied approaches to conceptualizing and studying psychological traits. The goal was to define personality in terms of specific types of traits that would provide an adequate basis for characterizing people. However, in an often cited study, Allport (1937) reviewed an unabridged dictionary and found more than 4500 terms that could be considered to represent human personality characteristics, or traits. Clearly, this number of terms represented an un-parsimonious and unfeasible approach to characterizing people. This led Allport to develop a three-tiered structure of traits. At the top are what he called cardinal traits which define nearly all of a person's behavior such as Jimmy Carter's humanitarianism, Robin Williams' comedic extrovertism, and Mohammad Ali's aggressiveness as a boxer. However, it is rare to find such dominating traits in a person. More common is that people will have a set of what Allport called central traits. People will have a cluster of between five to ten central traits that characterize their behavior in most situations. At the third level are what Allport called secondary traits in which are evident in most situations but not all. An example would be a supervisor who tends to be somewhat aggressive and domineering at work but relaxed and gentle at home and in social situations.

This approach provided a basis for classifying traits, but did not result in the identification of a generalized cluster of traits that could be used to characterize people's personalities. Beginning with the complete list of just over 4500 terms, Cattell (1950) reduced the list by removing synonyms and then applying factor analysis. This is a statistical technique that is used to examine the intercorrelations among people's ratings of all of the items in a list. This results in clusters of items, called factors, in which the items in each set are significantly correlated with each other. Using this method, Cattell reduced the original long list of specific characteristics to a shorter list of 16 personality factors (Cattell & Cattell, 1995) (Table 1.1). He used this list as a basis for a measurement questionnaire (the 16PF Personality Questionnaire) which has been used in many studies (Cattell, 1957) and continues to be used today.

Table 1.1. The 16 Personality Factors of Cattell (Extracted from Cattell &
Cattell, 1995).

Warmth	Liveliness	Vigilance	Openness to change
Reasoning	Rule-consciousness	Abstractedness	Self-reliance
Emotional stability	Social boldness	Privateness	Perfectionism
Dominance	Sensitivity	Apprehension	Tension

Cattell's work (Cattell, 1950, 1957) provided the foundation for the
development in the 1960s (Norman, 1963) of a still shorter list of five factors
which, according to McCrae and John (1992), did not attract much attention
until the 1980s. But, this model has now become known as The Big Five
(McCrae & Costa, 1987) and is the basis for much if not most of the current
research on personality. Although there is some variation in the exact terms
used to denote these factors, those that are most commonly used are the
ones introduced by Norman (1963): extraversion, agreeableness, conscien-
tiousness, neuroticism, and openness and each is characterized by adjec-
tives that give it fuller definition (Table 1.2).

Table 1.2. The "Big Five" Personality Characteristics (Sources: McCrae &
John, 1992, pp. 178-179; Paunonen & Ashton, 2001, p. 529).

Factor Name	Descriptive Characteristics
Extraversion	Active, assertive, energetic, enthusiastic, excitement seeking, outgoing (gregarious), positive emotions, talkative, warm
Agreeableness	Altruistic, appreciative, compliant, forgiving, generous, kind, modest, straightforward, sympathetic, trusting
Conscientiousness	Achievement-striving, competent, dutiful, efficient, organized, planful, reliable, responsible, self-disciplined, thorough
Neuroticism	Anxious, angry, depressed, hostile, impulsive, self-conscious, self-pitying, tense, touchy, unstable, vulnerable, worrying
Openness to experience	Artistic, aesthetic, curious, fantasy, feelings, ideas, imaginative, insightful, original, values, wide interests

These five factors have been widely accepted in personality psychology as a fundamental core of traits that has virtually universal cross-cultural validity (McCrae & John, 1992; Paunonen & Ashton, 2001). However, a limitation of trait psychology is that it was grounded primarily in methods of statistical analysis applied to lists of personality traits taken from an English dictionary which resulted in shorter lists in which items were clustered based on shared meanings. The human characteristics represented by these concepts can be found among people in virtually all cultures and so there may be a linguistic basis for these concepts in each language as exemplified by the words used in other cultures to describe human characteristics. Thus, even though traits were empirically determined, they were derived from people's associations of verbal constructs instead of being based on direct observations of behavior in relation to a hypothesized human characteristic.

The study of human motivation includes the concept of traits in the form of psychological constructs that define specific personality in regard to various aspects of personality such as the need to achieve, perceptions of control, curiosity, attributions for success or failure, and anxiety. Also, a distinction is made between trait versus state conditions in regard to virtually all motivational concepts. A trait is presumed to refer to a stable predisposition to behave in a certain way. In contrast, states refer to the disposition to demonstrate a given motive or personality characteristic at a given point in time or in specific types of situations. For example, with respect to the motivational construct of curiosity, people who have high trait levels of curiosity will act with curiosity in many different types of situations, but not all. In contrast, people with low trait-level curiosity will display little curiosity as a general rule, but may become highly curious in specific situations or, in other words, in certain state conditions. This is illustrated in Figure 1.4 where we see the differences between Carlos and Karl in eight different situations:

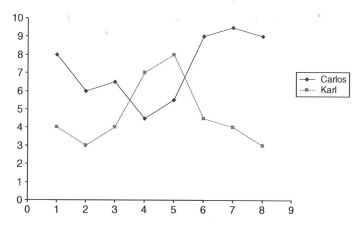

Figure 1.4. Illustration of Trait (Carlos) Versus State (Karl) Conditions.

1. Science
2. Literature
3. History
4. Dancing
5. Cars
6. Investment
7. Video games
8. Website development

Overall, Carlos has higher curiosity with an average score of 7.25 while Karl's average score is 4.69. From this we would conclude that Carlos has higher trait-level curiosity even though Karl scored higher in two specific areas (dancing and cars). This illustrates how people's behavior in specific situations (state-level behaviors) can be substantially different from their overall tendencies (trait-level characteristics).

This general principle is important because even though trait psychology as a formal school does not command much allegiance anymore, the use of the word trait in a more metaphorical sense to refer to a stable personality characteristic in contrast to situationally demonstrated characteristics, called *states*, is quite common and as indicated applies to virtually all motivational variables.

This concept has useful applications for motivational design. When designing a course or any type of learning event it would be useful to know what kinds of motivational predispositions to expect in the audience, which would allow one to prepare appropriate types of motivational strategies. The best predictor of a student's predispositions regarding the study of language, for example, would be knowledge of the student's motivation in previous settings of a similar type. In other words, knowledge of the learner's situation-specific motivation would be the best predictor. However, in situations where it is not possible to obtain state-specific knowledge of learners' previous experiences in a given type of situation, or when the learners have not studied a given subject area in the past, then the generalized or trait-level measure of academic motivation would be the best predictor. Also, this concept can help a teacher or designer avoid misdiagnosis of motivational problems with learners. For example, it is very easy to over generalize one's opinions about a student based upon that student's behavior in a specific situation. A teacher might conclude that a young boy who shows no interest in literature or language learning has little interest in school; hence, a low level of curiosity. It might be that the child has high levels of curiosity but the topics of study and the methods of engaging the children simply do not stimulate that child's curiosity due to a lack of perceived relevance or low confidence on the part of the student. Understanding and applying this concept, which is illustrated in Chapters 4, 5, 6 and 7 and in the design portion of the book, is directly related to knowing how to prepare accurate and holistic understandings of learner motivation and how to design effective motivational strategies.

Intrinsic Versus Extrinsic Motivation

Another issue that permeates the motivation literature is the distinction between intrinsic and extrinsic motivation. The meaning of these two concepts would seem to be somewhat intuitive based on the meaning of the two words and, in fact, there tends to be consensus among researchers on their formal meanings. According to Deci (1975), intrinsically motivated activities are "ones for which there is no apparent reward except the activity itself" (p. 23). That is, individuals with intrinsic motivation engage in tasks for the pleasure that comes from them. On the other hand, extrinsically motivated individuals engage in tasks for the rewards that follow from completing them, not for the pleasure coming from them. Extrinsically motivated tasks might be enjoyable, but by definition that is not the primary reason for engaging in them. Extrinsically motivated activities are undertaken because they have instrumental value; that is, they are necessary steps toward accomplishing goals that are valued. Thus, intrinsically motivated activities can be viewed as ends in themselves, while extrinsically motivated goals are means to ends. For example, a high school senior takes an advanced placement course in calculus to increase her chances of getting accepted into an engineering college, not because she is intrinsically motivated to learn calculus. After she arrives at the university, she spends all of her free time in the robotics lab even when she has no assignments there because she has long been fascinated by the possibilities of their prosthetic applications. Thus, the successful completion of her extrinsically motivated requirement led to the opportunity for her to engage in an intrinsically motivated activity. And, in fact, she found that she made use of calculus in programming the robots. Or, in a different setting, a young family man who is a supervisor at a large super-store enrolls in a night class in finance in the hope that it will help him move into management. He would like to make more money so he can enjoy his passion for wilderness camping with his family. In this case, the extrinsically motivated goal will help enable the young man to enjoy his intrinsically satisfying activities. Naturally, there can be a mixture of the two elements in a given situation, but as will be seen, there can also be conflicts between the two such that one interferes with the other.

Much of the early research on intrinsic and extrinsic motivation concerned their relationship to each other and it was found that the application of positive extrinsic reinforcements to intrinsically motivating tasks could decrease the frequency or duration of occurrence of the behavior. This was unexpected given the basic assumptions of reinforcement theory, which are described in Chapter 7. Briefly, Deci (1971) and Lepper, Greene, and Nisbett (1973), for example, unobtrusively observed subjects for a period of time to determine how much time they voluntarily spent on given tasks. Subjects were free to choose either one or none of the activities which, depending on the age group of the subjects, consisted of such things as reading, solving puzzles, or playing with water-based felt-tipped pens.

Then, the subjects were ushered into the experimental room and offered a reward each time they worked on the given task. In the third stage, subjects went back to the waiting room where there were, once again, the same kinds of activities they had been working on as well as alternative activities that they could choose. Unobtrusive measures revealed that subjects who had been rewarded spent less time on the designated tasks than they had previously and also less time than the unrewarded subjects. This was in contradiction to the expectations of reinforcement theory which presumes that rewarded activities will increase in frequency of performance, assuming that the subject is not satiated. Based on the controls implemented in the many studies conducted on this phenomenon, researchers have concluded that extrinsic rewards can have an undermining effect on intrinsic motivation (Condry, 1977). However, it is not a simple relationship and this topic will be covered in much more detail in Chapter 7.

The intrinsic–extrinsic concepts are often presented as a dichotomy indicating that one is either intrinsically or extrinsically motivated in a given situation. Theoretically, it is possible to be purely one or the other, but given the complexity of human beings and tasks, it is probably more common to find that there are elements of both that are intertwined in any particular situation. A colleague of mine raises orchids and also makes beautiful wooden bowls which he turns on his lathe from interesting blocks of wood. These are intrinsically motivated activities, without a doubt, but he also uses his crafting and gardening skills to produce products that he can sell to help support these hobbies. In contrast, another acquaintance of mine works for a university security force. He enjoys his work while he is there and takes pleasure from his ability to relate well to the students, but his primary motivation for staying employed there is his need for a job to support his family, and this job is more interesting to him than his other options. However, if he could, he would spend all of his time hiking, exploring, and writing poetry. And, still another acquaintance has, as he has gotten older, come to hate his job as an automobile mechanic and stays with it only because of the extrinsic necessity for income. Thus, there can be many variations in the blend of intrinsic and extrinsically motivated behaviors.

Finally we come to schooling which occupies many of a child's younger years. Is going to school an intrinsically or extrinsically motivated task? Educators tend to promote the value and the goal of having intrinsically motivated learners. They hope to see their students develop a desire to learn and to become lifelong learners. But, is this feasible, or even possible? How many children would go to school if they had a choice? And, one more question: how many of the students who went to school if they had a choice would do so because of intrinsic interest or because of its extrinsic value in helping them prepare for careers and life in general? Thus, there would seem to be very little intrinsically motivated activity in regard to schools. Yet, even though it seems paradoxical, one can visit a school and observe many children and young people who seem to be curious and absorbed in what they are doing.

Two researchers, Deci and Ryan (1985), have provided an explanation for this with self-determination theory (SDT) which adds several layers of elaboration to an otherwise simplistic distinction between intrinsic and extrinsic motivation. Their theory is explained in more detail in Chapters 5 and 6, but its basic characteristic is that it distinguishes among the conditions of amotivation, intrinsic motivation, and four types of extrinsic motivation. The most extrinsic of these is called "external regulation" and refers to tasks that are more or less totally regulated by extrinsic rewards, such as the mechanic I described above. The least extrinsic of the extrinsic conditions is called *integrated regulation* which occurs with a person such as the security guard whom I mentioned. He has internalized many of the values and goals associated with his job, but he is still motivated primarily by external requirements. In between these two extremes are two additional types of extrinsic motivation.

The point to be made here is that this is a complex issue and a challenge is to build intrinsic interest in one's subject without necessarily expecting all learners to become totally motivated by intrinsic interests and to respect the motivational orientations of students while, at the same time, trying to encourage positive growth.

Summary

The history of the study of motivation is long and deep. In fact, nobody knows how long it is. Recorded documentations of human investigations of motivation are relatively recent compared to the ponderings that people have engaged in for thousands of years. However, when one moves away from the musings of philosophers and insights of writers and artists into the realm of disciplined inquiry, there are only a very few hundred years of formal investigation. This history of the psychological study of motivation has yielded a huge quantity of knowledge, but since science aspires to be cumulative in its construction of knowledge we can gain an overview of major concepts and theories of motivation within a relatively short time. However, the word overview is critical. There are vast amounts of knowledge contained in specific research reports, reviews of literature, and theoretical papers that are available to serious scholars of motivation. The present book contains an introduction to this literature by synthesizing it into a conceptual structure that facilitates its application by designers, teachers, and others who are engaged in motivational problem solving.

The primary purpose of this book is to help you learn how to implement a systematic motivational design process which requires that you also acquire enough knowledge about human motivation to be able to use the process effectively. A synthesis of critical motivational concepts and theories is contained in Chapters 4, 5, 6 and 7 and this is followed by several chapters that will guide you through the motivational design process.

Chapter 2 – What is Motivational Design?

Forethought

When you think about the concept of motivation which picture would you choose as part of a metaphor representing it, dry leaves or a rock (Figure 2.1)?

Figure 2.1. Leaves or a Rock?
Leaves created from Arts and Letters. Rock is from a personal photograph

Introduction

Many people would choose leaves because motivation, like a pile of leaves, can be unstable, frequently changing, elusive, and easily modified by external forces such as "the winds of change." The metaphor is apt because students can be highly interested and engaged at one moment and "on another planet" at the next moment.

On the other hand, you might have chosen the rock because motivation, like a sturdy rock, can be viewed as being determined, single minded, strong willed, and resistant to change. People can overcome great obstacles and accomplish stunning achievements due to intense and unwavering personal motivation, as did Helen Keller and Lance Armstrong. But, it can also have a negative side as when people are highly motivated by self-destructive goals and resist efforts to help them change.

J.M. Keller, *Motivational Design for Learning and Performance,*
DOI 10.1007/978-1-4419-1250-3_2, © Springer Science+Business Media, LLC 2010

Thus, there can be contradictory views of what the inherent nature of motivation is. If it is more like leaves then it makes motivational design highly challenging. Even though you might be able to create a variety of motivational techniques, their effects might be short lived and it would be difficult to predict what motivational states would exist in the learners at any given time. On the other hand, if a person's motivation is already strong and stable then it would be easier to diagnose the person's motivational profile and prescribe strategies for change, but it might be more difficult to bring about the changes; you are not likely to motivate people to perform well in situations that are not consistent with their goals.

In fact, all of these sometimes seemingly contradictory attributes have to be taken into consideration in the motivational design process. Human motivation is complex and multidimensional, but a great deal has been learned about it and the knowledge can be incorporated into a systematic design process. The purpose of this chapter is to explain the concept of motivational design, describe a model for classifying approaches to motivational design, and discuss several related issues and challenges.

Characteristics of Design

What is design? This is a complicated concept but in a nutshell, as Koberg and Bagnall emblazoned on the back cover of early editions of their book (for example, Koberg & Bagnall, 1976), "design is a process of making dreams come true." This expression captures the sense of adventure and uncertainty that can accompany the design process, but more specifically it consists of a process of identifying a goal which is often based on a gap between the way things are and the way you would like for them to be, developing a strategy including activities and tools that you expect to help you accomplish the goal, exerting purposeful effort to achieve your goal, and finally evaluating and reflecting regarding your degree of success. Similarly, motivational design aims to enable the dream of educators, other behavioral change agents, and managers of human performance to stimulate and sustain people's efforts to make positive changes in their lives. More specifically, it refers to the process of arranging resources and procedures to bring about changes in people's motivation. Consequently, motivational design is concerned with connecting instruction to the goals of learners, providing stimulation and appropriate levels of challenge, and influencing how the learners will feel following successful goal accomplishment, or even following failure.

Motivational design can be applied to improving students' motivation to learn, employees' motivation to work, people's motivation to pursue a chosen career path, and improvements in their volitional, or self-regulatory, skills. It can also be used to bring about changes in specific motivational components of a person's personality such as increasing one's curiosity level, developing more positive self-efficacy, or overcoming feelings of anxiety and helplessness. Motivational design is systematic and aims for replicable principles and processes. In that regard, motivational design is based on the scientific literature on human motivation and stands in contrast to the *charismatic* motivational speakers and workshops whose aims are largely in the area of emotional arousal and are grounded in personal experience, intuition, and adages. Certainly, the successes of motivational speakers or anyone else who attempts to influence the motivation of another can be explained or investigated, even if on a post hoc basis, in terms of motivational constructs. The difference is that motivational design seeks explanation and predictability while charismatic approaches tend to be grounded more in the unique talents of individuals who have achieved success.

In this book, the primary focus *of motivational design* is on people's motivation to learn and refers specifically to strategies, principles, processes, and tactics for stimulating and sustaining the goal-oriented behaviors of learners. When explaining various aspects of motivational design, it can be difficult to maintain a clear distinction between the concepts of strategies versus tactics. Strategies are general guidelines and overall approaches to achieving a goal, while tactics are specific activities that contribute to implementing the strategy. A strategy for maintaining reader interest could be to systematically and consistently employ Rudolf Flesch's principles for readability based on human interest factors (Flesch, 1948). Tactics would include the inclusion of gender specific words instead of neuter plurals (their, they, its), sentences with quoted dialog, and other such things. In this book, an effort has been made to maintain this distinction, especially in Chapters 8, 9, and 10 which cover the motivational design process, but there are times when it is awkward to maintain an exact distinction. In those situations, the word "strategies" is sometimes used more generically to refer to activities to bring about positive motivation.

Motivational design, as illustrated in Figure 2.2, does not occur in isolation from other influences on learning such as the instruction itself and the learning environment. Thus, even though motivational design is a distinct process in and of itself, it is used in conjunction with the systematic approach to instructional design and adds another dimension to it. Some instructional designers might believe that if instruction is well designed, it will, ipso facto, be motivating. However, it is easy to explain how instruction can be well designed but might not be motivating. The traditional view of *instructional design* is that it encompasses processes and techniques for producing efficient and effective instruction. Efficiency refers to economy in the use of learners' time, instructional time, materials, and other resources. It is not generally viewed as relating to the motivational aspects of instruction except in a negative way. If an instructional event makes inefficient use of time and resources it can be boring or irritating to the audience. But, efficiency of delivery does not add to students' intrinsic interest in the situation.

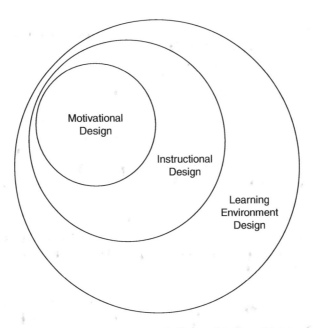

Figure 2.2. Motivational Design as a Subset of Instructional and Learning Environment Design.

Effectiveness, however, is sometimes regarded as including motivation. The argument is that instruction cannot be effective if it is not appealing to people. But in practice, instructional designers tend to have an unstated assumption that effectiveness refers to how well people can learn from an instructional event *given that they want to learn*. If the learning objectives are clear and appropriate, the instructional content is consistent with the objectives, and there are examples, practice, and tests that are all internally consistent, then the instruction will be effective if people are motivated to study, which adds an independent dimension to effectiveness. Thus, instructional design models often include two traditional motivational components consisting of getting the learners' attention as specified in Gagné's first event of instruction (Gagné, 1965; Gagné, Wager, Golas, & Keller, 2005) and providing reinforcement for correct responding (Skinner, 1954). However, none of these elements provides a sufficient explanation of motivation to learn.

The desire to succeed in a given instructional setting may not come from the instruction itself; it may come from long-range goals, institutional requirements, or many other sources (J. M. Keller, 1983b). Students might succeed, hence confirming the effectiveness of the instruction, because of purely extrinsic rewards such as a certificate, advancement to a higher grade or position, or avoidance of termination even if they do not have a desire to learn. Thus, instruction, like a trip to the dentist, can be very effective without being at all appealing, but the experience will be avoided unless absolutely necessary. In contrast, motivational design strives to make instruction more intrinsically interesting.

At the other extreme, instructional materials can be very appealing without being effective, especially when their appeal comes purely from their entertainment value as illustrated in the following dialog:

Child: "Boy, that textbook had a lot of good cartoons in it."

Teacher: "Yes, it did. What were the authors telling us about global warming?"

Child: "Uh, uh, that it is getting hotter?"

To be effective, motivational tactics have to support instructional goals. Sometimes the motivational features can be fun or even entertaining, but unless they engage the learner in the instructional purpose and content, they will not promote learning. As a classroom management technique, the teacher can introduce fun activities as an extrinsic reward for achievement or effortful behavior as Malone (1981) did in his research on learning and motivation in computer-based instruction. These extrinsic rewards can contribute to the students' overall good feelings about the course and the teacher, but they will not in and of themselves promote learning. If used improperly and too frequently, these entertainments can actually have detrimental effects on students' motivation to learn because the students will begin to work only for the extrinsic rewards (Deci & Porac, 1978). Thus, motivational design is concerned with how to make instruction appealing without becoming purely entertaining.

An additional distinction of importance is the one between motivational design and behavior modification. Teachers and employers sometimes have to deal with people who have severe personal adjustment problems due to low academic ability, emotional immaturity, or anti-social behavior. Solutions to these problems generally fall into the categories of behavior modification or, when it is not possible to change the person's behavior, expulsion from the situation. Assistance with these problems comes from areas such as counseling, psychological education, psychotherapy, and personnel specialists. This is outside the boundaries of motivational design as covered in this book, even though motivational design draws upon many of the same underlying concepts and theories of motivation. Yet, motivational design can lead to improved behavior by creating improved motivational states and traits for some students, especially when the motivational designer is focusing on the development of skills in self-motivation and self-regulation in students; however, motivational design is concerned primarily with improving the appeal of instruction or a work environment for people who fall within reasonable boundaries of readiness to learn or to work. More challenging situations can be approached using the same methods that are presented here, but their application would require expertise in human behavior modification that goes beyond the contents of this book.

From a broader perspective, learning environment design requires one to consider both motivational and instructional influences on learners, and both of these activities require consideration of learner goals and capabilities together with cultural and environmental factors that affect attitudes and performance. It is no wonder that the design of effective, efficient, and appealing learning environments is a complex enterprise. Even though there is a growing technology, in the sense of systematic knowledge of how to create learning environments, there is also an art to being able to successfully design and teach. The art of design and teaching is based on both knowledge and experience and refers to the necessity for personal judgment and problem solving. Many of the challenges faced by teachers and designers cannot be solved *by the book*. They can be solved by a combination of systematic problem solving and personal judgment based on one's overall experience and professional expertise. However, by learning and applying systematic problem-solving processes, and by learning how to recognize and classify various types of problems, one can increase one's expertise and judgmental capacity. The process described in this book will not lead you to automatic answers to motivational problems, but it can help you systematically and predictably improve the motivational qualities of your instruction and overall learning environment.

Motivational Design Models

Motivational design models can be categorized into four groups (Keller, 1988, 1994). The first three are grounded in psychological theories of human behavior. They can be classified as person-centered theories, environmentally centered theories, and interaction theories. Models in the fourth group, called omnibus models, have more pragmatic or pedagogical origins and incorporate both motivational design and instructional design strategies without distinguishing between the two. These omnibus models tend to grow out of successful practices that have been validated as to their effectiveness but are not based on any particular theoretical framework and can be based on a specific technique or theme.

Person-Centered Models

Person-centered models are grounded primarily in psychological constructs or theories that represent one or more motivational dimensions of personality. Their aim is to make positive changes in these characteristics which result in better psychological adjustment and improved learning. This approach can also be called psychological education which had a period of rapid growth and development in the 1960s and 1970s. Flanagan (1967) reported that a study by the American Institutes for research of 440,000 high school students concluded that high schools fail to help students develop a sense of personal responsibility for their own actions including their personal, educational, and social development. Evidence such as this contributed to the development of psychological education to supplement the teaching of vocational and academic skills to enable students to be better prepared for their futures. According to Alschuler (1973), there are four common goals that can be observed in the procedures employed within a psychological education course, keeping in mind that the word *course* refers here to a unit of instruction that can be anything from a stand-alone workshop to a component of a regular course in mathematics, language, or any other topic.

1. The first goal refers to procedures that are included to stimulate curiosity and fantasy. In this context, fantasy refers to such things as visioning oneself doing something differently or accomplishing a goal.
2. The second goal is illustrated by activities in which the participants experience a new way of thinking or behaving instead of just learning it cognitively. Games, role playing, and simulations are employed in this regard.
3. The third goal focuses on emotional development. Students engage in experiences that stimulate emotional responses and learn how to examine and manage their emotions, which is a desirable part of reaching maturity and developing self-determination (Goleman, 1995).
4. The fourth goal includes procedures that help students learn to live fully and intensely in the here and now. The psycho-therapeutic literature is replete with examples of how much time people spend regretting past actions and fearing future events which Kabat-Zinn (1990) calls a state of "full catastrophe living." However, as he points out, past events cannot be changed and most of the feared events never materialize, so it is much healthier to come to terms with the past, plan for the future as much as feasible, and focus on the present. This leaves one much freer to be emotionally integrated and open to learning. This concept of *mindfulness living* was expressed beautifully by an 85-year-old woman (Kabat-Zinn, 1990): "Oh, I've had my moments, and if I had to do it over again, I'd have more of them. In fact, I'd try to have nothing else. Just moments, one after another, instead of living so many years ahead of each day" (p. 17).

An example of a person-centered model is the motive internalization process created by McClelland in working with adults to improve their achievement motivation (McClelland, 1965) and applied in a school setting by Alschuler (Alschuler, Tabor, & McIntyre, 1971). The achievement motive is characterized by having a desire to achieve challenging goals and often includes a sense of competition. People who are entrepreneurs or who work in competitive environments such as sales normally have high levels of the achievement motive. It can also be demonstrated by wanting to outperform someone else or achieve self-imposed standards of excellence as when a marathon runner finishes the race with a new personal best time. In this case, the competition is with one's own standards instead of competing with other people. Other indicators of the motive to achieve are a desire to perform well over a long period of time in a process of reaching an achievement goal or doing something unique as with inventors and researchers.

Based on McClelland's (1965) extensive work on developing achievement motivation in adults, Alschuler (Alschuler, 1973; Alschuler, Tabor, & McIntyre, 1971) created a model for the development of achievement motivation in adolescents. His approach contains a six step process for arousing and internalizing a motive:

1. Attend. Get and sustain students' attention by using moderately novel changes in approaches
2. Experience. Allow students to vividly experience the thoughts, feelings, and actions associated with the motive.
3. Conceptualize. Help students learn how to conceptualize the motive by naming the parts and describing it.
4. Relate. Help the students conceptualize how the motive is related to their images of themselves, their basic motives, and the demands of their lives.
5. Apply. Provide opportunities and guidance for the students to practice applying the motive and experiencing the thoughts and feelings associated with it.
6. Internalize. Promote internalization by gradually withdrawing support while continuing to provide opportunities for students to exercise the motive with more voluntary and personal responsibility.

Typically this process is taught in a workshop setting and is supported by a variety of self-report measures, reflective activities, and games that help participants experience behaviors associated with the motive. A typical game used to illustrate the achievement motive is the ring toss game in which participants are given an objective, choose their own goals and challenge level, play the game, and then reflectively interpret the results. The game has numerous variations but in its basic form the participant is told that the objective is to throw as many rings onto a free standing pole as possible. The participant is given four or six rings and is given a free choice as to how close or far away to stand. Logically, one would expect the participants to stand above the pole and drop the rings on it in order to maximize the probability of success, and some participants do this. But many of the participants choose a position a few feet away from the post and then adjust their position closer or further away depending on whether or not they succeed on individual throws. This illustrates the achievement motive in which people like to set a moderate challenge for themselves. There are variations on this and other games that are used to illustrate how the addition of incentives and competition affect participant's goal orientations and decisions.

The relationship between achievement motivation and performance is not always clear, especially in school classrooms where

achievement in the form of compliance to externally imposed standards is frequently the primary requirement for success. In this setting, desire for success takes the place of the achievement motive which is activated when people have an opportunity to exercise a degree of autonomy in setting goals, defining their standards of excellence, and having control over resources required to achieve their goals. The situation is also complicated when, as often happens, one is trying to work on more than one task at a time. As motivation increases, there is a tendency for there to be a decrease in secondary task performance and an increase in primary task performance (Humphreys & Revelle, 1984).

Another area of psychological education that is directly related to the development of student attitudes and habits that can result in improved performance is volition, or as it is also called, self-regulation and these terms are used interchangeably in this book. This is not a psychological construct in the formal sense, but rather a concept that refers to a collection of behaviors and attitudes that are related to persistent effort to accomplish a goal. It is one thing to have an intrinsically motivated goal or an extrinsically imposed requirement that is instrumental to achieving important personal goals, but it is something else to employ behaviors that help one resist distractions and discouragement and to maintain persistent efforts to achieve the goal. This "something else" is summed up in the concept of volition and is illustrated in slightly varying ways by different theorists. One well-known model is that of Kuhl (1984, 1987) who lists six strategies, which he calls "action control strategies," that can be used to maintain task orientation. They are

1. Selective attention, also called the "protective function of volition" (Kuhl, 1984, p. 125): it shields the current intention by inhibiting the processing of information about competing action tendencies.
2. Encoding control: facilitates the protective function of volition by selectively encoding those features of incoming stimulus that are related to the current intention and ignoring irrelevant features.
3. Emotion control: managing emotional states to allow those that support the current intention and suppress those, such as sadness or attraction, in regard to a competing intention that might undermine it.
4. Motivation control: maintaining and reestablishing saliency of the current intention, especially when the strength of the original tendency was not strong ("I must do this even though I don't really want to.")
5. Environment control: creating an environment that is free of uncontrollable distractions and making social commitments, such as telling people what you plan to do, that help you protect the current intention.
6. Parsimonious information processing: knowing when to stop, making judgments about how much information is enough and to make decisions that maintain active behaviors to support the current intentions.

Kuhl's action control theory has been proven to provide valid strategies for establishing and maintaining self-regulated behavior (Kuhl, 1987), but the majority of research on this approach have been experimental, laboratory-type studies and in changing maladaptive behaviors. Of more immediate relevance in learning environments, especially with children, is the work of Corno (1989) and Zimmerman (1989).

For example, Corno and Randi (1999) proposed a design theory for self-regulated learning in a classroom setting. Their approach was to build self-regulatory skills implicitly by designing a unit of instruction in such a way as to expose students to these strategies as an integrated element of the course design, and also by means of the assignments they were given. For example, the study was conducted in a literature class with a thematic assignment dealing with quests. Specifically, the students analyzed the behaviors of Odysseus, from Homer's *Odyssey*, that led to the successful completion of his quest. The list produced by the students matched well with Corno and Randi's five indicators of self-regulatory behavior (Table 2.1), which were similar in some respects to Kuhl's action control strategies and to other characterizations of self-regulation strategies (Boekaerts, 2001).

Table 2.1. Self-Regulatory Strategies and Examples.

Self-Regulation Strategies	• Examples of parallel Strategies from Quest Analysis
Metacognitive control	• Planning
	• Monitoring/setting benchmarks
	• Evaluating progress
Motivation control	• Focusing/positive thinking
	• Endurance/self-reliance
Emotion control	• Visualization/mental imagery
Control the task situation	• Resource use/sorcery
	• Use of own cleverness/trickery
Control others in the task setting	• Getting help from confidants
	• Controlling his men

In an effort to help students build transfer from this activity to their own lives, Corno and Randi did a follow-up activity in which students wrote essays describing quests that they had undertaken. They then analyzed the essays for evidence of self-regulatory strategies and the researchers found that nine of ten students included at least eight examples of self-regulatory strategies in their essays. Even though they obtained positive results from this innovative teaching approach, the study was limited by the fact that there was no confirmation that students used these strategies in a newly experienced challenging situation. However, this design model was interesting in that it began with a somewhat discovery learning approach and then shifted to a more explicit examination of the characteristics of self-directed learners.

The approach taken by Corno and Randi was different from Alschuler, but these two examples of person-centered models had a similar goal which was to assist students in the development of motivational and volitional attitudes and habits that would improve their self-reliance and performance.

Environmentally Centered Models

Environmentally centered models are grounded in the principles of behavioral psychology which assume that behavior can be adequately explained in terms of an organism's responses to environmental influences. From this perspective, the concept of motivation is defined by Sloane and Jackson (1974) "as the extent to which certain stimulus objects or events effect the occurrence or nonoccurrence" (p. 5) of a given behavior. No reference is made to internal states of cognition or emotion. The primary ways to influence motivation are through the manipulation of deprivation and satiation. It is a well-established principle that people are more likely to repeat a behavior that has pleasant, desirable consequences than one that has unpleasant or no consequences and, furthermore, pleasant consequences are usually associated with receiving something of which you have less than you desire or which you desire more than what you are currently receiving (Premack, 1962). Satiation consists of receiving something which you no longer wish to have. Thus, if a teacher withholds positive, personal recognition from a student unless the student has exhibited a desirable behavior, then the student is more likely to exhibit those behaviors than ones which are ignored or result in undesirable consequences. However, if a student has resorted to using undesirable behaviors as a way of getting attention, then the teacher can use satiation by giving lavish attention to the student to reinforce desirable behaviors and ignore the undesirable ones. These examples, even though they are oversimplifications of real settings, illustrate the basic principles.

There are numerous behavior modification models (Gardner et al., 1994; Medsker & Holdsworth, 2001) that incorporate the principles of contingency management and most of them include five steps. The first is to identify the behavior that you wish to change, the second is to establish its baseline level by measuring its frequency of occurrence before you introduce any interventions, the third is to plan the contingencies of reinforcement which refers to the pattern of administering consequences based on the occurrence or nonoccurrence of the desired behavior, the fourth is to implement the program, and the fifth is to evaluate results to determine if there has been an acceptable level of change in the frequency of performance compared to the baseline. However, these principles were applied to behavior change in general, not specifically to instruction and learning.

It was the work of people such as Pressey (1926) and Skinner (1954, 1968) that led to the systematic application of these principles to motivation and instruction in a learning environment. Skinner who is probably the best known, applied these concepts to education (Skinner, 1968) in a form that can be called motivational design even though his model does not specifically differentiate the learning theory component of his approach from the motivational components. The primary result of his work became known as programmed instruction which is a combination instructional design and motivational design model. It uses the motivational principle of immediate positive reinforcement following correct responses, and it requires that instruction be structured to insure correct responses to the fullest extent possible. This early work led to the development of many principles of instructional design (Markle, 1969), but there were persistent problems with descriptions of the role of positive reinforcement which took the form of providing knowledge of results. This reinforced learning and was also considered to have a motivationally rewarding effect. However, research did not strongly support the combined influence of reinforcement and feedback on learning and motivation. Tosti (1978) helped clarify the issue by distinguishing between motivational and corrective feedback and the optimal timing for each.

With respect to motivational design models based on reinforcement principles that focus primarily on motivation to learn, one of the best known is the Personalized System of Instruction (PSI) developed by Fred Keller (1968). It incorporates programmed instruction, other instructional activities, and a complete instructional management system. It is self-paced and allows students to take tests when they are ready and to retake them if they do not succeed the first time. His system was initially appealing to faculty and students, but with experience problems emerged even though it was proved to be a highly effective form of instructional design (J. Kulik, Kulik, & Cohen, 1979). Regarding problems, faculty found that the time required to develop high-quality instruction and to manage the implementation of the class was far greater than they expected (Gallup, 1974). Many students took advantage of the self-paced aspect of the class to complete their work in a timely manner but many others procrastinated and their performance suffered (Gallup, 1974). Thus, extrinsic reinforcements that were available as an instrumental motivation to perform were not sufficient to stimulate the behavior of many students. The professors had to implement deadlines and other controls to influence the regulation of the procrastination-prone students.

In a different approach, Sloane and Jackson (1974) provided a model which describes how basic concepts of conditioning and reinforcement can be used to control the motivation of students. The model also attempts to describe how to move students from an external reinforcement system to an intrinsically rewarding condition. This can be a challenging goal because of the potentially negative influences of extrinsic control on intrinsic motivation (Lepper & Greene, 1978), but has promise for succeeding when there is initially no intrinsic motivation on the part of the learner. The work of Deci and Ryan (1985), as described in Chapter 1 and elsewhere in this book, provides a more comprehensive explanation of a design process associated with their self-determination theory that promotes different levels of internalized extrinsic motivation in addition to promoting intrinsic motivation.

Interaction-Centered Models

These models assume that neither the personal nor the environmental assumptions provide an adequate basis for understanding or explaining human motivation. In this approach, sometimes called social learning theory, or expectancy-value theory (J. M. Keller, 1983b), human values and innate abilities are seen to both influence and be influenced by environmental circumstances. Currently, *interaction-centered models* are probably the most widely used in the study of human learning and motivation in an educational context (Eccles & Wigfield, 2002; Pintrich & Schunk, 2002). In this regard, Hunt and Sullivan (1974) have offered theories and reviews of motivational research that focus on the interactions of individual traits with environmental influences on behavior, including social factors such as teaching style and the manner of using praise (Brophy, 1981).

Working within the general context of expectancy – value theory, deCharms (1968) developed an applied model with two major variables: achievement motivation representing the value component and personal causation representing the expectancy component. DeCharms' model is patterned after the work of McClelland and Alschuler (Alschuler, 1973; McClelland, 1965), but by including the concept of personal causation, it becomes an interactive model. It is concerned primarily with changing individual behavior to help students feel more confident and more in control of their destinies, and it includes many motivational strategies that can be used in a general instructional design process.

Wlodkowski (1984) provides a comprehensive, applied approach to motivation. He includes a large number of motivational factors including both humanistic and behavioral principles and he divides motivational strategies into six categories: attitudes, needs, stimulation, affect, competence, and reinforcement. He puts these into a process model which specifies things to do at the beginning, during, and at the end of a lesson or module of instruction. This model is based on a logical organization of components and does not have an integrative theoretical foundation. His presentation of his model includes numerous specific descriptions of motivational strategies, for the middle and secondary school levels as well as adult education level (Wlodkowski, 1999).

The model that provides the foundation for this book (J. M. Keller, 1983b) is an interactive motivational design model that is grounded in expectancy-value theory, reinforcement theory, and cognitive evaluation theory (Figure 1.2). These theories are integrated by means of a systems portrayal of when and how each of them is related to effort, performance, and satisfaction. This model contains four categories of motivational variables: attention, relevance, confidence, and satisfaction (ARCS) (J. M. Keller, 1987b). These were derived from a comprehensive review and synthesis of motivational concepts and research studies. A distinctive characteristic of the ARCS model, in addition to its four-category synthesis of motivational concepts, is its systematic design process that uses learner motivational analysis as a basis for determining what kinds of motivational strategies to use (J. M. Keller, 1987c, 1999). This is in contrast to approaches that prescribe specific categories of strategies to use at specified points in an instructional sequence.

Omnibus Models

Omnibus models are best described as complete solutions to given instructional goals. They are not motivational design models, but are included here because they offer excellent examples of motivational strategies in situ. The models sometimes have a theoretical underpinning, but their primary basis is pragmatic in that they incorporate a complete system of teaching and instructional management that is designed to accomplish a specific type of instructional purpose. Motivational strategies are embedded in the totality of these models, but are not usually highlighted or labeled as such. Instead, they are listed as subheadings under the functional category they serve. These might include such things as *getting attention, clarifying values, monitoring progress,* or *rewarding achievement.*

Joyce and Weil (Joyce & Weil, 1972; Weil & Joyce, 1978) and others (Medsker & Holdsworth, 2001) provide compilations of these models. They use a consistent format to present different teaching models that are grouped under one of four categories depending on whether the primary purpose of the model is social interaction, information processing, personal growth, or behavior modification. Examples of these models are *Social inquiry: An inquiry model for the social sciences, Inquiry training model: Theory-building as a source* (for teaching scientific inquiry and theory-building for children), and *Synectics: A model to build creativity.*

This category also includes many of the constructivist approaches to learning environment design (Duffy, Lowyck, & Jonassen, 1993) which focus on how to help learners develop meaningful, contextualized bodies of knowledge. Their concerns include the development of authentic learning experiences in which the lower levels of learning, such as declarative knowledge, are integrated into personally and socially meaningful structures of conceptual understandings, problem-solving skills, and complex cognitive skills (Van Merriënboer, Kirschner, & Kester, 2003).

Process Versus Models: Benefits of a Holistic, Systems Approach

Most of the preceding motivational design models are either procedural guidelines associated with a specific motivational concept or theory or structural models illustrating the relationships among variables and outcomes. In other words, they represent specific approaches to solving motivational problems or, conversely, achieving motivational goals in specific situations. However, motivational design, with emphasis on the word *design*, can also be viewed as referring to a generalizable process incorporating systems analysis and systematic problem solving. From a systems perspective, motivational characteristics and states are influenced by many overlapping and interacting sub systems and supra systems in an environment. For that matter, a person's motivation is itself multidimensional. For example, kids' motivations in a given class may include motivation to learn, to exert influence over other people, to be liked by other people, to avoid notice, and so forth. These motivations are influenced by their family and culture; role models such as their peers; their teachers; the physical environment including such things as temperature and noise; and characteristics of the instructional environment including stimulus richness, clarity of instructional goals and content, and challenge level to mention a few. All of these elements of a learning environment and its context can, in principle, be mapped into a systems model and studied with respect to their influences on motivation and performance. And, the results of theory and research on the relationships among these various components can also, in principle, be fitted into a systems perspective (see J. M. Keller, 2008b for an example).

Design Challenges With Regard to Motivation

There are many problems related to developing a formal approach to the study and practice of motivational design, but two are of particular interest. The first concerns the multidimensional nature of motivation, many aspects of which are rather unstable. Like ability which is a fairly stable and predictable human characteristic, motivation also has some reasonably stable characteristics. For example, people tend to have fairly stable orientations and motive profiles. That is, a person with a high need for achievement will tend to prefer predictably different kinds of activities from a person high in need for affiliation and low in need for achievement. Yet, both of these motives can be overridden by a motive, such as the need for physical security if it assumes a higher priority in a given situation. And, other aspects of motivation are highly volatile. For example, a person who is paying full attention to a lecture one moment can be easily distracted by an unexpected noise or interference from a nearby person. Furthermore, the intensity of one's motivation can vary tremendously over short periods of time. This variation in intensity, or arousal, tends to have a curvilinear

relationship to performance. Low levels of arousal tend to result in low
levels of performance due to lack of interest, boredom, and low levels of
effort. As one's motivation, or arousal, increases the quality and quantity of
one's performance increases, but only to an optimal level (Figure 2.3).
Beyond that, performance begins to deteriorate as motivation continues
to increase. This is comparable to moving from a state of boredom through a
state of optimal arousal to a state of debilitating anxiety. Performance is
less than optimal at either end of the curve. The articulation of this relationship is generally attributed to Yerkes and Dodson (1908) and is called the
inverted U-curve, or Yerkes-Dodson Law. The multiplicity of concepts that
are subsumed under the concept of motivation, the variability of many of
these constructs, and their curvilinear relationship to performance present
real challenges to anyone who tries to develop models of motivational
design!

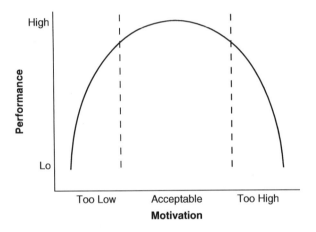

Figure 2.3. Curvilinear Relationship Between Arousal/Motivation and
Performance.

The second problem, which is that of measurement, is closely related
to the preceding. Just as it is difficult to obtain a functional holistic theory of
motivation, it is difficult to **measure** the important elements of influences of
motivational design because there are four, and probably more, sets of
variables that have to be considered. First are the human characteristics
that pertain to motivation, second are the design strategies intended to
influence motivation, third are the social and environmental conditions that
might influence the effectiveness of the motivational strategies, and fourth
are consequences, which present special problems. Sometimes changes in
achievement are used as the primary or only dependent measure in studies
of motivational effects. It is better to use measures of effort, such as time-
on-task, intensity of effort, or latency of response, because these are
direct measures of motivation. Achievement is an indirect measure that is

influenced by many non-motivational factors such as ability, prior knowledge, and instructional design factors. Measurement issues and examples of useful surveys are included in Chapter 11 and measures of specific constructs are described in context in Chapters 4, 5, 6, and 7.

Isolating and Defining the Motivational Problems

Too often, problems are presented without elaboration as "motivational" problems. However, motivation has many components, and a key component of motivational design is to identify the specific and concrete elements of motivation that are problematic in a given situation. A key part of the motivational design process presented in this book is the analysis phase (see Chapter 8). During the analysis phase the motivational constructs presented in Chapters 4, 5, 6, and 7 are used as a basis for diagnosing the motivational profiles of learners to identify specific ways in which their motivation might be satisfactory in a given situation and ways in which there are deficits. The deficits then become the targets for applying strategies to improve those motivational problems. Also, the inverted U-curve provides a basis for doing this analysis because it provides guidance for specifying when students are under motivated or over motivated. Thus, rather than focusing on the global concept of motivation and trying to modify it, the motivational designer can be far more effective by isolating specific aspects of learner motivation where there are problems and then designing relevant strategies.

Deciding Whether to Change the Person or the Environment

Improvements in learner motivation can result from changing the attitudes and habits of people or by changing environmental conditions to accommodate people's existing characteristics. Correspondingly, some psychological schools of thought and educational philosophies focus more on the individual, as in humanistic frames of reference, while others focus more on environmental materials and conditions to promote learning, as in instructivist theories and behaviorist orientations. As previously described, this book adopts an interactionist approach which assumes that learner motivation, and other human behaviors are influenced by internal psychological and physiological conditions and also by environmental stimulation and conditions. People's special abilities, motives, educational and life goals, and energy levels will influence their motivation in given situations. Environmental influences such as availability of resources, clear instructions, equitable grading practices, and variation in instructional methods will also influence learner motivation.

A goal of the motivational design process is to move systematically from analyses of learners and environmental components toward the development of strategies that will either accommodate the learners' existing characteristics or bring about desirable changes depending on what is most appropriate in the situation. In other words, it would be both futile and dysfunctional to try to change people so that everyone had the same learning style. This means that learning environments should be designed to accommodate differences in learning styles. On the other hand, if people lack certain characteristics that could be improved with greater benefits to them, as in the development of self-regulatory skills in people with poor learning habits, then it would be desirable to change those individuals. However, in still another variation on this relationship, if a group of learners are incapable of developing effective self-regulatory skills due to emotional, neurological, or some other type of handicap, then it would be appropriate to try to design the environment to compensate for this problem by having more frequent deadlines, closer supervision, or "motivational messages" (J. Visser & Keller, 1990). These types of interactions between learner aptitudes and instructional methods were studied extensively by Cronbach and Show who published a comprehensive review of this literature (1976). They found little support for providing variations in most instructional approaches to accommodate people based on differences in learning styles, such as those who are more visually versus verbally oriented, because it is much easier to design heterogeneous approaches that accommodate multiple learning styles. For example, it is much easier to design instruction that contains both visual and verbal representations, which is what most teachers do, than to divide the students for specialized approaches. But, Cronbach and Snow (1976) did conclude that there was potential for developing alternative approaches to accommodate differences in learner motivation.

The Limitations of Motivational Design

Even though a systematic motivational design process can be highly effective, there are challenges and limitations to consider when attempting to implement it. One set of challenges concerns the attitudes of teachers and designers toward being responsible for learner motivation. This issue is important because many teachers believe their responsibility is to teach content and skills effectively, but it is the student's responsibility to decide whether or not to learn them. Teachers say they cannot control student motivation; that is, they cannot force students to learn if the students do not want to. This is true, but it is an oversimplification. Teachers cannot control student motivation but they certainly do influence it. They can stimulate students' desire to learn or they can kill learner motivation. There are countless stories of students who became interested in a subject because of the enthusiasm and commitment of the teacher or because of the personal attention given to the student by the teacher. Conversely, too many students have had serious difficulties with their confidence and motivation to learn because of teachers who were harsh, boring, or just not interested in their subject matter or the students.

For teachers and trainers to accept the challenge of motivating learners it is important to understand what their boundaries of responsibility are. Because there are many dimensions to motivation, there is a corresponding diversity of motivational problems. Motivation enters into every aspect of people's lives; it affects their desire to be alone or with other people, their interest in building relationships, their choices of jobs, their willingness to accept authority, their desire to learn, their self-perceptions and self-esteem, their personal management, and even their desire to live. As a teacher, even though you cannot affect students' motivations in all of these areas you can and will affect some of them.

The teacher's motivational responsibility: Within this broad frame of reference, there are three areas that teachers commonly encounter. These are the motivational characteristics that relate to students' willingness to cooperate, desire to learn, and self-perceptions. The first category, *classroom behavior*, is important because a teacher has to manage the students' behaviors in the classroom to create a positive environment for learning. The second area, called *motivation to learn*, is important because this is central to teaching and learning. The third area, *self-perceptions* is more problematic. Teachers can support the development of positive self-perceptions, but normally they cannot assist students with personal motivational problems. This is usually the responsibility of counselors in the school and other adults in the students' lives, such as parents, friends, or professional therapists. With regard to all of these areas of motivational concern, this book focuses primarily on the **motivation to learn**, both the internal characteristics of the learners that affect their desire to learn and the motivational tactics that may be used by teachers to create positive learning environments.

Summary

There are many approaches to bringing about changes in peoples' motivation. They range from clinical efforts to make changes in peoples' personalities, as in the work of McClelland, Alschuler, and deCharms (Alschuler, 1973; deCharms, 1976; McClelland, 1965) to change the basic motive structures of people, to design models such as those of Wlodkowski and Keller (J. M. Keller, 2008a; Wlodkowski, 1999) that focus primarily on creating learning environments that will stimulate and sustain people's desire to learn. These models can be categorized according to whether they are more person centered, environmentally centered, based upon interactions between the person and the environment, or more comprehensive as in the omnibus models that integrate motivational and instructional strategies in support of a particular type of goal-oriented learning environment. Furthermore, all of these approaches are feasible and have evidence in support of their validity. Each of them has a specific purpose and has proven to be valid when used appropriately.

The success of any approach depends in part on how well it is integrated into the overall learning environment. Adopting a systems perspective helps one identify all of the subsystems within a larger system that must be considered in order for an innovation to be successfully adopted and sustained over time. For example, if you implement a program of achievement motivation training that successfully increases the need for achievement among the students in a classroom or school, those motive changes will probably diminish or even extinguish if the dominant family or social culture does not support individual goal striving and competition. In the early 1990s, the government of Indonesia instituted their *Open University* to make higher education available to the large numbers of people who either could not afford to go to a residential institution or could not qualify for the relatively small number of openings in those institutions. One of the assumptions of an open university system is that students will be able to enroll, receive their materials, and study individually at their own paces. However, there were major problems during the early implementation of this system. In the social culture of Indonesia, students were accustomed to working together in cooperative groups in almost everything they did which was a reflection of the larger cultural mores. Now, suddenly they were expected to work in a totally individualistic environment in which they had to set their own goals and work schedules and work diligently to achieve their goals. Thus, the students did not exemplify a traditional need for achievement profile and numerous changes had to be made in this open university system in order for it to succeed.

This example also illustrates the importance of audience analysis in a motivational design process. There are many types of challenges to face when trying to systematically influence learner motivation, including the inherent characteristics of human motivation, but the process is made even more difficult in the absence of a thorough understanding of the motivational dynamics of your students. Students, like people in other parts of life, are busy and want to work in the most direct way possible to achieve their goals. This is especially true in settings like schools where most of the motivation tends to be extrinsically determined. Thus, students will resist if not actually resent frivolous activities designed to motivate them if those activities have no relationship to the learning goals. This is especially true in adult learning environments. For example, if your audience consists of a group of professionals who are attending a short course for the purpose of learning an important new job-related skill or process, they will become annoyed if you engage them in lengthy warm-up or icebreaking activities unless they perceive these activities to be in important part of developing the appropriate social dynamics in that learning environment. However, this is seldom the case and most of the time a getting-acquainted activity that is integrated as a functional part of the lesson's learning objectives is far more effective. This can take the form, for example, of having people recall and discuss experiences or challenges related to the tasks included in the workshop or course agenda. Not only are the participants getting acquainted during this activity, but the results of the activity can be used by the facilitator to help articulate the specific objectives and contents of the training event.

In conclusion, even though human motivation is complex and there exists a huge number of concepts and design strategies related to human motivation, it is possible to obtain an overview of this content in such a way that one can follow a systematic process of motivational design and strategy creation that helps predictably influence learner motivation and the design of appealing learning environments. The next chapter will describe such a process.

3

Chapter 3 – The Arcs Model of Motivational Design

Forethoughts

Here is an exercise that I frequently do when I am teaching motivational design. It helps to reveal some key issues related to motivational experiences versus motivational design (Figure 3.1).

Imagine that you just finished taking the most interesting, motivating class you ever attended and then list some of the things that made it that way.

I like it when ... [These are some things that get or hold my interest in a class.]
1.
2.
3.
4.
5.

Now imagine that you just finished taking the most boring, uninteresting, demotivating class you ever attended, and then list some of the things that made it that way.

I don't like it when ... [These are some things that bore or irritate me in a class.]
1.
2.
3.
4.
5.

Figure 3.1. Motivational Likes and Dislikes.

If you did this exercise, you have shown that you know a great deal about what makes a class motivating. The question is, when you design a lesson or a course or when you prepare to teach is this knowledge that is derived from reflection on your own experiences sufficient to guide you? Or, do you find that there are gaps in your knowledge of how to create a motivating learning environment?

J.M. Keller, *Motivational Design for Learning and Performance*,
DOI 10.1007/978-1-4419-1250-3_3, © Springer Science+Business Media, LLC 2010

Introduction

Typically, even though they have years of experience as students and can potentially list motivating versus demotivating events, people feel that they do not have a reasoned, systematic approach to dealing with the motivational aspects of instructional design and teaching. Some people have a great deal of talent and are highly successful based on their experience and, perhaps, charisma, but they might be more limited in their repertoire than they wish they were. The answers they give to the question about gaps in their knowledge are usually of two types:

> "I don't have a good understanding of all the factors that influence student motivation; I lack a clear grasp of the specific factors involved. There are too many things to think about, and it's too fuzzy."

> "I don't know how to determine what kinds of motivational strategies to use, how many to use, or how to design them into the lesson."

The specific aim of the ARCS motivation model (Keller, 1987b, 1987c, 2008a) is to provide guidance for creating answers to these questions. This chapter provides an introduction to the ARCS model and serves as a foundation for the remaining chapters which are, for the most part, elaborations of the points made in this chapter. The first part of this chapter contains a description of the motivational variables and sample strategies that comprise the four categories of the ARCS model, the second part covers the systematic design process, and the final part discusses the relationship between motivational design and instructional design. The ARCS model, per se, was first introduced in 1984 (Keller, 1984) and I have published numerous articles, book chapters, and workshop materials that describe the model (for example, Keller, 1987a, 1987b, 1987c, 1999, 2008a; Keller & Suzuki, 1988). Therefore, the material in this chapter is derived in part from this background.

Categories of the ARCS Model

Based on an extensive review of the motivational literature which led to a clustering of motivational concepts based on their shared attributes, Keller (1979, 1983b) found they could be sorted into four categories. After making some modifications to the original cluster titles, the ARCS model (Table 3.1) was introduced (Keller, 1984). These categories enable you to quickly gain an overview of the major dimensions of human motivation, especially in the context of learning motivation, and how to create strategies to stimulate and sustain motivation in each of the four areas.

The first category, Attention, contains motivational variables related to stimulating and sustaining learners' curiosities and interests. In

Table 3.1. ARCS Model Categories, Definitions, and Process Questions.

Major Categories and Definitions		Process Questions
Attention	Capturing the interest of learners; stimulating the curiosity to learn	How can I make this learning experience stimulating and interesting?
Relevance	Meeting the personal needs/ goals of the learner to effect a positive attitude	In what ways will this learning experience be valuable for my students?
Confidence	Helping the learners believe/ feel that they will succeed and control their success	How can I via instruction help the students succeed and allow them to control their success?
Satisfaction	Reinforcing accomplishment with rewards (internal and external)	What can I do to help the students feel good about their experience and desire to continue learning?

the context of motivation, attention means something different from when it is used in regard to instructional design and learning. In a learning context the concern is with how to manage and direct learner attention. This is done by using cues and prompts in such a way as to lead the student to focus on the stimuli or parts of stimuli that are specifically related to the learning objectives. But, before attention can be directed it has to be acquired and this occurs in the domain of motivation. Thus, the motivational concern is for getting and sustaining attention.

The next step is to ensure that the student believes that the learning experience is personally relevant. The student might ask the classic relevance question, "Why do I have to study this?", or an adult who was required to come to your training session might be thinking (or saying!), "I don't need this. It doesn't apply to my job, and I have no interest in it." In both of these examples, the students do not perceive any personal relevance for the instruction. Even if a student does accept the need to learn the content, he or she might simply feel alienated from other students or the learning environment. Before students can be motivated to learn, they will have to believe that the instruction is related to important personal goals or motives and feel connected to the setting.

Even if the students in your audience believe the content is relevant and they are curious to learn it, they still might not be appropriately motivated due to too little or too much confidence, or expectancy for success. They could have well-established fears of the topic, skill, or situation that prevent them from learning effectively. Or, at the other extreme, they might believe incorrectly that they already know it and overlook important details in the learning activities. For these situations you have to design the learning materials and environment, including the instructor's behavior, so that the learners become convinced that they can learn the content and experience actual success on an assignment.

If you are successful in achieving these first three motivational goals (attention, relevance, and confidence) then the students will be motivated to learn. Next, in order for them to have a continuing desire to learn, they must have feelings of satisfaction with the process or results of the learning experience. Satisfaction can result from extrinsic and intrinsic factors. Extrinsic factors are very familiar to us. They include grades, opportunities for advancement, certificates, and other material rewards. Intrinsic factors, although often overlooked, can also be very powerful. People like to experience accomplishments that enhance their feelings of self-esteem, experience positive interactions with other people, having their views heard and respected, and from mastering challenges that enhance their feelings of competence.

In summary, these are the four components of the ARCS model that encompass the major factors that influence the motivation to learn. These factors are related to two important questions that you must ask yourself as you are designing or preparing to teach a course. First, what will you do to make the instruction valuable and stimulating for your students? Second, how will you help your students succeed and feel that they were responsible for their success?

Research Support

The four motivational components are based on a general theory of motivation in relation to learning (Keller, 1983b), and on supporting studies from many areas of research on human motivation (for example, Brophy, 1981). Also, there are large numbers of specific strategies that can be used to achieve the appropriate motivational goals. In the process of developing the ARCS model, many of these were gleaned from practical guidebooks, observations, and published studies and inserted into the appropriate categories.

The ARCS model has been validated by numerous research projects and by other indicators of validity. For example, the extensive work of Wlodkowski (1984, 1999) provides concurrent validity in that it includes many similar strategies even though the general model is different. The practical utility of the ARCS Model has been supported in a field test (Keller, 1984), and by research studies in a variety of settings (Shellnut, Knowlton, & Savage, 1999). Theoretical validation has been provided by studies such as those of Small and Gluck (1994) and Naime-Diffenbach (1991). Over time, the strategies have been modified for specific kinds of instructional settings such as textual material (Keller & Kopp, 1987), computer-based instruction (Keller & Suzuki, 1988), and online instruction (Keller, 1999).

Subcategories and Major Supporting Strategies

Each of the four categories also has subcategories based on the major motivational variables subsumed by the categories. The subcategories are useful in diagnosing learners' motivational profiles and in creating motivational tactics that are appropriate for the specific problems that are identified. Following are descriptions of the subcategories and main supporting strategies for each part of the ARCS model. Additional, detailed descriptions are provided in subsequent chapters of this book.

Attention Getting Strategies

The attention category includes human characteristics such as the orienting reflex, curiosity, and sensation seeking. Each of these represents a specialized area of research which will be described in Chapter 4, but in spite of their differences, each of them helps explain factors affecting the arousal and duration of attention.

One important aspect of attention is its nemesis, otherwise known as boredom (Kopp, 1982). Sometimes, as in a quotation attributed to Dylan Thomas who said, "Someone is boring me. I think it's me," educators believe that the avoidance of boredom is primarily the student's responsibility. However, it is not totally up to the student to be self-motivated. No matter how interested the students are at the beginning of a class, it is possible to bore them if you try hard enough. We've all seen professors or trainers who lecture "full bore." To avoid this condition, there are specific kinds of activities that will help, and they tend to cluster into three general categories:

A1 Perceptual Arousal: What can I do to capture their interest?
A2 Inquiry Arousal: How can I stimulate an attitude of inquiry?
A3 Variability: How can I maintain their attention?

Perceptual arousal. This is a type of curiosity (Berlyne, 1965) that refers to reflexive reactions to stimuli. Almost any sudden or unexpected change in the environment will activate a person's perceptual level of curiosity. A change in voice level, light intensity, temperature, or a surprising piece of information as in Chicken Little's proclamation that the sky is falling, to use a less emotional example that could be taken from any one of many horrible headlines, will do it. Humor can also be used to arouse curiosity, but must be used with care. It can cause distractions rather than increasing interest in the subject matter. The arousal of perceptual curiosity is a first step in the attention process but it is usually transitory in that people adapt to the situation rather quickly. It needs to be followed up with the next stage of curiosity arousal.

Inquiry arousal. A deeper level of curiosity may be activated by creating a problem situation which can be resolved only by knowledge-seeking behavior. Instructors often do this by using a warm-up activity that engages the learners in a problem-solving experiential situation and by the use of questioning techniques. Environmental design factors that evoke a sense of mystery are also good curiosity arousers. Kaplan & Kaplan (1978) have shown how curving paths that disappear behind an obstacle, partially revealed objects, and interplays of light and dark can stimulate curiosity and exploratory behavior. In instruction, these effects can be incorporated in multimedia design, furniture arrangements, and the use of presentation techniques such as progressive disclosure.

Variability. To sustain attention it is beneficial to incorporate variability. In a setting where there is little variation in the stimulus characteristics, regardless of whether it is a monotone voice or even a more irritating tick-tock of Grandma's clock, people adapt and tune it out. Instructors who use the same instructional approach repeatedly, even though it is a "tried and true" method, will benefit from variation. Typically, trainers move from a warm-up activity into a short lecture which is followed by a demonstration and an exercise. This is an excellent sequence, but can become boring when used unvaryingly. To diverge with a mediated presentation, a YouTube clip, or group processing activity would be a welcome change of pace.

Relevance Producing Strategies

Relevance is a powerful factor in determining that a person is motivated to learn. "How," the student is consciously or unconsciously wondering, "does this material relate to my life?" If the student has a good feeling about the personal meaningfulness of the material, or consciously recognizes its importance, then the student will be motivated to learn it. People most often believe that relevance refers only to the utility of what they are learning, as when the content of the lesson can be applied on the job or in "real life," but it also has other important components.

Relevance, in its most general sense, refers to those things which people perceive as instrumental in meeting needs and satisfying personal desires, including the accomplishment of personal goals (Keller, 1983b). Responding to people's perceived needs, which may or may not be congruent with their actual needs, is a cardinal principle of organizational success, especially in the fields of selling and marketing, and it is equally important in learning and instruction (Sperber & Wilson, 1986). A successful instructor is able to build bridges between the subject matter and the learner's needs, wants, and desires as represented in the various subcategories of relevance:

R1   Goal Orientation: How can I best meet my learner's needs? (Do I know their needs?)
R2   Motive Matching: How and when can I provide my learners with appropriate choices, responsibilities, and influences?
R3   Familiarity: How can I tie the instruction to the learners' experiences?

Goal orientation. Setting goals and working to achieve them is a key component of relevance. Generally speaking, people will be more motivated to learn if they perceive that the new knowledge or skill will help them achieve a goal in the present or future. Goal orientation is frequently used by teachers and trainers who try to relate the benefits of their courses to college acceptance, getting a job, getting a raise, getting a promotion, avoiding getting fired, or improved job performance. This external goal orientation also applies to courses that are taken as prerequisites to other courses.

This type of utilitarian motivation is probably the single most influential relevance factor, and it is appropriate to build on it when possible. To do this, make sure the students understand how the concepts and skills are related to their goals. It might be clear to you, and it might become clear to them after they return to their jobs. However, to improve the perceived relevance of the instruction while taking the course, use authentic examples and assignments whenever possible; that is, use job-related examples, make sure the students see the connections between the concepts and the skills they are learning in the application examples, and ask the students to describe their own perceptions of the connections.

Sometimes, instructors will try to use goal-oriented or job-related relevance when it really is not appropriate. The connection between the instructional material and the student's future success may be loose and tenuous at best. In foundational courses such as geography or statistics, it might be extremely difficult to identify direct applications to the students' lives, especially if the learners, or trainees have been assigned to the course as a curriculum requirement that is unrelated to their goals. In these situations, when the instructor cannot generate meaningful utilitarian relevance, there are other ways to help establish feelings of personal relevance.

Motive matching. There are many different types of learning environments and students will differ with respect to the ones in which they feel comfortable or not. If students feel positive about the interpersonal structure and working relationships in a learning environment they will be more likely to feel a sense of relevance. Understanding the students' personal motive structures can lead to the development of compatible learning environments. For example, people who are high in the need for achievement motive enjoy defining goals and standards of excellence for themselves. They also like to have a great deal of control over the means of achieving the goal and to feel personally responsible for success. They are often uncomfortable in group work that requires consensus in planning and shared responsibility for the results.

In contrast, people high in "need for affiliation" enjoy being with other people in noncompetitive situations where there is more of an opportunity to establish friendly relationships and enjoy dialogue in collaborative learning activities. It is also possible for people to have a combination of the affiliation and achievement motives. They enjoy interacting and a degree of collaboration, but ultimately they like to have areas of responsibility that are under their control. The point is, that the use of teaching strategies that include cooperative work groups combined with individual competitive activities such as games can help make the instruction more appealing independently of the content.

Familiarity. On the one hand, people enjoy unexpected and novel events as indicated in the section on attention and curiosity, but on the other hand they tend to be most interested in content that has some connections to their prior experiences and interests. At one level, familiarity can be as simple as including human interest language in textual information or human figures in graphics. Text which includes the use of personal pronouns and people's names is more interesting to people than third person or references to mankind in general (Flesch & Lass, 1949). At a higher level, instructional material that confirms the learner's preexisting beliefs and interests will be seen as relevant. In instruction, the use of concrete examples from settings familiar to the learner can help to achieve relevance, especially when teaching abstract material. Some ways to accomplish this are to stimulate personal involvement in the class. Learn and use the students' names. Ask for experiences and ideas from the students. Let them share "war stories" and "a-ha!" experiences.

Confidence Building Strategies

A desire to feel competent is a basic human motive and the degree to which one feels competent (White, 1959) in a given situation is reflected in one's feelings of confidence. Like the other major components of the ARCS model, confidence is a complex concept that encompasses several motivational constructs ranging from those that explain perceptions of personal control and expectancy for success to the opposite extreme which is helplessness (Keller, 1983b). There is also the problem of overconfidence which is detrimental to learning because the overconfident person believes that he or she already knows the given content or skills and does not pay attention to new information.

It is fairly common for teachers and trainers to underestimate people's anxieties about being able to learn in a formal school context because students are very good at masking their feelings and may appear more neutral than they really feel. This is one reason why it is important to provide success experiences for learners as soon as possible in a workshop or course. The success experience will be meaningful and will stimulate continued motivation if there is enough challenge to require a degree of effort to succeed, but not so much that it creates serious anxieties or threatens failure. There are several concepts and strategies that assist in building confidence:

C1   Learning requirements: How can I assist in building a positive expectation for success?

C2   Success opportunities: How will the learning experience support or enhance the students' beliefs in their competence?

C3 Personal control: How will the learners clearly know their success is based upon their efforts and abilities?

Learning requirements. How often have you been a student in the course or participated in a workshop where you really did not know what the instructor wanted you to learn or what would be on the examinations? This is not uncommon and is definitely a source of anxiety. Thus, letting the learners know what is expected of them is one of the simplest ways to help instill confidence. If the students have the appropriate level of ability and prerequisites for a given course, they will have a much higher expectancy for success if the performance requirements and evaluative criteria are made clear.

Letting students know what is expected of them does not mean that the instructor has to list precise and specific learning objectives and then teach to the test. When teaching students to conduct and report a review of the literature or to analyze and describe the common themes in several works of fiction, the instructor may expect an element of creativity that cannot be precisely defined in a learning objective. However, the instructor can define the criteria that would be used to determine the quality of the final product by describing the appropriate uses of evidence, use of logical and cogent arguments for key points, and so forth. Also, providing examples of other people's work will help instill confidence.

Success opportunities. After creating an expectation for success, it is important for the learners to actually succeed at challenging tasks that are meaningful. These success opportunities should be somewhat different for people who are just learning new knowledge or skills than for people who have gotten the basics and are trying to achieve mastery. Persons who are learning something new generally like to have a fairly low level of challenge combined with frequent feedback that helps them succeed or confirms their successes. After mastering the basics, people are ready for a higher level of challenge, including competitions that help them exercise and sharpen their skills. The challenges to the instructor and designer are to move people quickly enough to avoid boredom, but not so quickly that the students become anxious, and to adjust the pacing as the learners' competency levels change.

Personal control. Confidence is often associated with perceptions of personal control over being able to succeed at a task and the outcomes that follow success (deCharms, 1976; Rotter, 1972). Yet, in a learning setting, the control is often clearly in the hands of an instructor. To enhance motivation, the controlling influence of the instructor should be focused in the areas of leading the experience and adhering to the standards that are expected. This provides a stable learning environment in which the learner should be allowed as much personal control over the actual learning experience as possible.

This can take many forms. The use of experiential learning activities and other methods that require the learner to do problem solving provide situations in which the learner has to exercise personal control to succeed. Something as simple as using a short-answer test instead of a multiple-choice test gives the learner more control by showing that you are willing to consider a variety of responses.

To help students improve their confidence, provide corrective feedback that helps them see the causes of their mistakes and how to take corrective action. This helps the instructor and the students to maintain a task orientation in which it is perceived to be okay to make mistakes and learn from them. When students get no feedback until they see their final, summative score or comments, the students' perceptions of control decrease and they become more focused on trying to please the instructor instead of understanding the task. This can cause the instructional culture to shift from task involvement to ego involvement (J. Nichols, 1984). An ego-driven culture is one in which people want to avoid or hide errors so they will look as good as possible to the instructor and other students. On the surface, there might be a high level of accomplishment, but underneath there is usually an increase in anxiety, a decrease in confidence, and a decrease in real learning. Another simple strategy is to give the learner attributional feedback that supports effort and ability as the causes of success. Tell the learner such things as, "See! You did it on your own. I like the way you came up with a solution to this problem." Do not say things such as "You really lucked out on that one," which suggest that success (or failure) was due to things the learner could not control. Also be careful about body language. Both verbal and nonverbal messages will influence the learner's self-confidence.

Satisfaction-Generating Strategies

How many of the following outcomes would give you satisfaction at the end of a class:

- To finish a course and have the satisfaction of being one step further along your goal-path?

- To receive an award or a certificate for the achievement?

- To have acquired a useful set of skills or body of knowledge?

- To have enjoyed working and socializing with other people?

- To have received a tangible reward such as more pay, time off, gift certificates to the bowling alley?

- To have been stimulated by feelings of challenge and accomplishment?

All of the above can be satisfying for some learners, at least some of the time. However, the misuse of these outcomes can be very unrewarding. The final step in the motivational process is to create satisfaction so there will be continued motivation to learn, and positive recommendations of the course to other people. The three categories of strategy in this section provide guidance in determining what kinds of strategy to use to promote satisfaction.

> S1 Natural consequences: How can I provide meaningful opportunities for learners to use their newly acquired knowledge/skill?
> S2 Positive consequences: What will provide reinforcement to the learners' successes?
> S3 Equity: How can I assist the students in anchoring a positive feeling about their accomplishments?

Natural consequences. For a student to be able to successfully perform a challenging task at the end of a class that he or she could not do at the beginning is a very satisfying experience. One of the most rewarding results of performance-oriented instruction is to use the newly acquired skills or knowledge. If the relevance of the course has been previously established, and the student has application opportunities, then the student's intrinsic motivation will be high and there will be less of a requirement for extrinsic rewards. Case studies, simulations, and experiential learning activities can be excellent vehicles for providing meaningful application opportunities.

Another type of natural consequence that supports learners' intrinsic motivation is praise if it is used properly. If praise focuses on specific aspects of performance that are praiseworthy, then students will feel good about this genuine appreciation of their work.

However, it isn't always possible to put the new knowledge or skills to use immediately. There is sometimes a fairly long process of learning specific bits of knowledge and skills before they become a useful package. Also, praise isn't always sufficient in order for students to have an overall feeling of satisfaction. Typically, students are taking courses for extrinsic reasons to become qualified for certificates and degrees or because it is a requirement of their job. Thus, it is also important to use extrinsic rewards appropriately to reinforce the development of new skills and for students to feel good about fulfilling their requirements.

Positive consequences. Incentives in the form of awards, monetary bonuses, trophies, and special privileges are satisfying outcomes for the people who receive them, providing they are used appropriately according the established principles of using reinforcements to stimulate, shape, and maintain behavior. These types of outcomes are useful when learners are not intrinsically motivated, when the learning task is inherently monotonous as in drill and practice exercises, and in situations that are highly competitive. However, a challenge to teachers is that schools seldom provide resources for extrinsic rewards of any substantial value. However, inexpensive, symbolic rewards such as certificates, school supplies, or items monogrammed with a corporate logo can be quite effective in providing external recognition of accomplishment.

Seldom, if ever, is it appropriate to use only intrinsic methods or only extrinsic methods. Even when people are intrinsically motivated to learn the material, there are likely to be benefits from extrinsic forms of recognition. For example, public acknowledgment of achievement, privileges, student presentations of products, and enthusiastically positive comments are generally welcome. A primary issue is control. Learners like to have some feeling of control over their situation and to see the various pieces fitting into a whole. At the same time, people appreciate the external recognition that helps support the value of what they are doing.

Equity. Sometimes a person will feel very good about the outcomes of an achievement until he or she finds out what someone else received. If the other person's outcomes are perceived to be greater but their task accomplishment to be less, then satisfaction quickly turns into disappointment or even stronger negative emotions. People do not look at rewards in isolation, or in terms of their absolute value, which is often difficult or impossible to assess anyway. People tend to make comparisons with other people and with their own expectations. For example, an instructor could accomplish the course goals very satisfactorily, but if the outcomes were not what the students were expecting, student satisfaction would be low. Similarly, a student might achieve a new "personal best," a score that is higher than any he or she ever achieved before. But, if it is lower than someone else's with whom the student was making a personal comparison, satisfaction might still be low.

The best way to handle the problem of equity is to ensure that course outcomes are consistent with initial presentations and discussions concerning purpose and expectations and to maintain consistent standards and consequences for task accomplishment. It is possible to make exceptions for people with unusual circumstances, but these people should not receive special recognition or awards at the expense of those who have excelled under the normal requirements.

Relationships Among the Categories

The ARCS model provides a typology that helps designers and instructors organize their knowledge about learner motivation and motivational strategies. Motivational interventions can be focused within one of the four categories of the model or even within one of the subcategories. For example, the use of a metaphor to connect unfamiliar material to a familiar experience, such as comparisons of electrical circuitry to a plumbing system, could be restricted to Subcategory 3, Familiarity, under Relevance. But, motivational strategies are not always limited in this way. More often a motivational activity will have several effects. For example, at the beginning of a Coast Guard training lesson on how to rig a sling for helicopter rescues the instructor could show a short video of a successful rescue that depended on the use of this sling. This strategy could affect three different areas of motivation by stimulating curiosity, demonstrating the relevance of the lesson content, and providing a vicarious feeling of satisfaction to the students. However, the process might appear to be dangerous and complicated which means that the instructor would need to include a confidence building strategy right away.

Some strategies might extend over several lessons. For example, in a course on quality improvement, let's assume that the designer and instructor decide to prepare a case study which allows the students to apply the course's abstract concepts and procedures to a concrete business situation. To enhance relevance, the case is built around a hypothetical financial organization similar to the institution in which the students are employed. But, if the case exercise also contains an attention getting device at the beginning, contains corrective feedback on the various decisions that are made, and the solution to the problem provides a satisfying sense of accomplishment then not only has the primary concern for relevance been served, but the other requirements of motivation have also been met.

Even though it is expected that any complete instructional method, lesson, or course should fulfill all of the motivational requirements, there will be some situations where a specific type of motivational intervention is required. For example, a technical course might be obviously relevant to newly hired workers, and the course might be achievable. But, the content might be inherently boring, because it is highly procedural and involves very little problem solving or human interaction. In this case, the designer and instructor will have to devise learning schedules, contests, unexpected events, and other activities that are focused almost exclusively on the problem of maintaining attention.

Thus, the four categories defined by the ARCS Model answer the first question posed in the *Introduction* to this chapter regarding an understanding of motivational concepts. These categories of motivational variables help you understand the major components of the motivation to learn and provide guidance for generating strategies to use for each category. But, by themselves the categories do not tell you how many or what types of strategies to use or how to design them into the instruction. These decisions are made during the systematic design process.

The Systematic Process of Motivational Design

In addition to the synthesis and classification of motivational concepts, the ARCS model contains a *systematic motivational design process*. A basic assumption of the ARCS design process is that it is a problem-solving process, not a prescriptive process. That is, it is assumed that in most situations it is not possible to have a prescribed set of strategies or sequence of strategies to implement. At an abstract level it is possible to formulate principles and overall strategies that can be prescribed for creating motivating learning environments, but it is not possible to give concrete, generalizable prescriptions for what will motivate a specific audience in a particular setting at a given time. There is too much variability among the attitudes, values, and expectancies of learners. This leads to a second assumption of the ARCS design process which is that a problem-solving, heuristic approach to motivational design is more appropriate than prescriptive and algorithmic approaches. In the future as increasing amounts of knowledge about motivational design are accumulated perhaps it will be possible to create precise diagnostic tools that lead to concrete tactic prescriptions. But, because of the many situation-specific factors that comprise learner motivation, it is questionable as to whether prescriptive models can be totally successful.

The design process that is contained here is based in system thinking and follows a systematic problem-solving process. A critical success factor in this process is audience analysis which provides the basis for answering the second question in the *Introduction* to this chapter which was concerned with how many and what kinds of motivational strategies to use and how to design them into a lesson or course. Even though this process will help you be more systematic, do not expect it to be completely mechanical or algorithmic; it still requires judgment and benefits from experience, intuition, and creativity.

Motivational Design

The motivational design process, which is similar to the traditional instructional design process, has 10 activities, or steps. The "waterfall" diagram in Figure 3.2 portrays the 10 steps and lists the primary activities associated with each step.

The first two steps in the process consist of obtaining information about the instructional goals and content, the audience, and any other information that will assist in the analysis and design process (see Chapter 8 for detailed explanations and procedures). Then, the next step (Figure 3.2, Step 3) consists of audience analysis which is of particular importance in motivational design and is analogous to task analysis and instructional analysis in instructional design. This analysis helps identify what the motivational problems are. It is assumed that it will be necessary to incorporate motivational tactics in a course to sustain learner motivation, but the most important requirement for successful motivational design is to determine what kinds of major problems there are, if any, that will require specific motivational enhancements to bring learners to an appropriate level. Step 4 is also an analysis step but it focuses on the instructional materials and other aspects of the learning environment to determine whether they have appropriate motivational characteristics and do not have inappropriate ones. The presence of inappropriate strategies can be demotivating. For example, students may become annoyed if you use a series of activities to convince them of how important a lesson is if they already know that it is important. The outputs of Steps 3 and 4 provide input information for formulating motivational objectives and assessments (Step 5).

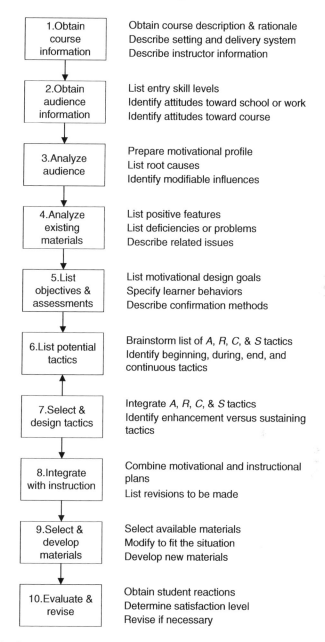

Figure 3.2. Steps in the ARCS Motivational Design Process.

The design and development phases are somewhat different from instructional design in that motivational design usually involves the enhancement of an already existing instructional product or learning environment or of a design document that already contains the instructional blueprint. If the instructional design specifications have already been determined, the question for the motivational design steps is how to create experiences that will fulfill the requirements that were identified in the analysis phase. Consequently, the motivational design phase generally begins with brainstorming, or another type of open-ended activity to generate a large number of possible solutions (Step 6). Subsequently, these are analyzed and the most feasible strategies are chosen (Step 7) and integrated into the instructional materials (Step 8).

After the motivational materials are acquired or developed (Step 9) it is appropriate to conduct a developmental try out, which Dick and Carey (1996) call "one-on-one" formative evaluation. When the materials are ready for a formal test, the final, integrated package of instructional and motivational materials are implemented in a pilot test or in the first offering of the course (Step 9) and formative evaluation is conducted (Step 10) before the materials are released from development for formal implementation.

These steps can also be listed as a set of activities subdivided into four phases based on the purpose of each activity (Table 3.2) as illustrated by the general questions listed for each activity. This ten-step process provides a comprehensive design model that is especially useful if you are designing a whole course or a section of a course that includes several lessons and when a team approach is used. The steps and documentation among team members facilitates communication and replicability in future projects. However, there is a simplified version of this process (see Chapter 10) that is useful when developing a single lesson or even several lessons when they are being motivationally enhanced by the instructor and subject matter expert.

The steps in the model can encompass many specific and complex activities, but in most training situations each step can be performed in a simple, straightforward manner to improve the motivational appeal of the course. Each step in the model is described in detail in Chapters 8, 9 and 10, but the following pages contain a brief elaboration of the process. This will provide a useful frame of reference as a foundation for Chapters 4, 5, 6 and 7. Following is a slightly more detailed overview (with a special emphasis on audience analysis) of how the motivational design process is conducted.

Audience Analysis

Audience Analysis provides the basis for the rest of the motivational design process. It is recommended that audience analysis be conducted prior to the beginning of a class while it is still being designed. This will

Table 3.2. Motivational Design Activities and Process Questions.

Activities	Questions
DEFINE	
1. Obtain course information	What are the relevant characteristics of the current situation including course description, rationale, setting and instructors?
2. Obtain audience information	What are the relevant characteristics of the audience, including entry-level skills and attitudes toward job and training?
3. Analyze audience motivation	What are the audience's motivational attitudes toward the course to be offered?
4. Analyze existing materials and conditions.	What kinds of motivational tactics are in the current materials or other source materials and are they appropriate?
5. List objectives and assessments	What do I want to accomplish with respect to the motivational dynamics of the audience and how will I know if I do?
DESIGN	
6. List potential tactics	How many possible tactics are there that might help accomplish the motivational objectives?
7. Select and/or design tactics	Which tactics seem to be most acceptable for this audience, instructor, and setting?
8. Integrate with instruction	How do I combine the instructional and motivational components into an integrated design?
DEVELOP	
9. Select and develop materials	How do I locate or create motivational materials to achieve the objectives?
PILOT	
10. Evaluate and revise	How can I detect the expected and unexpected motivational effects of the course?

allow the designer to anticipate the students' attitudes at the beginning of the class and to be prepared with the appropriate motivational tactics. Motivational analysis can also be conducted while a course is in progress to determine whether there should be adjustments to the motivational strategies.

The audience analysis is conducted by estimating student motivational levels for each of the 4 major categories of the ARCS model and for any of the 12 subcategories that might assist in developing an accurate profile of the learners. In keeping with the curvilinear nature of motivation, students can be too high or too low with respect to any of these motivational dimensions. For example, if students are too low in the attention category, it is probably an indication of boredom, but if they are too high they are probably going to be hyperactive. Thus, the audience analysis provides guidance on what types of strategies to use and also when it isn't necessary to enhance the motivational properties of the class.

The audience analysis can be based on several types of data ranging from a "best guess" estimate based on the designer's or instructor's personal experience to a judgment based on data collected from the students themselves. If more formal data are not available, even a "best guess" method can be extremely beneficial because it requires you to break away from the broad, general assumptions about the learners' motivational attitudes by carefully considering their attitudes with respect to each of the categories and even subcategories of the ARCS model. The subcategories of ARCS and associated "process questions" listed above are useful in this regard. If, due to lack of sufficient experience with or knowledge of the audience, a "best guess" method is not adequate, then it would be advisable to conduct interviews with members of the target population or other informed persons. Here again, the process questions associated with each subcategory can be used as guidelines for conducting interviews. Additional details about this process are contained in Chapter 8.

The results of the audience analysis are normally summarized in written descriptions, but they can also be portrayed on a diagram of the inverted U-curve that was introduced in Chapter 2 (Figure 2.3). An example (Figure 3.3) illustrates a frequently occurring profile for newly hired employees in a technical course and who have no prior knowledge or experience with this technical area. The students will enter the course knowing that it is relevant to their jobs. Also, due to the selection process most of them will be reasonably confident that they can achieve the objectives although some will have concerns which is why C is located on a line indicating the range of likely attitudes, and they expect to have a good feeling about completing the course successfully. But, many will regard the subject matter, which is highly factual and procedural, as essentially boring to learn. However, it is always important to assess the actual attitudes of prospective learners and not take stereotypical examples such as this for granted.

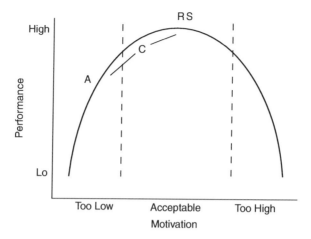

Figure 3.3. Graph of Audience Analysis Results.

A slightly different profile resulted when the author and his associate conducted an analysis of the expected audience at a session of an ISPI (International Society for Performance Improvement) annual meeting. First, we prepared verbal descriptions of our predictions (Table 3.3) and then plotted them on an inverted-U curve (Figure 3.4). This was a "best guess" analysis based on the experience of the two presenters (Keller & Kopp, 1987) with ISPI and similar conferences. Feedback from the audience confirmed that the analysis was accurate. However, it is also true that the

Table 3.3. Description of Anticipated Audience Motivation at a Professional Meeting.

Attention	Initially high. The audience will be very attentive at first, but will require changes of pace and participative activities to sustain attention.
Perceived relevance	Initially moderate to high. Since this is a volunteer audience, they will believe that the topic of motivation is important, but they will have concerns, even skepticism, about whether they will get something useful from this session.
Confidence	Some will have genuine concerns about their ability to motivate others, some will believe they can do it if they learn some good techniques, and others will already be skilled motivators, but they just want to check us out.
Satisfaction potential	Positive. If they find something applicable in the session, and are neither bored nor confused by the presenters, then they will feel that it was a useful 45 minutes.

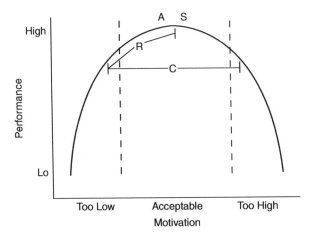

Figure 3.4. Illustration of Audience Motivation at a Professional Meeting.

results of this analysis are fairly general and could apply to many audiences at professional meetings.

The decision as to how specific to be will depend on the criticality of the decision, the anticipated obstacles, and the consequences of failure. For example, in preparing to meet with a captive audience the presenter might face hostility and risk being a scapegoat for the audience's irritation. In this case, the audience analysis is more critical; the presenter will have to give extra effort to identifying audience characteristics that will help in gaining attention to the learning process and establishing meaningful relevance.

In summary, the audience analysis provides an indication of what types of motivational strategies to use and where to place the greatest emphasis. In some categories, it may not be necessary or desirable to add any motivational strategies because you should never try to motivate an audience that is already motivated; just get on with the instruction and do not de-motivate them. For example, if the relevance of the material is clearly established in the students' minds before they ever set foot in the classroom, then do not add lecture material or exercises designed to establish relevance. It takes up valuable instructional time and irritates them. Instead, simply include a few comments to confirm the relevance of the material and use work-related examples and exercises.

Motivational Objectives

After completing the audience analysis and other analyses that might be relevant (Chapter 8), the next step is to list motivational objectives. These are your project objectives and might not be exactly the same as your affective objectives for the learners themselves. For example, if you anticipate that the learners will feel anxious and have a high fear of failure when they begin your class, you could write an objective that specifies that at the end of the first 30 minutes of training learners will have a more positive expectation for success in this class.

With respect to the preceding example of an analysis of an antici-pated ISPI audience, specific motivational objectives were written for con-fidence and relevance (Table 3.4), but not for attention because the audience did not indicate that attention would be a problem at the beginning of the presentation. Certainly, strategies were used to sustain curiosity, but it was not considered to be a problematic area. However, even though a given category of motivation might not be considered to be a problem for the audience, the presenter might find it beneficial to prepare objectives for the given area, such as stimulating attention and curiosity, especially if the presenter is inexperienced or uncertain about what to do. The criterion for determining how many objectives to write is a pragmatic one. If the designers or presenters believe it will be useful based on the analyses and their personal experience to write a particular objective, then they should do so. It is better within reason to have too many than not enough but without reaching a level of detail where they become trivial and unnecessarily costly.

Table 3.4. Motivational Objectives and Measures.

Objectives	Self-Report measures
Participants will indicate a higher degree of confidence in their ability to conduct motivational design.	My confidence in my ability to conduct motivational design has. a. Improved quite a bit b. Improved somewhat c. Stayed the same d. Not applicable (I didn't do enough of the pretest and/or exercise to have an opinion.) e. Other (Please describe.)
Participants will indicate that the session was interesting and worthwhile.	Overall, I found this session to be: (Check the lines where appropriate.) Interesting _____Boring Worthwhile _____Waste of Time

Motivational Measures

As in any type of project activity, it is useful to know if you have achieved your goals. When deciding what measurement methods to use and preparing the materials, it is possible to use the full range of measurement possibilities. These can range from direct observation of specified behaviors to self-report questionnaires. Straightforward self-report measures (Table 3.4) can be very useful when they focus on an identified area or concern. The important point, as in any measurement situation, is that the measures are consistent with the objectives and that the effects of bias can be taken into consideration in interpreting the results.

Motivational Strategy Design

It is not uncommon for designers or instructors, after they have developed their lesson blueprints, or lesson plans, to then reflect on what they can do to motivate the students and to then prepare a list of ideas. In this ARCS process, it is also appropriate to make lists of ideas, but it does not occur until all of the preceding steps have been taken. The importance of taking time for audience analysis has been empirically confirmed (Farmer, 1989; Suzuki & Keller, 1996). When designers do not conduct an adequate analysis and then apply the results to the final selection of strategies to use, they frequently incorporate too many and inappropriate strategies.

The strategy design phase has three steps which can be enjoyable, incorporating both creative and analytical thinking, if it is not rushed. The three steps are generation, selection, and integration.

The generation step is like brainstorming. The goal is to think of as many ways as possible to accomplish the motivational objectives. Look through other training materials, review published resources, recall examples from workshops you have attended, and talk to other people. Consider various types of material and strategies, such as cartoons, case studies, role plays, and experiential activities, which tend to promote interest and involvement. The point is to be in an open, creative frame of mind as you generate possibilities.

After assembling some ideas, it is time to be more analytical and to begin the selection process. It is important to consider the time and cost associated with incorporating any of the strategies, and to consider the personal styles of the instructors and students who will be associated with this course. It is also important to determine whether the motivational strategy will contribute to accomplishing the learning objectives. Some participative activities can be extremely clever and engaging while they are in process, but if the instructional effects are trivial, then the audience will be irritated and will become cynical of future efforts to use similar methods.

The third step is integration. After the motivational strategies have been chosen, it is time to adapt them to the specific setting and to write them into the instructional design plan. This also provides an additional opportunity to determine whether the motivational strategies are going to use an appropriate amount of the instructional time, and whether they will be internally consistent with the content and structure of the instruction.

Development and Pilot Test

During the development phase, the motivational material is prepared in conjunction with the instructional material. In fact, the distinction between the two often becomes blurred. A single activity, such as a case study introduced in the early part of the course, can help establish relevance at the same time that it is illustrating a concept or procedure.

When the materials are pilot tested, it is again important to think about motivation separately from instruction. The motivational criterion measures should be implemented along with the achievement measures and other indicators of course effectiveness that are used during the formative evaluation. If the motivational results are not what you hoped for, then respond as you would to deficits in instructional effectiveness, and begin to work on revisions.

Integration of Motivational Design and Instructional Design

The motivational design process is structurally similar to the traditional instructional design process and there have been several attempts to illustrate how they can be coordinated. Keller (Keller, 1983b, 1987c) described a way of coordinating them by illustrating how most of the activities in the two processes can be conducted in parallel (Table 3.5). The instructional design model depicted in the left-hand side of Table 3.5 is reasonably generic, particularly in regard to the sequence of steps. Some models distinguish between Define and Analyze as phases; others place Objectives under Design instead of Define or Analysis. However, these differences do not alter the basic relationships between the two processes under discussion.

As illustrated (Table 3.5), the audience motivational analysis can be conducted concurrently with the analysis activities in the instructional design process. Although individual designers will adapt models to suit their style and situation, the motivational analysis would normally occur after conducting the instructional analysis. Having identified the general body of knowledge or skills that the students are supposed to learn, it is time to estimate their motivational attitudes toward the material. Background information about the audience may have been obtained earlier when conducting a job or task analysis, but the actual analysis of the information is most effective after the instructional analysis is conducted. The results of the audience analysis can influence decisions about the learning objectives in addition to providing input to the writing of motivational objectives.

The interfaces during the Design and Develop phases are straightforward, and they involve parallel but different activities. The exception is developmental testing which is a formative evaluation activity. The drafts of the instructional materials, including the motivational enhancements, are presented to experts and representatives of the target population to

Table 3.5. The Parallel Processes of Motivational and Instructional Design.

Phase	Instructional Design steps	Motivational Design Steps
Analyze (define)	Pre-project analysis	
	Conduct task, job, or content analysis	
	Conduct instructional analysis	
	Identify audience entry behaviors	Conduct audience motivational analysis
	Write performance objectives and criterion measures	Write motivational objectives and criterion measures
Design	Design instructional sequences	Generate motivational strategies
	Instructional methods	Select strategies Integrate motivational and Instructional strategies
Develop	Helping the learners believe/ feel that they will succeed and control their success	Select or create Instructional materials Prepare motivational materials
		Enhance instructional materials
	Developmental test for learning and performance ("one-on-one" tryouts)	Developmental test for motivation
Implement & evaluate (pilot test)	Implement with target population representatives Conduct formative evaluation Certify or revise	

obtain feedback about the accuracy, clarity, time requirements, and effectiveness of the materials. At the same time, feedback should be obtained about whether the materials are appealing to the learners in terms of content and appearance ("Do the learners react positively to the 'look and feel' of the materials, whether in print or online?") and whether the motivational activities are feasible.

During the pilot test, or small group tryout (Dick & Carey, 1996), the entire package is implemented and formatively evaluated. The critical point here is to include formal assessments of the motivational effects of the instruction in addition to measures of learning and performance. This is commonly done with simple, "smiley face" types of self-report measures.

These can be valuable, but their value will be enhanced by having them correspond to the critical problem areas of motivation as defined during the audience analysis.

A final point is that the relationship between the two sequences in Table 3.5 should not be viewed as a formal prescription. In fact, the portrayed relationship is probably more representative of the expert than the novice designer. A novice designer, particularly one who has never given much thought to systematic motivational design, may choose to complete all of the instructional design steps prior to working on the challenge of motivational enhancements. This allows the designer to assess the entire instructional package in terms of its appeal to the target audience and to enhance it as appropriate. With experience, it becomes more efficient and effective to combine the two processes.

A different approach was taken by Main (1993). Recognizing the lack of motivational concerns in instructional design, he proposed that motivational design can be integrated into instructional design as shown in Table 3.6. In this approach, instructional designers need to ask about A, R, C, and S components simultaneously in every phase of the instructional design process. That is, "the ARCS model provides a framework for motivation considerations in each of the five phases" (p. 39). This means that there is an integration, which makes it difficult to distinguish instructional design process from motivational design process.

Table 3.6. Integrating Motivational and Instructional Design (Adapted from Main, 1993).

Motivational Categories	Instructional Design Phases				
	Analysis	Design	Development	Implementation	Evaluation
Attention Relevance Confidence Satisfaction					
	Validation and Feedback				

Okey and Santiago (1991) also proposed that motivational design in accordance with the ARCS model be incorporated into instructional design following the process of Dick and Carey's instructional design model (Figure 3.5). They described how the phases and activities of motivational design can be integrated into the procedures of instructional design, but in comparison to Main (1993), it would be more appropriate to say that

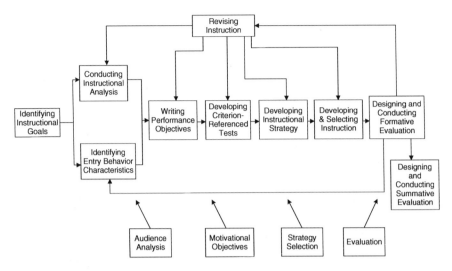

Figure 3.5. Relationships Between Motivational and Instructional Design
(Based on Okey & Santiago, 1991, p. 18).

their approach incorporates motivational design into instructional design. In
Main's approach, consideration is given to the four components of motivation throughout the instructional design process, but he does not specify
particular motivational design activities such as audience analysis which is
somewhat different from analyzing audiences with regard to entering level
knowledge and skills. In contrast, Okey and Santiago described how motivational design activities can be put into the process represented by the Dick
and Carey model and they discussed how this could be done.

ARCS and ISD: Point-by-Point Comparisons

A limitation of the Okey and Santiago approach is that the connections between the motivational and the instructional design processes are
defined only loosely. However, it is possible to be more precise in describing
the interfaces between the ten steps in the ARCS design process and the
instructional design process.[1] For example, eight key interfaces are illustrated in Figure 3.6. One could specify even more interfaces but these eight
represent the most important ways in which the two models can be symbio-
tically related to each other. However, before describing these interfaces,
it is helpful to point out that both processes draw upon the same base of

---

[1] I am grateful to Dr. Sang Ho Song who created an earlier version of this
point-by-point comparison approach while he was working with me as a
graduate student. I have modified it considerably, but appreciate his contribution of this idea.

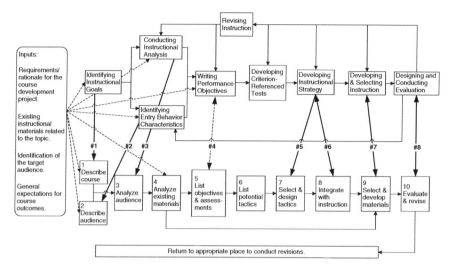

Figure 3.6. Point-by-Point Interfaces Between Motivational and Instructional Design Processes.

input information which usually includes information about the rationale for the course development project, existing materials related to the course to be developed, who the target audience is, and what the general expectations are as to what the course is supposed to accomplish.

Interface 1: Instructional Goals and Course Description

In instructional design, the output of a goal analysis includes a description of the current situation, a description of the desired situation, and a listing of gaps between the way things are now and the way you want them to be. In particular, the output of goal analysis describes the kinds of job-related competencies that must be represented in the workforce in order for the organization to achieve its goals. In a school environment, desired competencies are described more in the context of the requirements for students to be able to succeed at the next stage of schooling and in terms of the development of life skills that are appropriate for the given age level to help them in the present and future.

Interface 1 illustrates that the first stage of motivational design has a similar aim, but the focus is more on factors in the environment that are related to problems in the attitudes of learners or workers and the environmental factors that will influence the kinds of change strategies that will be feasible. The output of this first phase will provide guidance to the motivational designer as well as the instructional designer throughout the design process with respect to problems, goals, and practical decision- making regarding the selection and development of strategies.

One benefit of conducting this preliminary analysis is that designers can review the rationale for the course or other intervention that is to be developed to determine why there is a desire for it. In applied settings, education is usually directed at improving knowledge, skills, and attitudes that will lead directly to improved performance on the job. However, courses are also offered in applied settings for enrichment instead of the development of specific skills. In this case, they are usually called development courses rather than training. And, courses are also taught for such reasons as

- someone requires that they be taught, without reference to documented needs,
- they are part of a logically structured curriculum, or
- they are just a tradition ("our curriculum wouldn't be complete without it").

It is certainly helpful during the design process to know why a course is being developed so that the content and the motivational tactics and strategies can be consistent with the basis for the course.

Another benefit of this preliminary investigation is that the designer can obtain useful information from a variety of people and other information resources such as literature, instructional materials, students, teachers, employees, employers, subject matter experts (SMEs), administrators, staff members, vendors. This information can help them discover insightful ways to address the possible motivational problems when they get into the design phase of the process.

Interface 2: Entry Behavior Characteristics and Audience Description

Two major products are expected from the stage of "Identifying Entry Behaviors and Characteristics." One is a set of identified entry behaviors or skills that should have already been mastered by the target audience before beginning the instruction. The other is general knowledge of characteristics of students.

Identifying entry behaviors is important because it will give motivational designers more ideas on dealing with learners' motivation—especially confidence. We can easily notice that students with deficiencies of prior knowledge and skills will have difficulties in learning new material that goes beyond their existing schema. Therefore, information about students' prior knowledge can be used to determine how to bridge the new knowledge to be learned with what already exists.

Interface 3: Instructional Analysis and Audience Motivational Analysis

The instructional analysis phase of instructional development yields a description of the knowledge, skills, and attitudes that are related to the goals of the lesson or course. This product can be quite specific with detailed listing of steps in a process or a hierarchical presentation of higher and lower order concepts and skills to be included. Also, by knowing what the students are expected to learn, you can begin to estimate their motivational attitudes toward learning it.

The audience motivational analysis step also benefits from the knowledge about entry behavior characteristics combined with the other information contained in the Describe Audience step, which is Step 3 in the motivational design process. Trying to determine what the students' motivational attitudes will be at the beginning of instruction will depend in part on how competent and knowledgeable they are with regard to the lesson content. However, even though this information is useful, audience motivational analysis also includes other elements pertaining to the audience's past attitudes toward the subject matter and the results of peer group influences.

Interface 4: Coordinating Instructional and Motivational Objectives

It is desirable that Step 5 of motivational design (List Objectives and Assessments) be conducted concurrently or right after the "Writing Performance Objectives" stage of instructional design. There are two reasons for this. First, having appropriate levels of motivation greatly assists the accomplishment of the learning objectives. Also, good motivational objectives can help overcome deficiencies with the learning objectives and content of a class. In actual classrooms or training situations, the objectives of the instruction are not always clear and the content is sometimes not useful or necessary for the students to know. Even if things were done properly during design, they are not always executed properly. But, if the students are sufficiently motivated they are more likely to persevere in the face of instructional design challenges.

Interfaces 5 and 6: Designing Instructional and Motivational Strategies

It is sometimes assumed by instructional designers that the time to consider the motivational aspects of a design is when the instructional strategies are being developed (Dick & Carey, 1996). Although this approach might have positive results much of the time, it could also have negative results. If the appropriate motivational analysis has not been conducted, it is easy for instructional designers to add too many motivational strategies that are not related to specific motivational problems. Also, the process for designing motivational strategies is quite different from specifying instructional strategies.

The selection of instructional strategies is often a somewhat logical and prescriptive process based on the nature of the instructional objective. For example, if a student must recall specific items of knowledge or steps in a procedure, then an instructional strategy that includes memorization is appropriate, but if the instructional objective requires selecting and applying an appropriate procedure to solve a problem, then a problem-solving case study would be appropriate. But, the selection of motivational strategies to accomplish a goal of stimulating curiosity or improving confidence is not so straightforward. The motivational strategy design process begins with brainstorming to identify as many strategies as possible that might help achieve the desired outcome. Then, in a second phase of strategy design, one develops an analytical attitude and chooses strategies that can be achieved within the time constraints of the lesson and not detract from the instructional objectives. And, to the fullest extent possible, the motivational strategies should be transparent. For example, when beginning a lesson on troubleshooting in an electronics course, especially when the learners do not believe they should even have to take the course because they expect test equipment to tell them exactly what to do, the instructor could begin with a case study that requires the students to figure out how to proceed when the automated test equipment is broken. A case study based on an experience from real life can be motivating by building curiosity and relevance at the same time that it illustrates how the instructional content will be used.

As the final list of motivational strategies is occurring, the final step in the design stages of instructional and motivational development is to integrate motivational tactics into the instructional strategy (Step 8, Figure 3.6). So far, motivational tactics themselves have been selected or combined with each other. Now it is time to combine them with the instructional content, presentation methods, and learning activities that are in the instructional strategy. In some cases, designers will find a great deal of overlap between instructional strategies and motivational strategies. For example, providing review opportunities could be considered as an instructional strategy as well as a confidence building strategy. The important thing is to be aware of both the motivational and the learning requirements of the tactics. A review opportunity might not be necessarily, strictly speaking, if the learners have demonstrated mastery, but if their confidence is low, then an additional review opportunity could be included primarily for motivational purposes.

Interface 7: Develop Instructional and Motivational Materials

At this point, it is time to decide whether to develop new instructional and motivational materials or adopt and modify existing ones. In either case, the development of motivational materials need not be separated from the development of instructional materials. As indicated in the previous section, the greater the extent to which the motivational strategies are transparent in that they are fully integrated into the instructional materials the better. Even if a particular motivational activity is not integrated into an instructional activity it should still have a clear relationship to the instructional objectives or it can cause problems. For example, let's imagine that a newly assigned Coast Guard instructor is having trouble keeping his students engaged in a basic training class on the quick formation and rapid deployment of a helicopter-assisted rescue mission. The Coast Guard men and women on the rescue vessel have to repeat this course once a quarter, so they feel that they already know everything about the operation and the instructor is struggling to keep their interest. He talks to a visitor who is on the ship to conduct an inspection and discovers that the visitor recently participated in a dangerous rescue mission. He invites the visitor to talk to his class, which is a big success. The instructor would like to repeat this in his next class but knows that he won't always be so lucky as to have a guest speaker available. So, he searches the Internet to find videos of Coast Guard rescues. He succeeds in finding quite a few of them including a YouTube clip called the "Top Ten Coast Guard Rescue Videos" and the Discovery Channel series called *SOS: Coast Guard Rescue*. He includes a couple of them every time he teaches the class. At first they stimulate interest, but only while the video is showing. The students' interests do not transfer back to the training exercise. And, after awhile, the students even lose interest in the videos. In this example, the true stories are inserted into the lesson and they are related to the topic, but they are not tied directly to the learning tasks. The instructor would probably be more successful by building some scenarios and competitive games to engage the learners in proposing solutions to the scenarios that are presented as part of the learning task and then showing the videos of real-life situations dealing with that problem. In this way, the motivational elements would be fully integrated and perceived to be a natural activity because the students tend to like challenges and competition.

Interface 8: Evaluate and Revise

This interface illustrates that formative and summative evaluations are important for both processes and provide input to guide revisions to the instruction for both effectiveness and motivation. Evaluation for motivation can be planned and implemented in conjunction with evaluation for effectiveness including learner achievement. However, when implementing the plan, it is best to administer achievement tests before any motivational surveys are distributed. There are two reasons for this. The first is that you should avoid the possibility that the motivational survey would interfere with their performance on the achievement test and the second is that the achievement test is part of the overall instructional experience and might influence their motivational reactions.

Applying the Process

In summary, these eight major interfaces illustrate ways in which motivational design activities can be integrated with instructional design activities. However, as with all representations of a human-managed process, the actual implementation of it can vary depending on circumstances such as the kinds of inputs that are already available, timelines, budgets, and other resources. It can also vary depending on the personal style of the designer and the nature of the subject matter. For example, in an orientation course on a new sales strategy, the course designer would probably not employ a detailed application of all of these steps. But let's assume that a designer is responsible for developing a course to teach highly critical skills pertaining to safety procedures in a nuclear power plant which could result in catastrophic damages if they are violated. If, as actually happens, the learners are overconfident in believing that they already know all of the procedures even if they don't and they are bored with the idea of having to take the course, then the instructor will probably benefit from following all of these steps in detail! It is easy to understand this point in the context of such a critical situation, but even in the simpler situation it is also important to include all of the critical success factors such as audience analysis, preliminary motivational strategy list, final strategy list, and integration with instruction. The difference is that some of these steps can be done quickly and informally in the simpler case.

Summary

It is the design process that is built into the ARCS model that makes it a practical, application-focused theory instead of being purely a descriptive or prescriptive theory. It combines a descriptive synthesis of concepts and theories of motivation into the four major categories of ARCS with a systematic approach to motivational design. This problem-solving, design approach makes the ARCS model unique and gives it its broad base of application.

However, it is important to realize that it requires a good base of knowledge to apply the process effectively. Farmer (1989) and Suzuki (Suzuki & Keller, 1996) found that if designers and teachers are not proficient in doing a motivational analysis of the audience, or if they just skip it and start creating motivational ideas, then the resulting products are likely to de-motivate rather than motivate the learners. This is because the resulting products will probably have too many motivational strategies as well as strategies that do not directly address the actual problems.

The next four chapters describe the primary motivational variables to consider when analyzing an audience and contain numerous examples of motivational strategies and tactics. Then, the three chapters after that provide detailed explanations with examples of how to conduct the motivational design process.

Chapter 4 – Generating and Sustaining Attention

Forethought

Is curiosity a good thing?

Figure 4.1. Attitudes Toward Curiosity.

What do you think about this? Do you have an opinion one way or the other?

Introduction

A few years ago I would announce in my motivation classes that the study of curiosity had been neglected in the educational and psychological literature. But, that seems to have changed! Maybe it's because of the re-emergence of interest in multimedia, increased concerns about decreases in invention and patent applications in our society, or just because researchers have regained interest in this topic. Whatever the reason, this chapter tries to capture essential information about the concept of curiosity and the related concepts of boredom and sensation seeking. Following this review, the latter part of the chapter contains guidance for applying this knowledge. It describes three major subcategories of curiosity, or the broader concept of attention, and lists a selection of principles and strategies for generating and sustaining learners' attention and curiosity.

J.M. Keller, *Motivational Design for Learning and Performance*,
DOI 10.1007/978-1-4419-1250-3_4, © Springer Science+Business Media, LLC 2010

Psychological Basis for Attention

Learner attention is necessary for both motivation and learning. In motivation the issue is with how to **stimulate** and **sustain** the learner's attention. In learning, the concern is with how to **direct** the learner's attention to the concepts, rules, skills, or facts to be learned. In that regard, consideration is given to providing cues and prompts that will signal the key elements of instruction to the learners. In the context of motivation, and in particular within the ARCS model, the term *attention* represents a synthesis of several related concepts including arousal theory, curiosity, boredom, and sensation seeking. Most of the early research in these areas was done in the 1950s and 1960s (Berlyne, 1954b; Maw & Maw, 1966; Schachter, 1964; Zuckerman, 1971). For several decades there was little research on these topics, but there seems to be a resurgence of interest (Lowenstein, 1994; Renninger, Hidi, & Krapp, 1992). This is timely and relevant because of the contemporary interest in multimedia instruction, web-based instruction, and other forms of e-learning. In all of these delivery systems it is challenging to find and employ techniques for getting and keeping attention without distracting students from effective learning (Harp & Mayer, 1998).

Arousal Theory and Early Concepts

Arousal theory represents an effort to explain how behavior is activated and how it changes as one's arousal level changes. Much of the research and theory in this area is physiological. It attempts to understand how various bodily functions and systems function in relation to levels of arousal (Hebb, 1955) and stress (Selye, 1973). However, there are also formulations of arousal theory that involve both physiological arousal and cognitive attributions (Schachter, 1964). Arousal is assumed to be on a continuum ranging from very low levels, such as sleep, to extremely high levels of stress which can be expressed actively in emotional behavior such as rage or its opposite which would be paralyzing fear. However, the changes in behavior are not considered to be a linear, steadily progressing, increase in motivation and performance as arousal increases. The pattern is generally considered to be curvilinear in keeping with the Yerkes–Dodson Law, also known as the inverted-U curve (see Chapter 2). This pattern of low levels of arousal being associated with low levels of performance extending through a phase of optimal arousal and performance to a decline in performance resulting from excessive stress is an important component of the ARCS model. In particular, as was briefly illustrated in Chapter 3, Figures 3.3 and 3.4, this concept provides a basis for audience analysis and is also useful in helping to decide what types of motivational tactics to use. When analyzing learners and trying to identify specific problems, it is necessary to consider both the low motivation side of the curve and the high stress side. Both can result in less than optimal performance and disruptive behavior by students.

Curiosity

What is *curiosity?* On the one hand, everyone understands intuitively what it means to be curious, but on the other hand, we can find very different ideas about this concept. For example, consider the following perspectives:

- After the Olympian gods led by Zeus defeated the Titans, as told in the ancient Greek myth, *Pandora's Box*, Zeus created a man to live on the earth and have dominion over it and all its creatures. His name was Epimetheus and as time went by, his actions became totally predictable to the gods and to himself giving rise to high levels of boredom. So, in consultation with Poseidon, the god of the sea, Zeus decided to create a woman who would be like Epimetheus yet unlike him. He said, "Poseidon, this creature must be different in every way from man. Where man is hard, she will be soft. Where man is strong she will be weak. Where man is foolish, she will be wise. Where man is brave she will be timid. Where man shall be scared she will be brave" (Hoffman, 2007). After a time, boredom arose once again. This time, Zeus summoned Hades, the god of the underworld and asked him to gather the sprites, which are spirit-like creatures, of everything he could find in all the dark places (disease, hunger, hopelessness, cruelty, etc.). Zeus put these sprites into a beautifully decorated, sealed box which was carried to earth by an avatar in the form of a man. This man encountered Epimetheus and Pandora and asked them to watch over his heavy box because he had to hurry along on his journey. He cautioned them not to look inside the box or there would be terrible consequences. Eventually, Pandora's curiosity overwhelmed her and she opened it. Immediately almost all of the creatures swarmed out of the box, biting and nipping at her and then Epimetheus as they flew away. One of the sprites that had remained in the box came to Pandora, touched each hurt, and healed it. Then the sprite entered into Pandora's heart and gave her the gift of hope. This made Pandora realize that even though she could not undo the damage and pain she had caused, she could make it easier through the knowledge that one can have hope.
- Aristotle, as translated by Wheelwright (1951), begins *The Metaphysics* by saying, "all men [sic] by nature have a desire for knowledge." He goes on to say that this is evidenced by the joy we derive from our perceptions and insights quite apart from any practical benefits they might have.
- William James (1890) talked about there being two kinds of curiosity. The first is physiologically based as an instinct that is aroused by partially perceived, unexpected, or startling stimuli in the environment. The second is more cognitively based, such as scientific curiosity or metaphysical wonder.
- Berlyne (1954b) says that curiosity is a drive that is aroused by a stimulus such as a question and is reduced when the question or other stimulus event is resolved (Berlyne, 1954b).

What can you infer from these various conceptions of curiosity? Is it an innate drive, like hunger, that is activated when the appropriate stimuli are present and disappears when the body or mind's needs are met? Is it a self-activated behavior that arises because it is a pleasurable activity that is not satiated by success; that is, successful excursions of curiosity lead to increased amounts of curiosity-focused behavior? And, is curiosity a trait that works to the benefit of mankind, or is it a dangerous trait that must be managed carefully? In other words, is curiosity voluntary, a self-initiated quest for knowledge or an innate instinct or drive born of a need to resolve conflicts? And, is it a pleasurable state which also has positive benefits for mankind, or is it an unpleasant state and perhaps fundamentally evil force? Now, it is easy to see why the young woman in Figure 4.1 became so confused after being so confident!

Conceptual Foundations of Curiosity

All of these perspectives are represented in the study of curiosity, just as they are represented in the history of myth and philosophy. With regard to the psychological study of curiosity, there are basically three theoretical perspectives. The first is drive theory which assumes that curiosity results in a state of arousal which is considered to be aversive, or unpleasant, and results in exploratory behavior aimed at resolving the situation that led to curiosity arousal. The second is incongruity theory which assumes that curiosity is stimulated by perceived incongruities in the environment which, in moderate amounts, can be pleasurable, but otherwise tends to be aversive. The third perspective is based on the concept of competence in that curiosity is presumed to be a human characteristic related to the desire to achieve mastery of one's environment.

The empirical study of curiosity is relatively recent. Berlyne, who is one of the best known psychologists in this area, said (Berlyne, 1950), "Psychology has so far had surprisingly little to say about stimuli which influence behavior simply because they are new," p. 68. He introduced a preliminary theory of curiosity grounded in drive theory (Hull, 1943). Berlyne proposed that when an organism perceives a novel stimulus a drive-stimulus-producing response will occur. He also proposed that after a period of time curiosity will diminish. After habituating a group of rats to their environment, an experimental box, he removed them, placed three cubes in the box with one group of rats and three rings in the box with a second group. In both cases the rats approached the objects and investigated them for a while and then ignored them. In the next step, Berlyne replaced one of the cubes with a ring and one of the rings with a cube. Again in both cases the rats investigated the new object while ignoring the familiar objects. Thus, Berlyne concluded that novelty activates the curiosity drive resulting in exploratory behavior until the stimulus is no longer perceived to be novel.

In a subsequent study Berlyne (1954a) studied more complex forms of stimulus-generated exploratory behavior which he called *epistemic curiosity* (Berlyne, 1954b). This type of drive is aroused, for example, when a question is raised and reduced by obtaining its answer. In this study, one group of students was given a set of "fore" questions followed by instruction and then an after-questionnaire, while the other group was given only the instruction and after-questionnaire. He found that the pre-questions generated a higher level of curiosity and recall on the post-questions. He also found that interest was higher for questions about more familiar animals and whose concepts seemed incompatible. In this study, the preference for more questions about more familiar animals may have been due to the complexity of the study which led to excessively high levels of stress with the more unfamiliar material. However, questions and answers that had unexpected, or surprising, elements were most interesting. Thus, Berlyne found support for this more complex curiosity setting that was consistent with the earlier study; that is, curiosity was aroused by novel, unexpected stimuli and reduced after the objects or topics became familiar to the subjects.

Inherent in this theory is the notion that curiosity is stimulated by environmental stimuli. However, people may engage in exploratory behavior in the absence of a specific stimulus. Berlyne explained this by distinguishing between *specific* and *diversive* exploration (Berlyne, 1965). Specific exploration is stimulated by a novel or unexpected stimulus that results in either a reflexive response, such as a puff of air across the side of one's eyes which leads to blinking and then turning to identify the cause, or a perceived incongruity such as the blocks and rings that were presented to the rats in Berlyne's study of novelty and curiosity (Berlyne, 1950). Specific exploration, also called *perceptual curiosity*, focuses on a specific object and is information seeking. It abates when there is sufficient information to reduce the uncertainty associated with the object. Specific exploration is stimulated by what Berlyne calls the *collative variables* which refers to stimulus attributes such as novelty, change, surprisingness, incongruity, complexity, ambiguity, and indistinctness (Berlyne, 1965).

In contrast, diversive exploration results in settings that are monotonous or boring and do not have a specific object. The organism searches for anything that is interesting or novel and is not distracted by specific information gathering. Thus, diversive exploration is related more to boredom relief than to curiosity. However, the phrases "specific curiosity" and "diversive curiosity" are used in the literature. Day described specific curiosity as "an approach and exploratory response" that is high in collative characteristics such as novelty and ambiguity (p. 491). He also characterized a divisively curious person, as quoted in Vidler (1977), as being "restless, easily bored, continuously seeking change, but possibly fails to concentrate on these situations until full understanding is reached" (p. 25).

These distinctions between perceptual and epistemic curiosity and between specific and diversive exploratory behavior are well established in the literature and also fit well with our everyday experiences of being curious. We can easily distinguish between a momentary event that captures our attention briefly until we recognize and then dismiss the source of the intrusion and the experience of having a desire to investigate a topic of interest until we find the answers we seek. We can also distinguish between a focused type of curiosity that has a specific object and casual, somewhat random, visual explorations of our environment due to monotony or boredom. Even though these concepts grew out of a drive theory orientation to the study of curiosity, they are relevant to our general experience.

Another conception of curiosity is grounded in the concept of incongruity. According to Kagan (1972) the desire to remove uncertainty is a motive. It is similar to Berlyne's concept of epistemic curiosity, but it is not the result of a state of deprivation or any tension reduction process; hence, it is not considered to be a drive. As a motive it represents a human tendency to try to make sense of the world. This motive is supported by Festinger's (1957) work on cognitive dissonance as well as gestalt psychology. Cognitive dissonance occurs when two ideas or behaviors are perceived to be inconsistent or contradictory. This creates an aversive state and activates the motive to eliminate the incongruity by removing the cause of the discrepancy or modifying one's cognitive interpretations of the situation. For example, if a young boy believes that his father is strong and self-controlled, but observes his father losing his temper at his Little League ball game, yelling at the umpire, and being told to leave the ball field, the boy is in a state of cognitive dissonance. He can resolve the situation by modifying his concept of his father's character or by justifying his father's behavior as an expression of his father's principles regarding football games.

This assumption of a human motive to make sense of the world is also a cardinal principle of gestalt psychology which was founded in Germany in 1912 by Max Wertheimer (Koffka, 1935). With many experiments, they demonstrated that the whole can be more than the sum of its parts due to human tendencies to close gaps by organizing their perceptions into meaningful and familiar shapes and patterns. For example, they would present a line in the shape of a circle but with the two ends not touching each other. In recall tests, subjects tended to draw a complete circle. Even though this school of psychology is no longer active other than in the study of perception (Banks & Krajicek, 1991), its basic principles, like those of cognitive dissonance, are consistent with and support the incongruity theory of curiosity. Other researchers whose theory and experiments support this perspective, as described by Lowenstein (1994), include Hebb, Piaget, and Hunt.

A third theoretical perspective is also based on curiosity as a motive rather than a drive and focuses on human beings' desires to be competent and achieve mastery of their environment. It is reflected in the often cited description of curiosity provided by Maw and Maw (1964). Based on their review of existing literature on the topic and investigations with elementary school children, they concluded that curiosity is manifested when a person

1. reacts positively to new, strange, incongruous, or mysterious elements in his environment by moving toward them or manipulating them;

2. exhibits a need or a desire to know more about himself and/or his environment;

3. scans his surroundings to seek for new experiences;

4. persists in examining and exploring stimuli in order to know more about them (p. 31).

Their description of curiosity implies that it is a positive quest for knowledge and information that will answer questions, lead to deeper levels of understanding, and increase one's level of competence and mastery. This is different from both the drive theory explanations of curiosity which are grounded in the reduction of an aversive state of mind caused by uncertainty and the incongruity theory which is based upon the supposition of a motive-based behavior but still has the assumption that uncertainty is an aversive state of mind. From the perspective of motivational design, each of these theories will support certain types of analyses and strategies to be incorporated into a learning environment as will be explained later in this chapter.

Research on Curiosity

Research on curiosity includes studies designed to establish its validity as a psychological construct. These include studies to determine whether it has predictive validity; that is, do people who are higher in curiosity behave in the ways they are expected to behave relative to people low in curiosity. This research also includes studies of its concurrent and discriminate validity which determine whether curiosity is correlated with other constructs which would be expected to be correlated and not correlated with constructs that are expected to be independent from curiosity. One of the issues in establishing the validity and theoretical foundation of a construct is to answer underlying questions about what it should or should not be related to. For example, is curiosity correlated with intelligence or not? Should it be expected to be correlated? These issues are not always clear from the theoretical basis for the concept and must be determined by empirical studies. The following sections summarize some of the research findings regarding curiosity in relation to intelligence, learning, parental attitudes, schooling, self-concept, creativity, tolerance for ambiguity and perceptual rigidity, achievement, motivation, and anxiety.

Curiosity and Intelligence

One would expect curiosity to be positively related to intelligence, because we think of people with high levels of curiosity as being more inquisitive and having a higher desire to learn new things. However, the research has not demonstrated that there is a particularly strong relationship between curiosity and intelligence. Maw & Maw (1964) found significant but moderate correlations, ranging from 0.43 to 0.67, between IQ as measured by the Lorge–Thorndike Intelligence test and teacher judgments of curiosity for 148 5th graders in five different classes. The correlations of IQ with peer judgments of curiosity among the same 5th graders were also significant, ranging from 0.32 to 0.65, but less so. This led the researchers to control for IQ in the development of their curiosity assessment development and construct validation studies.

In contrast, at about the same time, Penny and McCann (1964) found almost no relationship between curiosity and intelligence. They were developing and validating a measure of reactive curiosity which they defined as "(1) a tendency to approach and explore relatively new stimulus situations, (2) a tendency to approach and explore incongruous, complex stimuli, (3) a tendency to vary stimulation in the presence of frequently experienced stimulation" (p. 323). They wanted to distinguish between the state of being curious and actually acting on one's curiosity. In a study with 120 boys and 154 girls in the 4th, 5th, and 6th grades, they found positive but insignificant correlations ranging from 0.06 to 0.14 for the boys. The correlations for 4th and 5th grade girls were 0.03 and 0.07, respectively. The correlation for 6th grade girls was much higher (0.24) but still not significant.

Day (1968b) administered an instrument consisting of 28 visually complex patterns originally developed by Berlyne (1963) to measure specific curiosity with a large group of 7th, 8th, and 9th grade students. He found no relationship between specific curiosity and IQ ($r = -0.01$, $n = 395$). However, he (1968a) reported finding positive correlations in a number of different studies with a self-report measure of curiosity that he created and the verbal portion and total IQ scores of the WISC. In a study of curiosity and intelligence in relation to creativity, he (Day & Langevin, 1969) found no correlation between curiosity and intelligence as measured by the overall score on the Hartford–Shiply IQ test, but there was a small but significant correlation at the 0.05 level with the verbal subtest ($r = 0.26$, $n = 75$). In a study of the relationships among curiosity, test anxiety, convergent thinking, divergent thinking, and intelligence Vidler (1974) found only a small positive relationship between curiosity and intelligence that just reached significance at the 0.05 level.

In summary, the literature shows that there might be no relationship or only a moderately positive relationship between curiosity and intelligence. However, it is difficult to draw a firm conclusion because this research has used many different methods for measuring curiosity. Until there is a more consistent, widely accepted definition of curiosity, there will still be uncertainty as to how strong this relationship actually is. For the time being, it is probably best to follow the example of Maw and Maw and to control for IQ in research and development studies involving curiosity.

Curiosity and Learning

As with the relationship between curiosity and intelligence, it is logical to assume that there would be an overall positive relationship between curiosity and learning and this assumption is supported by the research. There appears to be a moderate to strong correlation of curiosity with learning and the relationship might be even stronger than with intelligence, but the research is not altogether clear on this. Maw and Maw (1961) found that delayed retention of two large samples of 5th grade students was higher for high curiosity than low curiosity children independently of IQ. Many of the high curious children with higher retention scores were below average in IQ. Caron (1963) also found a positive relationship between curiosity and learning, both rote learning and comprehension, but especially on comprehension. His measurement of curiosity was a composite score consisting of subjective expectancy for acquiring the given knowledge and degree of involvement in the learning task. He found significantly positive results with a group of 1000 college sophomores, but he also found that past academic performance was correlated with the outcome. Thus, it was clear that curiosity did make a contribution to learning in this setting.

Another relevant concern pertains to the distinction between intentional and incidental learning. Research has shown rather consistency that anxiety and other elevated drive states can result in aversive levels of anxiety which is related to reductions in the range of cue utilization in learning. This research has shown that task related learning, or intentional learning, can improve under these conditions but incidental learning decreases. Incidental learning would be facilitated by attending to cues in the learning environment that are tangential to the specific task-related demands of the learning environment. The question is, how does this relate to curiosity? The drive reduction theories consider it to be, like other drives, an aversive state. But, other theories regard it as being a motive that is characterized by positive affect and approach behaviors. Paradowski (1967) investigated this question by testing the effects of novel versus familiar stimuli on intentional and incidental learning with undergraduates who were given pictures and text of common animals and unfamiliar animals in a counterbalanced design. The unfamiliar animals were designed to arouse curiosity and he found that the high curious group scored higher on both intentional learning as tested by details about the animals and incidental learning which was tested by asking questions about the background designs and colors. These results were unexpected given the traditional drive theory explanations of curiosity which postulate that curiosity arousal creates anxiety and reduces the processing of extraneous cues and confirmed the more positive conceptions of curiosity as a motive. However, these results to not rule out that there can be both drive-induced and motive-induced aspects of curiosity.

Developmental Influences: Parental Attitudes and Schooling

As with other personality characteristics, one can question whether there are developmental influences on children's curiosity. A fairly commonly held opinion is that children are naturally curious but it becomes diminished after they are in the school system for a while. Yet, many people persist through the school system and into adulthood with high levels of curiosity. Maw and Maw (1966) asked whether there are parental attitudes that are correlated with children's levels of curiosity. Using a combination of teacher and peer judgments, they identified high and low curiosity 5th grade boys and girls in a middle-class suburban area. Parents of these children completed the Parental Attitudes Research Instrument (PARI) (Schaefer & Bell, 1958). The researchers found several relationships between parental attitudes and curiosity for boys but not for girls. The fathers of high curiosity boys scored significantly lower than fathers of low curiosity boys on fostering dependency, harsh punishment, ascendancy of husband, and suppression of sexuality. Fathers of high curiosity boys scored significantly higher than fathers of low curiosity boys on the equalitarianism subscale. Mothers of high curiosity boys scored significantly lower than mothers of low curiosity boys on three subscales: fostering dependency, excluding outside influences, and intrusiveness. No differences were found with respect to girls. However, the number of pairs of girls and parents, 30, was much smaller than with the number of boys and their parents, 57. Thus, the parents of high curiosity boys tended to support higher levels of independence, more egalitarianism among the two parents and the child, and less suppression of their gender-based behavior.

Saxe and Stollak (1971) studied the behavior of 40 1st grade boys consisting of four groups. Each group represented a specific personality characteristic (high curious and prosocial, low curious, high aggressive, and high neurotic). Each child and his mother entered a play room outfitted with a variety of familiar and novel objects and toys. Mothers were told they would be observed for the purpose of seeing how her child interacted with the toys and she could play with him or not as she chose. They found that mothers of curious high prosocial boys displayed more positive feelings, fewer restrictions, and less inattention than mothers of aggressive boys. Mothers of curious high prosocial boys also displayed more positive feelings than mothers of low curious boys and mothers' positive feelings were correlated with their boys' attentiveness, manipulation, and offering of information. A child's curiosity toward novel stimuli was most highly correlated with mother's novel curiosity. Also, there was a moderate but significant correlation between education level and quantity of question–answer interactions.

All in all, both of these studies demonstrated a clear relationship between parental attitudes and behaviors and curiosity as well as other personality characteristics. Socioeconomic factors can have an influence but in these studies those factors did not appear to be nearly as influential as the personalities and parenting style of the mothers and fathers.

Independently of parental behaviors, questions have been raised about the influence of schools on curiosity. Curiosity tends to decline with age (Vidler, 1977) but it isn't clear whether this is due to maturation or environmental influences such as the schools. There is broad agreement that curiosity is one of the personality characteristics that should be fostered in school (Maw & Maw, 1977; Messick, 1979; Piaget, 1952; Wohlwill, 1987), yet there is evidence that teachers do not always encourage curiosity even though they say they value it. Torrance (1963) found that among teachers who say they value curiosity the students they identified as being best were not the most curious. And, Arnstine (1966) found that most classrooms do not include elements of the collative variables (novelty, paradox, surprise) that stimulate curiosity. Also, with regard to environmental influences, it might be that classrooms become less conducive to curiosity development as children progress through the grades. Several researchers have found that there is a substantial decline in the percentage of teachers in the intermediate grades who encourage expressions of curiosity compared to the primary grades (Englehard, 1985; Goodlad, 1984; Torrance, 1965). In a quasi-longitudinal study, Engelhard and Monsaas (1988) measured school-related curiosity of elementary students in grades 3, 5, and 7 in two public and one Catholic schools. There was a decrease in school-related curiosity across grade levels, but there was no influence due to type of school.

Based on the available evidence it is easy to want to blame the schools for the decreases in curiosity. As children progress through the grade levels there tends to be a stronger emphasis on getting right answers to specific questions and to acquiring established paradigms of thought. However, it isn't clear that this is a necessary condition as opposed to simply being the status quo. It would be interesting to examine classrooms that incorporate innovative educational approaches such as constructivist learning models and problem-based learning to see if there are measurable differences in levels of curiosity compared to more traditional instructivist approaches.

Curiosity and Creativity

It has been argued based on theory and conceptual definitions that there should be a relationship between curiosity and creativity (Day, 1968a) and there is some evidence to support this contention. Torrance (1969) asked a group of 75 highly gifted 6th graders to generate unusual questions about ice. One half of them had been identified by their teachers as being their most curious pupils and the other half the least curious based on a set of criteria that followed Maw and Maw's characteristics of the curious child. He asked the students to produce questions that would lead people to think about ice in new ways. One half of the children were given five minutes to produce as many questions as they could and the other half were given small notebooks called "Idea Traps" to take home and bring back the next day. He found that there was no difference between groups on the number of questions produced during the timed conditions but that the low curious children actually produced slightly more divergent questions than the high curious children even though the difference was not significant. However, under the untimed, take home, conditions the high curious children produced significantly more divergent questions. This confirmed the researcher's expectation that high curious children require more time for pursuing a problem and processing it in order to produce creative results.

Several other studies tend to support the relationship between curiosity and creativity. Based on a factorial discriminant analysis conducted on a battery of tests administered to 416 5th grade boys and girls who had been rated by their teachers and peers as high or low in curiosity, Maw and Magoon (1971) found that highly curious children were also higher in creativity. The association between curiosity and creativity was also found by Vidler (1974) who obtained positive relationship between curiosity and divergent thinking which is associated with creativity. His study included 212 undergraduate students in introductory education classes. Day and Langevin (1969) found positive correlations between curiosity and two measures of creativity with 75 female undergraduate nursing students. And, in a factor analytic study of 224 5th grade boys who were classified by their teachers and peers as to curiosity level, Maw and Maw found a positive correlation between creativity and a general curiosity factor.

One of the challenges in assessing these relationships is that neither curiosity nor creativity has clear, unambiguous definitions Maw and Maw (1970a). Using discriminant function analysis, the researchers found that higher levels of curiosity were associated with effectiveness, loyalty, reliability, accountability, intelligence, creativity, social attitudes, tolerance for ambiguity, a sense of personal worth, and responsibility. These results were based on 26 different measures of cognitive abilities, personality characteristics, and social action indices.

Curiosity, Tolerance for Ambiguity, and Perceptual Rigidity

It seems that to possess high levels of curiosity one must be open to new ideas and experience and not be too upset by experiencing a fair amount of uncertainty doing so. It is difficult to avoid ambiguities and other sources of uncertainty while exercising ones curiosity. The only way to avoid this would be to already have the answers before you start and that, of course, would be contradictory to the concept of curiosity.

In some ways the relationship between curiosity and ambiguity seems to be reciprocal. Smock and Holt (1962) studied children and found differences in the type of conceptual conflict introduced by different types of stimuli with some eliciting more curiosity than others. They also found a negative relationship between perceptual rigidity and curiosity motivation. Children with more rigid schemata tended not to perceive as much incongruity, perhaps because they were not open as much to new or discrepant information. In other words, children who were perceptually rigid avoided the unpleasantness of ambiguity by not perceiving incongruities in the same stimuli in which curious children did perceive them.

When students are comfortable with their surroundings and the nature of the learning task, they seem to be more open to expressing curiosity, probably because they have less anxiety than when the setting and task are unfamiliar or uncomfortable to them. Lenehan et al. (Lenehan, Dunn, Ingham, Signer, & Murray, 1994) found that students who were provided homework prescriptions based on their identified learning style preferences compared to a comparison group that received conventional study skill guidelines achieved higher grades, demonstrated more curiosity about science scores, and had lower anxiety and anger scores.

Curiosity, Self-Concept, and Anxiety

One can investigate the relationship between curiosity and many other personality characteristics. For example, Maw and Magoon (1971) found that higher levels of curiosity were associated with effectiveness, loyalty, reliability, accountability, intelligence, creativity, social attitudes, tolerance for ambiguity, a sense of personal worth, and responsibility. These results were based on a discriminant function analysis of 26 different measures of cognitive abilities, personality characteristics, and social action indices. However, the focus in the present setting is on relationships that are particularly useful in the context of designing and creating motivating learning environments. In addition to the relationships that have already been described, it is useful to consider curiosity in relation to self-concept, achievement motivation, and anxiety.

Self-Concept: A positive relationship between curiosity and self-concept appears to be a relatively stable finding. Maw & Maw (1970b) identified 15 high curiosity boys and 14 low curiosity boys from 19 different 5th grade classrooms. They measured a variety of factors, such as self-reliance, sense of personal worth, sense of personal freedom, feeling of belonging, and lack of withdrawing tendencies to estimate self-concept, and all of these factors were positively correlated with curiosity. Maw and Magoon (1971) found that several factors indicating positive self-concept loaded on the curiosity factor in their discriminant function analysis with a group of 5th grade boys and girls.

Anxiety: With respect to anxiety, its relationship to curiosity is usually inverse; that is, low levels of anxiety are associated with higher levels of curiosity. As Day (1968b) points out, high anxiety, especially as measured by Manifest Anxiety Scale, is associated with tendencies to withdraw from a situation and with feelings of helplessness which means that exploratory behavior will have ceased. If the state of anxiety is strong enough, it will depress curiosity in both high curious and low curious people. Peters (1978) found that high curious college students asked questions more than three times as much as low curious students when the instructor was perceived to be nonthreatening. But in the condition where instructors were perceived to be threatening, there were no differences between the two groups.

Vidler (1974) studied the correlations among curiosity, test anxiety, convergent thinking, divergent thinking, and intelligence. He found that both convergent and divergent thinking are negatively related to test anxiety and positively related to curiosity. He also found that convergent thinking is closely connected with traditional measures of intelligence and divergent thinking with creativity. He found a negative relationship between test anxiety and intelligence. He found a small, positive relationship between creativity and intelligence. He found a moderately positive relationship between curiosity and creativity.

In summary, there are many dimensions to the concept of curiosity and this is, without a doubt, a human characteristic that is of great interest to people. Furthermore, it is clear that people are not united in a desire to promote curiosity. One of the challenges to educators and counselors is to understand the conditions that promote curiosity development in order to know how to assist clients, students, teachers, and parents in developing this important survival skill.

Boredom

Eric Fromm (1955) said, "... one of the worst forms of mental suffering is *boredom*, not knowing what to do with one's self and one's life" (p. 253) (quoted in Healy, 1979, p. 38). This thought has been expressed throughout the ages in many ways. Carl Jung, the famous psychoanalyst who was a contemporary of Freud, expressed it from a different point of view (Figure 4.2).

The human characteristic of boredom has been studied independently from the study of curiosity for the most part. But, like curiosity, the concept of boredom has been a topic of philosophical, sociological, and psychological thought for a long time! For example, boredom, or ennui, combined with anomie, which refers to feelings of normlessness or a loss of values, was a central theme in Federico Fellini's famous film "La Dolce Vita." Released in 1960 and set in the era of the 1950s closely following two world wars and when there was a constant awareness of the possibility of a nuclear holocaust, it portrays a bored group of well-to-do "drifters" who have lost faith and allegiance to the Church and other traditional values and are always searching for thrills to escape momentarily from an overriding sense of purposelessness and boredom. This group is set in contrast to an intellectual who fills his apartment with philosophers, poets, and artists,

"I'M SOMETIMES DRIVEN
TO THE CONCLUSION THAT
BORING PEOPLE NEED TREATMENT
MORE URGENTLY THAN
MAD PEOPLE."

DR. CARL JUNG

Figure 4.2. Carl Jung on Boredom (Source: Personal Collection).

but their musings are ultimately pretentious and empty resulting in a tragic action by the host. This film is considered to be brilliant and even profound as a work of cinematic art but also because of the powerful way in which it captured key sociological characteristics of this era.

This sociological perspective on concerns about disassociation and boredom is also captured in a treatise by Sean Healy called *The Roots of Boredom* (Healy, 1979). His central thesis is that although boredom has always been a topic of consideration in human affairs "its incidence and character has radically changed in the course of the last three centuries, and that what was a rarity has become a pervasive aspect of Western culture ..." (p. 1). One can wonder if Healy would draw the same conclusions today because, thanks to the many distractions offered by technology and social networking opportunities and the number of two-parent families in which both are working, people seem to be anything but bored. However, many of these alternatives to boredom might be escapist in nature rather than meaningful engagements with life and intellectual development.

These considerations, while not grounded in empirical research, are valuable in that they illustrate cultural orientations and values that influence peoples' motivation and behavior. With regard to psychological research, Geiwitz reviewed the available literature on boredom (Geiwitz, 1966) and found four constructs that tend to be mentioned in conjunction with it. The first was *arousal* which was generally considered to have an inverse correlation with boredom. In other words, low levels of arousal are associated with high levels of boredom. The second was monotony which was considered by many to be positively correlated if not actually synonymous with boredom. However, some of the previous research found that reported levels of boredom could vary independently of the level of reported monotony but that boredom was associated with *repetitiveness* which was an element of monotony. A third construct, constraint, was presumed by some to be related to boredom but had not been empirically demonstrated. And, the fourth construct was unpleasantness or negative affect.

How is this related to schooling? Imagine sitting in a class in which you are finding it almost impossible to stay awake. Assume that it is a class that you do not want to take (unpleasantness), you can't leave until the bell rings (constraint), the teacher speaks in a monotone voice (low arousal), and is very redundant (repetitive). It is the perfect scenario to induce boredom! And sleepiness. Is this scenario realistic or an exaggeration of reality? I will let you answer that question.

As a result of his experimental study, Geiwitz (1966) found that there are differences among the four constructs with respect to their effects on boredom. After performing several episodes of a highly repetitive task (making check marks on sheets of paper) the subjects reported high levels of arousal, repetitiveness, constraint, and unpleasantness and all were significantly correlated with boredom. However, when holding three of these variables constant and studying each one independently in relation to boredom, he found that low arousal and high constraint were independently related to boredom. Unpleasantness was somewhat related to boredom when there was repetitiveness. Thus, the three conditions of low arousal, high constraint, and high unpleasantness were most closely associated with boredom.

Independently of Geiwitz's (1966) work, Mehrabian and O'Reilly (1980) proposed a similar three-dimensional model consisting of three pairs of characteristics that could be used to characterize various dimensions of temperament. They are pleasure–displeasure, arousal–nonarousal, and dominance–submissiveness, which are similar to constraint in Geiwitz's model. Examples of emotional states and their characterizations by the three sets of constructs are exuberance (pleasant, arousable, dominant); anxiousness ((unpleasant, arousable, submissive); relaxed (pleasant, unarousable, dominant); and disdainful (unpleasant, unarousable, dominant). Boredom, as characterized by Kopp (1982) is low on arousal, pleasantness, and dominance, which he called self-determination.

These studies attempted to define boredom in terms of its associated characteristics which are helpful to understanding the critical attributes of the concept. But a limitation of these definitional efforts is that they are indirect based on inferences drawn from correlations. Another direction in the study of boredom is represented by efforts to develop self-report measures that provide direct, albeit subjective, estimates of it. Vodanovich (2003) reviewed 25 years of research on the measurement of boredom and describes several instruments that are relevant to learning and work settings.

A conclusion to be drawn from these various studies is that boredom can be conceived as being below one's optimal level of stimulation. This reductionistic representation of the concept is helpful, but it is even more helpful to have knowledge about the attributes of boredom and ways of assessing it in different settings, especially when one tries to diagnose the causes of boredom in a learning environment and design strategies to alleviate it.

Sensation Seeking

In contrast to boredom is the concept of sensation seeking (Zuckerman, 1971, 1978, 1979) which refers to the extent to which people seek unusual or novel experiences. Would you, for example, prefer to ride in a hot air balloon or watch a travelogue on your television set? High sensation seeking needs are associated with a variety of risky behaviors such as fast driving, gambling, excessive use of alcohol, promiscuousness, and even using controlled substances. But, this represents the risky extreme forms of behavior and these risky behaviors are not the goal of high sensation seekers but rather the consequences of pursuing behaviors that satisfy their desires for novelty, change, and excitement. Other forms of behavior that satisfy needs for sensation seeking include physically challenging activities such as mountain climbing or hang gliding, emotionally engaging entertainments such as horror movies or other kinds of suspense movies, high levels of social activity, and even adventure such as travel to foreign places (Zuckerman, 1979).

Traditionally, the primary method for measuring sensation seeking tendencies was with Zuckerman's "Sensation Seeking Scale" (SSS) which originally had 34 items but was later expanded to 72 items (Zuckerman, 1971). This instrument has pairs of forced-choice items which ask you to choose between such things as

a. I enter cold water gradually, giving myself time to get used to it.
b. I like to dive or jump right into the ocean or a cold pool.

Sensation seeking is not a unidimensional construct. The measurement scale provides a general SSS score as well as scores on four factors: thrill and adventure seeking, experience seeking, disinhibition, and boredom susceptibility. The propensity toward high levels of risk taking would characterize only some people and be reflected in a high score on the thrill and adventure seeking subscale. One of the subscales, boredom susceptibility, suggest that some people are motivated more by a desire to avoid boredom that to seek high levels of risk, which illustrates why there can be such a wide range of behavior among people scoring high on the SSS.

Research on both sensation seeking needs and boredom illustrate that people vary in the amount of stimulation that is optimal and that there are both trait and state differences in these characteristics. An instructional pace that will be considered relaxing by a person low in arousal needs might be insufferably boring to a person high in sensation needs. This is another reason why audience analysis combined with variation in approach is useful in motivational design. You need to know how much variation there is in your audience, and what level of stimulation will be appropriate.

Strategies for Attention and Curiosity

By now, you know how important the category of attention is. Before any learning can take place, the learner's attention must be engaged. The best-designed instruction will be completely wasted if the learner's mind is elsewhere. Even if students want to learn, they will find it difficult if their minds are dulled by an environment that is too bland or repetitive or they are distracted by the features of an environment that is too noisy. The challenge with attention is to find the right balance of consistency, novelty, and variation for your learners, because people differ in their tolerance of stimulation. Some people get bored very quickly while others prefer a relatively more stable environment. By understanding how people differ, what tactics to use, and how to adjust the tactics for your audience, you will be able to keep them focused and interested. There are several different sub-components of attention (Table 4.1), each of which has a central question and supporting tactic that helps define it. Also, each of these is based on one of the major supporting concepts of attention. The first, perceptual arousal, is based on Berlyne's concept of the same name and incorporates other basic elements of arousal theory. The second, inquiry arousal, is directly related to Berlyne's concept of epistemic curiosity, and the third, variability, incorporates the issues surrounding boredom and sensation seeking.

Table 4.1. Subcategories, Process Questions, and Main Supporting Strategies for Attention.

Concepts & Process Questions	Main Supporting Tactics
A1. Perceptual arousal What can I do to capture their interest?	Create curiosity and wonderment by using novel approaches, injecting personal and/or emotional material.
A2. Inquiry arousal How can I stimulate an attitude of inquiry?	Increase curiosity by asking questions, creating paradoxes, generating inquiry, and nurturing thinking challenges.
A3. Variability How can I maintain their attention?	Sustain interest by variations in presentation style, concrete analogies, human interest examples, and unexpected events.

A.1. Capture Interest

Jim began the workshop, "Safe Operation of the Forklift Truck," with a true story of Fred who decided driving the forklift had to be a snap and tried it out after watching a friend drive it. Luckily Fred survived, but both the forklift and three aisles of stored merchandise were lost. Jim told the story with dramatic gestures and facial expressions, using good story-telling techniques. If available, he could have shown a video dramatization as an alternative.

An unexpected noise or movement will automatically attract a person's attention. This phenomenon can be and is used by teachers when they pause dramatically, yell "pay attention," slap a book on the desk, or use any number of other tactics to regain their students' focus. However, these tactics are effective only if used sparingly and even then their effects are usually momentary. There has to be something to excite a deeper level of curiosity or the moment is lost.

Another and more powerful element of perceptual arousal is concreteness. Generally speaking, people are more interested in specific people and events than in abstractions. For example, compare the following statement

Just before the beginning of the Revolutionary War, a famous American patriot said that people should be willing to die if necessary to obtain liberty for the citizens of this county.

to this one:

On the eve of the Revolutionary War, the famous American patriot Patrick Henry exclaimed, "I know not what course others may take; but as for me, give me liberty or give me death!"

Which one, in your opinion, is the more attention getting sentence? I hardly need to point out that research shows that it is the second one. It has a much higher level of interest because it mentions a specific person and contains a quotation of an emotionally charged statement of his.

All of the tactics in the following list are examples of ways to get or regain the attention of learners as a result of exciting their senses or their expectation that something interesting is going to be presented. These tactics can apply to the way you prepare printed or multimedia materials, and to your own presentation style.

1. Include references to specific people rather than "mankind," "people," or other such abstractions.
2. Illustrate general principles, ideas, or other abstractions with concrete examples or visualizations.

3. Make complex concepts or relationships among concepts more concrete by use of metaphors or analogies.
4. Present items in a series of list format rather than paragraph format.
5. Make step-by-step procedures or relationships among concepts more concrete by use of flow charts, storyboards, diagrams, cartoons, or other visual aids.
6. Ensure that the instructor establishes eye contact and exhibits enthusiasm.

A.2. Stimulate Inquiry

> Susan asked her students in widget production what they would do if they received a request to produce 300 widgets in two days and the electricity went off during the first afternoon.

It is critical to get students' attention, but the bigger challenge is to keep it. The learners will have a greater desire to pay attention if you can awaken a deeper level of curiosity than simply exciting their senses. The other components of motivation also contribute to maintaining learner motivation, but within the frame of reference of this category, the concept of curiosity arousal is a key element. This level of curiosity, which is called epistemic curiosity (Berlyne, 1965), occurs when you have awakened the learners' desires to know the answer to a problem, to learn something new.

There are, as with all of the categories of motivation, many ways to accomplish this goal. A good question to ask yourself is, "Can I violate the learners' expectations?" Many topics can be introduced problematically; that is, in a way that arouses epistemic curiosity if you give it some thought. For example, you might say something startling such as, "Junk food is important to your diet." Then, ask the students if they know why this could be true. Afterward, explain how certain ingredients of junk food are nutritionally beneficial even though other ingredients are not, and if a person is not getting the beneficial ingredients in other parts of his or her diet, then the junk food can be beneficial. In a more advanced science class, you could present conflicting principles or facts. For example, begin a lesson on properties of light with a description of light first as a wave then as particles.

After introducing a topic in a manner that arouses epistemic curiosity, it is effective to have an assignment that allows the student to investigate the problem and produce an answer or opinion. In this way, they are learning numerous research and communication skills in addition to the content of the lesson. It would take far too much time to teach every topic in this manner, but by using this technique from time to time, you will get a higher level of inquiry-focused curiosity in the learners. The following four suggestions can help you think of ways to approach this goal:

1. Introduce or develop topics problematically (that is, stimulate a sense of inquiry by presenting a problem which the new knowledge or skill will help solve).
2. Provoke curiosity by stimulating mental conflict (for example, present facts that contradict past experience; paradoxical examples; conflicting principles or facts; or unexpected opinions).
3. Evoke a sense of mystery describing unresolved problems that may or may not have a solution.
4. Use visuals to stimulate curiosity or create mystery.

A.3. Maintain Attention

> Elaine introduced the relationship between marketing personnel and outside computer retail operators by doing the following: First she showed a video introducing retail concepts with brief examples of actual operations; second, she gave a lecturette on details of the concepts and procedures associated with them; and third, she asked the class to read and discuss a brief scenario of a problem between a marketing person and a retail operator.

What do people do when they want to go to sleep? They try to avoid any unexpected or unusual stimuli. They try to manage their environment so that it is quiet or that all the sounds are familiar. When they are young, they like for someone to read to them. The steady, quiet voice of another person lulls them to sleep.

Unfortunately, these sleep-inducing conditions are often produced in a classroom. The immobility of the students who are sitting at their desks, the absence of windows or rules prohibiting the students from noticeably looking out of them, and the regular cadences of a teacher's voice can be very effective in creating boredom and sleepiness.

This subcategory of attention refers to factors in the environment that can be used to overcome boredom and meet people's sensation seeking needs by providing changes of pace, changes in approach, and using media that provides visual or auditory appeal.

Variation in Format

1. Use white space on paper or screen space in multimedia to separate blocks of information (text and/or illustrations).
2. Use a variety of typefaces to highlight titles, quotes, rules, key words, etc., but maintain a consistent style.
3. Use variations in layout; that is, variation in spatial location of blocks of information.
4. Include variations in types of material (for example, alternations between blocks of text, figures, tables, pictures).

Variation in Style and Sequence

1. Have variation in writing function (for example, exposition, description, narration, and persuasion).
2. Include variation in tone (for example, serious, humorous, exhortation).
3. Include variation in the sequence of the elements of the instruction (for example, vary a sequence such as "introduction," "presentation," "example," and "exercise" varied by changing the order, adding an extra exercise).
4. Include variation between content presentations and active response events (e.g., questions, problems, exercises, and puzzles).

Summary

The attention dimension is critical because, to state it in the extreme, students have to be awake to be motivated to learn. At the same time, they cannot be appropriately stimulated to learn if they are hyperactive. If there are too many distracting stimuli in the environment, then they need to be simplified. Once this basic level of attention is achieved, then the use of inquiry arousing activities will provide a deeper level of motivation and will lead to the next requirement, which is relevance.

Chapter 5 – Establishing and Supporting Relevance

Forethought

If there is one question that signifies an issue with the relevance of instruction it is, "Why should I have to study this?" The traditional answer in school is either the one portrayed in the cartoon (Figure 5.1) or a comment about the subject matter being required by the curriculum. In the workplace, the number one answer is "Because it will help you on the job," or the trainer, like the teacher, will simply point out that it is required. Most of the time these are not very satisfying answers because if it were apparent that the content was useful the student probably wouldn't be asking the question! Another problem is that frequently the instructor might not have a good answer other than to say that it is a required subject. To build a true sense of perceived relevance in the learners the teacher must have a clear understanding of the importance of the instructional content. It is great to say that the content is useful if it is, indeed, true and if it can be demonstrated convincingly to the students. However, even if the content isn't particularly useful in a literal sense there are other things that are important in the learning environment that can be used to build relevance. But one thing is certain: the teacher or trainer must have a clear belief in the relevance of the content before being able to convince the students!

Figure 5.1. Trying to Answer the Relevance Question.

J.M. Keller, *Motivational Design for Learning and Performance,*
DOI 10.1007/978-1-4419-1250-3_5, © Springer Science+Business Media, LLC 2010

Introduction

Why do people choose to do the things they do? From a radically concrete perspective, there are as many reasons as there are situations. Every situation could be viewed as having something unique about it. But, from a more general perspective, peoples' choices can be understood in terms of a variety of psychological concepts and theories, one of the most broadly accepted of which is expectancy-value theory (Steers & Porter, 1983; Vroom, 1964) which was briefly introduced in Chapter 2. This theory postulates that people choose to pursue a given goal when the expected outcome is something they desire and they have a positive expectancy for achieving it. This relationship is considered to be multiplicative in which behavior potential is a function of expectancy times value [$BP = f\,(E \times V)$]. This means that both terms must have positive values or the result will be zero behavior potential. The second term in the equation which is based on goals, motives, and values is the part that applies to relevance.

But, as we know, participation in school is a requirement and seldom the result of a voluntary choice based on one's values and expectancies. What, then, are peoples' expectations of a course with respect to relevance? This chapter contains several psychological concepts that help explain relevance and the other part of the equation, expectancies for success, will be discussed in the next chapter on confidence.

What Is Meant By Relevance?

Relevance refers to people's feelings or perceptions of attraction toward desired outcomes, ideas, or other people based upon their own goals, motives, and values. The greater the attraction associated with a given goal, the greater the likelihood that a person will choose to pursue that goal assuming that it is perceived to be achievable. Relevance is often viewed from a purely pragmatic perspective. When students, including adult participants in training, ask why they should be studying a given topic they most often want to be told or shown how it will be useful to them in their jobs or have a practical application in some other part of their lives. This is a legitimate expectation but not one that can always be fulfilled as an immediate consequence of a lesson or course. Learning the concepts of torque and acceleration in an auto repair course and how to apply them can have immediate practical benefits, but this will probably not be true when the same concepts are taught in a theoretical physics course at the high school level.

However, it is possible to create a sense of relevance in the absence of immediate utility because there are many other psychological characteristics that are related to relevance. People can have a high level of intrinsic motivation in a topic even when there is no practical benefit. For example, one of my sons developed a keen interest in dinosaurs when he was 4 years old and he acquired detailed knowledge of their names, habits, and habitats. His expertise was acknowledged by his preschool teacher in a newsletter in which she described a unit of work on dinosaurs that she had taught and she commended my son as their "resident expert whose knowledge greatly exceeded my own." For some reason, this particular interest can be observed in many preschool and elementary school children. What, then, are some of the factors that help explain the concept of relevance?

Psychological Basis for Relevance

Key Question for Relevance:

In what ways will this learning experience be valuable for my students?

Certainly, a sense of relevance occurs when the content to be learned is perceived to be useful to one's work, but it can also be enhanced when there is a match between teaching and learning styles, when there is a match between the content and one's personal interests, when one can relate prior knowledge and experiences to the current content, and when the content and performance requirements are consistent with one's personal and cultural values. Thus, the foundation for relevance lies in understanding such concepts as the dynamics of goal choice, psychological needs and motives, future orientation, interests, intrinsic motivation, personal and social values, and a host of affective and emotional states such as feelings of connectedness and perceived empathy.

Goal Choice

Typically, people have many goal choices but at any given moment in time the achievement of some goals will be desired more strongly than others. People choose goals that have the highest perceived benefit relative to other potential goals with respect to intrinsic interest and perceived benefits of the expected outcomes. One way of characterizing a person's affective attitude toward a goal is by using the concept of *valence* (Vroom, 1964). If a person prefers the attainment of a certain outcome to not attaining it then that outcome has a positive valence. It will have a negative valence if the person wishes to avoid it or is indifferent toward attaining that outcome. The strength of the valence results from the instrumental value of the goal; that is, the perceived connection between accomplishing the given goal as a means to accomplishing subsequent goals, and the intrinsic value of the goal; that is, the degree to which the goal is valued as an end-in-itself. Together, instrumental value and intrinsic value contribute to the expected satisfaction to be obtained by achieving the outcome. In other words, expected satisfaction is influenced by both intrinsic and instrumental consequences. An outcome can be valued for its own sake and for its perceived connection to the attainment of other valued outcomes. For example, an apartment dweller in a large city with good public transportation may not have a functional need for a car but greatly desires one because of the anticipated satisfaction of driving the car as a pleasurable experience in and of itself. In the more typical situation, a person will desire a car because it will enable one to fulfill several outcomes after acquiring it, such as a mother with several children who will use it to transport them, go to the grocery store, go shopping, and visit friends. For her, having a car would be a goal with a very high valence. And in a still different situation, a young professional man might desire a sporty car for both intrinsic and instrumental reasons including the pure pleasure of driving it, his expectation of being admired for having such a car, and for its functional uses in going to work and so forth.

Early psychological theories that attempted to explain goal-oriented behavior were reductionistic in nature, which means that the psychologists tried to reduce explanations of behavior to their most elemental component. Two of these approaches were the *instinct* theories and *drive* theories. Instinct theorists such as James (James, 1890) and McDougall (McDougall, 1908, 1970) tended to regard all motivated behavior, as opposed to learned behavior, as instinctive. This theory was developed primarily from the study of animals but presumed to also apply to humans. However, in humans, it was assumed that even though some behaviors were instinctual in nature, they did not always result in exactly the same kind of behavior. Food seeking would result in similar behaviors but would be modified by a given culture's concept of what constitutes edible food, but other so-called instincts, such as gregariousness, were much vaguer and not universal among humans, which they must be in order to be a true instinct. Thus, instinct theory was weak because virtually any observable behavior could be given a label and designated as an instinct. Some examples are listed in Table 5.1. Furthermore, attaching a label to a behavior does not constitute an explanation of it. By identifying something as an instinct, it

Table 5.1. Examples of Instincts Listed by James (1890) and McDougall (1908).

Examples of Instincts			
James		**McDougall**	
Rivalry	Curiositye.	Parental care	Sympathy
Pugnacity	Sociability	Combat	Self-association
Sympathy	Shyness	Curiosity	Submission
Hunting	Secretiveness	Food seeking	Mating
Fear	Cleanliness	Repulsion	Constructiveness
Acquisitiveness	Modesty	Escape	Appeal
Constructiveness	Jealousy	Gregariousness	
Play	Parental love		

precludes having a theory of motivation that can be subjected to prediction and validation. Also, there was no overarching theory or taxonomical rules to guide the creation of lists of instincts; psychologists could create unending lists of behavioral descriptors and call them instincts.

Another set of theories that provided explanations of some aspects of motivated behavior were known collectively as drive theory. The basic principles of drive theory are based on the concept of homeostasis which means that the organism tries to maintain a sense of balance. Motivation results from a state of imbalance caused by deprivation in regard to physical and psychological needs and desires. It is important to note that not all needs automatically result in drives, and drives can result from desires, not just needs. Thus, it was necessary to have a theory to explain the origin and operation of drives, and the best known was that of Hull (1943). However, it was Woodworth (1918) who introduced the concept of drive and he proposed that it has three characteristics: *intensity*, *direction*, and *persistence*. Intensity refers to the level of activation of the drive and its accompanying emotional level. Direction refers to the object, or goal, of the drive, and persistence to the tendency to continue the goal-seeking behavior until it is achieved and the state of equilibrium is restored.

Hull formalized drive reduction theory by expressing it in terms of a formula which stated that the strength of a behavior depends on the strength of the drive combined with habit strength. Habit strength refers to how well the pattern of behavior that leads to drive reduction has been learned, drive refers to the need or desire that is in a state of disequilibrium. In other words, a state of disequilibrium such as hunger will not automatically lead to food seeking behavior unless the organism has learned a set of relationships, habits, between food seeking behaviors and the acquisition of food which then reduces the strength of the hunger drive. Hull also postulated the relationship to be multiplicative: behavior = drive x habit.

As with other theories of motivation and behavior, drive theory can explain some aspects of behavior such as those that are relatively fixed and mechanical, but many aspects of motivated behavior are explained more effectively other kinds of theories such as cognitive theories that are more holistic in nature. Cognition refers to the thought processes that occur internally when we try to understand our actions, interpret the world around us, and engage in decision making.

Tolman: Purposive Behavior

One of the early cognitive theories that offered an alternative to drive theory was that of Tolman (1932). Instead of postulating a drive mechanism, Tolman's basic assumption was that behavior is *purposeful* in that it is always directed toward or away from some particular outcome. This is another way of saying that behavior is goal oriented and tends to be *persistent*, *patterned*, and *selective*. Regarding the first of these three characteristics, people tend to persist in their efforts to achieve a goal until it is obtained, but this simple assumption has complex implications. This is because people have multiple goals and goal conflicts might occur during the process of trying to achieve an initial goal. For example, a person who is trying to lose weight will vow when going to bed and first arising the next morning to strictly follow a healthy diet during that day. But as the day progresses, this goal is frequently supplanted by other goals related more to eating habits that provide immediate gratification and stress reduction. A dramatic and humorous example of this can be illustrated with the so-called "stress diet." There are many variations of this, but a typical one would be something like the one in Figure 5.2.

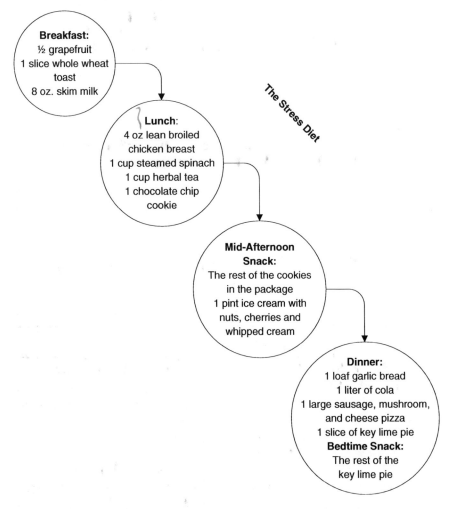

Figure 5.2. Illustration of a Goal Shift on Diet.

A characteristic of behavior that contributes to persistence is Tolman's second assumption that there tend to be *consistent patterns of behavior leading to goal attainment*. For example, most of us have habitual routes that we follow from our homes to our places of work and consistent patterns of behavior at work. That is why we might never see acquaintances with whom we are in relatively close proximity but who have different daily patterns. It also explains one of the reasons why it is difficult to change behavior. Having established a pattern such as the one represented in Figure 5.2, it is extremely difficult to change because it is habitual and satisfies powerful goals related to stress reduction.

Tolman's third characteristic is *selectivity* which means that we make deliberate decisions about the paths to follow to obtain our goals. It also implies that we tend to choose the easiest or most direct path, especially for pragmatic goals such as getting to work on time. For different types of goals, we might choose different paths, such as maximum exposure to historical sites in the available time if our goal is to tour Civil War battlefields. But, even here, the principle is the same. We select the most effective and efficient path to achieve our goal.

Tolman also introduced the concept of *expectancies* in reference to the expectation that a given set of behaviors will lead to a specific goal. His concept of expectancies is rigorous in that it is based upon learning a set of behaviors that lead to the goal, not faith or "hunches." These expectancies are developed over a period of time during which the organism develops a *cognitive map* of the environment. The cognitive map includes acquired knowledge as to the location of a goal and a series of steps that lead to goal attainment. These concepts do not necessarily imply metacognition but simply reflect a learned set of relationships. These concepts were validated in the study of infra human subjects such as rats, but they also apply to psychological situations and human performance. For example, much of this book is based upon a cognitive map of the primary motivational influences on learning and their relationships to each other which resulted in the macro models of learning and performance presented in Chapter 1. This cognitive model supports the development of expectancies that one can achieve given motivational goals by following a set of steps prescribed by the motivational design process embedded in the theory and model. Cognitive maps and the closely related concept of *mental models*, which can be developed to articulate people's perceptions, decisions, expectancies and cognitive maps (Craik, 1943; Johnson-Laird, 1983), continue to be the subject of active research in instructional theory and the learning sciences (Johnson-Laird, 2005; L. Westbrook, 2006).

Lewin: Field Theory

In contrast to drive theory which is primarily an environmental theory and the cognitive theory of Tolman, Lewin (Lewin, 1935, 1938) introduced *field theory* which is an interaction theory based on expectancy-value concepts. Lewin's theory attempts to account for the many forces that are interacting at any given time to influence behavior and how a given behavior is the result of these multiple influences. Lewin (1935) postulates that a person's behavior is the result of interactions of the person and the perceived environment, or life space which refers to one's psychological reality. It is important to note the role of perceived environment versus physical environment in this theory. For Lewin, a person's reality consists of the totality of perceptions, attitudes, prior knowledge, and so forth which can vary substantially from the actual physical environment. This concept is also a central assumption in constructivist theory (Duffy, Lowyck, & Jonassen, 1993) which emerged much more recently than Lewin's work. In Lewin's theory a person's life space can be represented geometrically by a figure with an outer boundary that is subdivided into parts (Figure 5.3). The parts are called regions and are separated by boundaries which vary in terms of their permeability. The various regions are related to each other in terms of "tensions," or magnitude of connectedness.

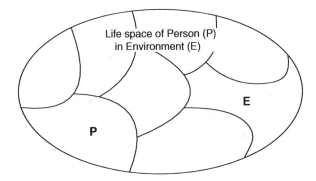

Figure 5.3. Example of Lewin's Life Space Representation (Based on Lewin, 1935).

A person tries to reduce tensions between regions by achieving the relevant outcomes. For example, the mother who lives in an environment in which car ownership is accepted and has multiple outcomes that can be achieved by obtaining a car would have a strongly positive valence for car ownership because these goals would have only a thin separation from each other and the acquisition of the car would neutralize the tensions among those regions. This is illustrated by the four adjacent regions in the center and upper left part of Figure 5.4. There might be a slight reduction in tensions among the other regions because the mother would have less need to grow vegetables, it would be relatively easy to get provisions for dinner, and she might have more time for personal recreation such as reading. But, a traditional Amish farmer whose religion forbids the use of cars and even electricity for personal comfort would have a strongly negative valence toward owning a car because its potential utilitarian benefits would

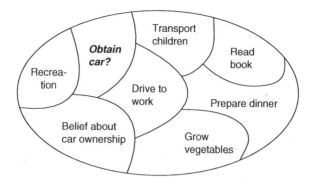

Figure 5.4. Examples of Regional Activities and Attitudes.

not create a tension between the two sets of goals and beliefs. The boundary between car ownership and fulfilling one's transportation needs would be impermeable. This person would have a different goal, such as owning a horse and buggy or a good pair of shoes that would take the place of owning a car.

Lewin's work laid the groundwork for a better understanding of the interactive effects of multiple goals. With respect to students and their motivation to learn, there are many types of goals, some of which are desirable in a school situation and some are not. For example, we want students to be motivated to achieve; we do not want them to be motivated to cheat or procrastinate. We want them to be motivated to be cooperative and persistent; we do not want them to be motivated to be uncooperative or lazy. Our challenge as educators is to relate our instruction to the desirable goals that students already have and to shape or modify goals that are undesirable. Subsequent researchers have provided additional guidance and clarification.

Motives

Research on the goal directedness of behavior, including Lewin's work, has a long history. It includes the early drive theories (Hull, 1943) which suggest that motivation results from deprivation with regard to elemental drives which are primary physical, but can be psychological by means of association. If people are hungry, thirsty, afraid, or lonely, for example, they will be goal directed to satisfy those needs. When they succeed in reaching a state of satisfaction, or homeostasis, they will no longer be motivated to pursue goals related to those needs.

Tolman (1949) worked from a different set of assumptions. He postulated that behavior is purposive, that people have motives and goals that result from needs and desires that activate behavior, but that these needs are not necessarily the result of deprivation. His work builds on many of the ideas of Lewin (1935) who suggested that there are forces in the environment as well as within ourselves that help define our goals and stimulate us to action. This perspective is also present in the work of Murray (1938) who viewed motivation as resulting from a combination of internal needs and external, environmental, pressures.

All of this work helped set the stage for the well-known work of Maslow (1954) and McClelland (1976). One of the problems in the earlier research was that there was no taxonomy of needs. Researchers would create new "needs" every time they observed some new aspect of behavior. Maslow brought order to this situation by proposing a theory which postulated that there is a hierarchy of needs and that lower order needs must be satisfied or sufficiently under control in the "eyes" of the individual before higher order needs will be pursued. The five levels of needs are

- physiological, which refers to hunger and thirst,
- safety and security, referring to the continued ability to provide for housing and basic physiological needs,
- love and belongingness, which includes companionship as well as long-term relationships,
- self-esteem, as obtained from achievement and recognition, and
- self-actualization, which is defined in terms of reaching one's highest potential.

This list has had great appeal to practitioners in the workplace and in education, but has received criticism from researchers because it is difficult to validate. But, from a practical application perspective, this theory helps us understand that motivation to succeed in school, which relates primarily to the fourth level, self-esteem, cannot be fully activated if a child never gets enough to eat, is afraid, and is isolated from his or her peers. However, a challenge to this theory is to understand what is meant by a satisfied need. This is a highly subjective issue. For example, a first semester freshman in college might expect to have a comfortable apartment, a car, and a generous allowance before feeling that his lower level needs have been met. But, when people are highly motivated to achieve they can endure high levels of deprivation. For example, artists and aspiring actors may be satisfied with only minimal levels of food and shelter while pursuing their dreams, but even then, there is a level at which their lower order needs must be met before they are motivated to learn.

In contrast to the work of Maslow, McClelland (1976) focused on three needs: achievement, affiliation, and power and his conceptual foundation is different from the need deprivation concept of many earlier theories. Deprivation does not account for why a need, or motive, can grow instead of diminishing even as it is being realized. For example, people high in the need for achievement do not move into a state of equilibrium following success as would be predicted by need theory. Instead, they tend to be stimulated to achieve more and higher levels of success. Therefore, McClelland postulated that equilibrium is transient and occurs when one approaches the fulfillment of a desired affective state, and following the achievement of a goal one's desires can change causing a new state of disequilibrium. That is why some people can never seem to get enough with respect to a desired goal. Salesmen constantly try to surpass last year's goals and athletes continually strive to achieve new "personal bests."

Achievement, Affiliation, and Power

The three motives studied by McClelland and his colleagues can be extremely useful in helping to understand the behavior of people in school and work and to match instructional environments to individual learning styles. People who are high in the *need for achievement* enjoy moderate challenges because they like to take risks, but they want to succeed. If a task is too easy, they get no pleasure from success. If it is too difficult, they do not get to experience success and they do not like to fail. They set personal standards of excellence and try to achieve them in competition with others, by doing something unique, or by simply reaching a higher personal level of accomplishment. They tend not to like to work in groups, as they want to set their own direction and be personally responsible for their outcomes.

The most traditional method for measuring need for achievement is the Thematic Apperception Test (TAT). It is a projective test which consists of presenting an ambiguous stimulus and then asking the respondent to fantasize and create a story about it. Projective tests can be highly unstructured as in the Rorschach test, popularly known as the inkblot test in which the respondent is shown an abstract figure of black ink on a white background made by putting a few drops of black ink on a large sheet of white paper, folding it, and pressing it. The resulting image is somewhat abstract and used by clinical psychologists to evoke stories that reveal their clients' innermost feelings, thoughts, and values. They can be useful when used properly by a trained therapist, but are not designed to conduct research on specific psychological constructs such as the need for achievement. The TAT uses pictures or verbal leads as a stimulus and then asks respondents to make up vivid, imaginative stories. Four questions are used to help stimulate the imagination of the respondent. The first question is, "What is happening? Who are the people?" The respondents have approximately 5 minutes to respond to each of the six stimuli that are typically administered. The stimulus materials resulted from extensive research on pictures, and later verbal leads that had an effective combination of situational cues and ambiguity to evoke a variety of motive predispositions. Scoring of the resulting stories was based on a strictly defined rubric and trained reviewers can achieve inter-rater reliability estimates of .90 and higher.

In contrast, people high in *need for affiliation* are more interested in personal relationships. They like to have warm, satisfying relationships with other people. This refers to friendships, not just romantic attachments. They think about their friends, they nurture the friendship, and they get upset if there are problems or departures. They enjoy working in groups and letting the group take credit for results without having to have personal recognition in a way that sets them apart from the group. They tend not to make good leaders because they are more concerned about whether people like then than whether they are setting and enforcing rules and standards.

Finally, people high in the *need for power* feel good when they have been able to have an influence on the behavior of others. With immature people, this influence can be self-serving and destructive. But, mature people with a high need for power enjoy exerting their influence in a way that benefits their organization and other people. This characteristic is associated with good managers and teachers.

These needs are not mutually exclusive. A given person can have high or low levels on all or any combination of them. Teachers sometimes encounter challenges from children with a high need for power. They might challenge the teacher's ability to control the behavior of the children in the classroom. In this situation, the teacher will have to establish leadership before other motivations, such as achievement, will be exhibited by the learners. Children with any combination of these needs can be accommodated by using a variety of assignments and working conditions, such as group work, that allow students' needs to be met most of the time even if they are frustrated some of the time.

Competence

The concept of competence was introduced by White (1959) as a fundamental motive which refers to "an organism's capacity to interact effectively with its environment" (p. 297). Like the other "motive theorists," White moved away from the drive theory assumptions of motivation based on the alleviation of deprived states which did not explain voluntary actions that led to pleasurable states. He postulated that the attainment of competence could not be attained from the energies associated with drives or instincts and, furthermore, a state of equilibrium in humans if not other species is not a desirable state for it results in boredom. As White points out, when people are under excessive stress as in wartime or with excessive workloads, a period of stress reduction and equilibrium appears to be highly desirable. But once it is achieved, people soon become restless and seek external stimulation. Instead of desiring an absence of stress, people seem to not only desire but need an optimal level of stimulation. Hebb's (1958) extensive research on the behavior of people under conditions of stimulus deprivation illustrates that people will begin to produce their own stimuli in the form of hallucinations when there is virtually no input from the external environment. Research on people such as orphans and infants who experience severe social deprivation do not mature properly. As Hebb (1958) put it, "The animal reared in isolation is a permanent screwball at maturity: motivationally, socially, intellectually abnormal" (p. 109). He is referring primarily to research on dogs and people. Thus, the development of competence by means of exploratory behavior is an important component of cognitive and social development.

White (1959) introduced the concept of *effectance* motivation to explain the mechanism that leads to the development of competence. For example, even in play activities children seem to enjoy discovering the effects they can have on the environment and, conversely, the effects the environment has on them. Feelings of satisfaction result from these interactions and not from solving them in a process leading toward homeostasis. White defines the result of these activities as *feelings of efficacy*, which should not be confused with the concept of self-efficacy (Bandura, 1977) which refers to one's expectations of being successful in pursuing a goal. Feelings of efficacy refer to the satisfying feelings of mastery or insight as one interacts with the environment. Furthermore, people are more likely to engage in competence-building explorations when the stimulus environment is moderately complex relative to the challenge level of the task. If the task is too easy, boredom sets in; if too difficult, then cognitive processing becomes more narrowly focused and one is less attentive to all of the potentially relevant cues in the environment (Tolman, 1949).

Even though they have had separate lines of development, the competence motive has some things in common with the achievement motive. Elliot & Dweck (2005a) argue that competence is the core of achievement motivation. They claim that the concept of achievement has not been clearly defined in the literature and they identify two fundamental weaknesses in the literature. First, they say that it "lacks coherence and a clear set of structural parameters" (p. 4). The concept is difficult to operationalize and the achievement motivation literature contains multiple conceptualizations and methodologies that are not consistently related to a central concept. Second, they say that the achievement motivation literature is too narrowly focused and does not incorporate many aspects of behavior that could fall under the general question of understanding achievement-striving behavior. With these assumptions as a starting point they propose that the concept of competence motivation be used to replace the concept of achievement motivation. They, and the numerous authors in their book (2005b), present conceptual and empirical papers which explore this basic issue. It is too soon to know whether the vast literature on achievement motivation will be reconceptualized as they propose, and one could question some of the characterizations of both achievement motivation and competence motivation as they are portrayed in various parts of this book, but it is certainly an intriguing proposal and contributes to a more holistic approach to understanding this literature which is, in itself, useful.

Future Orientation and Future Time Perspective

Another influence on the valence of a goal is one's *future orientation* which Raynor (Raynor, 1969, 1974) defined primarily in terms of the instrumentality of an immediate goal with regard to future goals. That is, if an immediate goal is perceived to be connected to the attainment of future outcomes then the perceived utility of the immediate goal will be stronger depending on the value of those outcomes. Thus, goals that require the completion of prerequisite courses or certification exams before one is allowed to continue along a desired academic or professional path can have high valences, even to the point of causing anxiety because the higher the instrumentality the higher the cost of failure. This relationship also applies in achievement-focused situations in which a cluster, rather than a linear progression, of accomplishments must be completed in order to achieve a final goal, as in the Boy Scouts where one must earn a combination of required and elective merit badges to attain the prestigious level of Eagle Scout. This is a refinement and expansion of Tolman's field theory concepts of goal strength being related to the tensions between a given goal and contingent goals.

Another concept related to future orientation is *future time perspective* (FTP) which refers to one's perceived temporal distance between the present and a future event. Some people perceive future events to be much closer in time than other people do. Those with a short FTP focus more on the present and their motivation to accomplish an immediate goal is not strengthened by the perception of possible future benefits. In contrast, those with a long FTP see a much closer connection between current activities and future goals and the expectation of future benefits strengthens their immediate motivation. De Volder and Lens found that 11th graders' motivation was positively correlated with the value they attached to future goals and to their perceived instrumentality of their current schoolwork for helping to achieve those goals.

However, these correlations have to be qualified by considering students' attitudes toward the future. Van Calster et al. (1987) found in a study with 230 Dutch-speaking male high school student between 17 and 19 years old that regardless whether perceived instrumentality (PI) was high or low, there was a relatively low correlation with motivation to learn among the students who had a negative attitude toward the future (Figure 5.5). However, as the attitudes toward the future became more positive there was a steadily growing increase in

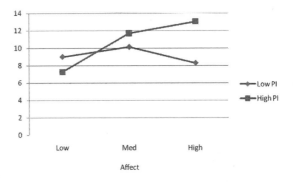

Figure 5.5. Correlation of Attitude toward Future and Perceived Instrumentality with Motivation To Study (Based on Data from Van Calster, Lens, & Nuttin, 1987).

the correlations between PI and motivation to learn. In contrast, they found that students with positive attitudes toward the future but low PI had a much lower correlation with motivation. The group of students who had medium-to-high positive attitudes toward the future but low PI had the greatest number by far of underachievers. Thus, the authors conclude that efforts to raise the PI of immediate tasks can increase motivation for students with positive attitudes toward the future but is not likely to do so for those with negative attitudes.

In an extensive review of the literature on gender and orientations toward the future, Greene & DeBacker (2004) found gender differences in each of five different theoretical orientations: achievement motivation, future time orientation, perceptions of future selves, expectancy-value theory, and social cognitive research on perceived instrumentality. Even though there was cross-cultural diversity among the studies they reviewed, they found a fairly consistent and historically stable pattern for men who tended to have a longer future time perspective but with a somewhat narrow focus on goals related to employment and financial security. In contrast, women tended to have greater diversity in their goal orientations for the future. Their goals focused more on marriage and family but it has become more commonplace for them to include goals related to employment and a career. There also appeared to be a strong sociocultural influence on the overall future orientation and goal orientations among men and women.

Still another aspect of future orientation that can have an influence on the design of motivating learning environments relates to whether individuals see their futures as being limited or open-ended and this tends to be related to age (Lang & Carstensen, 2002). When people have more long-term or open-ended time perspectives they tend to focus more on knowledge acquisition goals that are instrumentally related to desired future states. When future time perspective is more short-term and limited, the focus shifts more toward managing personal networks. In a study conducted in Germany with 480 adults ranging in age from 20 to 90 years of age, Lang and Carstensen (2002) affirmed that younger people tended to have a more open-ended time perspective in contrast to a more limited time perspective with older people and the goals of the two orientations differed as one would predict. People with a limited time perspective tended to reduce the size of their personal networks focusing more on socially and personally satisfying relationships. The personal networks of people with an open-ended time perspective tended to be larger and included people who could contribute to their knowledge related goals and future achievements. However, factors other than age can influence this future time orientation. Fredrickson and Carstensen (1990) found that age differences in goal selection disappear based upon the conditions people find themselves to be in or imagine themselves to be in. For example, young people who are anticipating a major change such as relocating to a new environment or older people who imagine the creation of a life extending medical advance will form goals independently of their actual ages. Also, conditions that influence one's life expectancy independently of age also have influences on goal selection that are the same as found with age differences. Carstensen and Fredrickson (1998) found that within a group of young men who were HIV patients, those who still had a relatively open-ended life expectancy also had more of a long-term future time orientation while those who were closer to the end of their lives displayed the characteristics of older adults. Thus, as people approach their actual or perceived end-of-life they tend to focus more on emotionally meaningful goals rather than career focused goals. In spite of this, there can be age-independent orientations as with young people who fear the future acting more like old people and older people who remain psychologically young having a life space that is filled with multiple and contingent goals.

Goal Orientation

Several motives that affect people's behavior have been described, and another is *goal orientation*. This refers to whether people are focused more on the outcomes of their goal striving behavior or the activities in the process leading toward the goal. The two most frequently described sets of concepts in this regard are task versus ego orientation and mastery versus performance orientation.

Nichols (1984) studied the development of attributional behaviors in children and he noted a distinctive difference between children, and adults for that matter, who are task oriented versus ego oriented. *Task-oriented* people tend to focus on how to accomplish the task and other elements of getting the job done. *Ego-oriented* people tend to focus more on what is going to happen as a result of doing the task. They worry about external evaluations and what people are going to think about them.

Similarly, Dweck (1986) made a distinction between *learning goals* and *performance goals*. A person who is motivated by learning goals likes to seek challenging tasks, believes that skills can be learned, focuses on task mastery, and believes that abilities can be improved with effort. In contrast, a person who is performance oriented is more concerned with appearing to be competent, wants to succeed with minimal effort, believes that ability is fixed, and is concerned about social comparisons and symbols of success.

Greater levels of anxiety are associated with ego, or performance, orientation. The fear of failure or, at the very least, of not succeeding at a high level, can become so strong that people are almost unable to make any progress at all. Their fear of potentially negative outcomes paralyzes them. In contrast, the person who is task, or learning, oriented is better able to concentrate on achieving as well as possible under whatever the existing conditions are.

Even though these characteristics are often presented as a dichotomy, there are many qualifying conditions to take into consideration. For example, extreme orientations in either direction can be maladaptive as was illustrated above in relation to performance orientation. But, even a task or learning orientation can become maladaptive when one's standards become so high, so perfectionistic, that they become unattainable. However, people generally possess both types of orientations in varying degrees. A person can be contemplating the consequences of success of failure without having it become debilitating. This person might be perfectly well able to focus on the task and, in fact, a moderate degree of performance orientation can heighten arousal and lead to better performances.

It is useful to keep this pair of concepts in mind when designing learning environments. If people are learning skills for which they have little background or confidence, it is best to design the environment to maximize task orientation while minimizing a focus on the performance requirements. Later, after the learners begin to achieve a level of mastery, the performance conditions can be increased to help them strengthen their skills. For example, if the students know they will be faced with a challenging test such as the Scholastic Aptitude Test, their preparatory instruction can begin with a focus on practicing the skills to be performed on the test, such as analogies. As the instruction progresses, the students can be given practice tests with not time limits. And then, the conditions can be changed to be identical with the conditions under which they will take the test. Similar strategies are used when teaching such things as playing a musical instrument or a skill such as gymnastics.

These concepts are especially useful when diagnosing performance problems. Often, a student's difficulties in learning a new skill can be grounded in an excessively high level of ego-orientation or performance anxiety. Helping the student to focus on the task itself and engaging in some desensitization activities regarding the performance environment can help reduce anxiety.

Interest

John Dewey is credited with introducing the concept of *interest* in relation to learning in his monograph entitled "Interest and Effort in Education" (Dewey, 1913). His thesis was that effort by itself does not result in effective learning; interest must be coupled with effort before real learning will take place. He said, "Practically the appeal to sheer effort amounts to nothing. When a child feels that his work is a task, it is only under compulsion that he gives himself to it. At every let-up of external pressure his attention, released from constraint, flies to what interests him. The child brought up on the basis of 'effort' acquires marvelous skill in appearing to be occupied with an uninteresting subject, while the real heart of his energies is otherwise engaged (p. 1)."

His concept of interest was somewhat different from current conceptualizations and research, but in many ways he anticipated the current
research. To some degree, he was equating interest with intrinsic motivation and effort with extrinsic motivation with the implication that interest
leads to approach behaviors and extrinsic motivation leads to avoidance
behaviors. It is certainly desirable to have intrinsic interest in a learning
situation, but people can be highly motivated and learn effectively even
with extrinsic goals.

One of the areas relevant to instruction and learning in which
interestingness has been studied is discourse processing or, in other
words, learning from textual materials. Schank (1979), who made several
early contributions, especially in regard to story-telling narratives, postulated that events which deviate from our normal expectations arouse interest more than expected events. For example, a 83-year-old man who dies of
a heart attack while making a purchase in a convenience store would not
attract much interest, but if his heart attack occurred while trying to help
the clerk foil a robbery it would be of interest. Shank distinguished between
firm and predictable interest arousing events such as death, danger, power,
and sex which he called "absolute interests" in contrast to "relative opera-
tors" such as unexpectedness or novelty which are contextual in relation to
an individual. Shank listed several conditions that help elicit interest, two of
which (when there are violations of expectations and when relevant information is missing as in detective stories) are related to Berlyne's work on the
curiosity concept (Chapter 4). The third one in which the content of the
event is related to salient themes such as the ones he called absolute
interests is more centrally a part of the relevance category. Even though
the concept of interest has elements of curiosity arousal, its most central
attributes are related more to relevance issues such as personal goals, past
experience, and established interests.

Much of the early research on interestingness, including Shank's
(1979) was in the context of learning from text, or discourse analysis,
which is relevant to instructional design and learning. Hidi & Baird (1986)
conducted a literature review in which they divided the existing studies
according to whether they dealt with stories or, in other words, narratives
whose primary purpose is to entertain and which employ many of the
attributes of curiosity arousing events (Berlyne, 1954b) or expositions
whose functions are more to inform, explain, or persuade. In their discussion of storytelling narratives, Hidi and Baird (1986) point out that interest
has both emotional and cognitive components. The former are aroused more
by human dramatic situations (Wilensky, 1983) or Shank's absolute interests, while cognitive interest tends to result more from curiosity stimulating
stimulus characteristics such as incongruity, unexpectedness, novelty,
paradox, etc. which Berlyne (1954b) called "collative variables." Hidi &
Baird (1986) also point out that in contrast to some writers who distinguish
between interest arousal being primarily in the external stimulus or in the

individual, their position is that it results from the interaction of the stimulus and the person which helps account for variations among people's reactions to similar stimulus events.

The research on interestingness in expositions was hampered, according to Hidi & Baird (1986), because little was known about the kinds of passages that readers find interesting in this type of text and because most of the existing research had been done on college-level textual material and specially constructed passages designed for research. Little had been done with kindergarten through 12th grade materials which tended to include anecdotal stories and passages high in human interest. Flesh (1948) had developed a human interest formula that could be used to rate text material, but it seems not to have been used in these studies.

Another complication exists with regard to the effects of interestingness on recall, especially when the interesting content is auxiliary to the important content. Hidi & Baird (1986) found that students had the highest recall for content that was interesting to them or had personal meaning to them regardless of whether this information was part of the important, superordinate, content of the reading or just subordinate content. Hidi, Baird, & Hildyard (1982) tested free recall of content from three types of material from actual school textbooks: expositions, interesting narratives, and mixed versions in which interesting but unimportant passages were inserted into the important expository content. They found that in the mixed text material, there was significantly less recall of important information. They concluded that the narrative insertions actually reduced the recall of important information.

Garner, Gillingham, and White (1989) introduced the concept of "seductive augmentation" to refer to information which they called irrelevant; that is, interesting but unimportant. As this expression has been used in this body of literature (for example, Harp & Mayer, 1998) it refers to information that is irrelevant to the primary message in the passage or to the learning objectives in an instructional program, but not necessarily irrelevant to the general topic. This is a more restricted use than in the broader literature in which material considered to be irrelevant would have no relationship to the topic. In the present context, seductive augmentation such as an anecdote about seacoast homes in Mississippi that were destroyed by Hurricane Katrina or a picture of endangered sailboats, or a picture of trees bent over from the force of the wind (Figure 5.6 right) that is inserted in text that is describing the principles of hurricane formation would be irrelevant to the central purpose of the text even though it is tangentially related to the topic by illustrating the destructive force of hurricanes. In contrast, an illustration of the cloud formations in a tropical storm preceding a hurricane (Figure 5.6 left) would be relevant. Garner et al., (1989) extended the work of Hidi, et al., (1982), by comparing recall of key points from an expository passage and the same passage with interesting content (seductive detail). The experiment was conducted with college-age adults

Figure 5.6. Relevant Versus Irrelevant Illustrations in a Lesson About Hurricane Formation.

and with 7th graders. In both cases, the presence of seductive detail interfered with recall of key points.

Intuitively, it would seem that adding material to make text, especially scientific text, more interesting would engage the reader into a more careful reading of the material which would then lead to greater learning. However, the previous studies did not obtain this result because, it was assumed, that the irrelevant but interesting material diverted attention from the central content of the passages. Harp and Mayer (1997) proposed making a distinction between emotional interest, which referred to the kinds of seductive details included in previous studies, and cognitive interest which referred to information that added explanatory detail to the content. They also used a combination of text and illustrations. Seductive detail in the text included interesting but irrelevant information such as the following: "Approximately 10,000 Americans are injured by lightning every year. Eyewitnesses in Burtonsville, Maryland, watched as a bolt of lightning tore a hole in the helmet of a high school football player during practice. The bolt burned his jersey, and blew his shoes off. More than a year later, the young man still won't talk about his near-death experience" (p. 94).

Seductive illustrations consisted of pictures of the same events described in the text and cognitive interest consisted of a series of drawings illustrating six steps in the lightening formation process. Their results were consistent with previous research which illustrated the interference effect of seductive detail and previous research on learning from text which illustrates the beneficial effect of relevant illustrations (Fleming & Levie, 1978). Harp & Mayer in a subsequent publication (Harp & Mayer, 1998) concluded that the interference effect of seductive details results from their prompting of inappropriate organizational schemas rather than distracting or disrupting the reader.

From a completely different perspective that is an expansion of the work on interest in text, two linguists (Sperber & Wilson, 1986) have postulated that relevance is a central requirement, if not the most important element, in communication and perception. In any setting, we will pay attention to novel stimuli only to the extent that we perceive a connection to something important in our own lives. If there is no connection, then we tend to ignore them. For example, if you enter a room and a group of people is already there, you will tend to scan the room. You will tend to notice people who are potentially threatening or intimidating either because of their size, their appearance, or their manner. As long as you feel this threat, you will continue to pay attention to them, even if it is indirect. However, additional information sometimes dissipates the potential threat and you lose interest. For example, if an average man observes a particularly handsome male whom he imagines to be a potential threat to his relationship with his wife or girl friend he will feel anxious. But if he then sees that the man is happily married and does not have a "roving eye," then he will soon ignore him unless there is some other basis of association. However, people whom you recognize as friends, friends of friends, etc., will attract your attention. Other people will be neutral; there will be nothing about them that leads you to a second glance. You might not even recognize them on the street the next day. If you start talking to someone you have not previously known, you will try to determine whether you have enough shared interests and experiences to stimulate further conversation and a possible acquaintance. If not, you move on. Underlying all of these actions, according to Sperber and Wilson (1986), is the principle of relevance. Both our visual and verbal communications function according to this principle. We establish and maintain visual and verbal communication when there is relevance to our lives.

Intrinsic Motivation

The concept of *intrinsic motivation* is different from interest in that it refers more to self-initiated attraction toward particular goals or activities because of their intrinsic interest and the need satisfaction that results from pursuing the given intrinsic interest, particularly in regard to the needs for competence and self-determination (Deci, 1975). In contrast, as we have seen, interest refers to the attraction or concern we feel toward events or objects because they touch upon our most basic needs and fears, or absolute interests (Schank, 1979). Interest can also be generated when events include characteristics such as novelty, unexpectedness, and other curiosity arousing features. Thus, interest tends to be more situational in nature than the broader concept of intrinsic motivation.

One can develop intrinsic interest in a topic even when the goal or task was extrinsically motivated at first. For example, when I was in graduate school and the end of the semester approached together with the huge pressures to write papers and prepare for exams, I found that I would become intensely interested in the topic I was researching even if I had previously been somewhat indifferent toward it. I would find numerous references to documents that were directly related to my topic but went beyond my immediate requirements, and I would see references to tangential topics that intrigued me. I made notes of the references and planned to read them after the semester ended. Which I never did! Later, when I began to teach theories of learning, cognition, and motivation, including the topic of intrinsic versus extrinsic motivation, I recalled those experiences and tried to explain them to myself. They didn't seem to fit either category because the course requirement was extrinsic and success in the class was instrumental to obtaining my doctoral degree. But, I would develop a high level of what seemed to be intrinsic motivation but it would disappear when the semester ended. Thus, I called it "situational intrinsic motivation" because it was necessary to develop a high degree of interest in order to put forth the tremendous effort required to meet all the deadlines. While in that state I regarded these interests as being deep and abiding, as in a condition of intrinsic motivation. Yet they faded quickly after the semester ended. It wasn't until I read self-determination theory (Deci & Ryan, 1985) that I found a formal explanation in terms of internalized extrinsic motivation. In my case, the motivation did become somewhat internalized, but just not as intensely as during the final weeks of the semester.

Deci (1975) explained that intrinsic motivation is tied to basic need satisfaction, in particular the needs for competence and *self-determination*, or *autonomy*. However, Deci and Ryan point out (Deci & Ryan, 2000) that intrinsically motivated activities are not undertaken for the purpose of satisfying these needs, but because they "are freely engaged out of interest" (Deci & Ryan, 2000, p. 233). In order for intrinsic motivation to be sustained, there must be satisfaction of the needs for competence and autonomy. It should not be assumed that the converse of this condition is true; that is, engagement in intrinsically motivated behaviors is necessary for the satisfaction of these needs which can also be met by activities that are not intrinsically motivated, but it is necessary to experience feelings of competence and autonomy to remain intrinsically motivated. These concepts are embedded in *self-determination theory* (SDT) (Deci & Ryan, 1985) which accounts for goal selection and the psychological needs that underlie the maintenance of goal-directed behavior. Thus, SDT incorporates the concept of interest combined with competence and autonomy which form the basis of the dynamics of intrinsic motivation.

It is not uncommon in the literature for the distinction between intrinsic and extrinsic motivation to be portrayed as a dichotomous contrast. However, in the context of an SDT sub-theory called Organismic Integration Theory (OIT) Deci & Ryan (Deci & Ryan, 1985; Ryan & Deci, 2000) present a taxonomy of human motivation with six categories that include amotivation, four types of extrinsic motivation, and intrinsic motivation (Table 5.2). This taxonomy was developed to explain different types of extrinsic motivation and the kinds of contextual factors that contribute to the development of a particular motivational orientation.

Table 5.2. A Taxonomy of Human Motivation According to Deci and Ryan (Based on Deci & Ryan, 1985; Ryan & Deci, 2000).

Type of Motivation	Characteristics
Amotivation	Lacking an intention to act or, in other words, a condition of indifference toward a goal or activity.
Extrinsic motivation (four types):	
External regulation:	Motivated by an external demand or requirement. This is the traditional view of extrinsic motivation which was contrasted with intrinsic motivation in early studies (Condry, 1977).
Introjected regulation:	Externally controlled but the person is motivated internally by a desire to obtain approval and esteem by performing well. This is consistent with Nicholls' (1984) concept of ego orientation.
Identification:	This is regulation through identification; that is, the requirement is external but the person identifies with its importance which results in a degree of intrinsically generated motivation. For example, a military recruit who must undergo physical fitness training but embraces it because of its importance for survival in combat.
Integrated regulation:	Motivation in this case is characterized by a behavior that is required but has become completely internalized. Thus the person has become self-motivated. This is similar to intrinsic motivation but the behavior is still being performed for instrumental reasons to accomplish external outcomes.
Intrinsic motivation:	This is the condition of a behavior being performed for its inherent pleasure and not because of instrumental contingencies.

It is important to realize that this is a taxonomy, not a hierarchy. It is not necessary to move through a lower level, with regard to degree of internal regulation, before going to a higher level. Frequently, behaviors that are totally externally regulated become more internally regulated as one becomes more familiar with the characteristics of a situation. For example, a new employee's compliance with rules regarding punctuality, politeness in communication, dress code, and personal appearance (facial hair, etc.) might initially be motivated totally by a desire to avoid unpleasant consequence; hence, extrinsically controlled. But, after gaining experience and seeing the disruptions that occur to the work environment when people are not willing to be "team players," this employee might move to the level of identification which combines a degree of internal regulation with the external requirements. In summary, a person's initial motivation for an activity or task can be in any category of the taxonomy and it can jump to any other category depending on the person's experience in that situation.

One of the important conclusions from the research on interest and intrinsic motivation is that in a learning environment your instruction does not have to have an immediately practical outcome in order for the learners to experience relevance. If you can make connections between your course content and their intrinsic interests or, at the very least, their situational interest, their motivation to learn is likely to be positive.

Flow

The psychological concept of *flow* (Csikszentmihalyi, 1975) refers to being completely absorbed in an activity to the point that you are not conscious of distractions, you are in a high level of intrinsic motivation, you are not thinking about success or failure, your attention is totally focused on your task, and you progress unconsciously from one thought or activity to the next. Being in a state of flow is to have achieved a maximum state of perceived relevance. According to Csikszentmihalyi (1990), the three primary factors that represent a state of flow are interest, concentration, and enjoyment.

Research on flow has been done in many different contexts including education, gaming, sports, and various professions. Many of the studies focus on what happens when people are in a state of flow (Csikszentmihalyi, 1975), but there is also curiosity about how to achieve this state. According to Csikszentmihalyi (1990), achieving a state of flow is facilitated by over-learning so that one is able to approach tasks holistically as a singular integrated action rather than as a series of discrete actions to be performed. This state can be achieved in the context of a well-learned performance activity such as playing a solo on an instrument or even in an orchestra, but it can also be achieved in tasks that are not so well structured. For example, in the process of doing research, taking notes, and generating themes for a research paper, one can become so absorbed in the task that a sense of the passage of time disappears.

However, overlearning a task or becoming highly task oriented in a goal-oriented process does not explain why flow sometimes occurs and sometimes not. In an effort to gain a greater understanding of the relationship between flow and its relationship to other factors in the environment,

Shernoff et al., (Shernoff, Csikszentmihalyi, Schneider, & Shernoff, 2003) studied conditions that are related to the positive engagement of students in high school classrooms. They collected data from 526 high school and middle school students in a longitudinal study. Data were collected from 12 different research sites across the country during the first, third, and fifth years of the study. The students who participated were randomly selected and stratified by academic performance, gender, race, and ethnicity. Data were collected by means of an Experience Sampling Method (ESM). Each participant had a package of response forms that contained 45 items on the front and back of a single sheet of paper. Participants wore wristwatches which could be buzzed by an electronic paging system. Upon being signaled, the participant was expected to immediately pause and fill out one of the response forms. They were asked to describe their location, the activities they were engaged in, and their thoughts by responding to a series of Likert-type items ranging from 0 (low) to 9 (high).

One measure was degree of engagement in the given task. This was assessed by asking about their levels of interest, concentration, and enjoyment, which are the components of flow. A second category was attention for which they simply indicated whether they were thinking about school-related topics (math, taking notes, how to write their paper, etc.) or non-academic topics (friends, eating, going home, romantic interests, or nothing at all). The final category, quality of experience, included four sub-variables: mood (happy, sociable, strong, proud, active), esteem (self-worth, ability, accomplishments, meeting expectations, and personal control), academic intensity (challenge, importance of topic to personal goals, concentration, and personal importance), and intrinsic motivation (interest, enjoyment, desire to engage in the activity).

These measures were correlated with three categories of independent variables (Table 5.3). One was challenge/skill level which had four levels: flow, anxiety, relaxation, and apathy. Another was type of classroom activity that was occurring at the time of the response and this had five levels. The third category was school subject in which nine different sub-categories of subjects were included.

In general, the results of this study confirmed the theoretical expectations that flow states defined as high in challenge and high in skill were associated with overall higher levels of engagement including the three sub-components of engagement (Table 5.4). Higher levels of engagement were also associated with higher levels of relevance and control. With regard to how students spent their time in school, they were involved with group work, including labs, 15% of the time, engaged in discussion 9%, and watching TV or videos 7%. The rest of the time they were engaged in individual work (23%), listening to lectures (21%), doing homework or studying (7%), and taking exams (13%). Students reported the highest levels on all dependent variables when doing group work and taking exams. They also reported high levels of attention when doing individual work. With respect

Table 5.3. Independent Variables and Levels (Based on Shernoff, Csikszentmihalyi, Schneider, & Shernoff, 2003).

Challenge/Skill	Classroom Activity	School Subject
Flow (high challenge, high skill)	Lecture	Math
Anxiety (high challenge, low skill)	TV/video	English
Relaxation (low challenge, high skill)	Exam	Science
Apathy (low challenge, low skill)	Individual work Group work	Foreign language History Social studies Computer science Art Vocational education

to school subjects, the major relationships that were found are listed in Table 5.4, and it can be observed that overall students reported their academic classes to be more intense and their non-academic classes to be more intrinsically interesting.

In summary, this study illustrated many cogent relationships among school characteristics and emotional characteristics. The study is particularly valuable in illustrating the different kinds of strengths and problems across the various subject areas and instructional methods in school classroom settings. However, it is also of interest to examine factors that influence flow in online activities due to the prevalence of computer-based self-directed learning programs and e-learning courses which often combine self-directed learning with instructor and student-to-student interfaces.

Studies of flow in the context of engagement in web activities can offer insight into relationships that may affect web design for optimal online learning experiences, especially in the context of self-directed learning. Chen, Wigland, and Nilan (1999) investigated whether the concept of flow could be meaningfully applied in a web context and if so what conditions on the web are associated with being in a state of flow. Csikszentmihalyi (Geirland, 1996) said that,

> A Web site that promotes flow is like a gourmet meal. You start off with the appetizers, move on to the salads and entrées, and build toward dessert. Unfortunately, most sites are built like a cafeteria. You pick whatever you want. That sounds good at first, but soon it doesn't matter what you choose to do.

Table 5.4. General Summary of Major Findings in Shernoff et al. (Based on Shernoff, Csikszentmihalyi, Schneider, & Shernoff, 2003).

Dependent Variables	Independent Variables			
	Challenge/Skill	Instructional Relevance and Control	Classroom Activities	School Subjects
Engagement	In all of the dependent variable categories, the flow condition (high challenge, high skill) had the highest correlation and the apathy condition (low challenge, low skill) the lowest. With few exceptions, the other conditions were as expected.	Higher levels of relevance and control were associated with higher levels of engagement.	Students reported higher levels on all dependent variables in relation to doing group work and taking exams. In addition, they reported high levels of attention when doing individual work.	Engagement was highest for art and computer science followed by vocational education and social studies.
Interest				Same as above for interest and enjoyment, but not concentration.
Concentration				
Enjoyment				
Attention				Highest in math, science, and computer science. Lowest in history, English, and social studies.
Quality of Experience				
Mood		High control was associated with more positive levels of mood and also with esteem.		Art was correlated with mood, intensity, and motivation, but not esteem. Math and science rated as most intense but not most motivating.
Esteem				
Intensity		High relevance was associated with high intensity.		
Motivation				

> Everything is bland and the same. Web site designers assume that the visitor already knows what to choose. That's not true. People enter Web sites hoping to be led somewhere, hoping for a payoff.

Analogies such as this are useful in helping conceptualize and understand the emotions associated with the situation, but they need to be supplemented with a more precise definition. When working on the Web one can experience many different emotions including such things as frustration, fun, and skepticism. In order to distinguish flow states on the Web from these other conditions, Chen, Wigand, and Nilan (1999) defined four characteristics:

1. it must provide immediate feedback;
2. it must offer clear rules allowing Web users to follow and clear goals to pursue;
3. it must provoke enough complexity which should not be easily exhausted; and
4. it must create dynamic challenges, not static ones (p. 589).

They prepared a questionnaire which they distributed to active web users and received 327 replies. The questionnaire presented three descriptions of flow states that had been created by Csikszentmihalyi (1975) and used in other studies (McQuillan & Conde, 1996). These descriptions were from a rock climber, a composer, and a dancer:

> My mind isn't wandering. I am not thinking of something else. I am totally involved in what I am doing. My body feels good. I don't seem to hear any-thing. The world seems to be cut off from me. I am less aware of myself and my problems.

> My concentration is like breathing. I never think of it. I am really quite oblivious to my surroundings after I really get going. I think that the phone could ring, and the doorbell could ring, or the house burn down or something like that. When I start, I really do shut out the whole world. Once I stop, I can let it back in again.

> "I am so involved in what I am doing. I don't see myself as separate from what I am doing."

The questionnaire asked the respondents whether they had ever experienced a state such as this while working on the web. People who answered "yes" where then asked what they were doing and to provide additional explanation about how they felt the last time they experienced this feeling. The questionnaire also asked them if they had experienced feelings of time going by too fast, enjoyment, being in control, and challenge. Each time, they were asked to describe what they were doing when they felt this way.

The researchers found that three categories of activities accounted for the majority of conditions in which respondents experienced flow: research on the Web, information retrieval on the Web, and creating Web pages. While this is interesting, the important finding was that the antecedents of flow; that is, the conditions that led to flow were clear goals, immediate feedback, and matched skills and abilities. However, more recent research raises questions about uses of the Internet at work for personal enjoyment. In other words, workers sometimes if not frequently use the web as a digression from work and find it enjoyable. Questions arise about the relationship between flow and these procrastination activities. The researchers found that popular diversionary activities such as online games, online chat, online telephony, and blogging are the best predictors of problematic use of the Internet which refers to socially unacceptable and even criminal Internet uses, Internet procrastination from work, and flow. Their study signals the need for additional inquiry into these issues and this would certainly be an issue in education. Many instructors have a policy against the use of laptop computers in the classroom because students use them, whenever they can get away with it, for divergent activities such as shopping and social networking.

It is interesting to note that the three antecedents of flow identified by Chen et al. (Chen, Wigand, & Nilan, 1999) are also goals of, if not actual characteristics of, web-based learning activities. However, one could question whether these three antecedents by themselves would differentiate flow from procrastination. A challenge in web-based instruction is that there are many types of distractions that can, on the one hand, keep students fully engaged in Web activities but, on the other hand, distract them from the learning goals. Deimann and Keller (2006) describe several of these such as *lost in hyperspace, cognitive overload*, and *seductive details* which all refer to various types of distractions when working on the Internet and also describe how volitional; that is, self-management strategies must sometimes be employed to help students stay on task. This raises interesting questions about flow as an inherently beneficial state of mind versus a sometimes diversionary state of mind and how to promote flow within a designated goal-oriented activity!

Transition

Clearly there is a rich foundation for the concept of relevance. The various theories and concepts provide a basis for specifying several subcategories and many specific strategies for helping to instill a sense of relevance in the learners. As can be seen, these go far beyond the simple concepts of usefulness or authenticity to encompass elements of personal style and background experience. The following section provides a taxonomy of relevance subcategories and examples of strategies.

Strategies for Relevance

"Why do we have to study this?" How many times have you heard this question, or asked it yourself? This is the classical "relevance" question. As we have established, it is very difficult for students to be motivated to learn if they do not perceive there to be any relevance in the instruction. If the extrinsic rewards, such as recognition, promotion, or material rewards are strong enough, then students will see the instruction as being relevant to accomplishing these goals, but these rewards will not make the content of the instruction more personally relevant. There are almost always extrinsic rewards associated with performance in school, but the type of motivation that results from this could be called motivation to achieve instead of motivation to learn. To stimulate the motivation to learn, it is best to build relevance by connecting instruction to the learners' backgrounds, interests, and goals. Following (Table 5.5) are three major categories of relevance strategies, examples of the primary question to be asked in regard to each, and samples of the kinds of tactics that are related to each category. The first category can include both extrinsic and intrinsic goals, but the second and third are primarily intrinsic in nature.

R.1. Relate to Goals

> When teaching a course on data processing, Jim used application examples and practice exercises based on the types of data and clients that the learners would find on their jobs.

All of the motivational self-help books and how to achieve success books tell us that having a clearly defined goal is a necessity. Think about the times in your own life when you have been highly motivated. Did you have a goal that you were excited about achieving, such as a vacation that you were

Table 5.5. Subcategories, Process Questions, and Main Supporting Strategies for Relevance.

Concepts & process questions	Main supporting tactics
R1. Goal Orientation How can I best meet my learner's needs? (Do I know their needs?)	Provide statements or examples of the utility of the instruction, and either present goals or have learners define them.
R2. Motive matching How and when can I link my instruction to the learning styles and personal interests of the learners?	Make instruction responsive to learner motives and values by providing personal achievement opportunities, cooperative activities, leadership responsibilities, and positive role models.
R3. Familiarity How can I tie the instruction to the learners' experiences?	Make the materials and concepts familiar by providing concrete examples and analogies related to the learners' work or background.

longing to take, attracting the attention and interest of a "special someone," obtaining a degree or special award? Most of the time the answer will be, "yes." When people have clearly defined goals, it is much easier to determine whether you can build a connection between them and what you are teaching, even if the connection is somewhat remote.

But what if your learners do not have clearly defined goals, or if there is no clear and immediate connection between your content and the kinds of goals that they might develop? Many of the tactics implied by the following process questions will help learners see connections to actual or potential goals. Two specific tactics are "before and after" comparisons and future wheels. You have observed before and after comparisons all of your life. They are one of the most popular advertising techniques for showing the benefit of a new product. You can use the same technique to illustrate how mastery of your content can lead to good things in the future.

A related technique is to use a future wheel when students do not perceive any future value for the present subject. A nice feature of this technique is that they generate the potential connections to their future needs and goals, not you. This technique is somewhat like mind mapping. Have each student draw a circle in the center of a blank sheet of paper. Give the following instructions: "Imagine that you successfully learn this material. How might this benefit you in the future? Think of all the things this might lead to, or help you with. For each one of them, draw a line out from your circle, put another circle at the end of the line, and put the item in it. Draw a separate line and circle for each item you can think of." After they complete this task, then have them repeat the process for each of the new circles. And, do it one more time. When the students have finished, they will be amazed to see how many potential benefits there are to the current subject. You may also be surprised at the number and kinds of connections they make.

Not all goals are projected into the future. Some can be very close at hand. The following list contains tactics for highlighting the present worth of the content as well as projecting it into the accomplishment of future goals.

Present Worth

1. State the immediate benefit of the instruction if it is not self-evident.
2. Include comments, anecdotes, or examples that stress the intrinsic satisfactions of the subject of instruction.

Future Value

3. Include statements describing what the learner will be able to do after finishing these instructional materials.

4. Ensure that at least some of the examples and exercises are clearly relate to the knowledge and skills that the students will need in the future.
5. Tell the student how the successful accomplishment of this instruction is related to future goal accomplishment (e.g., is success in this instructional situation important for admission to subsequent courses, selection of a major area of study, or admission to advanced levels of study, salary increase, job retention, or promotion).
6. Tell the learner how this instruction will improve his or her general life coping skills.
7. Encourage the learner to think of this instruction as contributing to the development of an intrinsically interesting area of study and development.

An Example

The activity presented in Figure 5.7 illustrates how a facilitator can discover what issues and problems the learners have in regard to the topic of a lesson or workshop. This activity allows the facilitator to do some "on the spot" needs assessment to find out how to connect his or her course objectives to the needs and interests of the learners. In this exercise, participants individually list problems in Part 1. Then, the facilitator calls upon each participant to mention one problem in turn and keeps rotating through the class until no one has any more items to contribute. Next, the class discusses the list and combines similar items. In Part 2, every one copies the list onto their worksheets and then rates each item as follows:

Y = This is a motivational problem that I believe I should be responsible for solving.

N = This motivational problem is outside my control. There is nothing I can do about it.

?? = I'm not sure how to classify this problem.

After everyone has finished, the facilitator has everyone compare notes and they discuss their various opinions. The facilitator relates the problems to the objectives of the class and points out that there might be ways to deal with some of the "uncontrollable" problems, which is what typically happens after the class learns the motivational design process.

R.2. Match Interests

In a course on basic marketing concepts and techniques, Mark allowed groups to select their own marketing objectives and strategies during competitive group exercises.

There is more to relevance than utility; that is, connecting instruction to goals is utilitarian in that it based on achieving external outcomes. To

---

Have You Ever Had A Problem with Student Motivation?

Part 1: List of Motivational Problems

What kinds of motivational problems do you encounter in the classroom or with the materials you produce? List three or more motivational problems faced by you or other developers of instructors in the courses you deliver. In other words, what kinds of motivational problems are presented by the participants (students) or situation?

1. _____
2. _____
3. _____
4. _____
5. _____
6. _____

Part 2: Ratings of Motivational Problems

(Instructions will be provided by your facilitator.)

Y = _____

N = _____

? = _____

Y	N	??	Group List of Problems
__	__	__	1. _____
__	__	__	2. _____
__	__	__	3. _____
__	__	__	4. _____
__	__	__	5. _____
__	__	__	6. _____
__	__	__	7. _____

What techniques can you use to build a stronger sense of relevance?

Figure 5.7. Hooking Into Learner's Concerns.

develop a holistic approach to relevance, and to compensate for situations where the instructional content is only weakly related to learner goals, there are several things you can do to engage the learners. People are more motivated to achieve in situations where they receive personal recognition and are valued as both human beings and for the contributions they can make. In classrooms, learners will feel more interest and relevance when they feel that the teacher knows them, takes a personal interest in them, and cares about whether or not they succeed. This is why teacher behaviors such as eye contact, knowing the students' names, and unobtrusive conversations with students all make the student experience higher levels of relevance in that setting.

The use of role models and stories about the challenges faced by real individuals who had to work and strive to achieve personal goals in fields of study that are relevant to the subject matter are tactics that undoubtedly have their origins in antiquity. But, they still work. That is why this is a common theme in literature, movies, and even advertising. Also, a teacher's emotional displays of enthusiasm and other feelings of challenge and achievement can help inspire some students, awakening vicarious interests in the content that may persist as a new, internalized interest and even career focus. Even when we do not adopt the interests of an enthusiastic person, we tend to be motivated by that person and are interested in what they have to offer.

The way in which you teach a subject can also inspire a feeling of relevance, at least for the duration of the unit of work. For example, people who have a strong desire for achievement will feel a higher level of relevance for a topic if you organize competitions or other opportunities for them to set personal goals and excel. Many students will respond positively to cooperative group work that provides a relaxing context in which to talk and collaborate with other students. However, some of the students who have a high desire for personal achievement will probably not enjoy group work if their grades are dependent on the performance of the group. Your challenge as a teacher is to use a variety of teaching methods that allow the needs of the various students to be met. This will increase their overall sense of relevance of the requirements of the situation to their needs and will make them more receptive to learning even if the relevance of the topic itself is not readily apparent.

Basic Motive Stimulation

1. Use personal language to make the learner feel that he or she is being talked to as a person.
2. Provide examples (anecdotes, statistics, etc.) that illustrate achievement striving and accomplishment.
3. Include statements or examples that illustrate the feelings associated with achievement.
4. Encourage the learner to visualize the process of achieving and succeeding, and the feelings associated with it.
5. Include exercises that allow for personal goal setting, record keeping, and feedback.
6. Include exercises that require cooperative work groups.
7. Include puzzles, games, or simulations that stimulate problem-solving, achievement-striving behavior.

8. In the exercises (including puzzles, games, and simulations), encourage the learners to compete against each other, themselves (i.e., trying to beat their own record), or against a standard.

Role Models
9. Use anecdotes about noteworthy people in the area of study, the obstacles they faced, their accomplishments, and the consequences.
10. Use examples, testimonials, etc., from persons who attained further goals after successfully completing the course of instruction.
11. Include references to, or quotations from, people who can convincingly describe the benefits of the particular skill/knowledge area.

R.3. Tie to Experiences

> Leslie began a workshop on accounting software applications by asking each participant to describe the amount of experience each had with any kind of accounting software.

Quite a few years ago, one of the largest international hotel-motel companies, headquartered in the United States, used an advertising slogan of "no surprises." They were trying to establish the concept that you, the customer, could always expect the same, predictable high-quality service and familiar amenities of their hotels. This would relieve the weary traveler of the stresses of dealing with unfamiliar surroundings and not knowing what to expect. This slogan reflected the tendency of people to be interested in things that are related to interests that they already have. It has long been known that most of the participants in the audience to hear a controversial speaker already agree with the speaker. The participants desire confirmation of things they already believe.

A primary goal of education, which is to expand students' minds and stimulate both critical and creative thinking, would seem to contradict the desire for familiarity. One way to achieve both goals is to find ways to connect new, unfamiliar content to past knowledge and experiences of the learners. Then, transition them into new knowledge and perspectives (see the activity in Table 5.6). The following analytical questions offer some suggestions in this regard.

Connection to Previous Experience
1. Include explicit statements about how the instruction builds on the learner's existing skills or knowledge.

2. Use analogies or metaphors to connect the present material to processes, concepts, skills, or concepts already familiar to the learner.

Table 5.6. An Example of Linking the Unfamiliar to the Familiar.

CASE: THE SOCIAL STUDIES CHALLENGE

In his 9th grade social studies class, Gil Perkins had to teach a thematic unit on cities. It focused on politics, economics, education, and other aspects of a city's infrastructure such as distribution systems (food and merchandise) and communications. He had trouble motivating the interest of the students in his rural Midwestern school with respect to this module. Almost none of them had ever been to a large city. Their impressions were formed by the excitement, drama and, usually, violence of television programs set in large cities. In contrast, this social studies information was not interesting or relevant to them.

After reading some material about "inquiry teaching," Gil began his unit this year by asking the class, "What would happen in a town of 12,500 people if the food supply were cut in half overnight?" The students were both surprised and intrigued by this question, which referred to a town the size of theirs. A lively discussion followed in which speculation turned into thoughtful discussion based on their knowledge of the close interactions of people in the town and the surrounding farms, ranches, and dairies.

After 20 minutes, Gil interrupted and asked the class what would happen if the food supply were cut in half overnight in a city of 1,250,000 people, and he named some cities of that approximate size. The discussion took a very different turn. It was much more speculative and reflected the values and beliefs of the students based on their home backgrounds, travel experience, and television preferences. It soon became obvious that they were dealing purely in speculation and could not meaningfully analyze the situation.

At that point Gil introduced the new module and explained how the things they would learn would help them better understand what might happen. Before beginning, he and the class summarized a list of their key questions and predictions. As he taught the material, Gil had the students relate it to the small town situation and to the list of questions and predictions.

Options for Individualization

3. Give the learner choices in the content of assignments (e.g., is the learner allowed to choose examples and topics of personal interest for at least some of the assignments).
4. Give the learner choices in the type of assignment (for example, allow the learners to select from a variety of means to accomplish a given end).

Summary

This principle of relevance has strong application in a classroom. Children will process information much more effectively and efficiently, and be more motivated to pay attention and learn if they perceive personal relevance. There are many ways to transmit this sense of relevance. It can come from the content of a communication, the personal warmth, attention, and enthusiasm of the teacher who generates a vicarious sense of interest in the students and from activities that are deliberately designed to build bridges to the students' past experiences.

Some researchers in motivational design (Means, Jonassen, & Dwyer, 1997) have, like Sperber and Wilson (1986) who are from a different professional discipline, postulated that relevance is the most important component of motivation. However, they found that the other dimensions of motivation are also important. As illustrated in the various concepts of motivation and their synthesis into the ARCS model, there does not appear to be any single motivational concept that is by itself most critical. That is why a holistic approach is desirable. However, there is no denying that relevance is one of the most important influences.

Chapter 6 – Building Confidence

Forethoughts

Why is the fellow in Figure 6.1 so confused? Maybe it's because he is trying to answer these questions:

What are the implications of the following quotation from the presocratic philosopher Heraclitus (540–475 B.C.) with regard to his attitude toward prediction and control? *Time is a child moving counters in a game; the kingly power is a child's.*

What, if anything, does Heraclitus' comment have in common with the famous question asked

Figure 6.1. Pondering Difficult Questions.

twenty-five hundred years later by Einstein (1879–1955)? *Does God play dice with the universe?*

And finally, how are these issues related to your own outlook and expectations in life?

Introduction

In the present context, confidence refers generally to people's expectancies for success in the various parts of their lives. There are many psychological constructs and attitudinal concepts that help provide explanations for people's expectancy-related beliefs regarding the degree to which they can predict and even control the outcomes of their behavior. This also includes the "downside" of the concept which refers to lack of confidence or low expectancies for success.

A central issue in this regard seems to be perceptions of control. Life can be frightening and depressing if you feel that you have no control over your daily events and future goals. It is much more comforting to begin each day knowing what to expect and ending each day with a satisfying feeling of accomplishment than to have no idea whether you will be safe or whether you will encounter unfair, frustrating actions from other people who are more powerful than you are. Yet, even when you have an overall positive sense of confidence based on a perception of having things under control, there are unexpected events that occur, some of them beneficial and some not. A car wreck is not something you expect at any specific point in time even though you know that there is always a possibility of a crash if driving is part of your life. Thus, if a crash does occur and it is not physically or financially devastating, you will probably adjust to it and carry on. It is an undesired but not totally unexpected event in your overall view of life. However, this expression of a reasonable view of the probabilities of an uncontrollable event is not shared by everyone. Let's assume you are a highly successful salesman and the top producer in your department. You are fully expecting to be promoted to sales manager, but the job goes to a newly hired MBA with little actual experience. This is an unexpected and inequitable consequence that can have devastating effects on your sense of prediction and control, not to mention your emotional attitudes! Experiences such as these, combined with the totality of experiences in your life and your overall personality traits, can have a huge impact on the degree to which you believe you can control all aspects of your life versus being subject to random and uncontrollable events. Furthermore, your underlying religious and philosophical beliefs can exert a strong influence on your feelings of being in control or having a somewhat more fatalistic attitude.

A concern for control and predictability is an age-old human concern which is reflected in all mankind's musings and speculations about life as reflected in psychology, literature, and philosophy, and opinions vary greatly. Even in ancient Greece among the presocratic philosophers there were diametrically opposite points of view (Wheelwright, 1966). For example, Heraclitus, as quoted in the Forethoughts, expressed the point of view that change and randomness, if not outright whimsy, are characteristics of life. He is also well known for his statement that, "You cannot step twice into the same river, for other waters and yet others go ever flowing on," which suggests that change is constant even though things might appear to have a measure of stability. In contrast, Parmenides, another Greek philosopher from the same era, held the opposite point of view. He postulated that the physical world is an ungenerated, indestructible, permanent, and unchanging whole. Hence, knowledge can be obtained by applying reason to distinguish reality from appearances which results in predictability and control. That which we perceive to be change is only illusion, or appearances. The true underlying reality does not change.

This point of view was echoed to a degree by Einstein as indicated by his answer to his question about God playing dice with the universe was that "God does not play dice with the universe." In other words, he believed that there are immutable truths that would explain the permanent underlying reality of things. In contrast, just as in the opposing views of Parmenides and Heraclitus, the contemporary physicist Steven Hawking points out that from the point of view of quantum mechanics and the uncertainty principle in physics there is randomness in the universe which means that perfect prediction is impossible. This led Hawking (2005) to say, "Thus it seems that even God is bound by the Uncertainty Principle, and cannot know both the position, and the speed, of a particle. So God does play dice with the universe. All the evidence points to him being an inveterate gambler, who throws the dice on every possible occasion" (p. 1).

These few comments are intended to illustrate the agelessness of this issue of predictability and control and to underscore the relevance of this concern in people's lives, not to represent a rigorous exploration of presocratic philosophy and modern science!

In psychology, inquiry into the question of prediction and control tends not to be so dichotomous, but it is the basis of many concepts and theories concerning expectancy for success. The early part of this chapter contains explanations of many of the most salient concepts regarding the issues of confidence and personal control and the later part contains specific guidelines for creating strategies that help students build positive expectancies for success!

Psychological Basis for Confidence

Key Question for Confidence

How can I help the students succeed and believe in their ability to control their successes?

Anxiety and fear are much greater parts of students' lives than teachers realize. In an unpublished study by the author of this text, middle school children responded to a survey of motivational attitudes, one of which was fear of failure. Their teachers filled out a similar questionnaire in which they were asked to estimate the motivational attitudes of each student. There were many variations due to differences in subject matters and differences in students' actual opinions versus teachers' estimations of the students' opinions. For example, students in art classes rated their classes as being less relevant than English classes while the art teachers overestimated the students' perceptions of relevance. Both the English and the math teachers underestimated the students' opinions; that is, the students considered the classes to be more relevant than the teachers predicted. However, there was one comparison that was consistent throughout the study: *virtually all of the teachers underestimated the fear of failure and anxiety expressed by the children*. The prevalence of anxiety and fear manifests itself in many ways, ranging from various types of avoidance, such as absenteeism and procrastination, to rebellious responses such as misbehavior in the classroom and aggression or bullying against other students outside the classroom. Even highly successful children who have a deep-seated fear of failure and of disappointing their parents or other social-reference groups are adversely affected by such feelings. When these fears are taken to the extreme, suicide is not an uncommon result.

For the majority of students, anxiety and fear are manageable and do not have detrimental effects on performance. In fact, a moderate amount of arousal in the form of anxiety or fear is normal when faced with a challenge, regardless of whether it is in a classroom, on a playing field, in the workplace, or in a recital hall. This is one of the things that stimulate people to maximum performance. However, it can become a debilitative force within anyone, and some students live with it all the time.

How can we understand this phenomenon and what can we do to help students overcome it by developing greater levels of confidence? Our goal in relation to building the motivation to learn in students is to help them develop positive expectancies for success. These positive expectancies can result from the students' perceptions of having some control over the outcomes of their behavior, their attributions for success and failure, their beliefs in their capacity for being effective, their self-fulfilling prophecies, the extent to which they have feelings of helplessness, and their sense of optimism.

Locus of Control

People differ in the degree to which they believe that they are responsible for the outcomes of their behavior or that external forces are the primary cause. For example, let's assume that Charlie is expecting a grade of *A* on a term paper but receives a *B* and he immediately blames the instructor for not providing clear instructions or grading the paper fairly. In contrast, Carolyn who was also expecting an *A* and got a *B*, immediately assumes that she did not read the instructions carefully or simply did not try hard enough. If we can assume that the two papers were highly comparable and the grading standards were objective, we could conclude that Charlie and Carolyn have very different views about the controlling influences in their lives. This characteristic was called *locus of control* by Rotter (1966). People who believe they will be rewarded appropriately by means of grades, recognition, money, privileges, or other tangible outcomes if they do a good job are considered to have an internal locus of control. In contrast, people who believe that being rewarded depends on luck, personal favor, or other uncontrollable influences, regardless of how well or poorly they achieve, are considered to have an external locus of control. Naturally, there are some situations where almost anyone would predict that he or she would be rewarded for doing well as in a game of skill such as jump rope with a fixed reward for a specified level of performance, and other situations that most people would perceive they have little control over getting a reward as in guessing the outcome at a roulette table where luck is the primary influence if the machine is not being manipulated. But, what Rotter and other researchers found was that regardless of objective degree of control in a situation, some people will on the average have a more internal set of beliefs while others are more external. That is, they differ predictably in their tendency to interpret their control over the outcomes of their behavior as being internally or externally determined.

Rotter's introduction of this concept (Rotter, 1954), especially after he published the freely available *I-E Scale* that could be used to measure it (Rotter, 1966) resulted in a landslide of studies within a very short time (Phares, 1976; Rotter, 1972) and it continues to be of interest (Declerck, Boone, & DeBrabander, 2006; Ifamuyiwa & Akinsola, 2008). The role of locus of control in behavior has been studied in virtually every walk of life, but the focus here is on studies that established the meaning and validity of the concept and its role in motivation and learning.

In this regard, Rotter and others demonstrated that learning which occurs under conditions where the outcomes are perceived to be under the control of others can be very different from that which the learner perceives the outcomes to be under internal controls such as ability, skill, or effort. This is illustrated by learning outcomes under skill conditions that are quite different from the traditional findings of behavioral conditioning studies. It was a well-established principle (Bandura, 1969) in behavioral conditioning studies of reinforcement and performance that if one group of subjects receives reinforcement following every correct response (100% reinforcement) but a second group receives intermittent reinforcement after only 50% of the correct responses, there are different extinction patterns following a point where no reinforcements are given any more. Both groups would continue responding for awhile, but the group that had received 100% reinforcement would stop responding sooner than the group that had received 50% reinforcement. This was presumed to be because the 100% group was quicker to conclude that there had been a change in the rules than the 50% group (Rotter, Liverant, & Crowne, 1961).

However, when the concepts of skill versus chance are introduced the outcomes are different. If one group of subjects is told that success at an ambiguous task is so difficult that it is largely a matter of luck, but another group is told that success is due to skill and that previous research has shown that some people are better at the task than others, then the group receiving skill instructions has extinction patterns that are the opposite of the general results in behavioral conditioning studies. In the group receiving skill instructions, those who received intermittent reinforcement stopped working on the task sooner than those who had received 100% reinforcement when reinforcement was withheld. In other words, those who had been getting 100% reinforcement took longer to give up the perception that success truly was due to their skills than the group that had been successful only 50% of the time. In the group that was told success was a matter of luck, the results were the same as in traditional studies; that is, if they were getting 50% reinforcement, they would attribute a string of successes or failures to luck and would keep trying longer than if they had been getting 100% success and it suddenly stopped. It is important to note that under all of these conditions, success was under the control of the experimenters and due to the ambiguous nature of the task it was possible to convince the subjects of the skill versus luck components (Holden & Rotter, 1962; Rotter, Liverant, & Crowne, 1961).

This has interesting implications for school learning environments. Phares, in Chapter VII ("Locus of Control and Achievement in Children") of his book (Phares, 1976), reports on many studies done during the late 1960s and early 1970s that show an overall consistent relationship between internal locus of control and higher levels of school achievement even though there are some variations in the findings. There was even a positive relationship between locus of control and creativity that was found in one study (DuCette, Wolk, & Friedman, 1972). Most of these studies used the Intellectual Achievement Responsibility Questionnaire (IAR) (Crandall, Katkovsky, & Crandall, 1965) or the Bialer (1961) Locus of Control Scale. These results suggest that in spite of some of the inconsistencies in results and even though teachers are "powerful others" in this environment and are not always clear or equitable in their grading standards, there is still an overall perception that students have control over the grades they receive.

One reason that internals might have superior achievement is that internals tend to be superior in several aspects of cognitive processing. They were quicker than externals to deduce the relevant cues and rules in an ambiguous learning situation (DuCette & Wolk, 1973). Also, internals tend to be better at incidental as well as intentional learning. Wolk and DuCette (1974) presented textual material to subjects and found that internals remembered more of the content of the material, which was an indication of incidental learning, as well as performing higher on the intentional task of finding errors. In three studies conducted over three successive semesters, Dollinger (2000) found that internals had greater knowledge of incidental knowledge related to his course in Personality Psychology. During the third week of class, called Research Day, the students responded to a battery of questionnaires that would be incorporated into lectures at later times in the semester. One of these was a "Trivia Test" which included such things as the instructor's office hours, points needed for an A, the date of the next exam, color of the supplementary Course Packet at the bookstore, major topics in the class, the instructor's wife's name which was included because she is also a psychology instructor, and other things which had been mentioned in passing during the first two weeks. In each one of the three semesters he found that internals had greater recall of incidental information and also performed better on tests even after controlling for GPA.

However, there are differences in perceptions of control in specific situations as well as differences in how internally oriented students react to success and failure compared to externally oriented students. Yeigh (2007) examined the relationship between trait-level locus of control and attributions for success or failure under conditions when participants responded to the operation-word task (Turner & Engle, 1989) which maximized the information processing load in their working memories. In this task participants are presented with a set of words followed by a relatively simple math problem to solve in their heads. After doing so, they are asked to recall the words. This task is repeated numerous times with increasing levels of difficulty. Yeigh found that participants with high trait–level perceptions of control attributed success outcomes to their efforts and abilities, both of which are internal causes. But, they attributed failure primarily to an external cause; in this case it was task difficulty. In contrast, students with low trait-level perceptions of control were divided between attributing successful outcomes to an internal cause, ability, and to two external causes - luck, and task difficulty. It is interesting to note that they did not attribute success to effort. But, following failure, they attributed their outcome primarily to internal causes (ability and effort) and partially to the external cause of task difficulty.

Yeigh concluded that with respect to the recall task, high trait-level internals were internalizing success and externalizing failure, while low-trait-level internals (which is to say, high trait-level externals) were externalizing success and internalizing failure. Furthermore, the high internals performed better initially, perhaps due to lower anxiety based on the expectation that they could control performance outcome. But, when they were faced with negative feedback their performance deteriorated. This could have been because of lowered confidence, but it could also be due to excessive cognitive load (Sweller, 1988, 1994). The internals have normally developed causal schemata in school settings in which they perceive ability and effort to be the primary causes of performance outcomes. But, as a result of experimenter manipulations in this situation, they found themselves failing at tasks at which they believed they should have been successful, so they engaged in internalized causal searches to find explanations for their failures. This type of metacognitive activity put an increased load on their working memory, which has a limited capacity, and interfered with their problem-solving activities.

This research has clear implications for instructional design in that interactions between motivational factors such as perceived controllability and information processing activities in the working memory can influence cognitive load and student capacities for effective learning. This relationship is illustrated in Keller's theory of motivation, learning, and performance which specifically illustrates mental resource management at the interface between motivation and information processing (Keller, 2008b, Figure 5, p. 94). To design truly effective learning environments, teachers will need to consider student's causal models, including perceived self-efficacy, in relation to the challenge levels of the task and the types of feedback that are offered.

It may also be important to consider ethnic and cultural differences. Previous research has shown that people's locus of control perceptions are moderated by ethnic influences which are at least in part a reflection of socioeconomic status and by cultural backgrounds. Jessor, Graves, Hanson, and Jessor (1968) in a comparison of Anglo-Americans, Latin-Americans, and Native-Americans found that Anglo-Americans had the highest level of internality followed by Native-Americans. Latin-Americans scored the lowest. Numerous studies (see Phares, 1976, p. 152) find that African-Americans score in a more external direction than Anglo-Americans but that low SES students score more external than high SES students regardless of race. Muller, Stage, and Kinzie (2001) examined the relationships among ethnicity, locus of control, and science achievement among precollege students including ethnic representation from African-Americans, Asian-Americans, Latinos, and White males and females. They found that at the 8th grade level locus of control was strongly related to science achievement for every subgroup except Asian-American males. Furthermore, the differences at this grade level tended to remain stable through high school and combined with the overall lower level of participation of African-Americans and Latinos in high school science and math classes, are reflected in a large underrepresentation of these ethnic groups in science and mathematics classes in college.

With respect to cultural differences, Parsons, Schneider, and Hansen (1970) found no difference between American and Danish students. They had expected that the Danish students might score more externally because of the stronger central government authority in Denmark, but that was not the case. In a different kind of cultural comparison, Hsieh, Shybut, and Lotsof (1969) found that a group of Anglo-American high school students in Chicago scored more internally than a group of Chinese students in Hong Kong, but that American-born students in Chicago with at least one Chinese parent were more like the Anglo-Americans. The researchers explained that in the Chinese culture luck, chance, and fate are very much a part of life and that people consider their situations in life to be governed largely by things outside their control. This tendency toward externality in Asia could also be influenced by the overall religious/philosophical beliefs exemplified in Buddhism and some other belief systems which postulate the importance of accepting ones circumstances. In a different study of Asian and American cultures, Brown, Aoshima, Bolen, Chia, and Kohyama (2007) compared locus of control and learning approaches among students in the United States, Japan, and Taiwan. They found that both Japanese and Taiwanese students scored higher on externality than the students from the United States but that they are not more likely to attribute learning outcomes to external versus internal factors.

These studies from the early 1970s and from the last few years illustrate the rather stable relationships between locus of control orientation, cultural and ethnic group affiliation, and school achievement. But, care must be taken in interpreting these results. There tend to be high levels of variance within each specific group. Thus, within a group that has a more external orientation than the others, there will be many people who are very internal in their locus of control perspective. This is one of many reasons why it is important to avoid type-casting anyone based on these categorical characteristics. However, it can be helpful in designing instruction to know the locus of control orientations of your students, especially if there are extremes. But, this requires collecting data from students in specific situations and not relying on generalizations from research.

Origin–Pawn Theory

The *origin-pawn concept* refers to the degree to which people believe they have control over their lives. Pawns, like the most restricted pieces in a chess set, feel that the locus of causality for their behavior is outside of themselves. In other words, according to deCharms who introduced this concept (de Charms, 1968), "A Pawn feels that he is pushed around, that someone else pulls the strings and he is the puppet" (deCharms, 1976, p. 4). Pawns tend to avoid challenges, behave defensively, feel powerless, and are negatively motivated. In contrast (de Charms, 1968), "An Origin is a person who feels that he is in control of his fate; he feels that the cause for his behavior is within himself" (deCharms, 1976, p. 4). Origins feel potent, optimistic, and confident, and they are accepting of challenges and positively motivated.

Like other motivational characteristics, people do not always behave as if they were Origins or Pawns in all aspects of their lives. It would be irrational to do so because there are situations where one has little or no control such as being a passenger in an airplane versus those situations that require high levels of control such as driving your own car. However, the value in this concept, like other motivational concepts, lies in identifying differences in *perceived* personal control that differ from the objective reality and have positive benefits for individuals or result in maladaptive behavior and underachievement. In this regard, the validity of this concept was established in several studies (reported in deCharms, 1976, p. 16) which illustrated that Origins had higher levels of achievement, people had more positive feelings about themselves and others when they felt like Origins, and they had more positive feelings toward others who demonstrated the qualities of Origins. Not only that, people remembered the productions (presentations) of Origins for a considerably longer period than the productions of Pawns. Viney and Caputi (2005) summarize a variety of studies confirming that people's responses to Origin–Pawn measures are correlated with the actual degrees of controllability in a situation, yet there are individual differences reflecting people's Origin–Pawn orientations. Origins were shown to have more positive attitudes and higher status at work and more positive interpersonal coping strategies. Their scores were negatively correlated with fatalism.

This concept is normally measured by using content analysis of protocols created by the respondents. As in the Thematic Apperception Test, individuals provide tape recorded, handwritten, or e-mail responses to a stimulus such as

> I'd like you to talk to me for a few minutes about your life at the moment—the good things and the bad— what it is like for you. Once you have started, I shall be here listening to you, but I would rather not reply to any questions you may have until the 5-minute period is over. Do you have any questions you would like to ask now, before we start? (Viney & Caputi, 2005)

Or, specific leads might be used as in the following examples (deCharms, 1976) with school children: "When a child won't join in group activities ...," "Sometimes he/she wished that ...," or "The thing I like best about myself is ...."

All of the stories resulting from these stimuli are evaluated by means of a content analysis rubric that produces separate Origin and Pawn scores. As can be seen by the lists of characteristics in Table 6.1, raters look for clear distinctions between indicators of Origin and Pawn orientations. Trained raters can score the protocols with high levels of inter-rater reliability ranging from 0.87 to 0.93 (Westbrook & Viney, 1980).

This concept is sometimes compared to, or even equated with, locus of control. The two concepts do have some attributes in common, but there are also important differences. The Origin–Pawn concept focuses on a general sense of being in control of one's life and the things that happen in contrast to locus of control which is defined primarily by the degree to which people believe they have control over the consequences of their behavior. Also, this concept is presumed to represent a belief or attitude and is not considered to be a trait as is locus of control. Another difference in the formulation and measurement of this characteristic is that each dimension is scored separately. Locus of control, as introduced by Rotter and measured by Rotter's I-E Scale (Rotter, 1966), contains numerous pairs of items in which one item in the pair will represent more of an internal orientation and the other more of an external orientation. The respondent has to choose one item from each pair. This forces the results into a point along a continuum when, actually, people might have complex blends of internality and externality. The method used to score the Origin–Pawn concept is more likely to reveal these mixtures of beliefs.

Table 6.1. Indicators of Origin and Pawn Characteristics in Content Analysis (Based on Westbrook & Viney, 1980).

Indicators of an Origin orientation	Indicators of a Pawn orientation
1. Self-expresses intention (says that he or she intended, planned, decided; mentions plans, purposes, goals, e.g., "I planned the party," "we decided to have a child.").	6. Self-indicates that he or she did not intend an outcome (e.g., "I did not plan to have this baby," "I was in a car accident").
2. Self-expresses exertion or trying (describes his or her efforts to achieve some stated or implied result, e.g., "I'm trying to find out," "it took quite a bit of energy to load the boxes").	7. Self-indicates that he or she did not try to bring about an occurrence (e.g., "I wasn't trying to fix it but when I bumped it, it started to go," "I made no effort to look after the orchids, but they bloomed profusely").
3. Self-expresses ability (comments on his or her skill, competence, e.g., "I became school champion," "I'm managing very well").	8. Self-expresses lack of ability (describes self as powerless, ineffective, incapable, a failure, e.g., "I couldn't attract a man," "I just couldn't help it").
4. Self-describes overcoming or influencing others or the environment (e.g., "I didn't let them stop me," "the hill was steep but I managed to climb to the top").	9. Self-describes being controlled, forced, prevented by, at the mercy of external forces such as other people, environmental forces, chance (e.g., "He wouldn't let me take the kiddies," "I don't want to be locked up in a place like this").
5. Self-perceived as cause or origin (e.g., "I took control during labor," "I produced the play").	10. Self-perceived as a pawn (events are described as unpredictable or uncontrollable (e.g., "The sickness struck me," "my car hit one side of the bridge and careened to the other side").

Considering that people with an Origin orientation tend to achieve better in schools, deCharms (deCharms, 1976) designed and implemented a large-scale study to see whether student's Origin perceptions could be strengthened and if this would result in higher achievement. He trained teachers in methods that would help create a learning environment to support Origin behavior. The classroom learning activities and assignments gave students a great deal of freedom and autonomy with the teacher playing more of a managerial role. He found that 6th and 7th graders who received Origin training for 1 year had a significant improvement in their Origin scores compared to a control group and that students who received the Origin training during their 6th and 7th grades were significantly higher than those who received it for 1 year. There was a tendency in the school in which this study was conducted for the students to fall farther and farther behind the national norms as they progressed through school. This trend was reversed with the students who received Origin training, and that their gains persisted for at least 1 year, which was all he measured, following their training. This is in sharp contrast to the negative data received in most follow-up studies. Thus, there seem to be clear benefits from having or developing an Origin orientation and it appears to be possible to develop this orientation with the appropriate guidance and practice.

Self-Efficacy

Another concept related to the belief in personal agency is *self-efficacy* (Bandura, 1977) which is typically referred to as a person's belief that he or she can succeed in performing a given task. While true at one level, there is more than this to the concept as Bandura articulated it. More specifically, Bandura (1986) defines self-efficacy as "people's judgments of their capabilities to organize and execute courses of action required to attain designated types of performances" (p. 391). In other words, a person's self-efficacy is comprised of a combination of beliefs related to three questions: Am I capable of doing the things that are necessary for success, developing a plan that will lead to success, and persisting in my efforts long enough to achieve success? The resulting strength of a person's self-efficacy is hypothesized to "determine whether coping behavior will be initiated, how much effort will be expended, and how long it will be sustained in the face of obstacles and aversive experiences" (Bandura, 1977, p.191).

Thus, personal estimates of self-efficacy have several influences on behavior. One of these relates to goal choice. There are aversive consequences to pursuing goals that one is not capable of accomplishing and rewarding consequences for success. Thus, there is positive coping value for people to develop personal estimates of their probability of success in pursuing specific courses of action and making rational choices to maximize success and this is also related to the amount of effort that one will exert. High self-efficacy leads to higher and more persistent effort, especially when faced with obstacles, and this leads to higher attainments. Thus, a positive spiral of expectancies, effort, and success which reinforces the positive expectancies is established.

Self-efficacy has been shown to be predictive of school achievement. Overall, students with higher self-efficacy perform better than students with low self-efficacy (Schunk, 1996). Thus, it serves as good indicator of academic performance. But, there are other factors to consider in regard to behaviors associated with self-efficacy and learning. For example, self-efficacy influences the way in which people approach preparatory activities prior to undertaking actual task performance activities, especially when one also considers success uncertainty as it relates to the challenge level of the task. If people have high self-efficacy and low uncertainty, they are most likely to work directly toward task accomplishment without engaging in much if any preparatory activities. However, if people have a high sense of personal self-efficacy but experience some uncertainty about success due to the challenge level of the task, they are more likely to expend more time in planning and learning prerequisite skills that will help improve their probabilities of success (Bandura, 1982). Success uncertainty combined with high self-efficacy can actually stimulate higher levels of effort than when there is little or no success uncertainty. They will keep their attention focused on the task itself and ways of best overcoming obstacles and challenges. Salomon (1984) found that students high in self-efficacy spent more effort learning from material perceived to be difficult, such as learning from text, than from material perceived to be easy such as TV. With the easy material, the high self-efficacy students exhibited overconfidence, invested less mental effort in learning the material, and actually underperformed. With regard to people who have lower self-efficacy combined with success uncertainty, they are more likely to focus on themselves than on the task. That is, they focus on perceived personal deficiencies and also see obstacles as being more formidable than they actually are.

With respect to the origins of self-efficacy perceptions, Bandura lists four sources (Bandura, 1977). The first is actual *performance achievements.* Generally speaking, successful mastery experiences tend to build positive self-efficacy and failures lower them. Furthermore, an accumulation of mastery experiences across a variety of types of tasks in one's life strengthens a generalized sense of mastery that can help a person develop higher levels of persistence and success at tasks for which the person traditionally had low self-efficacy. For example, let's assume that a young man named Bob is uncomfortable in mixed gender social situations with his peer group. He feels that he is not good a casual conversations or at dancing. But, he is good in school tasks and in general handyman tasks. He enjoys using tools and doing projects at home as well as mastering his school subjects. As he progresses in school, his general sense of self-efficacy grows because of these successes. Then, he gets a job requiring a combination of problem-solving skills and repairing equipment. This requires him to interact with many different people at work, and he finds it easy to interact with them about job-related matters. His generalized self-efficacy continues to grow. Then, at an office party, he decides to make an extra effort to be outgoing and he succeeds. Here, in contrast to a purely social situation, he has many things in common with his coworkers. His self-efficacy about casual social interaction improves and over time, he is able to transfer his confidence to other situations that are not tied to work.

However, success does not always lead to improved perceptions of self-efficacy. If the task was perceived to be extremely easy or success was due to luck, then self-efficacy probably won't improve. Conversely, if a person fails at a task, self-efficacy might not decrease if the person felt that he simply didn't try very hard to succeed. However, generally speaking, repeated successes at a given class of tasks will lead to positive self-efficacy and repeated failures to lowered self-efficacy.

A second source of information that can lead to improved self-effi- cacy is *vicarious experience*. Social comparisons that lead to the conclusion that "if he can do it, I can do it" are among the most common types of vicarious experiences that affect self-efficacy. However, simply observing another person perform a task will not necessarily affect one's self-efficacy. Bandura's extensive work on observational learning (Bandura, 1969) illus- trates that there are many conditions of the models and the environment that determine whether the observer will experience a change in attitude or behavior. For example, the observer must feel a sense of personal identifica- tion with the model based on age, values, station in life, and so forth.

The third influence is *verbal persuasion* which can be self-induced or come from other persons. We see examples of this with mentors, cheer- leaders, coaches, and others who exhort us to try harder. We can also use self-talk to build our belief that we can accomplish a task. However, verbal persuasion will have little long-term effect if it is not followed by actual success. Verbal persuasion can also be a powerful source of low self-effi- cacy, especially for people whose self-concept is not strongly positive. Criticism from others who are perceived to be more powerful or superior in one way or another can be devastating to a person who has not yet developed a high level of inner strength in regard to perceived self-efficacy.

Emotional arousal is the fourth source of information that affects self-efficacy. Emotional arousal that is too high can have an adverse effect on self-efficacy due to heightened levels of fear of failure, embarrassment, or other similar reactions to a situation. This level of arousal can interfere with your cognitive processing and your motor skills causing you to be "tight," self-conscious, and not capable of smooth, reflexive responses to stimuli. Emotional arousal that is too low can also interfere with perfor- mance, but this condition would probably be characterized more by lack of desire than by feelings of low efficacy as in, "I could do it if I wanted to, but I don't want to."

It is interesting to consider potential interrelationships between self-efficacy, and goal orientation (Chapter 5), especially with regard to the interactions of emotional arousal, self-efficacy, goal orientation, and success. People with low efficacy are, by definition (Bandura, 1977), less able to organize their environments and plan courses of action that they expect will lead toward success. If a person is concerned about his or her likelihood of succeeding, then this person may have heightened emotional arousal to the point that it becomes debilitative. The person's worries about succeeding could lead toward a high level of performance (Dweck, 1986) or ego (Nichols, 1984a) orientation and low levels of mastery or task orienta- tion with regard to accomplishing the goal. On the one hand, moderate levels of performance/ego orientation can stimulate a person to higher levels of accomplishment if the person is basically confident and competent in the given set of tasks. However, as doubts about succeeding increase, the increased worries could detract from productive task oriented behaviors that would increase the probability of success. Thus, a reasonable approach to reducing negative emotional arousal that interferes with the development of positive self-efficacy could be grounded in coaching activities that focus on increasing task oriented behaviors while desensitizing the person's fears of failure. This coaching could be combined with feedback that encourages the person to reflect on the positive consequences and to attribute success to improvements in their self-efficacy skills.

        Even though self-efficacy as a concept has some things in common with other concepts in this category of confidence, there are distinctive differences. The origin–pawn concept has overlap in that it includes expressions of ability and responsibility for achieving one's goals, but self-efficacy differs in its focus on planning, action, and persistence in accomplishing goals. Also, the concept of locus of control is similar in that it deals with personal agency, but it is quite different in its fundamental focus. Locus of control refers to a person's belief that he or she has control over the outcomes of his or her behavior (Figure 6.2.A), but self-efficacy refers to perceived control over behavior; that is, whether or not one expects to succeed at a given task (Figure 6.2.B). It does not include the concept of having control over the outcomes of performance.

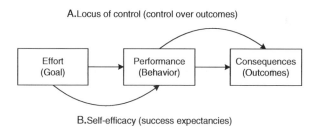

Figure 6.2. Relationship of Locus of Control & Self-Efficacy to Behavior and Outcomes.

Effects of Self-Efficacy

        It has been well established that there tends to be a positive relationship between self-efficacy and academic achievement (Pintrich & De Groot, 1990; Schunk, 1981, 1985). Students who are high in self-efficacy appear to have more flexible learning styles and coping strategies as indicated by their use of metacognitive strategies which incorporate more cognitive skills and by their greater persistence (Nichols & Miller, 1994). In other words, if they believe in their capability to succeed, they demonstrate more adaptive learning strategies by using metacognitive strategies, complex cognitive skills, and greater amounts of effort as indicated by their persistence at the task (Paris & Oka, 1986; Schunk, 1985).

These relationships were also investigated in a study of motivation and performance among learners working in dyads on a computer-based modeling task (Sins, Joolingen, Savelsbergh, & Hout-Wolters, 2008). According to Sins et al. (2008) the majority of research on self-efficacy, achievement goal orientation, and cognitive processing is based on self-report measures taken from individuals working on individual tasks. In their study, Sims et al. (2008) used self-report measures for achievement goal orientation and self-efficacy, at both the individual and group levels. They assessed cognitive processing behavior by analyzing the chat data from the log file histories of the various teams. Cognitive processing was classified as either deep or surface level based on the protocol analysis scheme of Sins, Savelsbergh, and Joolingen (2005). Surface processing was indicated by evaluating, quantifying, and analyzing activities with no reference to knowledge. Deep processing was indicated by these same activities combined with references to knowledge and by incorporating inductive reasoning and explaining activities. The researchers found that self-efficacy and mastery achievement goal orientation were positively related to deep processing, which implies the use of multiple metacognitive strategies and complex cognitive skills, and to achievement. There was no relationship between surface cognitive processing and achievement.

Attribution Theory

A related area of research that has superseded locus of control is *attribution theory* (Jones et al., 1971). This research builds on the observation that people vary with respect to their attributions of the causes of success and failure. Some people have a tendency to attribute success or failure to their ability. For example, they frequently use the phrase, "I can do that." Others who doubt their ability may say, or think, "No matter how hard I try, I won't be able to do this." As with locus of control, there are situations in every individual's life where both of these statements would be objectively true, but despite the objective probabilities, some people more characteristically use one set of attributions or another, especially when the objective probabilities are not clear to them.

Weiner (1992, 1974), who has extensively developed the concept of attribution theory, lists four primary attributions: ability, effort, task difficulty, and luck (or other external forces). The first two are internal attributions and the other two are external. However, he introduced another observation. Two of the attributions (ability

Table 6.2: Weiner's Attributional Elements in Relation to Stability and Locus of Control (Based on Weiner, 1992; Weiner, 1974).

		Locus of Control Dimension	
		Internal	External
Stability Dimension	Stable	Ability	Task Difficulty
	Unstable	Effort	Luck

and task difficulty) are relatively stable, not easily subject to change (Table 6.2). The other two (effort and luck) are easily changed and unstable. If people have confidence in their ability and do not see the tasks they face as being unnecessarily difficult, then their anxiety levels will be relatively low and they will tend to be persistent in working to achieve their goals. Because these are rather stable conditions, we would not expect there to be sudden changes in the person's behavior, at least not in the contexts where these beliefs are held. On the other hand, if a person's attributions are of low ability and high task difficulty, it can be difficult to change the person's behavior in a positive direction because these are stable attributions. In contrast, it is relatively easy to encourage a person to exert more effort, or to help them learn that luck is not the cause of success, if in fact that is not the case. Efforts to change a student's attributions often begin in the effort and luck categories, and then proceed to helping them develop stronger perceptions of their abilities and of task mastery.

Self-Fulfilling Prophecy

Self-fulfilling prophecy refers to a special type of expectancy belief. In short, it is commonly defined as a belief that although initially false becomes true as a result of believing in it (Merton, 1948). Two of the most commonly used examples of this principle are the bank failures during the Great Depression of the 1930s in the United States, and the transformation of a common flower girl on the streets of London into a fine lady. In the former instance, the banks were solvent but people believed them to be in jeopardy of failing. This belief led to a headlong rush to withdraw money from the banks which they were ill equipped to handle because of the time it would have taken to retrieve assets to provide the refunds. Thus, the belief caused the crash. Similarly, but happier, Henry Higgins in the musical *My Fair Lady* is able to complete the transformation because of his belief that he could instill an elegant dialect of speaking and fine manners in the flower girl. It was because of his belief in his capabilities to do this, and not her belief that she could do it, that led to the transformation. This story is based on the Greek myth of Pygmalion which is why the self-fulfilling prophecy is often called the Pygmalion effect. Pygmalion was a gifted sculptor in Cyprus who found a flawless piece of marble and decided to craft a beautiful woman from it. Prior to completing his statue he had no interest in women, so the story goes, but after viewing his creation he fell in love with it. He then went to the temple of Aphrodite and asked her to help him find a woman who would be as ideal as his statue. Intrigued, Aphrodite went to the sculptor's studio while he was away and was enchanted by his statue which, to her delight, looked like her! She rewarded the sculptor by bringing his statue to life.

The self-fulfilling prophecy has been studied in both learning and work settings. It was induced experimentally by Rosenthal and Jacobson (1968) in a classic study in which they administered a test of nonverbal intelligence to a group of 1st first through 6th sixth grade elementary school children at the beginning of an academic year. They randomly selected 20% of these children and identified them as intellectual bloomers based on the test results; that is, that they had high potential for a spurt of intellectual growth. These children were identified for "information purposes only," and the teachers were told not to do anything special; just teach their classes in their normal manner. The results demonstrated that these children showed greater intellectual growth and higher reading achievement than the control students. At the end of the study, teachers were interviewed and they could not identify anything they had done differently for the bloomers than for the other students, yet the effect was there. Somehow, they were communicating higher levels of support or applying other techniques that benefited the bloomers. The children were not told that they had been classified as "bloomers" and so the results were attributed to the teachers' self-fulfilling prophecies. The early study of Rosenthal and Jacobson had methodological problems, but the effect has been replicated although not always strongly. For example, Schrank (1968) randomly assigned children to classes and told some of the teachers that their students had high learning potential while telling others that their students had low learning potential. The students in the so-called "high potential" classes learned more than the other students. In a follow-up study, Schrank (1970) told the teachers that the students had been randomly assigned to their classes, but told some of the teachers to teach their classes as if the students had high ability and others as if their students had average ability. No differences in learning were found. Thus, when teachers believed the students had higher ability, as in the first study, they had higher expectations of their abilities to achieve higher results from these students and that is what happened. However, attempting to "pretend" that students can achieve at a higher level was not effective.

An example from a work environment is provided by Livingston (1969) which he attributes originally to Rosenthal & Jacobson (1968). The interesting thing about this story is that it is true, not a fictional musical. As explained by Livingston (1969):

The importance of what a manager believes about his training and motivational ability is illustrated by "Sweeney's Miracle", a managerial and educational self fulfilling prophecy:

> 'James Sweeney taught industrial management and psychiatry at Tulane University, and he also was responsible for the operation of the Biomedical Computer Center there. Sweeney believed that he could teach even a poorly educated man to be a capable computer operator. George Johnson, a black man who was a former hospital porter, became janitor at the computer center; he was chosen by Sweeney to prove his conviction. In the morning, George Johnson, performed his janitorial duties, and in the afternoon Sweeney taught him about computers.
>
> Johnson was learning a great deal about computers when someone at the university concluded that, to be a computer operator, one had to have a certain I.Q. score. Johnson was tested, and his I.Q. indicated that he would not be able to learn to type, much less operate a computer.
>
> But Sweeney was not convinced. He threatened to quit unless Johnson was permitted to learn to program and operate the computer. Sweeney prevailed, and he is still running the computer centre. Johnson is now in charge of the main computer room and is responsible for training new employees to program and operate the computer.'

Sweeney's expectations were based on what he believed about his own teaching ability, not on Johnson's learning credentials. What a manager believes about his ability to train and motivate subordinates clearly is the foundation on which realistically high managerial expectations are built (85–86).

The concept of the self-fulfilling prophecy seems to have been derived from a more generalized conceptualization originally posited by Thomas (Thomas & Thomas, 1928) as pointed out by Merton (1948) and, more recently, Krishna (1971). Thomas's theorem as quoted by Merton (1948) is that, "If men define situations as real, they are real in their consequences (p. 193)." This incorporates the self-fulfilling prophecy, but it also explains situations in which peoples' beliefs, even when not necessarily true, govern their own behaviors. For example, if a storekeeper believes that a certain type of customer is likely to steal something, he will behave as though his belief is true even if it doesn't come true. And, by his projection of negative expectations, he can actually induce the behavior that he suspects.

But, this takes us back to the self-fulfilling prophecy! Parents can also be caught up in this same situation as when their fears that a child will engage in socially unacceptable behavior communicates a set of expectations to the child that results in the undesired behavior. From the child's, or customer in the suspicious shopkeeper's establishment's point of view, they might conclude that, "if they are already convinced I am going to do it, I might as well do it."

Another way in which prophecies can influence the outcomes of social behavior is illustrated by what John Venn (1888) referenced in Merton (1936, p. 904), called the suicidal prophecy. In some ways this is the opposite of the self-fulfilling prophecy. Suicidal prophecies are those in which it may be presumed that the prophecy leads to the nonoccurrence of the predicted behavior or outcome. For example, as illustrated in an example used by Merton (1936, p. 904), Marx predicted that in capitalism there would be a progressive concentration of wealth in the upper classes with a corresponding increase in misery in the lower classes. However, the popularity of socialist teaching and propaganda in the 1800s led to an unexpected occurrence. Laborers who could easily be treated unfairly when negotiating individually began to organize into labor unions. As a result, their collective bargaining power led to a slow down, "if not eliminating (Merton, 1936, p. 904)" the developments predicted by Marx. One could add a footnote to Merton's conclusions which is to say that maybe he just didn't wait long enough. During the later part of the 20th century and the first part of the 21st century in the United States an accelerating movement of wealth to the top 1% of Americans has been occurring together with a breakdown in organized labor and steadily lowering standard of living for the wage-earning citizens. Perhaps the economic breakdown will lead to some remediation of this process!

Happily, the self-fulfilling prophecy can work in a positive direction, and it has been shown that students of teachers who have generally positive expectations about how their students will perform do achieve at higher levels. Furthermore, this relationship between high self-efficacy teachers and student performance has been found regardless of differences among their students with respect to initial motivation and past performance (Jussim & Eccles, 1992).

Teacher (Manager) Self-Efficacy

An issue related to the research on self-fulfilling prophecies is how to establish and maintain such expectancies. Simply telling a teacher to assume that a group of people can improve and to teach them accordingly is not sufficient (Schrank, 1970). Even though there is an implication in this research that the leaders (teachers or managers) believe that the other people can change, the critical attribute of this concept is the leader's perceived locus of causality; that is, it is their belief that they can cause the change that is critical. But, the research on the self-fulfilling prophecy tends not to offer specific guidance for developing these expectancies. The teachers in the Rosenthal and Jacobson (1968) studies did not think they were treating the "bloomers" any different from the other students. However, in studies of teacher self-efficacy, which is a belief that is fundamental in the self-fulfilling prophecy, it has been possible to identify specific teacher behaviors associated with learner success.

Teachers with high self-efficacy spend more time helping students persist in their efforts, design challenging assignments, support students' ideas, have a positive classroom environment, try out new instructional techniques, engage children in more self-directed activities, give students more freedom, give more help to students having difficulties, and involve all students in discussions (Ashton & Webb, 1986; Gibson & Dembo, 1984; Tschannen-Moran, Woolfolk Hoy, & Hoy, 1998, 1990). In contrast, teachers lower in self-efficacy are more likely to ignore the less able students while focusing on the ones with a higher probability of success and to blame external factors such as insufficient materials, lack of parental support, and lack of control over student assignments (Ashton & Webb, 1986; Gibson & Dembo, 1984) for their lack of success. Efforts to improve teacher self-efficacy include strategies for helping teachers examine their own teaching practices and to shift their focus away from external factors onto their own attitudes and practices (Weinstein, Madison, & Kuklinski, 1995).

Efficacy beliefs are also related to success in other areas of leadership such as management and nursing. Wood and Bandura (1989) found that business school students with higher perceived self-efficacy performed better in a complex simulation activity requiring managerial decision-making and goal-seeking behavior. Success also required social mediation by means of the efforts of a group of employees in the simulated organization. And, in another example, a measure of self-efficacy was obtained from 89 junior-level managers in a large clearing bank in the United Kingdom and measures of their performance were obtained from two supervisors for each manager (Robertson & Sadri, 1993). The results showed that managerial self-efficacy was related to performance ratings.

In a different professional area, Spence Laschinger and Shamian (1994) found that managerial self-efficacy affected staff nurses' and nurse managers' perceptions of job-related self-efficacy. Based on a path analysis of data pertaining to self-efficacy, professional practice behaviors, structural empowerment, and nursing leadership, Manojlovich (2005) found that self-efficacy mediated the relationship between structural empowerment and professional practice. These results, like the preceding one, confirm the utility of self-efficacy in affecting one's own behavior and the behavior of others.

Learned Helplessness

All of the preceding concepts related to expectancies and outcomes assume that people, or infrahuman subjects, do in fact perceive there to be a relationship between what they do and what happens as a consequence. But, what if a person perceived there to be no relationship? That is, what if a child saw no relationship between his efforts to learn to read, play board games requiring strategy application, or play piano and the outcomes of those efforts? Success or failure would be regarded by this child as a random occurrence. This extreme condition is known as *learned helplessness*.

This type of helplessness is called "learned" (Seligman, 1975) because it results from a two-stage process. In the first stage helplessness is real, unavoidable, and inescapable. Nothing the subject in this setting does or tries to do will alleviate the experience of failure. For example, if a young child in kindergarten or primary school is expected to learn computational mathematics but, due to an undiagnosed and undetected developmental lag, is unable to read, the child will experience an unrelenting experience of failure. After a period of time the child will conclude that for him there is absolutely no relationship between his efforts and the experience of success or failure. Consequently, the child will resort to random responses, getting some answers correct due to chance or rote memorization but missing others due to no discernable pattern. Attempts on the part of a teacher or parent to encourage the child by telling him to try harder simply reinforce his feeling of helplessness because he believes that he is trying as hard as he can and he continues to fail. Now, let's assume that after the summer break, the child has matured a bit and could now learn to do the math if he put all his effort into it. In other words, the child now has the ability to succeed. But, due to the deep helplessness conditioning, the child will interpret each mistake as evidence of his inability and will continue to fail.

This is a very difficult condition to overcome, but it can be done with a carefully controlled environment and cognitive restructuring. From an environmental perspective, it is necessary to build a series of tasks that are carefully graduated from the person's entry level of competence to a more advance level. Then, with encouragement to begin, the person is reinforced for each success and also told that his success was due to his own efforts and ability. For this to work, the person does have to experience a small degree of challenge and success in order for the feedback to be believable. This training was called reattribution therapy by Dweck (1975) because the person is learning to perceive rational connections between his behavior and its consequences and to attribute success to ability and effort. Dweck worked primarily with the topic of mathematics but similar results can be obtained with the development of reading ability (Keller, 1983a).

Learned Optimism

On a more positive side is the phenomenon of *learned optimism*. Seligman (1991), during more than 20 years of clinical research on learned helplessness and depression began to note some characteristic differences between people who are more susceptible to depression compared to those who are not. One of the fundamental differences was pessimism versus optimism. Numerous studies demonstrated that pessimists tend to have more illnesses, not be as persistent, give up more easily in the face of challenges, and have more depression. Optimists, on the other hand, are more successful, and are liked more by others, frequently exceed expectations on aptitude tests, are healthier, and are happier. He has developed measures of optimism and depression, which reveal that far more people are pessimistic than even realize that they are. Furthermore, he has demonstrated that people can learn to be more optimistic, not by simple, popular self-help inspirational reading and books, but by a well-researched and validated process of cognitive restructuring. It involves a set of attributional exercises and other activities designed to help you develop new, more productive patterns of thinking and behaving. To integrate some of these tactics into a learning environment is beneficial for children, especially when the teacher is modeling the behavior!

Ability Beliefs

People's beliefs about their abilities will influence their expectancies for success, attributions, and performance. One set of beliefs, called an *entity concept of ability*, is that it is relatively fixed and unchangeable. From this perspective, people believe that you either have an aptitude for a given activity or you do not, or, that you have a specific level of ability and that you can't change it to any meaningful degree. Thus, they believe that some people have high ability to do math, learn to dance, write essays, or be a leader and other people have low ability. In contrast is the *incremental concept of ability* which is the belief that one's ability in any of these areas can be improved with effort, even if it is a slow process. Entity beliefs can keep people "locked into" much lower levels of learning and performance than they are actually capable of doing. For example, in mathematics many children, and adults for that matter, believe that they have low ability for math and they try to avoid situations requiring computation or other forms of math, and they give up quickly when they do not understand something. This is not to be confused with learned helplessness, because in this situation people do see a relationship between their behavior and its consequences. The problem is that they perceive it to be a poor relationship; that is, they attribute failure to low ability.

People high in self-efficacy tend to have an incremental belief in ability (Ashton & Webb, 1986; Woolfolk & Hoy, 1990). They are more likely to assume that they can learn strategies and skills that will help them succeed in their own goal pursuits and in helping other people succeed. However, when people have an entity belief that is unrealistic, it can be challenging to help them shift to an incremental perspective. A rather dramatic change in attitude and achievement was obtained by Dweck (2006) in working with middle school children in an inner city school. In her study, children were taught elementary neurology regarding how the brain works. They were shown videos illustrating how the brain grows by developing new neural pathways when it is engaged in learning new things. The children were then told to visualize their brains growing as they learned the math skills that were presented to them. The results were positive with regard to achievement and beliefs that ability can improve with effort and success. The anecdotal comments of some children illustrated their excitement of feeling that their brains were growing as they mastered new skills.

Transition

The following categories of strategies encompass the concepts from the preceding review and are used when conducting the audience motivation analysis. When designing strategies for confidence there is the problem of building confidence in people who lack it and not kill it in those who already have it, as is also true with the other three major categories of ARCS. There is also the problem of creating a "need to know" in people who are overconfident. If people already believe they know something, they will not notice when they are being presented with new material. A complete set of strategies must deal with all these issues!

Strategies for Building Confidence

A conclusion that can be drawn from the research literature is that one of, if not the primary, characteristics of confidence is the perception of control. This refers to the learners' perceptions about their own abilities in relation to the perceived and actual predictability of the outcomes of their actions. A tremendous amount of research with both humans and animals has demonstrated how one's perceptions of control influence both mental health and achievement. When people believe that they have little or no control over what happens to them, they experience anxiety, depression, and other stress-related emotions. In contrast, when they believe that they can predictably influence their environment by exercising their efforts and abilities in pursuit of their goals, then they are both healthier and more motivated to be successful. Following (Table 6.3) are the major subordinate concepts and tactics that help define confidence and how to influence it.

Table 6.3. Subcategories, Process Questions, and Main Supporting Strategies for Confidence.

Concepts and Process Questions	Main Supporting Tactics
C1. Learning Requirements How can I assist in building a positive expectation for success?	Establish trust and positive expectations by explaining the requirements for success and the evaluative criteria.
C2. Success Opportunities How will the learning experience support or enhance the learners' beliefs in their competence?	Increase belief in competence by providing many, varied, and challenging experiences that increase learning success.
C3. Personal Control How will the learners clearly know their success is based upon their efforts and abilities?	Use techniques that offer personal control (whenever possible), and provide feedback that attributes success to personal effort.

C.1. Success Expectations

> On the first day of a three-day course on servicing XYZ-111 copiers, Manuel gave the learners handouts which described the course project and how it would be evaluated.

One of the simplest ways to help students reduce anxiety and develop realistic expectations for success is to help them understand what will be expected and how they will be evaluated. What if you reported for work on a new job, and your boss just told you to go to work without explaining what was expected of you? You would be anxious, perhaps angry, and less than optimally productive. Now, consider how often this happens in a classroom: Students begin a new class or a new topic and are just told to start studying without being given a clear understanding of how to focus their efforts or what they will have to perform. Sometimes teachers will read the lesson objectives, but all too often, the objectives are written in language that the students cannot understand. That is, the objectives tend to incorporate technical language from the material that the students have not yet learned. By explaining requirements in everyday terms the students can understand, and stressing what the students will be doing, not just the outcomes, you can improve their confidence because it enables them to focus their efforts toward success. Also, as indicated in the following two tactics, students' confidence is likely to be even higher if they are allowed to develop at least some of their own goals and objectives.

1. Provide clear statements, in terms of observable behaviors, of what is expected of the learners as evidence of successful learning.
2. Whenever possible, provide a means for learners to write their own learning goals or objectives.

C.2. Success Opportunities

> During a one-day seminar on new accounting proce-
> dures, Lucille had learners practice off-line on small
> parts of a more complex procedure and then do the
> entire procedure on the computer.

Do you truly give your learners opportunities to succeed, to build positive expectations for success? What are the influences on their expectations? The answer is, "everything." Well, maybe not everything, but a great many things. For example, the readability and challenge level of the instructional materials, the body language and words of the teacher, and the frequency with which the students get to actually practice under nonthreatening conditions are just a few of these influences. It is important for students to be challenged from time to time, but the challenge should come from the learning activities themselves, not from obstacles in the characteristics of the materials or the teacher's behaviors.

Anxiety is to students' emotional states in the classroom as the common cold is to health and sickness in wintertime. Anxiety generally results from unknown threats in contrast to fear, which is associated with identified threats. Fear is preferable to anxiety because you know what your target is, you know what you have to do to either avoid or conquer the situation. But, when students have little understanding of what they will be required to produce and do not know how they will be evaluated, they become anxious. They can compensate for this by over-studying or by retreating into indifference or rebellion. By over-studying they hope to be prepared for any possible outcomes. Students who do not have the time, motivation, or ability to overlearn may try to "beat the system" by withdrawing, cheating, or becoming hostile. Instead of studying thoroughly, they assume that success has become a game of chance and they will try to guess what the teacher will put on the tests or what criteria will be used to evaluate their assignments. You can reduce anxiety by making the performance requirements clearer and by having well-designed lessons as described in the tactics listed below.

Challenge Level

1. Organize the content in a clear, easy to follow, sequence.
2. Sequence the tasks from simple to difficult within each segment of the materials.

3. Make the overall challenge level (reading level, examples, and exercises) appropriate for this audience.
4. Ensure that the materials are free of "trick" or excessively difficult questions or exercises.
5. Make the exercises consistent with the objectives, content, and examples.
6. Include methods for self-evaluation, such as answers to exercises.
7. Provide confirmational feedback for acceptable responses and corrective feedback for responses that do not meet criteria.

Restructure for Success

Following (Table 6.4) is an example of how to increase confidence by reducing the perceived challenge level. In this case, the learners perceived the task to be more challenging than it actually was. The *motivational* tactic in this case was to reduce the perceived challenge level by revising the *instructional* strategy. This increased the trainees' expectancies for success and their performance improved.

Table 6.4. A Strategy for Helping Reduce Learner Stress.

CASE: A PROBLEM OF STRESS INDUCED ERRORS
The trainees for a one-day course on a new computerized accounting system consisted of bookkeepers and secretaries responsible for entering travel receipts and other financial items. The instruction was online so that it would have high relevance to the actual performance conditions.
Lucille, the instructor, noticed that many trainees were making mistakes because of their nervousness about learning the new procedures and about working on the computer. Lucille knew that the mistakes were not due to lack of ability because the new procedures were actually simpler than the old ones.
She revised her approach by having the trainees learn and practice small parts of a more complex procedure off-line using pencils and worksheets. Then she had them do the procedure on the computer. Their confidence in their ability to do the accounting process and in using the computer increased more rapidly, and stress-related errors decreased immediately.

C.3. Personal Responsibility

Jason designed a computer-based instruction course that gave learners options of taking unit self-checks which allow learners to measure their own progress before module tests.

When you are successful, your confidence becomes stronger, right? Most people answer "yes" to this question. But, a much better answer is, "not always." It depends on your attributions for success. If the task was challenging and you believe that you were successful because of your abilities and efforts, then your confidence will improve. But if the task was easy, or if you believe your success was because of luck, helpful influences from someone else, or personal favoritism, then your confidence is not likely to improve.

When people have feelings of control over their performance and believe they have the ability to succeed their expectancy for success, which is a key part of confidence, is strong. There are numerous ways you can help students develop these perceptions. One is to organize your lessons in such a way that students do, in fact, have some meaningful areas of personal control. Another is to give them, in technical terms, positive attributional feedback; that is, let them know by your words and actions that you have confidence in their ability to succeed providing they work hard. Never tell them that they succeeded because you did them a favor, or because you "gave" them a grade. Instead tell them they got the grade that they earned. Consider all of the following techniques in your lesson planning and teaching, but use only the ones that are most relevant:

1. Give learners choices in sequencing; that is, explain how they can sequence their study of different parts of the material.
2. Allow learners to go at their own paces.
3. Give learners choices among ways of demonstrating their competency (that is, provide alternative methods of exercising and testing).
4. Give learners opportunities to create their own exercises of methods of demonstrating competency.
5. Give learners choices over work environment; for example, working in a room with other people or away from other people.
6. Give learners opportunities to record comments on how the materials could be improved or made more interesting.

Clearly, confidence is an important dimension of motivation. When the conditions of relevance are not met, learners will be indifferent. They might be stressed if the requirement to successfully complete a course is critical to their plans for the future, and this can cause them to perform less well than they are able. But, often, this level of stress carries over into confidence. The consequences of negative influences on confidence can be devastating to a person's self-esteem and productivity. This is one more example of why we say that all of the components of motivation are important. One component might be more important to a given individual or group at a given point in time, but all are critical in building and sustaining a healthy level of motivation to learn. This leads us to the final component, which focuses on how to reward and sustain one's motivation to learn in a way that leads to feelings of satisfaction.

A Confidence Booster

This example (Figure 6.3) is a group message that an instructor sent individually to each student as a potential confidence booster. The message reaches the students outside of class at a time when the instructor knows they might be having problems.

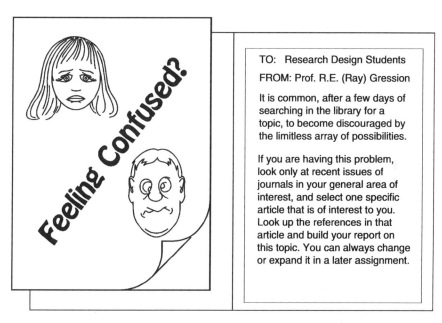

TO: Research Design Students

FROM: Prof. R.E. (Ray) Gression

It is common, after a few days of searching in the library for a topic, to become discouraged by the limitless array of possibilities.

If you are having this problem, look only at recent issues of journals in your general area of interest, and select one specific article that is of interest to you. Look up the references in that article and build your report on this topic. You can always change or expand it in a later assignment.

Figure 6.3. Example of a Group Motivational Message to Boost Confidence.

Summary

Even though each of the concepts included in this section has distinctive characteristics, bodies of related research, and specific areas of behavior for which it provides the best explanation, it is also true that these concepts have shared attributes. The things they have in common center around the concept of perceived control and its influence on a person's confidence. Although there are differences among people as to how much anxiety and lack of perceived control that they can tolerate, it is the loss of perceived control that appears to be at the base of many psychological problems such as fear, depression, and helplessness. Dramatic events such as loss of income or other causes of financial instability, failure on a major exam, being deceived by someone you thought you could trust are all causes of a loss of perceived control, but so are more mundane things such as having excessive disarray in your home or office, not being able to find bills that are due to be paid, and being embarrassingly far behind in your communications with other people. And, in a learning environment, on the positive side, helping students understand what is expected of them and how to maximize their likelihood of success are ways to improve perceptions of control.

7

Chapter 7 – Managing Outcomes for Satisfaction

Forethought

One of my favorite quotations from the professional literature of instructional design is by Don Tosti who asked at the beginning of one of his articles (Tosti, 1978), "If feedback is desirable, why do people go to such lengths to avoid giving or receiving it" (p. 19)?

Assuming that he is correct, why do you think this is? Is it because, as illustrated in Figure 7.1, we usually associate feedback with criticism? What do you think?

Feedback can be a powerful tool for building positive motivation and also for killing people's motivation. The principles covered in this chapter help explain uses of feedback together with other factors that influence intrinsic and extrinsic motivation.

Figure 7.1. Effects of Feedback on Motivation.

Introduction

What makes us either persist or lose interest in a goal and what makes us feel good about our accomplishments? For many years psychological research focused primarily on the effects of external consequences on behavior (rewards, punishments, and indifference) while educators tried valiantly to maintain a belief in the importance of intrinsic satisfactions of learning. Now, there is ample evidence to support both positions as being important to understanding why people are or are not satisfied with the consequences of their behaviors.

J.M. Keller, *Motivational Design for Learning and Performance*,
DOI 10.1007/978-1-4419-1250-3_7, © Springer Science+Business Media, LLC 2010

Intrinsic motivation, which can also be called intrinsic satisfaction, can result from feelings of mastery and from the pleasure of having succeeded at a task which was meaningful and challenging. If you design instructional content and learner activities that are at an optimal level of challenge and for your audience and are perceived by them to be worthwhile, then you have set the stage for intrinsic satisfaction. This appears to be rooted in several innate characteristics of people. As indicated by the research that supports the first three components of the ARCS model, people like a certain amount of novelty, they like to feel competent, they like to build knowledge and skills in areas of personal interest and importance, and they like to experience a degree of control, or autonomy. When all of these conditions are met in a learning environment, then intrinsic satisfaction will result or be sustained from successful achievement. When these conditions are not met, students lose interest. For example, children love to learn new tasks, such as how to tie their shoes. They will play with them repeatedly until they master the task. Once mastered, they are not interested in tying their shoes for fun anymore, only when they need to. In other words, the intrinsic pleasure is gone after they achieve mastery. Researchers (McMullin & Steffen, 1982) have confirmed what parents know from experience, which is that children are more interested in tasks, such as puzzles, when the difficulty level increases slightly as their competence increases.

Why, then, do these conditions that support intrinsic motivation not occur more often? It would require an ideal environment to constantly achieve this standard. There are many reasons why children and adults are in the courses they take, and the choices of content in those courses are based on decisions ranging from tradition through convenience to actual needs. The most common reason why people are in a given course is because it is required. This is true for children in school, for adults who are trying to earn degrees or certification, and for adults who are responding to the requirements of their workplace. In many of these settings, it is the extrinsic rewards that "motivate" people to attend. These rewards can be positive as in obtaining degrees, certificates, and pay raises, or negative as in avoiding punishment or other undesirable outcomes. Furthermore, in school settings, teachers are required to "grade" students to indicate who has achieved certain levels of competency and who is superior to whom. Consequently, it is not the exclusive or even primary role of the teacher, from an institutional perspective, to promote intrinsic satisfaction. Also, people want things in life; they want more than just "feeling good." To do this, they have to be competitive and acquire the skills and credentials to support their goals. For all of these reasons, teachers are challenged to manage the use of extrinsic reinforcements together with creating conditions for intrinsic satisfaction.

Another complication with trying to design environments that result in positive feelings of satisfaction results from the interactions between extrinsic reinforcements and states of intrinsic motivation, especially when you compare your situation to other people's. You will be happy if the outcomes of your behavior meet or exceed your expectations but disappointed if your expectations are not met or if you perceive them to be unfair compared to what other people receive. These issues are the basis for this chapter's focus on conditioning theory, interactions between extrinsic reinforcement, and cognitive evaluation as they relate to satisfaction and continuing motivation.

Psychological Basis for Satisfaction

Key Question for Satisfaction

What can I do to help the students feel good about their experience and desire to continue learning?

Reinforcement and Conditioning

That the effects of *extrinsic reinforcements* can have a powerful influence on behavior is amply demonstrated by the *operant conditioning* literature. The use of positive reinforcements increases the frequency of the responses that lead to the reinforcement. This is generally true, but as the literature shows, there are many complicating elements. One of the first concerns the issue of what is a reward? An outcome that is rewarding for one person might not be so rewarding for someone else. After identifying outcomes that will have a rewarding effect, there is the issue of how often to give them; that is, what schedule of reinforcement to use. And there are the even more complicated issues of when to ignore undesirable behaviors so that they will extinguish, or to use punishment to decrease the frequency of a behavior. There is a vast literature on this subject (Beck, 1990), but fortunately there are a few basic principles that an instructional designer and teacher can use to help ensure the effective use of positive consequences. These have to do with recognizing success when it occurs, timely use of feedback and praise (Brophy, 1983), and using tangible rewards consistently, even if they are primarily symbolic rewards in the form of tokens and privileges (Pintrich & Schunk, 2002).

Behavioral psychology played a strong role in the development of instructional psychology and applications to the design of learning materials. Examples of these such as programmed instruction and a course design model called the Personalized System of Instruction are described in Chapter 2. Those early applications have evolved into more complex theories and models of instruction (Gagné, Wager, Golas, & Keller, 2005; Reigeluth, 1983, 1999), but the basic principles of behavioral conditioning contained within those models are still valid and must be managed effectively in an effective and appealing learning environment. Regardless of one's overall commitment to a given theory of instruction or learning, people generally tend to sustain or increase behaviors that have positive results relative to their values and goals and avoid those that have detrimental outcomes.

Classical Conditioning

Anne is in her car at an intersection waiting to cross a major thoroughfare. When the traffic light turns green she accelerates only to notice that an 18-wheel truck coming at a high speed from her right is not going to stop. She slams on her brakes and narrowly avoids being crushed. Afterward her autonomic nervous system reacts like an explosion of lights, raucous sounds, and ricocheting steel balls in a Japanese pachinko parlor. She has to pull to the side of the road to wait for her heart to stop pounding and her adrenaline to subside. Eventually, she continues to work thankful to be alive.

The next day she has to stop at the same intersection. When the light turns green she is far more cautious and proceeds safely on her way. Even so, she finds that her heart is pounding, her blood is pulsating, and she is short of breath.

What has happened? Why is she having these reactions even though she was in no danger? She is experiencing a type of conditioning called Pavlovian or Classical conditioning. It results when a normally irrelevant stimulus event occurs in association with a reflexive, or unconditioned, stimulus and response. In Anne's case, the intersection which previously had no particular significance to her is now associated with her naturally occurring bodily response to an unexpected near-death experience. For a few days, that intersection will trigger the same neurological responses in her body, but with less intensity and the effect will extinguish as time goes by unless it happens again.

This behavioral phenomenon was first reported by Ivan Pavlov (1906) who was a Nobel Prize winning Russian physiologist. While studying the digestive processes of dogs, he would put meat powder on their tongues to induce the involuntary response of salivation. After a period of time, as a dog would become more familiar with the experimental conditions, he observed that the dog would begin to salivate before the meat powder was placed on its tongue. With continued observation, Pavlov noticed that there were cues such as the clinking sound of the metal bowl used to carry the meat powder that signaled the onset of salivation. Thus, it appeared that the dog had learned to associate the clinking sound with the arrival of meat powder and this produced salivation before the dog could detect the smell or taste of it. He called these learned salivation responses "salivary secretions" and this process became a major focus of his research (Pavlov, 1927). It refers to the conditioning of a reflex, which by definition is not normally under voluntary control, so that it is stimulated by a previously neutral stimulus.

Formally, this process of conditioning reflexes begins by identifying an *unconditioned stimulus* (UCS) and *unconditioned response* (UCR) which means that the UCS evokes the UCR without any previous conditioning.

Examples of this other than dogs salivating in the presence of food include the familiar flexing of the lower leg in response to a tap on the patellar tendon, a feeling of relaxation after smoking a cigarette due to decreased flow of oxygen to the brain, a feeling of pleasantness after viewing an aesthetically pleasing stimulus, and heart palpitations and shortness of breath following an unexpected and dramatic threat.

The next step is for a neutral stimulus to occur regularly in the presence of the UCS → UCR pairing. Based on the frequency and intensity of this association, the neutral stimulus will begin to evoke the response and is then known as a *conditioned stimulus* (CS). The UCR now becomes a *conditioned response* (CR) which means that it is still a reflexive response, but it can now be stimulated by a CS.

Classical conditioning can occur in many ways in everyday life. A child who is ridiculed by a teacher or other children in a math class may react with shame and embarrassment. If this happened fairly often or was traumatic enough, then the math classroom itself could become the conditioned stimulus and the child would begin to have the negative feelings while approaching and entering the room. Similarly, a reflexive reaction to a choking sensation is for the throat muscles to contract. If choking is not a common problem for a person, but it happens one time when trying to swallow a tablet, the person can develop difficulties in taking medicine. The appearance of the pills (CS) can result in a tightening of the throat muscles (CR) which then increases the difficulty of swallowing the pills. In reality the relaxed human throat can easily swallow a palm-full of pills but the conditioned response interferes.

The conditioned response can become stronger as a result of *stimulus generalization* which occurs when the conditioned response to a specific stimulus also occurs in response to similar stimuli, which is what happens in the development of a phobia. For example, the student who evidenced an anxiety reaction when approaching the math classroom could develop a similar reaction when approaching a science classroom, especially if math were included in the science instruction or if something causes him to experience embarrassment in that room. This generalization could continue to spread until the student developed a generalized state of anxiety in reaction to attending school.

Conditioned responses can be weakened and *extinguished* by following a process of disassociating the CS with the CR. For example, the student could spend time in empty classrooms. Gradually, the conditioned response would disappear, just as it did with Anne after repeated crossings through the intersection without incident. And, assuming that a counselor was involved with the process, the student could be assured that he would not be ridiculed upon reentering the normal classroom.

Classical conditioning can be a factor in students' motivation to learn. If we consider the previous example, students can develop reactions of fear and withdrawal because of an unpleasant experience in a particular learning situation. On the other hand, learning environments can be arranged to foster feelings of relaxation and happiness. When elementary school teachers decorate their rooms with colorful and happy images, part of the intent is to develop these pleasant associations. While this can be helpful, it is most important for teachers to be sensitive to the influence of their words and actions on students. Teachers who mistake patronizing or sarcastic comments for cleverness can cause a strongly unpleasant emotional reaction in their students. Mindfulness of their power and influence is critical in avoiding these kinds of situation.

Operant Conditioning

Anne has just purchased a cup of coffee from a vending machine. When she reaches into the coin return pocket to get her change she discovers that it contains an extra fifty cents which was probably left by a previous customer. She is delighted by this small but unexpected "find." On her way out of the self-service canteen she checks the coin pockets in the other machines but they are all empty. The next day she doesn't get extra coins in her change but she does find twenty-five cents in one of the other coin pockets. Every day for a week she checks all of the coin pockets without success. Then, she gradually stops checking them.

Once again Anne's behavior has been influenced by an unexpected event in her environment. Is the same type of thing happening here that happened at the intersection? In both cases her behavior was conditioned by a stimulus event following her behavior, but the second example is quite different from the first one. In the first case, a response that normally occurs only automatically as a reflex became associated with an environmental stimulus that continued to trigger the response until it extinguished. In the second case, a naturally occurring behavior (reaching into the coin pocket for change) became associated with a rewarding consequence (getting some extra money).

This type of learned association is called operant conditioning and it consists of managing the consequences of a behavior to either increase or decrease the frequency of that behavior. The relationship between a behavior and its consequence is known as a contingency and contingency management refers to the implementation of specific types of relationships. There are four types of stimuli that can be used as consequences of a behavior:

+S$^+$ Administer something pleasant. This is *positive reinforcement*. It consists of receiving a reward such as food, tokens, awards, or praise after performing in behavior that meets the requirements of the person who is managing the reinforcement system.

−S Take away something unpleasant. This is known as *negative reinforcement* and it occurs when a person is allowed to move from an aversive, or unpleasant, conditioned to a more positive one. And for example, a teenager who has had to endure several hours of silence in his room because he was not doing his homework is allowed to turn the stereo back on after completing his assignments. It is important to note that negative reinforcement is reinforcement, not punishment, because it leads to an increase in the frequency of the desired behavior.

$+S^-$ Administer something aversive. This is one type of punishment and it consists of inflicting something unpleasant on the person whose behavior is being managed. Examples of this type of positive punishment are spankings or having to pay a fine for speeding ticket.

$-S^+$ Take away something pleasant. This type of *negative punishment* is used frequently. It consists of such things as requiring a child to study in his or her room after misbehaving ("time out"), taking away a child's cell phone or iPod if they misuse it, or a spouse who withholds affection after being ignored for too long. This type of punishment often precedes negative reinforcement which consists of reinforcing correct behavior by ending timeout, returning the equipment, or once again being affectionate.

Another component of contingency management pertains to the stimuli that precede the occurrence of a behavior. For example, sometimes children behave properly in a school classroom and sometimes they don't. Typically, they behave properly if the regular teacher is in the classroom assuming that the teacher has good classroom management skills, but the children might misbehave if the teacher leaves the room for an extended period or if they have a substitute teacher. In this example, the presence of the teacher is the discriminative stimulus (S^D); that is, the characteristic of the environment that signals that a given contingency is in effect. In other words, if the teacher is in the classroom, students know that they will be rewarded for good behavior and punished for inappropriate behavior. Actually, the teacher would like for the children to behave properly as soon as they enter the classroom regardless of whether she is there or not. In other words, the teacher would like for the classroom to be the discriminative stimulus that signals to the children that good behavior is called for. But, the children learned that if the teacher is not present there is no consequence for misbehavior. This does not mean that the children will misbehave, but it means that other elements in the children's personalities and values will exert the primary influence on their behavior. Thus, the classroom itself becomes a *non-discriminative* (S^Δ) or neutral stimulus.

When a parent, teacher, or other behavioral specialist is trying to establish a new behavior, it is customary to provide continuous reinforcement; that is, to reinforce every occurrence of the desired behavior or at least a close approximation of it. Sometimes it is necessary to shape the behavior from an initial rough approximation to the exact behavior that is desired. For example, if a supervisor is attempting to use positive reinforcement to improve a newly hired, inexperienced employee's behavior who does not always return from breaks on time or get back to work right away, the supervisor will first make a positive comment each time the employee is back at his desk on time. If this is successful, the employee will have a more regular pattern of promptness but might continue to waste time with frivolous activities before actually getting back on task. In this case, the supervisor will stop reinforcing the employee for promptness and watch for a time when the employee begins working immediately after returning from the break. The supervisor might say, "Jack, it's great to see that you jumped right back into that project immediately after your break!" Thus, shaping refers to rewarding successive approximations of a performance that become closer and closer to the ultimate target behavior. This process is used with great success in training animals.

In actuality, *continuous reinforcement* is seldom used for very long. If every occurrence of the behavior is reinforced, the behavior will normally extinguish rather quickly if the reinforcements cease. More sustained patterns of behavior can be achieved by using schedules of reinforcement which have two dimensions. One dimension consists of interval versus ratio frequency of reinforcement and the other consists of fixed versus variable intervals. Interval schedules are based on time; that is, a reward is given for the first response after a specified amount of time. In a ratio schedule the reward is given after a specified number of responses. An interval schedule can be fixed or variable; that is, the interval can be specified as five minutes, two hours, or any appropriate period of time. Or it can be a variable interval which means that the reward is offered at unpredictable moments during a specified amount of time before or after the interval limit. If the interval is 10 minutes, the reward can be offered after, for example, two minutes or 14 minutes. Similarly, in a variable ratio schedule in which reinforcement is given on the average after every 20 responses, the reward may occur after 5 responses or 19 responses. Behaviors are maintained for longer periods of time with variable schedules because it is more difficult to determine if one is in a long interval or large ratio or if extinction has actually set in.

Token Reinforcement Systems

A token economy is a system that incorporates the systematic use of reinforcements to manage behavior, encourage learning performance, or increase learner motivation. In these systems target behaviors are specified and tokens are awarded for those behaviors. When enough tokens are accumulated by one of the participants they can be exchanged for a tangible reward such as a small toy, a school supplies item, or a special privilege. These systems can be used in school classrooms, custodial centers for adults with developmental problems, or other supervised environments. Parents sometimes use these systems to establish regular patterns of behavior such as habits of personal hygiene. The expectation is that by providing extrinsic rewards until the behavior becomes well established the behavior will eventually become intrinsically satisfying. The extrinsic rewards are gradually withdrawn during this process. Thus, there are three primary components to a token reinforcement system (Jenson, Sloane, & Young, 1988, p. 170): (1) the tokens to be dispensed, (2) the rules for earning the tokens, and (3) the backup reinforcers to be earned.

Tokens can be anything that does not already have value, such as coins, associated with them. Commonly used tokens are shiny stars, plastic chips, or marks on a progress chart. The rules for earning them must be clearly specified to the students as when students receive a token for every 10 minutes they work quietly on an assigned task. Tokens can also be awarded based on the amount and quality of work completed and displaying appropriate behavior in the classroom. For these different contingencies, there are two basic methods of using tokens. The first is to reward students with tokens for behaviors that you want to increase, such as raising their hands before talking. The second type of goal is to decrease undesirable behaviors. This can be done by giving the students an amount of tokens and then charging them a penalty for doing the target behavior, such as touching their neighbor or texting during class. Also, tokens can be awarded for every occurrence of the target behavior or on a schedule as in any other application of behavioral management contingencies. Then, at specified intervals tokens can be exchanged for the backup reinforcers such as small toys, edible items, or special privileges such as getting to spend a certain amount of time playing an Internet game. It is usually best for there to be a range in value in the assortment of reinforcers. Having some high-value gifts along with lower valued ones provides the learners with an incentive to earn more tokens or to save their tokens until they acquire a sufficient amount to get their desired prize.

Token reinforcement systems grew rapidly in popularity in the 1960s and in 1972 Kazdin and Bootzin published an evaluative review (Kazdin & Bootzin, 1972) of the work done up until that point in time. They observed that this methodology had been employed with diverse settings and audiences including psychiatric inpatients, the mentally retarded with regard to ward, self-care, and classroom behaviors, children in classroom settings, delinquents, and autistic children. They found some applications to be effective and others less so, but they identified several problems that can become obstacles to success. One is staff training. They found that it was not uncommon for staff members to fail to implement the token system appropriately. Staff would become indifferent, not fully understand the contingency structure, and not provide tokens consistently. They also found instances of client resistance which might be expressed in the form of disruptive behavior, breaking rules, complaints, and anger. In school settings, children might react negatively by simply not cooperating or actively trying to disrupt the system. Another problem that they identified was client nonresponsiveness to the contingencies. This could happen for several reasons including failure to perceive the contingencies or inability to remember them with the more severely disturbed or retarded ones or because they did not find the system to be compelling enough to excite their interest. This would be more of a problem with finding appropriate backup reinforcers and an effective schedule than with capability problems. Still another area of problems has to do with being present to observe and reward the target behaviors when they occur or simply not observing them. This was especially true in residential centers, but it is a challenge even for a teacher in a classroom due to the many challenges of teaching, monitoring behavior, and meeting individual needs. In a follow-up review, Kazdin (1982) found that the same challenges to implementation still existed, especially in regard to staff preparation. Successful programs required great attention to staff training and supervision to ensure that the programs were implemented as designed. He also found that there were few successful programs outside the realm of research and demonstration projects. Institutional programs which were his major focus simply required too many resources with regard to personnel, supervision, and availability of backup reinforcers. Smaller programs, such as those that a teacher might implement in a classroom, were more frequent, but even those tended to have limited life spans due to the extra demands placed on teachers to supervise and maintain the project after the novelty effect wore off.

Token economies are used most often for managing behavior to improve personal habits and discipline, but they can also help to improve learning. O'Leary and Drabman's (1971) thorough review of the literature describes many successful applications of this process even though there were failures. The studies they reviewed were predominately positive in terms of decreases in disruptive behavior, increases in study behavior, increases in academic achievement, and beneficial unexpected outcomes such as better attendance and bartering for tokens among the students. In a more recent review of literature and experimental study, Truchlicka, McLaughlin, and Swain (1998) developed a token system to improve the spelling and other areas of academic performance of middle school special education students with behavior disorders. The students could also earn points for completing homework, being on-task behavior, and behaving properly in the hallways. They used a combination of reinforcements for these behaviors and response costs (penalties) for unacceptable behavior such as "wasting time, playing with objects, incomplete assignments, not following directions, talk-outs, swearing, cheating, fighting, coming to class late, and failing to bring academic materials to class" (p. 3). They implemented the system with three of these special students and obtained positive results with each of them. Their review of literature focused on more recent studies, relative to the earlier (Kazdin, 1982; Kazdin & Bootzin, 1972; O'Leary & Drabman, 1971) reviews, which confirmed many of the positive applications of token systems in academic settings. Finally, similar positive results were obtained by Filcheck et al. (Filcheck, McNeil, Greco, & Bernard, 2004) in the use of a token system to manage disruptive behavior in a preschool classroom. They also considered reviewed methodological issues and generalizability and concluded with several observations regarding critical success factors in these systems. Like Kazdin and Bootzin (1972), they pointed out the importance of careful design and rigorous implementation on the part of the teacher and other members of the project.

Even though there are many positive examples of token systems, there are also those that do not succeed. O'Leary and Drabman (1971) indicate that there are three primary reasons for this. The first concerns problems with the program itself, which Kazdin and Bootzin also discuss in detail. The second is problems associated with the teacher, which is similar to problems with implementation due to problems with the staff as described above. For example, it can be extremely challenging to implement a token system effectively in regular classrooms which typically have quite a few students. The students monitor the teacher and can become quite competitive. They are likely to make social comparisons in which they challenge the teacher to provide them with the same reward that was given to another student. For example, Billy might complain to the teacher that Sally raised her hand four times to answer questions and got three tokens but he raised his hand four times and only got one token. Thus it can be extremely time-consuming for the teacher to manage the token reinforcement system effectively to avoid complaints and at the same time not have it detract from the learning environment. The third area consists of problems with the specific population used in the token system. Some groups will not respond positively to it due to negative peer pressure and other issues.

Relationship Between Extrinsic Reinforcement and Intrinsic Motivation

Generally speaking, as discussed in Chapter 5, intrinsic motivation seems to be comprised of a personal interest in a given task or subject (Schank, 1979) combined with perceptions of increases in competence (White, 1959) and personal control over one's choices and courses of action (deCharms, 1968). The achievement of personal goals under these conditions of personal control, which White calls *effectance motivation* in relation to one's desire to satisfy the need for competence, lead to a positive emotional outcome which he calls *feelings of efficacy* (p. 322). In contrast, the use of reinforcement contingencies to manage another person's behaviors tends to take personal control away from that person and put it in the hands of the performance manager and it has long been noted that extrinsic controls and incentives can have a detrimental, undermining effect on intrinsic motivation and learning (deCharms, 1968; Harlow, 1953; Hunt & Sullivan, 1974; White, 1959). Among the best known early studies of this issue were those conducted within the framework of *cognitive dissonance theory*. Festinger and Carlsmith (1959) demonstrated that there was greater behavior change among subjects who were paid small amounts of money to lie about how interesting a dull experiment was than among subjects who were paid a large amount of money. The low-paid subjects actually begin to enjoy the experiment more than they had prior to being paid. A large number of studies, summarized by Condry (1977, p. 460) confirmed in various ways that the larger the extrinsic influences and rewards the less change and internalization there is. They explained the results in terms of cognitive dissonance theory which presumes that people try to obtain internal consistency between their thoughts and actions and that they will change their behaviors or interpretations of them when there is dissonance. Thus, when people received a large amount of money for lying they could accept the fact that they were doing it for the money. But with a small reward it perhaps continued to bother their conscience to lie and so they changed their opinion about the object of the lie. From the perspective of social learning theory, deCharms (1968) observed that when a task is perceived to be undertaken for instrumental reasons (that is, to achieve an external goal or externally controlled incentive) it becomes less intrinsically interesting and satisfying.

Continued research on this topic illustrates that there are complex relationships between the implementation of extrinsic reinforcers and intrinsic motivation. Studies of reinforcement generally followed a pattern of measuring the frequency of a target behavior to establish a baseline, measuring the frequency after implementing a reinforcement schedule, and then withdrawing the reinforcement schedule at which time the frequency was expected to return to the baseline. But Deci (1971, 1972) conducted several studies which indicated that the use of intrinsic rewards can actually decrease intrinsic interest. He used several different methods, but in a typical one, when subjects who were allowed to freely play with puzzles or magazines were put into a situation where they were rewarded (paid) for solving puzzles, the amount of time they spent on puzzles versus magazines decreased below the baseline when they were put back into the play situation. There were speculations that the subjects had simply satiated their interest in puzzles, but subsequent research has confirmed that extrinsic rewards can have an undermining effect on intrinsic interest (Condry, 1977; Deci & Porac, 1978; Lepper & Greene, 1975). But, extrinsic rewards do not always decrease intrinsic interest as when people get paid for their work and also love what they are doing. The extensive research on this topic has revealed several concepts that help explain the interactions of extrinsic rewards and intrinsic interest.

A key element in determining whether a reward will have a positive or detrimental effect on intrinsic motivation is related to whether the reward has an *informational* or *controlling effect*. A reward such as praise that informs a person of successful achievements on optimally challenging tasks can increase intrinsic motivation providing the praise attributes the outcomes to the performer's actions. For example, telling a student that, "I am impressed by the creative way you solved the design challenge posed by our client" will increase the architectural student's feelings of efficacy and intrinsic motivation. Telling the student that you are pleased because he implemented the exact solution that you told him to could be perceived as having a controlling influence and decrease intrinsic motivation (Brophy, 1981).

The *timing of a reward* can influence its effect on intrinsic motivation. For example, several researchers have compared a condition in which one group of students are told in advance that they will receive a reward after completing a learning task, while a comparison group is given a reward unexpectedly after doing the task. In the expected reward condition subjects were less interested in the task afterward and their performance was sometimes lower than in the unexpected reward group. The task interest of those receiving the unexpected reward was not affected except those whose initial intrinsic interest was low. These students showed a substantial increase in interest following the experiment (Lepper, Green, & Nisbett, 1973). In these studies the reward was *exogenous* to the task. That is, the reward was not logically connected to the task, as in receiving a candy bar after finishing a math homework assignment.

In contrast, a condition in which expected rewards are not likely to reduce intrinsic motivation is when the reward is *endogenous* to the task; that is, when the reward is a natural component of the task as in winning money at poker or getting paid for your work. However, Condry (1977) questions whether these outcomes can be called rewards since they are an integral part of the task–outcome relationship. Winning money at poker is not a "reward" that is being administered by someone else according to their contingency rules, assuming that it is a fair and honest poker game. Winning money is an expected result of having and exercising sufficient skill in relation to the element of luck that is inherent in the game. Getting paid at work is the natural result of contractual relationship of exchanging one's effort and talent for remuneration. Demotivation can occur when the contingencies governing this relationship are violated and performance can be affected by the relationship, as in piece rate methods of payment, but the outcomes are not "rewards" that are extrinsic to the expected results of the task performance.

In considering these relationships between extrinsic reinforcements and intrinsic motivation it is important to remember that they apply to situations where subjects already have a degree of intrinsic motivation. When they have no intrinsic interest in a task, and in the frequently used example of getting a child to brush his teeth, extrinsic rewards in the form of tangible rewards (tokens that can be exchanged for a trip to the toy store) or controlling type of praise ("You will make daddy very happy if you brush your teeth," and "That's great! You made daddy very happy by brushing your teeth,") can be used to establish the behavior which will presumably become self-sustaining.

However, these issues take still a different dynamic in fields such as performing arts and sports. In the performing arts, including film actors and pop music stars, the extrinsic rewards can be enormous. Yet, in many of the arts it requires years of effortful practice (Ericsson, 2006) to be accomplished and competitive. It is doubtful that the expectation of extrinsic rewards could, in and of themselves, sustain the motivation and diligence of these aspiring performers. Even in sports it often takes an extremely high level of competitive spirit and intrinsic motivation to persist in the effort to attain a prestigious, and financially rewarding, assignment. The interplay of intrinsic and extrinsic motivation in contexts such as these is complex and of interest for further study.

Cognitive Evaluation and Satisfaction

On pay day at work, when your graded paper is returned in a class, when a judgment is rendered against you after a close call in a weekend softball game, and in most situations where there are outcomes related to your performance you have a reaction. You might feel happy, angry, disappointed, relieved, or indifferent, or you might experience judgmental reactions about the fairness, appropriateness, or stupidity of the outcome. Reactions such as these are not based purely on the outcomes; they are based on your expectations and social comparisons relative to the outcomes. In other words, people compare what actually happens to them to what happens to others and to their own expectations. For example, you might experience considerable anxiety about a task such as learning to dance, passing a math test, or traveling to a foreign country only to find that it is much less threatening than you expected. Hence, you will feel relief. On the other hand, you might experience either exhilaration or disappointment depending on how the experience compares to your expectations. If you receive a raise in pay at work or avoid a pay cut during a period of economic recession you will be happy. If the raise is quite a bit more than you expected you will be ecstatic. However, if it is less than you expected or believed that you deserved you will be disappointed if not angry. Similarly, if you learn that someone else got a larger raise for doing the same or less work as you, well, I don't have to tell you what emotional reaction will probably occur! In a school setting it is not uncommon for students to be assigned to a group project with each person in the group getting the same grade. As often happens, some people do almost all the work, while others do little or nothing. The "workers" will most certainly have negative feelings about the project.

Your feelings of satisfaction are influenced greatly by your subjective evaluation of an outcome based on your expectations and social comparisons. When the outcomes are not what you expected you will probably modify your attitudes or feelings regarding the situation and this will influence your future motivation for that task or activity. For example, if a trip to a water park is not as enjoyable as you expected, then you will probably lower the value you attach to that activity in the future. In contrast is a college freshman who takes a literature course only to satisfy a general education requirement but discovers that he loves the readings, discussions, and reflective papers that are assigned. His expectations will have been exceeded and he might increase the value he attaches to this activity to the point where he majors in literature. In other words, adjusting expectations can directly influence satisfaction and continuing motivation. As the "modern" mother read in a bedtime story to her young daughter, "So the prince and the princess lowered their expectations and lived reasonably contentedly ever after."

There are several psychological theories that help explain one's cognitive (attitudinal) and emotional reactions to events. Three that are included here are cognitive dissonance theory, balance theory, and equity theory and all of them have direct application to the design of learning environments that are appealing and stimulate a desire to learn.

Cognitive Dissonance

Most of the time, people have internally consistent beliefs and behaviors. That is why people who believe in being honest do not steal or keep things that do not belong to them and when they find themselves in an incompatible position, as when they discover in the parking lot of a department store that they received too much change, they may be indecisive and uncomfortable about whether to keep the money or return it. This condition can be characterized as *cognitive dissonance*, a concept introduced by Festinger (1957), which occurs when there is an inconsistency among attitudes, or cognitions. He stated two basic hypotheses as a basis for his theory (p. 3). The first is that dissonance serves as a motivator in that it is a psychologically uncomfortable state and the person will try to reduce it to achieve congruity of attitudes and behavior, which he called consonance. The second one stated that people will "actively avoid situations and information which would likely increase the dissonance" (p. 3). This theory will not tell us what decision a person will choose, only that there will normally be an effort made to resolve the dissonance. Considering the example at the beginning of this paragraph, will the person return the money? It will probably depend on the strength of the person's belief in honesty and the amount of money. If this is a strongly held belief, the person will return the money to achieve consonance, especially if the amount is relatively large such as receiving a $10.00 bill instead of a one. But, if the amount is small, such as an extra dollar bill, the person might consider the response cost of having to take time to return it versus rationalizing that one dollar doesn't really make any difference, especially if there are competing conditions such as being late for an appointment, tired, or needed to hurry home to cook dinner. In this case, the person chooses to live with a small amount of discomfort due to the greater comfort of not having to retrace steps.

These assumptions were confirmed in an experiment that has become a classic in the history of social psychology (Festinger & Carlsmith, 1959). The experimenters had a group of male students from the introductory psychology class fulfill two hours of their research participation requirement by spending the first hour on extremely dull and boring tasks (Table 7.1). Each participant was given a tray full of spools and told to empty the tray, put the spools back again, remove them, and repeat this process for 30 minutes. The experimenter, wearing a lab coat and holding a stop watch, observed and made notations on his tablet continuously. After thirty minutes, the subjects were then given a board containing 48 square pegs and told to turn the pegs one-quarter turn at a time. The experimenter continued to observe.

At the end of these tasks while the subject was presumably waiting to be interviewed, the experimenter told the subjects that there was another condition in the experiment and he would describe it for their interest. The experimenter said that in that condition a student who worked for him would pretend that he had just finished the experiment, meet the next subject outside the entrance and say what an enjoyable experiment it was, that it was fun, interesting, intriguing, etc. The subject was then asked to wait in the outer office for the interviewer (Table 7.1).

Table 7.1. A Three Phase Study of Attitudes and Affect in Relation to Dissonance (Based on Festinger & Carlsmith, 1959).

Phases	Conditions		
	One Dollar Condition ($7.60 in 2009 Dollars)	Twenty Dollar Condition ($152.00 in 2009 Dollars)	Control Condition
Preliminary Task (Boring, monotonous)	All subjects spent one-half hour placing spools on a tray, removing them, and then doing it again. Another half-hour was spent turning square pegs one-quarter turn at a time.		
Dissonance Inducing Activity	Subjects in both of these groups were induced to tell the next subject in private that the experimental task was fun.		
Interview and Rating of Task Interestingness	All subjects met with interviewer, one at a time, and discussed and rated their feelings in regard to four questions about the interestingness and usefulness of the experimental tasks done in the preliminary segment.		

After a few minutes the experimenter would call the subject back in and apologetically explain that the hired student didn't come to the lab. He then asked the subject to meet the next student to explain how interesting the experiment is. One group of subjects was offered $1.00 ($7.60 in 2009 dollars) for their services and the other experimental group was offered $20.00 ($152.00 in 2009 dollars). If subjects hesitated the experimenter used a variety of persuasive comments to get them to comply. The $1.00 group was the high dissonance group. Festinger's theory was that higher levels of dissonance result when the pressure, or inducement, to say something contrary to their beliefs was minimal. When the inducement became large as in the $20.00 group, which is equivalent to $152 dollars in 2009, there should be less dissonance. He predicted that in the low dissonance group there would be little changes in attitude toward how boring the task was as indicated by their ratings in the final phase of the study. They would have low dissonance because they could simply rationalize their lies by the large amount of money they received and the rationalization that they weren't hurting anyone. In contrast, he predicted that subjects in the high dissonance group would resolve their conflict by deciding that the task was actually somewhat interesting.

In the final interview phase, subjects were asked four questions of which one was presumed to be directly related to the influence of the dissonance conditions. This question asked the participants if they thought the tasks were interesting and enjoyable. Both the Control group and the Twenty Dollar group rated the tasks as somewhat uninteresting which was consistent with the nature of the tasks. In contrast, the One Dollar group rated them as rather interesting, significantly more so than the other groups, which supported the dissonance reduction hypothesis. A second question which was expected to be indirectly affected by the dissonance treatments showed the same differences as the first question but not at a level that reached full significance. Participants were also asked whether the experiment gave them an opportunity to learn about their ability to perform such tasks and whether they thought the experiment was measuring anything important. No differences were expected on these questions which served as a check on the possibility of a generalized response to the situation rather than one that was specific to the dissonance effect. The three groups did not differ significantly in their ratings of these questions. Overall, the Twenty Dollar group responses were very similar to the control group which suggests that the large reward was considered a sufficient justification for telling the lie and there was no need to change their opinions about the boring nature of the task. The group that received only $1.00 modified their opinion to reduce dissonance resulting from willingly telling a lie. It is interesting to note that 11 of the 71 participants were dropped from the analysis because they refused to be hired or communicated the truth to the next participant!

There have been challenges to the concept of dissonance theory. For example, Wicklund and Brehm (1976) indicated that perceived personal responsibility based on self-concept underlies dissonance reactions. This would result from an internal psychological conflict resulting from the assumption that one is a good and intelligent person but who also has to

face with the reality of having done something that had undesirable characteristics or consequences. Thus, changing one's attitudes can be explained
as an ego defense mechanism. Also, there are aspects of dissonance theory
that can be related to older theories of the self that are rooted in ego-related
cognitive processes (Allport, 1943; Hilgard, 1949; Rogers, 1954) which consider peoples' tendencies to maintain their psychological integrity using self-
deception, selective attention, and other ego protecting devices. This
research can be related to the contemporary distinctions between performance versus mastery orientation (Dweck, 1986) or ego versus task orientation (Nicholls, 1984) as discussed in Chapter 5, but dissonance theory still has
distinctive characteristics that cannot be subsumed under these other concepts. Greenwald and Ronis (1978) review the status of dissonance theory 20
years after its inception and illustrate how certain predictions and relationships within the original conception of dissonance theory could not be enter-
tained within the revised version of the theory. Aronson (1992) discusses
cycles of high versus low interest in this theory and reviews it in relation to
other theories that deal with aspects of cognition and motivation. He also
points out the difficulties in doing the kind of research that provided a basis
for many of the early social psychological theories that required deception
and a degree of discomfort for the participants which were carried to an
extreme in the Milgram (1965) studies of obedience to authority in which
subjects were induced into believing that they were administering painful
electric shocks to another person. But, even though it is more difficult to use
deception as a paradigm for the study of dissonance, there are other ways to
investigate this theory as illustrated by the following study.

Festinger's dissonance theory (Festinger, 1957) distinguished
between the induction of dissonance which he characterized as something
akin to a state of arousal or tension and its reduction as a result of actions
taken to eliminate the psychological state of conflict. Elliot and Devine
(1994) pointed out that the research on dissonance had tended to focus on
its arousal properties as exemplified in the work of Brehm and Cohen (1962)
and others (Croyle and Cooper, 1983), but there had not been direct empirical tests of the reduction of psychological discomfort following the implementation of a dissonance reduction strategy. They put undergraduate
students into groups in which they wrote essays in favor of or against raising
tuition by 10% the following semester. All of the students in the study had
previously indicated in an unrelated context that they were against raising
tuition, as might be expected! Students in the high dissonance group were
strongly encouraged to write counter-attitudinal essays in which they would
list reasons in support of the tuition hike because it would be helpful to the
university to see what they had to say; however, despite the encouragement, this was considered to be a free choice on their part. Students in the
low-dissonance group were told to write arguments against the increase.
Students in one of the groups in the high dissonance condition were asked to
respond to an affect measure followed by an attitude scale before writing
their essays. Students in the other high dissonance group wrote their essays

first and then responded to an attitude scale followed by an affect scale. The sequence of the scales was important because the experimenters were testing to see whether attitude change would be followed by dissonance alleviation. Their hypothesis was confirmed and the researchers were thereby able to confirm the workings of both affective and cognitive processes in the dissonance induction and alleviation sequence.

It is important to keep in mind that Festinger was focusing on the psychological disturbance caused by dissonant perceptions and actions and the actions taken by people to reduce the discomfort, and this can help explain students' reactions to a learning event. For example, to have successfully completed a course does not automatically mean that a student will be satisfied with the outcomes of the course. This will be illustrated in some examples following an explanation of the remaining two theories to be described in this section.

Balance Theory

A different method of identifying and analyzing dissonance is provided by Heider's (1946, 1958) *balance theory* which was used to explain whether people will have positive feelings of satisfaction toward each other or not. Like cognitive dissonance theory, balance theory is based in part on the assumption that people strive for consistency among their attitudes, but it predates dissonance theory and is grounded in concepts related to person–environment interactions. For example, he proposed that we can understand the positive or negative relationship between two people by examining the attitudes between the primary person of interest (P), the other person (O), and their attitudes toward given entities (X) which can be situations, events, ideas, things, and so forth. The various relationships can be expressed in terms of to like, to value, to esteem, to love, and their opposites. He considered these relationships to be additive, not multiplicative as in other, expectancy-value, formulations of person–environment interactions. This led to his concept of balance theory.

Heider (1946) analyzes and predicts interpersonal liking in terms of cognitive fields containing the three elements of the person (*P*), another person (*O*), and an object (*X*), and these relationships can be depicted graphically using a technique introduced by Cartwright and Harary (1956). A balanced state exists when, for example, *P* likes *O*, *P* likes *X*, and *O* also likes *X*. For example, if Bob (P) likes June (O), and both Bob and June enjoy watching football (X), a balanced state exists which would contribute positively to Bob and June liking each other. But if June dislikes football as illustrated in Figure 7.2b, a state of imbalance exists and both Bob and Jane will be motivated to resolve the dissonance.

Heider (1946) describes a variety of actions that can result from imbalance. One option is to simply accept the discomfort resulting from the dissonance, but to achieve balance one of them could change their attitude

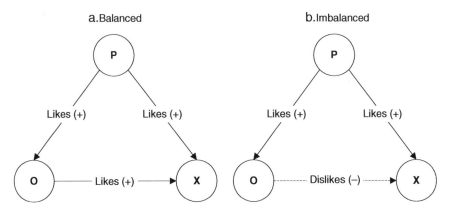

Figure 7.2. Balanced Versus Imbalanced States.

toward football, they could identify something else that they both enjoy doing so much that it overrides the football conflict, especially if Bob moderates his interest in football, or they could stop seeing each other.

Using triads illustrates the options clearly but over simplistically. There will be multiple objects (X) toward which Bob and June have attitudes of liking or disliking. Cartwright and Harary (1956) illustrate how these multiple-object relationships can be diagrammed, and in a more recent study, Hummon and Doreian (2003) developed a simulation program that can model complex sets of relationships. The use of balance theory has been useful in the study of small group behavior as well as in dyads and triads, but the advanced levels to testing and application of this model become quite complex. In the present context, the theory is useful because of the ways it can help motivational designers analyze factors that contribute to dissatisfaction with the outcomes of a learning event. Considering the high degree to which group-based and collaborative learning activities are now promoted and used in learning settings, the work begun by Heider and elaborated by others provides a rigorous foundation for research and design. Hummon and Doreian (2003) refer to numerous studies pertaining to this.

Equity Theory

The effective use of intrinsic factors and extrinsic rewards has a strong influence on satisfaction as do issues related to dissonance and imbalance, but there is one more area of influence to be included here. We have various types of interpersonal relationships and there are many exchanges that occur in them. These exchanges occur in many types of social situations such as work, parents and children, lovers, teammates, volunteer organizations, and even adversarial situations such as opponents in a game or hostile neighbors. Adams (1965) studied the elements of exchanges in social situations the conditions under which they would be viewed as fair or unfair, and what people do as a consequence of equitable or inequitable exchanges. In his *equity theory*, Adams describes exchanges in terms of the ratio of input to output conditions that lead to perceived or actual inequity and the consequences that follow.

Inputs can be anything that an individual perceives to add value to an exchange, such as hours of labor, technical skill, longevity, level of education, experience, work ethic, age, leadership, ethnic identification, gender, influential others, and even things such as social status and physical appearance. However, Adams makes a distinction between the *recognition* versus *relevance* of these attributes. Both the employee and the employer might recognize the presence of these characteristics, but they might not agree on which ones are relevant in the given situation. A job interviewee might have a high opinion of his formal qualifications in terms of a prestigious academic degree but the employer might focus more exclusively on the applicant's experience, evidence of competence in the specific skills required on the job, and evidence of a positive work ethic. One of the challenges to a person who is seeking to build a positive exchange is to identify what the salient personal characteristics are, and this applies in personal relationships as well as the workplace. A man might try to impress a woman by doing things for her and showing her how he can solve problems for her. He considers these to be positive expressions of his interest in her, but she might regard his overtures as overbearing since she values a friendship based on listening and empathy.

Based on the individual's perceptions of the quantity and importance of the inputs that are relevant in a given situation, such as work, he expects a fair return from the employer in terms of pay, status, authority, respect, and advancement opportunities. These are considered to be the outcomes of the person's inputs. The most satisfying kinds of outcomes in a job setting include such things as status symbols, responsibility, meaningful work assignments, feedback, and respect. Outcomes also include the *absence* of undesirable characteristics such as monotony, isolation, surveillance ("micro management"), and lack of recognition of accomplishments. One of the challenges in management, parenting, or maintaining a relationship is to provide outputs that are perceived by the person to be appropriate. As with inputs, outputs can be evaluated in terms of recognition versus relevance. Many years ago when I joined a frequent flyer organization for a major airline, I received an attractive, framed certificate proclaiming my status as a member of that organization. A colleague had one of these on display in a prominent place in his office. I thought it was silly to do so; it was not an award in recognition of some achievement; it was more in the nature, in my mind, of a receipt acknowledging that I had paid money to become a member. I would have preferred free frequent flyer miles or a free tote bag, tablet binder, or something useful with the airline monogram on it. I recognized the airline's intentions and to me it was not a relevant outcome but since the outcome I received was consistent with other new members I did not experience feelings of inequity.

Perceptions of equity versus inequity result from social comparisons of perceived outputs in relation to inputs. A state of perceived equity exists when the ratios are perceived to be equal (Figure 7.3). It is important to think it terms of ratios because a first-level manager will make less money than a midlevel manager, but he will perceive the situation to be equitable if he also perceives that the inputs required to be a midlevel manager are correspondingly greater.

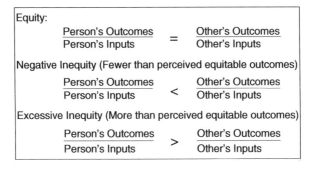

Figure 7.3. Illustrations of Perceived Equitable Versus Inequitable Relationships.

Inequity occurs when the relationship between inputs and outcomes for one person are discrepant from those of another, at least as perceived by the person. Also, inequity can be in a negative or positive direction, which means that a person receives less than he considers to be equitable relative to the input/outcome relationship, as in being underpaid, or that he receives more of an outcome relative to his inputs in comparison with others, as in being overpaid.

Inequity creates dissatisfaction which Adams compares to feelings of dissonance as in Festinger's cognitive dissonance theory and this results in efforts to reduce these negative feelings. There are several ways to do this. The first is to alter one's inputs. If a person feels that his outcomes are too low relative to his inputs, then he might be motivated to reduce his inputs. This is more likely to be observed with hourly work than with piece rate work. An hourly worker can reduce his level of effort without affecting his pay, but a reduction in productivity for the piece rate worker will have an immediate negative effect on his income. Theoretically a person who perceives that he is being overpaid might attempt to increase his productivity to justify the overpayment, but this is not as predictable as reducing one's inputs when being underpaid. Another possibility is to modify one's outcomes to achieve equity, but this is more difficult to do because out-comes are usually under the control of someone else. A third approach is to simply change one's attitudes toward one's input–outcome ratio or toward the other person's ratio. This is called rationalization and requires cognitive reinterpretation of the ratios in order to modify one's perceptions to match the reality of the situation. Still another solution is simply to leave the situation, as in quitting, breaking off the relationship, or getting divorced.

One of the challenges with using this theory is that people differ in how they interpret a satisfactory set of ratios. That is, some people prefer their input/outcome ratio to be less than that of their partner. To explain differences in personal preferences, Huseman, Hatfield, and Miles (1987) introduced the concept of equity sensitivity. They identified three funda-mental patterns:

Benevolents: This person prefers that his input/outcome ratio be less than his perception of the other person's input/outcome ratio. These are people who would typically be characterized as preferring to give than to receive and would be observed most often in helping relationship types of situations. Also, some religions stress a philosophy of giving and sacrifice without expecting material returns.

Equity Sensitives: This represents the traditional equity model in which people expect there to be parity between their ratio of inputs and outcomes compared to those received by other people.

Entitleds: This third group of people expect to have higher levels of outcomes relative to others for the same or fewer inputs. This would be characteristic of the colloquial meaning of "spoiled child" and others who feel that they deserve a higher return or a "better deal" on everything they do. Sometimes, people with low self-esteem have to feel that they got a special advantage in order to feel good about themselves. For example, some children will use devious methods to get larger portions of desirable foods or more toys in comparison with their siblings.

These various components of equity theory are highly relevant to learning environments in which personal and product evaluation occur on an almost continuous basis. Students make social comparisons with respect to the personal attention, grades, and privileges received by other students in the degree to which those rewards are deserved relative to what they are receiving. They also make comparisons of the equity of their outcomes relative to their own expectations. That is, students might believe that a course was well thought, had good assignments, and was interesting, but still have a very negative attitude toward the course because of a highly excessive workload which hurt their performance in other areas of their lives. Also, they might feel that an examination was inequitable because it was not consistent with what the instructor focused on or had indicated to be the important points of content in the course. Thus, to achieve student satisfaction in a learning environment, many factors must be balanced relative to the quality of the teaching, the internal consistency of objectives, content, and examinations, and grading practices that are equitable across students.

Transition

There are numerous tactics that you can use to support satisfying feelings of accomplishment in the majority of your learners. These range from using exercises that are authentic with an optimal challenge level, by providing feedback on results, and by grading in a manner that is fair and consistent with a stated set of criteria.

Strategies to Promote Feelings of Satisfaction

To have a successful outcome of your efforts to learn and perform well in a class is pleasant, but it does not always result in feelings of satisfaction. For students to have an overall, positive feeling about their learning experience, several conditions have to be met, and these conditions are related to the expectations of the students. One of the most important elements of satisfaction is intrinsic motivation; that is, if learners believe that they achieved a desirable level of success while studying topics that were personally meaningful, or in other words, relevant, then their intrinsic satisfaction will be high. But, if part of their motivation is based on extrinsic factors, such as getting a good enough grade to be recommended for some special honor, and they do not get it, then their satisfaction will be depressed in spite of positive intrinsic satisfaction. Conversely, if they achieve well enough to obtain a desired extrinsic reward, but also believe that the learning experience was a waste of time, then their satisfaction will be less than optimal. Finally, another component of satisfaction is based on social comparisons and comparisons to expected outcomes. If learners feel that the results they obtained were not equitable based on the amount of work they had to do, or if some students feel that they were not treated fairly compared to other students, then their satisfaction will be lowered despite the actual intrinsic and extrinsic outcomes they obtained. These components of satisfaction (Table 7.2) are reflected in the concepts and tactics listed in the following table.

S.1. Intrinsic Satisfaction

After they finished the final application exercise in a self-study course on electronic troubleshooting for the Series 300 Mini-Computer, Robert showed a videotape in which actual service representatives expressed the good feelings they experience after solving identical types of problems in the field.

Table 7.2. Subcategories, Process Questions, and Main Supporting Strategies for Satisfaction.

Concepts and Process Questions	Main Supporting Strategies
S1. Intrinsic Reinforcement How can I encourage and support their intrinsic enjoyment of the learning experience?	Provide feedback and other information that reinforces positive feelings for personal effort and accomplishment.
S2. Extrinsic Rewards What will provide rewarding consequences to the learners' successes?	Use verbal praise, real or symbolic rewards, and incentives, or let learners present the results of their efforts ("show and tell") to reward success.
S3. Equity What can I do to build learner perceptions of fair treatment?	Make performance requirements consistent with stated expectations, and use consistent measurement standards for all learners' tasks and accomplishments.

A primary goal of most educators is for their students to develop an intrinsic interest in learning and, if possible, to stimulate their interest in the teacher's subject matter. This is extremely difficult unless the students already had a high level of intrinsic motivation even before entering the teacher's classroom. This is because culture and family values have a strong influence on the value that a child places on school and learning. With these positively motivated students, the teacher's challenge is to sustain or increase their intrinsic motivation. Even with students who have this positive outlook, it can be difficult to sustain it because, in most situations, students are required to be in your classroom; they have not taken your course voluntarily by choice. Therefore, to sustain and build their intrinsic motivation, the tactics listed below can be helpful. These tactics focus on reinforcing students' pride of accomplishment together with affirming the value of what they have learned. This tactics will also help you with students who do not have a high level of intrinsic motivation. Every student and every teacher can think of at least one situation where the relevance of the content or the enthusiasm of the teacher sparked a degree of intrinsic interest. When that happens, the teacher must recognize it and reinforce it to nurture and sustain the student's interest. These tactics must be used jointly with the other tactics in this section to achieve high levels of satisfaction in the learners.

Positive Recognition

1. Give the student opportunities to use a newly acquired skill in a realistic setting as soon as possible.
2. Provide verbal reinforcement of the learner's intrinsic pride in accomplishing a difficult task.
3. Include positive, enthusiastic comments in the materials or in your feedback, which reflect positive feelings about goal accomplishment.
4. Provide opportunities for learners who have mastered a task to help others who have not yet done so.
5. Give acknowledgments of any actions or characteristics that were necessary for success.
6. Give acknowledgments of any risks or challenges that were met.

Continuing Motivation

7. Provide information about areas of related interest.
8. Ensure that the learners are asked or informed about how they might continue to pursue their interest in the topic.
9. Inform the learners about new areas of application.

S.2. Rewarding Outcomes

> During a two-day course on instructor skills, Karen writes "motivational messages" to learners praising them for specific skills they have shown in making presentations.

The most traditional concept of outcomes that make people feel satisfaction are extrinsic rewards, which refer to such things as money, grades, certificates, awards, symbolic objects (emblems, monogrammed school supplies, coffee cups, key chains, etc.), and tokens that can be exchanged for desired object such as candy or school supplies. In addition to these material objects, which are not often available to the classroom teacher, you can use activities that are enjoyable and fun as a reward to finishing learning tasks and assignments. For example, to motivate students to persist at tasks that can be routine and boring, such as memorizing a body of facts, you can use games such as a "homemade" version of *Jeopardy*, or a computer game as a means of review and practice. One challenge with extrinsic rewards is to use them sparingly and intermittently. If they become commonplace, they will lose their reinforcing value.

1. Include games with scoring systems to provide an extrinsic reward system for routine, boring tasks such as drill and practice.
2. Use extrinsic rewards to reinforce intrinsically interesting tasks in an unexpected, non-controlling, manner.
3. Include congratulatory comments for correct responses.
4. Give students personal attention while working to accomplish the task, or after successful task accomplishment.

5. Use reinforcements frequently when learners are trying to master a new skill.
6. Use reinforcements more intermittently as learners become more competent at a task.
7. Avoid threats and surveillance as means of obtaining task performance.
8. Use certificates or "symbolic" rewards to reward success in individual or intergroup competitions, or at the end of a course.

Pleasant Surprises

Following (Figure 7.4) are examples of the use of extrinsic rewards ranging from extra play time for children to a corporate coffee cup for adults. They can be very effective when used appropriately. Even a 39 cent bag of M&Ms can have a very positive impact when used as a fun reward in a competitive learning activity.

Figure 7.4. Examples of Inexpensive Extrinsic Rewards.

S.3.　Fair Treatment

> At the end of a course on safe lifting procedures, Ken reviews learners' performances using a checklist based on the course objectives and gives each learner a copy of the completed checklist.

Have you ever received a positive reward which made you happy, only to realize later that someone else received a greater reward or higher level of recognition for doing the same thing or less? Suddenly your positive feelings become negative ones. This is because people make comparisons, either with other people or with their own expectations. If the recognition or reward you receive is not commensurate with the effort and success you achieved, then your level of satisfaction will be decreased even though the "absolute value" of your outcome is positive. Similarly, as in the opening example, if your perception is that someone else received a greater reward for the same or less accomplishment, then your satisfaction level will be adversely affected. There are cultural differences in regard to perceptions of equity. In some cultures, for example, students would not expect to be treated equally in the same way that students in another culture would expect. In some cultures, it would be embarrassing for a student to receive personal recognition that was excessive in relation to his or her status, or to give recognition in a way that isolates a student from the group. However, even though the specific manifestations of equity will differ, there will be an expectation of equity that influences satisfaction. Following are two tactics that refer to equity in the context of lesson planning and delivery. These tactics call attention to the importance of consistency as a form of equity. That is, are the exercises and tests "fair" given what was actually taught?

1. Ensure that the content and types of problems in the final exercises and posttests is consistent with the knowledge, skills, and practice exercises in the materials.
2. Ensure that the level of difficulty on final exercises and posttests is consistent with preceding exercises.

Summary

People tend to evaluate everything that happens to them. Even before they arrive at a classroom or open a web-based tutorial they will have attitudes about what they are going to learn, and they continue to have attitudes throughout the process unless they experience periods of time in which they are totally engrossed in the experience. The principles and strategies in this chapter are organized and designed to help you know how to assist students to become focused on a lesson, develop curiosity about the content, and feel good about their learning experience.

8

Chapter 8 – Identifying Motivational Problems

Forethought

A fundamental premise of this book is that one can employ a systematic motivational design process to predictably improve the motivational appeal of instruction.

What are the implications of this regarding creativity, spontaneity, and innovation? Does "systematic motivational design" imply that the process is mechanistic, like an assembly diagram for a barbeque grill? Does it mean that the person doing motivational design

Figure 8.1. Is Motivational Design Mechanistic?

becomes robotic (Figure 8.1)? And, to put it another way, is it possible to follow a systematic process and also be creative?

What do you think? You will find my perspective on this in this chapter.

Introduction: Beginning the Design Process

Earlier in this book (Chapter 3) the twin questions of how to determine how many and what types motivational strategies to use were raised. An issue regarding the implications of these questions was whether motivational design could even be approached systematically or whether it is more of a creative and intuitive activity. This process, which will be reviewed briefly as an introduction to this chapter, is neither mechanistic nor creative. The process simply represents a set of activities joined in a systems perspective as to how to identify motivational problems and goals and then how to develop learning environments that will stimulate and sustain learner motivation. Mechanism versus creativity results from ways in which people apply the process and the particular problems they are trying to solve.

The complete process has ten steps which have been implemented in many different cultures and schools at all levels from kindergarten through adult continuing education and training. Also, there is a simplified approach (Chapter 11) that does not require completion of all ten steps, but it does require an understanding of the full process.

As illustrated in Table 8.1 which maps the *motivational design process* next to the *instructional design process,* you will begin by recording information about your course (Step 1). This will include a brief

Table 8.1. Summary of Motivational Design in Relation to Instructional Design.

Generic Design	Motivational Design Steps	Instructional Design Steps
Analyze	1. Obtain course information 2. Obtain audience information 3. Analyze audience 4. Analyze existing materials	• Identifying problem for which instruction is the appropriate solution • Identifying instructional goals • Identifying entry behaviors, characteristics • Conducting instructional analysis
Design	5. List objectives and assessments 6. List potential tactics 7. Select and design tactics 8. Integrate with instruction	• Writing performance objectives • Developing criterion-referenced tests • Developing instructional strategy
Develop	9. Select and develop materials	• Developing and selecting instruction
Pilot Test	10. Evaluate and revise	• Designing and conducting formative evaluation • Designing and conducting summative evaluation • Revising instruction

description of the instructional event that you wish to motivationally enhance and the learning goals. Then, you will record information about the students in your target audience (Step 2), and based on this information, you will do an audience motivational analysis (Step 3) to determine where there might be motivational deficiencies versus satisfactory levels of motivation.

These results tell you what areas of motivation will require special attention as you prepare your lesson plans. This motivational analysis compliments the instructional design analysis of audience capabilities based on their abilities and prerequisite knowledge requirements.

Following the audience analysis, you will analyze the current status of your course materials (Step 4) to determine the ways in which they are satisfactory and the areas in which they will require motivational improvements. This is analogous to the instructional analysis that describes the knowledge and skills to be included in instruction. Based on these analyses, you will prepare objectives for your motivational design plans and you will indicate how you will know if these objectives have been accomplished. In other words, you will identify the assessments you will use to verify that your motivational objectives have been achieved (Step 5). In contrast to instructional design objectives which describe expected leaner outcomes, these objectives define your motivational goals.

The next three steps of the process (Steps 6, 7, and 8) constitute the design activities. The first of these steps consists of preparing a preliminary listing of motivational tactics (Step 6) that might help you succeed in accomplishing your motivational objectives. You will engage in brainstorming, either on your own or in a group, to identify as many tactics as you can in each of the four areas (attention, relevance, confidence, and satisfaction) and in relation to the beginning, middle, and end of the instructional period. This leads to the final selection of tactics (Step 7) where you will apply several analytical criteria to your brainstormed list to select the ones that you will actually use. After you finish this final selection step, you are ready for the final design step which is to integrate your motivational tactics (Step 8) into your lesson plan, or instructional strategy plan. These design steps differ from instructional design in ways other than just their purpose.

The final two steps can be completed jointly with the last two phases of instructional design (Table 8.1), or they can be done independently if you are preparing motivational enhancements for an existing course. In Step 9, you will develop the motivational tactics by selecting existing materials, developing new materials, or modifying the instructional strategies to include motivational elements. Then, in the final step, you will pilot test them by trying them out, formatively evaluating them, and revising them if necessary (Step 10).

These steps represent the complete systematic process that one might follow. It can be used in a formal manner with documentation of each step, or it can be used as a general heuristic guide to thinking and planning. In formal design settings, where decisions might be reviewed, personnel assigned to the tasks might change, or modifications might be made to the instruction, it can be helpful to have documentation that explains what happened at each step. But, if you are following the process for your own course, then you might require only a few notes which will serve as reminders when you prepare to offer this course in the future. The important thing is the process represented by these steps, not the specific questions in the worksheets. As you use these worksheets, I expect that you will modify them to fit your situation. In the remainder of this chapter, each step is introduced and a detailed description of the worksheet is provided.

In summary, what are the implications of this process? Does it seem to be excessively structured with negative effects on creativity, spontaneity, and innovation in the process of teaching, as was asked in the Forethought? Some people do, in fact, resist systematic design processes because they believe formalized processes will inhibit their freedom and creativity. And, who knows, maybe it will for some people. However, that is because of their personal style and not because of the design process itself. The design process consists of guidelines that help you make best use of your time in trying to accomplish a goal. As was quoted in Chapter 3, "design is a process of making dreams come true" (Koberg & Bagnall, 1976). When Don Koberg and Jim Bagnall first began publishing *The Universal Traveler: A Soft Systems Guide to Creativity, Problem-Solving, & the Process of Reaching Goals*, they were on the faculty of the School of Architecture and Environmental Design at a California University. One of the distinctive characteristics of this book which has been through numerous editions is that the authors describe many attributes that make one a creative user of the design process. These include qualities such as awareness of life and everything around you, enthusiasm, self-control, a positive attitude, and the ability to overcome fear. Fear, they maintain, is the biggest enemy of creativity and design. Fear causes you to become narrow and safe in your approach to problem solving and generating solution ideas to develop and test. You must not abandon an idea that you feel excited about even if others do not agree with you. To be an effective designer, you must be willing to try out new things, make adjustments when things do not go as planned, and to find ways to be enthusiastic about the process that you are undertaking! As you begin to work on your motivational design project, you must become enthusiastic about it. If not, then the results of your project are not going to inspire you or anyone else. Conversely, if you are enthusiastic, then there is a high probability that you will generate some creative ideas that are appealing to your audience! This attitude applies to instructional design and motivational challenges just as it does to every other field in which design plays a role!

Step 1: Obtain Course Information

Overview

The selection and development of motivational tactics that are appropriate for a given course depend on many factors that include, but are not limited to, characteristics of the learners and their goals. Motivational tactics require time and expense to develop and they take time to implement. If they take too much time, they can actually detract from the learning objectives and course content. When this happens, the motivational tactics become demotivational. To ensure that the motivational tactics are appropriate for the situation, it is necessary to collect background information about the course that is to be offered and about the audience.

Step 1 focuses on several characteristics of the course and how it will be delivered. As illustrated in Worksheet 1 (Table 8.2) there are four

Table 8.2. Motivational Design Worksheet 1.

OBTAIN COURSE INFORMATION
Title of Instructional Unit (Course, Module, Lesson, etc.):
Description of Content and Conditions
1. What is the purpose (major goal or objective) of this unit? 2. Provide a brief description of the content (actual or expected) of this unit. 3. Will you teach this unit more than once this year and will you teach it in subsequent years? 4. How much time is there to revise or create this unit of instruction?
Curriculum Rationale
1. What curriculum need or requirement is supposed to be met by this unit of instruction? 2. What are the benefits to the students?
Context
1. How does this course relate to other courses taken before or after this one? 2. What delivery system (method of presenting the instruction) will be used (e.g. classroom presentation and discussion, lecture-lab, self-paced print, etc.)?
Instructor Information
1. How much subject matter expertise do you or the other teachers of this course have? 2. What kinds of teaching strategies are you or the other teachers familiar and comfortable with? 3. What kinds of teaching strategies would be unfamiliar to, or rejected by you or the other teachers?

parts to this step: (1) course description, (2) rationale for the course, (3) context, and 4) instructor information. The course description asks for an overview of the course and its purpose, how many times and how frequently it will be taught, and how much time you have to work on lesson planning and design before having to teach the material. This helps you decide how much effort to put into designing motivational tactics. Describing the rationale for the course and its context (relationship to other courses and method of delivery) helps with the design of motivational tactics that are relevant to the purpose of the course.

The characteristics of the instructors should be taken into consideration when designing and developing course materials for an instructor-led setting even though this is not typically done by instructional developers or curriculum specialists. This applies to both the instructional tactics and the motivational tactics that are used. Ultimately, the personal style, knowledge, and experience of the instructor have strong influences on the course and on the tactics that will be successful. Instructors may require training in how to adapt and use tactics such as games and role-plays before they will use them. If you can obtain answers to the four questions in this section during the first phase of your work, you will be more effective in selecting tactics and designing materials that will be comfortable for the instructors to use.

If you are a teacher who is applying this process to your own instruction, then you will be more likely to consider these elements. Just keep in mind that there is not one best way to teach or to motivate students. The best approach is to understand your own personality and preferences and to develop methods and a style that are comfortable for you.

An important principle in regard to these worksheets is "adapt and apply." Each worksheet has an overall purpose and you should feel free to modify them based on your audience, the nature of your project, and the degree of design and development that will be required. After you have applied the process once or twice, you will become comfortable with making revisions to the questions and customizing the worksheets in other ways that meet your needs. However, it is strongly recommended that you not skip steps. Each step serves an important function in the overall process. Even if it takes only a few minutes to consider any of the steps, your thoughts and documentation pertaining to that step will contribute to a stronger more effective outcome!

Instructions for Worksheet 1: Obtain Course Information

This worksheet (Table 8.2) and the second one (Table 8.5) are designed to help you get background information about the setting and the audience that will help you analyze the motivational characteristics of the audience and to prepare for selecting effective motivational strategies. Some of the information is very general and does not have a direct one-to-one relationship with a particular motivational decision, but it definitely helps you understand the general motivational framework which will be useful in doing the audience motivational analysis (Worksheet 3). In designing motivational strategies, this general information will help you choose appropriate analogies, learner activities, and other aspects of motivational design.

Description of Content and Conditions

1. Try to state the overall purpose or objective of the unit in one or two sentences. This will serve as a reference point when deciding whether or not to include motivational strategies and tactics that are listed for consideration during the design steps.

2. Writing a brief summary of the content also provides a reference point for identifying and selecting motivational tactics, and it also helps you list and focus on the most essential parts of the unit.

3. Some motivational tactics can be implemented quickly and easily, but others, such as case studies or experiential learning activities, take much longer. By giving some thought to how many times this course will be taught, you will be better able to decide how much effort to put into motivational tactics. For example, if you or others are going to teach this unit several times and for more than one year, it is worthwhile to develop motivational tactics that require more design and development time.

4. Teachers and trainers often say they do not have enough time to think about motivational activities. In fact, they often say they don't even have enough time to think about good learning activities. This question asks you to indicate just how much time you do have. In Step 7, you will apply several practical criteria to the selection of motivational tactics. Time will be one of them.

Curriculum Rationale

1. Units of instruction are developed and delivered for many reasons ranging from prescribed curriculum requirements to individual educational plans for children with special needs. If a given unit of instruction is a prescribed element of a curriculum, there is sometimes a rationale based on the philosophy or the curriculum or the structure of the subject matter. It will help your own motivation to teach the material as well as the students' motivation to learn it if you know and accept the curriculum rationale for the content.

2. If a student should ask, in regard to this unit that you are developing, "Why should I study this?" how would you answer him? Can you think of something more meaningful than to say, "It's required?" In other words, what benefits are there, if any, for the students to learn this material? Sometimes there are clear benefits to the students. For example, students in a college preparatory program

of study will clearly benefit from learning the content and test-taking skills to help them do well on competitive exams. For students who are not in a college preparatory program, it will be more difficult to think of specific benefits for some of the academic material they are required to learn. Sometimes it is difficult to identify the benefits to students because you may have been wondering about that yourself; that is, some of the units that we, as teachers, have the most difficulty teaching are the ones for which we, ourselves, do not see a real benefit. Try to identify specific benefits in this section. It will help you focus on certain aspects of learner motivation in the motivational design process. However, if you cannot think of specific and meaningful benefits, do not worry about it at this time. As you proceed through the motivational design process, there will be other places where you can address this problem.

Context

1. What is the relationship of this unit of instruction to other parts of the course or curriculum? Does it build on previous content or skills? Think about related topics, not just the specific prerequisites or next steps within the defined content and skill area. For example, if you are working on a history course that covers Egypt, consider whether the students have read about Egypt or neighboring areas in other courses such as social studies or geography. Also, consider how and when they might encounter this content or topic again in the future. This will help you later when it is time to develop motivational tactics to make the instruction relevant to students' interests and experiences.

    Another type of contextual relationship to consider is the connection to skill development. Are there skills to be learned in the present unit that build on past skills or contribute to future requirements? For example, if students in your unit of instruction have to analyze historical documents to look for the presence of certain themes or metaphors that helped define a culture at a particular time, such as the concept of balance and harmony in ancient Greece, have they done assignments in other classes that require similar skills? Or, might they have to do so in a future course? For example, in literature classes, have they had to, or will they have to, analyze a literary work in terms of major themes or metaphors and write a paper that explains and supports their observations? If you can make these kinds of connections, it will help you add motivational value to the lesson.

2. Delivery system refers to the primary way in which instruction is delivered to the students. Common delivery systems are instructor-led classroom instruction, self-paced print instruction, computer-based instruction, and web-based instruction. Delivery systems

should not be confused with media selection. Within any delivery system, you can choose what type of media to include. For example, in a classroom, you might use a variety of media such as posters, videos, a white board, or Power Point slides. But different delivery systems have implications for motivational design based on their overall characteristics. For example, a teacher who is experienced and attentive to the dynamics in a classroom will be able to sense the need for changes in motivational tactics and respond accordingly. But, in computer-based instruction, you have to anticipate the motivational requirements of learners in advance and design the appropriate tactics into the instructional materials. The computer cannot respond to changes in motivation as flexibly and expertly as an experienced teacher can.

Instructor Information (This Section Applies to Instructor-Facilitated Courses)

Although typically not done, the characteristics of the instructors should be taken into consideration when designing and developing the course materials for an instructor-led setting. This applies both to the instructional strategies and to the motivational strategies that are used. Ultimately, the personal style, knowledge, and experience of the instructor have a strong influence on the course. If you can obtain answers to the questions in this section during the first phase of your work, you will be more effective in selecting and designing materials that will be comfortable for the instructors to use.

1. The level of subject matter expertise can be important when trying to make a unit of instruction more motivating. Teachers with a high level of knowledge and experience are usually better able to think of a variety of possible motivational tactics. But, sometimes, their familiarity with the subject matter limits their ability to see it in new and novel ways that might appeal to the background and interests of the students. Similarly, teachers who are teaching out of their primary content area will sometimes be able to bring new ideas and perspectives to the topic. In your own preparation, consider the degree to which you might need to find ways of looking at your subject matter with "new eyes" to make it more motivating. A variety of good tactics for opening your perspective and getting new ideas are contained in a generalized design book called *The Universal Traveler* (Koberg & Bagnall, 1976). The actual exercise of creating motivation ideas will occur later (Step 6). The only requirement here is to consider the level of your expertise and other members of your team if more than one person is working on this.

2. Try to list the various teaching strategies that you have used. For example, has most of your experience been in the form of

explanatory lectures followed by examples and exercises for the
students? Have you, or other teachers who might be working on this
project, used strategies such as discovery learning, inquiry teaching, simulations, games, or case studies? Include as many as you can.

3. Finally, list any teaching strategies you or others are uncomfortable
    with, or that you have heard about but never tried. This information
    in this section also helps prepare you to select and develop motiva-
    tional tactics that will be acceptable to you and other teachers who
    might be involved. There is no point developing a creative role-play
    exercise if the teacher is not confident and comfortable using such a
    strategy.

Sample Worksheets

Two sets of sample worksheets are included here and throughout
the description of this process. Both of these are based on actual situations
and while they provide good, concrete illustrations of how the worksheets
can be used in two very different situations, I have not tried to modify them
to the point of making them "perfect." Overall, they are fine, but sometimes there are parts that could be improved. I will point this out in the
appropriate places. If you are using this book as a text, you could build
exercises around these worksheets by having your students critique them
and suggest improvements. One of the reasons I left some of the problematic areas the way they are is because they represent characteristic
problems I have encountered among the students in my motivational design
course. It is helpful to the students to see the examples of what not to do as
well as positive examples.

The first sample (Table 8.3) is from a course that was being developed and motivationally enhanced for a training course in a corporation.
This example is based on a project in an actual company and was originally
reported in a class assignment by Julie Jenkins, one of my graduate students. However, I have modified numerous aspects of the situation and the
contents of the worksheets for this sample. The revisions do not detract
from the authenticity of the example, but they do provide better illustrations of various aspects of the requirements for each step.

The second example (Table 8.4) is based on work that was done by
Gail Hicks in a special program for gifted and talented students in an
elementary school in New Jersey. Her situation diverged from a typical
classroom or online course because she met with the children infrequently.
This program was designed to help them learn inquiry skills and it extended
throughout the semester, and there were numerous motivational issues to
consider. She followed the ARCS systematic design process, but many parts
of these structured worksheets were completed by me retroactively. Even
though some parts exceeded the level of detail that she required, they were
effective in providing a basis for documenting her project.

Table 8.3. Worksheet 1 Course Information Example: Corporate Training Environment.

Corporate Example: Worksheet 1:
Course Information

Course Title

ESE is Easy (ESE = enterprise support environment)

Course Description

Course Description

The lesson under survey is part of an interactive computer-based training course for Digital Magic's[1] Systems Integration Process Group. This four-hour technology-based training (TBT) was designed to teach Digital Magic's Systems Integration personnel how to use the Enterprise Support Environment (ESE) application to plan, manage, and archive projects using the Systems Integration Process (SI-Pro).

Purpose of Course

The course objectives, as outlined in the DDD, state that upon completion of the course, learners will be able to use ESE to

1. load enterprise models or enterprise templates,
2. adopt work products,
3. tailor the Work Breakdown Structure (WBS),
4. manage the Statement of Work (SOW),
5. manage a project plan, and
6. archive enterprise materials.

New or Existing?

The course under analysis currently is in the final stage of testing and is about to be released to the client for mass reproduction. Since this is a new Digital Magic application, this is the first course ever created for ESE.

Logistical Considerations

The course will be taught several times during the next two months. The frequency of modifications is dependent upon the client, however, negotiations are underway for a modified version of the ESE TBT to teach the next version of the application. Apparently, the next release of the application will contain the same features as the current version, but in addition, it will contain estimation features for project cycle time and project costs. The client has indicated the new TBT should include instructions for the new functions, but they would like any revisions we see fit incorporated as well.

---

[1] A fictitious company name.

Table 8.3 (continued)

Time Allotted for Revisions
  The new version of ESE is due to be released very soon. Since negotiations are underway for the new, revised TBT, we can most likely expect approximately 6–8 weeks to implement course revisions.

Rationale

Rationale for the Course
  This course is being taught to provide specific training for Digital Magic personnel who are part of the SI-Pro Competency. ESE has been designed to support the needs of these personnel (project managers and process exponents), so the ESE course had been created to teach how to use this very valuable tool.

Rationale for Course Revisions
  Since the *ESE is Easy* TBT is the first course ever created to teach this new tool, it was quite difficult for the instructional designer and project team members to construct the course in the time allotted by consultants. The effectiveness of the instructional design is uncertain, for the course has not been evaluated. In addition, revisions to motivational strategies are definitely required because the initial time constraints prevented the ID from being able to spend time implementing detailed principles of motivation.

Setting

Context
  ESE is an interactive, computer-based training course for ABCC personnel who are involved with project management. The course is being delivered via CDROM and has been designed using this delivery vehicle so employees can complete the course in the comforts of their own home, at the office, etc. The course is setup so that users may navigate through the course at an individual pace. The course not only allows the learner to backtrack, but actually prompts them to do so at specific points throughout the course. This course is not related to any other courses currently at Digital Magic.

Delivery System
  The course will be delivered either at the work site or at the ABCC employees' homes via CDROM.

Instructor Information
  [Not Applicable]

Transition

  All of the information you have recorded helps establish a frame of reference for the analysis and design steps that will follow. Also, when you have motivational design projects to undertake for other courses or for your current one at a future time, this kind of documentation will help you remember the

Table 8.4. Worksheet 1 Example: Elementary School Gifted and Talented Class.

Elementary School Example: Worksheet 1

Course (Unit) Information

Unit Title[2]: Independent Study Project

Unit Description

1. Brief description of this unit[3]:
   The instructional need to be addressed in this unit is the development of an independent project. The emphasis of the course is upon the expansion of independence, the introduction of the concepts and skills necessary for self-directed learning, problem-solving skills, communications, effectively using time, and the completion of an independent project. The target population for the unit is identified intellectually and academically talented and gifted 5th and 6th grade students.

2. Purpose (major goal or objective) of this unit?
   The thrust of the unit is to develop critical and creative higher level thinking skills, and to use these skills to creatively solve a problem, to develop greater facility in planning activities to research and to share a completed project with others.

3. Is this a new or existing unit? (Check One) Existing unit __X__ New unit _____
   This is a standard assignment for this target population.

4. What are the logistical considerations of this unit? Will it be
   a. taught one time or many? Taught annually.
   b. modified frequently or infrequently? Updated annually.
   c. taught frequently or at widely spaced intervals? It will be taught every year.

5. How much time is there to revise or create this unit before it will be taught? Three months.

Rationale for the Unit

6. What need or requirement is supposed to be met by this unit?
   One goal is to design the unit to promote student feelings of responsibility and persistence (in other words, a perceived sense

---

[2] **Note change in level of reference from course to unit.**
[3] Note modification to question.

Table 8.4 (continued)

of personal causation) during the entire process. The students must also be called upon to use problem-solving techniques in the development of an original independent project. The project will also help students learn to develop original and/or unusual ideas, especially as solutions to problems (U.S.O.E. definition of gifted and talented children). The students will then be able to draw upon these skills and use their potential to the fullest to realize their contributions to self and society (Wenonah School's talented and gifted policy philosophy).

7. What are the perceived motivational or instructional problems? The problem associated with the unit is the motivation of the students. Although in a talented and gifted program such as ours the initial motivation of students is not usually a problem, the difficulty frequently occurs in maintaining a high level of motivation throughout the entire time period. The students work individually and independently on their projects.

specific circumstances of this situation and the reasons why various motivational design decisions were made. The benefits of your work on this project will transfer to other projects. In the next section, we will take a close look at the characteristics of the audience, or students, for this unit of instruction.

Step 2: Obtain Audience Information

Overview

The information in this step (see Worksheet 2, Table 8.5), together with the preceding one, provides the foundation for the audience analysis to be conducted in Step 3. This step focuses on several factors that have a strong bearing on the initial motivation of students and how they are likely to respond to the content and instructional strategies of the course. For example, the existing reputation of the course, the extent to which the students have similar or divergent values, and the method of selecting or assigning students to courses help you anticipate the entry-level motivation of students. This information is extremely useful when designing the motivational tactics to use at the very beginning of a course.

Instructions for Worksheet 2: Obtain Audience Information

1. From one perspective, classes are always heterogeneous; that is, there will always be differences among the students based on their unique personalities and interests. However, in some classes

Table 8.5. Motivational Design Worksheet 2.

OBTAIN AUDIENCE INFORMATION
1. How well do the learners in this class know each other, if at all? Are they a reasonably homogenous group, or are there distinct subgroups?
2. What are the learners' overall motivational attitudes toward school?
3. What do you expect the students' general attitudes toward this unit of instruction to be? Is this an elective or a required unit? Do you expect them to regard this unit of instruction as being useful or of little personal value? Do you expect them to believe that it will be difficult or easy, boring or interesting?
4. What kinds of teaching strategies are the students accustomed to (e.g., lecture followed by exercises, collaborative groups, case studies, role plays, self-instructional printed materials, computer-based instruction, etc.)? Do you expect them to have any strong likes or dislikes with respect to various teaching strategies?

the learners will be generally homogenous with respect to their overall socioeconomic level, their values regarding school, and their attitudes toward the future. In other classes, there will be distinct subgroups based on differences in these same variables. Briefly describe the extent to which you believe your class to be generally homogeneous or to have distinct subgroups. This will have a direct effect on how you conduct your audience analysis in the next step.

2. Do the students in your class have an overall positive attitude toward school and its importance in their lives? Are there differences among subgroups in your class with regard to their attitudes toward school? Take note of these attitudes in your response to this question.

3. What do you think their attitude will be toward the subject matter of the unit of instruction that you are preparing in this design process? Will they regard it as being useful or not particularly useful? Do you expect them to regard it as an interesting subject, or basically somewhat boring? Describe any aspects of their attitude toward this subject that you can.

4. Finally, think about the teaching strategies that are familiar to these students and their attitudes toward the strategies with which they are familiar. Reflection on this issue will help you choose strategies that might be most motivating to these students.

Sample Worksheets

The corporate example (Table 8.6) illustrates a fairly common situation in training and also in educational institutions because this is a required course which means that the participants are what is commonly called a "captive audience." However, as indicated in the worksheet, not all of the participants are expected to have a negative attitude!

Table 8.6. Worksheet 2 Audience Information Example: Corporate Training Environment.

Corporate Example: Worksheet 2:
Audience Information

Questions Related to Audience Information

Who are the learners?
The target audience consists of project managers and process supervisors within the SI-Pro Competency Group. Both project managers and process supervisors have full authorization in ESE, and they are considered SI-Pro experts.

Do the learners know each other?
The target audience is dispersed across many locations, but many of them network with each other. However, this course is being offered to individuals as self-directed study, so they will not be interacting in a real or virtual classroom.

What are the learners' motivational attitudes?
Most of the learners have negative attitudes toward training. The negative attitude toward training is most likely a result of one of three factors: (1) the ESE training course is required, not voluntary or (2) previous self-directed, technology-based training courses were a negative experience for the learner, or (3) previous face-to-face training courses were a negative experience.

What are the learners' general attitudes toward this course?
Attitudes toward the course vary, but are predominantly negative. Most employees view training as boring or unnecessary. They would rather learn how to use the tool by their own means.

Do the learners have any strong likes or dislikes with respect to various types of delivery systems and teaching strategies?
However, some of the learners have never experienced technology-based training and are eager to participate in the new course. Other employees are reluctant to use the TBT or experience any type of training.

Even though the age level and organizational settings are extremely different, the elementary school example (Table 8.7) is a dramatically different

Table 8.7. Worksheet 2 Audience Information Example: Elementary School
Gifted and Talented Class.

Elementary School Example: Worksheet 2
Audience Information

1. Who is the target population for this unit?[4]
   Fifth and 6th graders in the academically talented and gifted
   program in an elementary school in the Northeastern United States.

2. What are the learners' motivational attitudes toward school, and
   their morale within their school?[5]
   These students generally enjoy school because they are able to be
   highly successful and their school supports them with good resources.

3. How well do the learners know each other, if at all? For example, will
   they know each other and have experience working together?[6]
   By the time this unit begins, all of the students who are participating
   will know each other as a result of being in the same special class, at
   least at the level of recognizing each other. Some of them will be
   friends and acquaintances. Some of them will have known each
   other from being together in previous grades.

4. What are students' general attitudes toward this unit? Did they volunteer
   or were they assigned? Do they think it is useful or unnecessary? Do they
   think it will be difficult or easy, boring, or interesting?
   This is a requirement of all students in this program. Based on an
   interview conducted by the special project teacher, the students
   believe that it is challenging, but that they can do it. They get enthused
   about having an opportunity to pursue something of their own interest,
   but they do not think the project is very useful to them for their future.

5. Do the learners have any strong likes or dislikes with respect to
   various types of delivery systems and teaching strategies?
   At this grade level, most of them like variety and get bored quickly
   with lectures, unless the lecture is a "special talk" on a topic of
   interest. The idea of an independent project appeals to them.

---

[4] Note change in the question compared to the corporate example.
[5] Again, note changes in this question to make it more appropriate for a
   school setting compared to the previous example.
[6] And, once again, the question was modified.

situation from the corporate one. Like the corporate example, this is a required course but the children are eager to participate. It is a novel experience compared to their normal routine and it even has an air of eliteness about it. But, as indicated in the worksheet, there are several motivational challenges confronting the teacher!

Transition

These first two worksheets contain your descriptions and reflections on the background information that you were able to acquire about the course and the students. This information has prepared you for the next step, which is a formal analysis of the audience, and for Step 4 in which you will do a motivational analysis of any course materials that currently exist for the unit of instruction that you are motivationally enhancing.

Step 3: Analyze Audience

Overview

Audience analysis is a critical step in the motivational design process. It requires decisions that will have a direct influence on defining your motivational objectives and selecting or creating tactics. The purpose of this step is to estimate what the motivational profile is for the whole class or for selected subgroups or individuals in the class.

One of the challenges in solving motivational problems is that the initial motivation of the learners can be too high as well as too low. If it is too low, their achievement will be low because they have little desire to succeed and they will not exert enough effort. If their motivation level is too high, then the quality of their performance decreases because of excessive stress that causes them to "freeze up;" that is, not be able to remember information or engage in ineffective problem-solving tactics.

The goal of motivational design is to identify and use motivational tactics that help keep learners in a happy medium between the two extremes. By analyzing the audience to determine specifically what types of motivational problems exist, it is possible to select tactics that solve these specific problems. This also helps avoid problems that can result from having too few or too many motivational tactics. It helps instructors rely on a rational method of motivational design instead of depending totally on past experience or trial-and-error methods.

These conditions can be represented in a graphic format (Figure 8.2) as previously illustrated in Chapter 3. The baseline is divided into three sections representing motivational levels that are too low, acceptable, and too high. The vertical axis represents performance or achievement. As illustrated by the plotted curve, which has the appearance of an upside-down letter *U*, performance is at a maximum when the motivation levels are

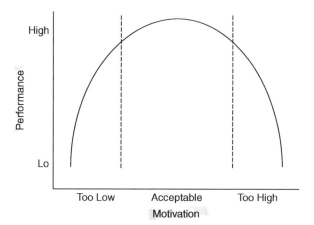

Figure 8.2. Curvilinear Dynamics of Learner Motivation.

acceptable, and it decreases when motivation levels are too low or too high. This is not, strictly speaking, a mathematical model, because the methods of measuring motivational levels are not sufficiently precise or stable to provide a basis for creating rigorous mathematical models that encompass all the dimensions of motivation. However, it is a useful method for graphically portraying the concepts and conditions of motivation and performance, and it becomes useful when recording the results of your audience analysis in Task 3 of this section (see Worksheet 3, Table 8.8).

This process of audience analysis assumes that you have studied the preceding chapters that explain the concepts, tactics, and subcategories representing each of the four major categories (Attention, Relevance, Confidence, and Satisfaction). Keep in mind as you do this analysis that you are trying to predict what the initial motivational characteristics of the audience will be when they begin the unit of instruction that you are motivationally enhancing. Consequently, in the audience analysis, each ARCS category is described in terms that reflect this focus on prediction. The information in Worksheets 1 and 2 is to be used as background on which to base your estimates of the *audience motivational profile*.

Instructions for Worksheet 3: Audience Analysis

1. In the audience analysis (Worksheet 3, Table 8.8), you will build a learner profile that incorporates each of the four ARCS dimensions. The first step is to determine whether there will be a dominant profile for the entire group, or whether there are distinct subgroups. If there are distinct subgroups, then you will develop a separate profile for each. You can record all of your results on this worksheet by labeling each subgroup as you describe it, or use separate copies of this worksheet for each one. Keep in mind that even if you divide the large group

Table 8.8. Motivational Design Worksheet 3.

ANALYZE AUDIENCE

1. Does this analysis pertain to the whole class or one subgroup (use separate forms or identify with a label as indicated in instructions)?

2. Based on the information in Worksheets 1 and 2, how do you characterize the audience on each of the following dimensions (describe each and use the graph to portray the results)?

> Attention Readiness:
> Perceived Relevance:
> Felt Confidence:
> Satisfaction Potential:

1. Graph of audience analysis. Use this graph to portray the results of your audience analysis. Draw additional graphs as necessary for additional subgroups or for individuals.

4. How would you characterize the major versus the minor problems?

5. Does the major cause appear to be modifiable? If not, which other conditions might be influenced to improve overall motivation?

6. Is there anything else that should be considered in the audience analysis?

---

into subgroups there will still be variations in motivation among the individuals in each subgroup. The purpose of this analysis is to identify the major characteristics of each group or subgroup.

2. Describe the audience's motivational profile to provide a basis for identifying motivational tactics to use. If the audience's motivation is too low or too high, then you will design motivational tactics to bring it into the acceptable range. If the audience's motivation is already acceptable, then you will use only as many motivational tactics as necessary to sustain learner motivation.

Student motivation can be too high or too low in each of the four major areas of motivational variables. Explanations and examples of each will help prepare you to determine the motivational profile of your audience.

Attention Readiness: Refers to the degree to which the audience will be likely to respond with curiosity and attention to the instructional material. At one extreme, the audience is likely to be under-stimulated (bored) and not likely to pay attention, or over-stimulated (hyperactive) and unable to keep their attention on any one stimulus.

If students are in your course because they have elected to study this subject, or if you expect that they will be alert and open-minded about the content of your course because of their intrinsic interest in the subject, then they will probably be in the acceptable range of attention readiness. However, we can sometimes predict that a certain type of subject matter will be viewed as uninteresting and boring by a given group of students even though the material might be relevant and important to know. For example, students in a physical education class frequently have to listen to instruction on the rules of a sport before they are allowed to play it. Typically, they are bored by this instruction because all they want to do is get on the playing field and start the game. In contrast, assume that it is the first day of class for a student who is interested in science. If, when the student goes into the classroom, the counters are filled with interesting experimental apparatus and the walls are covered with colorful posters of scientific illustrations and information, the student is likely to be hyper-active. The student will be trying to look at everything and will have a strong desire to walk around the room for a closer look and to touch the various items. This student will be excessively high on the attention dimension of motivation and it will be necessary for the teacher to calm him down before he will be ready to listen attentively to the lesson.

Perceived Relevance: Refers to whether the audience is likely to perceive any personal benefit from the course with respect to motive or goal attainment. At one extreme the audience will be indifferent or even hostile if they perceive no relevance. At the other extreme, perceived relevance may be so high due to the importance of this course to their future goal attainment (e.g. graduation, promotion, job retention, scho-larship) that they have high anxiety due to feelings of jeopardy.

For example, students frequently do not perceive the relevance of academic subjects. The students might accept the necessity of studying a subject because it is a required link to a future goal, which is one component of relevance, but they might not see how the subject has any meaningful importance in their lives. Consequently, they would be expected to be in the "low" category for relevance. In contrast, a student might be enrolled in a course that either has or is perceived to have a vital link to the student's future. The student might be so nervous about the consequences of not doing well in the course that his or her

performance will be less than possible due to excessive stress. In this case, the motivation level is clearly too high for relevance. If the students believe that the subject matter is important for the present or future in their lives, and that it has some personal relevance in their lives, then they are in the acceptable range for this category.

Felt Confidence: Refers to how likely the audience is to feel a comfortable sense of challenge in the course. If they feel too unconfident, they will experience feelings of helplessness. The students often experience it as "I can't do this no matter how hard I try". But, if the students are overconfident they will be arrogant and likely to overlook the gap between what they actually know and what the course is teaching.

It is not uncommon for students to develop helpless attitudes toward specific subjects. For example, some students might believe that they have a writing problem, that it is excessively difficult to write good essays or technical reports. Other students might have math anxiety because of fears they have developed toward this subject. If you suspect that such an attitude exists among some of the students toward your subject, then you would mark them low on confidence. In contrast, some students believe that they know more than they do. If you are going to teach subject matter that the students have previously studied, even though they studied it at a more elementary level, then you may have problems with the students being overconfident. Keep in mind that if the students believe that they already know the material, and they do, in fact, know it, then they are not overconfident. In that case, they are appropriately confident. If their overall expectation is that they can learn the material with a reasonable amount of effort, then they are in the acceptable range of motivation for this category.

Satisfaction Potential: Refers to the audience's preconceived ideas about how they will feel about the outcomes of the course. At one extreme, the reluctant learners may have a feeling of "sour grapes." It is the feeling that "No matter how well I succeed in this course, I'm still not going to like it." At the other extreme, they may be expecting too much from the course, a feeling of panacea as if the course were going to solve all their problems or help them achieve total mastery of the given skill.

It is quite possible that students' satisfaction potential can be too low even though they know the material is relevant and they are confident they can learn it. This sometimes happens in required courses. The students might have a bad attitude simply as a result of not having a choice, and not being intrinsically interested in the material. If this were the case, then the group would be in the low range for this category. The opposite condition exists when students' expectations are too high. For example, when students first get the opportunity to study a foreign language, they might be enthusiastic because they expect that within a short time they will be able to have pen pals and converse in the new language. This will not be possible at the end of a first unit of instruction in a new language, so the students will be disappointed with what they have learned even though they might have done quite well in regard to the realistic goals of the course. If you believe that students' expectations exceed what is realistic, then their satisfaction potential is too high. The acceptable range of motivation is when the students have realistic expectations and expect to have a satisfying feeling of accomplishment if they succeed.

3. Graph the results of the analysis. It can be helpful to portray the results of the analysis in a graphical format. Even though the graph is not, strictly speaking, a quantitatively based plotting of coordinates, it provides an illustration of results that can be comprehended at a glance and provides a handy reference in subsequent steps of the motivational design process.

To graph the audience profiles, refer to your verbal descriptions in the previous task. If the motivational level of the audience for a given component of motivation is at the maximum level of acceptability, then move your pencil across the horizontal axis of the diagram (Figure 8.2) until you reach the midpoint. Then move your pencil up until you reach the inverted U curve and write the initial at the top of the U-curve, as illustrated by the **A** and **S** in Figure 8.2. This indicates that you expect motivation to be at the optimal level, and by referring to the vertical axis of the diagram, that performance will be at a maximum to the extent that it is influenced by motivation.

If you believe the audience's motivation is in the acceptable range, but not optimal, then place the initial for the given motivational dimension at an appropriate point on the curve. Similarly, if you believe the motivational level to be too low or too high, put the initial at an appropriate point on the curve to indicate your estimate of the magnitude of the motivational problem. Initials placed near the extreme left or right will indicate a severe problem.

There are two other factors to consider when graphing your results.

- If there is a high degree of variation in the audience on one of the characteristics, represent it by a line instead of a point on the graph (see **C** in Figure 8.3). The example in Figure 8.3 illustrates that the majority of the students are in the acceptable range of confidence, but there are also some who are too low and some who are too high.

- If a characteristic is multidimensional for a given group, then represent it as two different points or lines on the graph, and subscript each to differentiate them. For example, relevance could be too high in a situation such as a remedial class where the students have to earn a higher grade than is normal for them in

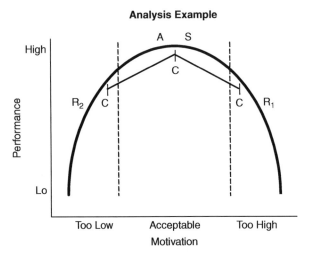

Figure 8.3. Sample Audience Analysis Graph.

order to both pass the class and raise their grade point average sufficiently to graduate. This makes the course highly relevant to their future and introduces an excessively high sense of relevance (R_1) because of their fears of what will happen if they do not achieve the higher grade. However, if these remedial students do not perceive the course to have any useful benefit in their lives, or do not find it interesting based on their past experience or current interests, their sense of personal relevance will be excessively low (R_2). Keep in mind that each of the four major categories of the ARCS model has subcategories, and an audience's motivation can be different for one subcategory than it is for another. When this is the case, use subscripts for each subcategory and provide an explanation of what each subscripted initial refers to.

4. For this item, record any *root* causes of the problem that you can identify. There may be several motivational problems resulting primarily from a single cause. For example, relevance might be too high due to fear of not graduating by not passing a course. This leads to high anxiety and could lead to lowered confidence among students who tend to withdraw instead of being energized by threats, and could also lead to hyperactive levels of attention (eyes darting around trying to see everything, unable to focus attention on specific items). Consequently, all of these motivational problems exist, but most are pushed to extremes by a debilitatingly high level of relevance due to the fear of not graduating.

5. Describe where motivational strategies can have the most effect. It may not be possible to do anything about the major problem, but the overall motivational climate can, perhaps, be improved to achieve a

more satisfactory level of motivation to learn. For example, you as a course developer or instructor cannot change the relevance issue in the preceding example; that is, the reality of a possible failure to graduate. But you can work on improving the other motivational conditions to counteract the effects of excessive stress. For example, you might be able to bolster confidence by incorporating a higher than normal number of motivational and instructional design strategies that help the students obtain concrete success experiences at frequent intervals. You might not be able to help everyone because it is possible that some people will not have the motivation or talent to succeed, but the goal is to help them maximize their own potential capabilities through careful design. Similarly, you may be able to help them improve their attention by removing distracters, adding more attention-focusing cues, and removing other environmental stressors.

> **Do not**, at this point, attempt to define the solutions (although it is perfectly appropriate to make notes of anything that occurs to you). The goal is to identify the areas in which you can have an effect on student motivation.

6. If you have any other information or observations regarding the audience that do not fit into the preceding sections, record them here. Always jot down any thoughts that occur to you about the audience and potential motivational tactics. These notes can be very helpful later when you get to the design steps.

Sample Worksheets

The corporate sample worksheet for Audience Analysis contains a good level of detail in describing the various motivational conditions of the audience. It is important to make your descriptions reasonably detailed. For example, if you simply say, "The audience will find the material to be boring," it does not reveal an understanding of why they might find it to be boring based on past experiences, boring content versus boring delivery, a lack of interest on the part of the learners rather than problems with the instruction itself, and so forth. Having a more in-depth analysis is tremendously helpful in identifying problems and generating motivational strategies.

Notice in this sample that the author states that the analysis will pertain to the entire group rather than specifying different subgroups. As you read the content for each part of the analysis, do you agree with this, or does it appear that there might be two subgroups that could be discussed separately? If so, the appropriate thing to do would be to have separate discussions and graphs for each subgroup Table 8.9.

The elementary school example also puts everyone into one group, and it seems to be appropriate in this case. Certainly there will be individual differences in motivation which the teacher can manage on a one-to-one

Table 8.9. Worksheet 3 Audience Analysis Example: Corporate Training Environment.

Corporate Example: Worksheet 3:
Audience Analysis

Target Audience

The following analysis is an estimated motivational profile for the entire target audience of project managers and process exponents.

Attention Readiness

Many of the learners' (see A1 on the graph) will most likely expect this course to be boring, because many of them have taken technology-based training in the past that was boring. They will expect it to have good production qualities in keeping with their company's overall image, but they will also expect the contents to be presented in a technical and linear manner. Also, the attitude of many is that they would rather just be given the tool to learn on their own, so they might have a tendency to not pay close attention to contents as they go through the lessons. However, there is also a group of newer employees who have positive expectations of technology (A2) and will be curious about this mode of training as well as being interested in the content.

Perceived Relevance

The learners' perceived relevance of the course will be high with respect to the relevance of the content to their job requirements (R1). However, the more experienced employees will expect the instruction itself to have a moderate to low level of relevance (R2). That is, in their experience, there is often a big gap between the way the material is taught and the way they actually have to apply it on the job.

Felt Confidence

The amount of confidence will vary depending on the learner's knowledge of the Systems Integration Process and the learner's computer navigation skills, but it will be moderate to low. Any project managers or process exponents who are not confident in their knowledge of the SI-Pro may be apprehensive about trying to learn ESE which is the new application to be used for managing SI-Pro projects. In addition, ESE serves as a single interface to four databases. Learners with a strong knowledge of computers and the SI-Pro will be more confident then learners with average knowledge. Similarly, the delivery mode for the course is new for some students and was not a successful mode for some of the others. Consequently, they may not feel sure they will be able to successfully complete a TBT course.

Satisfaction Potential

For many of the learners, there will be two attitudes in regard to satisfaction potential. On the one hand (S1), it will initially be moderate to low because of their attitudes about this training; that is, they would rather learn the tool on their own instead of having to work through a formal training package. However (S2), they will be pleased if they find that they do successfully learn this application because they know they will have to use it on the job. This second, more positive attitude, will be reflected in a more positive overall satisfaction expectation on the part of the newer employees who will expect to benefit from the training and to have a good experience (S2).

Graph of Audience Analysis

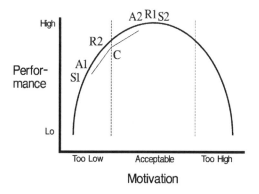

Characteristics of Major vs. Minor Problems

Some of the major problems include the learners' low attention readiness levels because they do not care about the training or feel it will be boring, and a low felt confidence because of fearfulness of a technology-based training course without any assistance from a live instructor.

Minor problems include low expected relevance of the way the material will be taught and a low satisfaction potential among some learners because of negative attitudes about this type of training and the time it will take to complete it.

Modification of Major Cause

Solutions to the attention readiness and relevance problems can be solved together by having interactive activities early in the training that are highly relevant and engaging. Confidence problems can also be solved by using instructional design tactics such as frequent exercises in which the challenge level is not too high and providing informative feedback. It will also help to use a sequencing strategy in which some interesting applications of the tool are taught early in the training. Solving these motivational problems will most likely remove any problems with satisfaction potential.

basis, but there are several issues that are characteristic for this age group with this type of task, especially with the extended deadlines and infrequent meetings. Notice also how the instructor identifies motivational character-istics of the group at the beginning of the process and also how they will change over time. In this case, the instructor had experience in teaching this course which gave her a basis for predicting the problems. The reason she wanted to learn about the ARCS model and apply it was not because of a lack of knowledge of the problems but because of a desire for guidance in solving them. But, even though she thought she knew the problems, by doing the systematic analysis represented in this worksheet she was able to refine her understanding and be more specific Table 8.10.

Table 8.10. Worksheet 3 Audience Analysis Example: Elementary School Gifted and Talented Class.

Elementary School Example: Worksheet 3

Audience Analysis

1. Does this analysis pertain to the whole class or one subgroup (use separate forms or identify with a label as indicated in instructions)? A, R, C, and S are being applied to the whole target population, because even though there are individual differences, there are some problems and characteristics that apply in a general way to just about everyone. These conclusions are based on interviews conducted with samples of students and their teachers.

2. Based on the information in Worksheets 1 and 2, how do you characterize the audience on each of the following dimensions (describe each and use the graph to portray the results)?

   Attention Readiness: Initially high. Students will be anxious to select a topic and will have many ideas on how they want to implement it into a project.

   Perceived Relevance: Low to moderate. The audience seemed to feel the only relevance was to complete an assigned task. They could not perceive a use in the future.

   Felt Confidence: High, but not excessively high. Those students who were satisfied with their independent project for this year had a high degree of confidence, and even those students who were not satisfied with the work they did this year seemed to have genuine confidence in their own abilities to do a good job in the future.

   Satisfaction Potential: Varied. Most students who finish the project successfully feel a sense of accomplishment at having succeeded at a task that required so much personal management and persistence (S_2). But, students who are not highly self-regulated tend to do a lot of last minute work and are usually disappointed with the results (S_3).

Over-motivation may be a problem because students will have so many ideas they may think they can accomplish more than is practical or possible. If their goals are too high, they may reach a level of frustration (S_1). Some of the students seem to display intrinsic satisfaction with the idea of completing the independent project (S_2), but others seemed to need an external motivator (S_3).

Graph of Audience Analysis

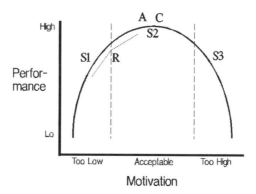

3. How would you characterize the major versus the minor problems?

   The major problem is to sustain their motivation over time. They are enthused at the beginning, but the necessity to maintain their independent effort over time becomes a challenge. They tend to lose interest which affects attention, and they do not see the relevance as being particularly high to their overall lives or future goals.

4. Does the major cause appear to be modifiable? If not, which other conditions might be influenced to improve overall motivation?

   Yes, the major causes are modifiable. Some direct interventions to help sustain attention and build relevance should be helpful. Also, some efforts to incorporate satisfaction tactics at key points during the project should also help.

5. Is there anything else that should be considered in the audience analysis?

   One more item is realistic goal setting. Sometimes the students want to do more than they can possibly accomplish. The special project instructor needs to help them set interesting but realistic goals.

Transition

Just as a chain needs all of its links, all of the steps in the motivational design process are important. However, the audience analysis step is, in some ways, the single most important one. It provides the foundation for all subsequent decisions. Another reason for its importance pertains to the variable nature of personal motivation. Motivational strategies that are successful at one point in time might not be effective at a later time. This can result from overuse, from changes in the lesson content, interference from outside the classroom, or any of many other causes. Therefore, it is helpful to continuously monitor learner motivation. The use of Worksheet 3 in this section has been in a context of trying to predict what the motivational profile of learners will be. After you actually have experience with them, you can use this same audience analysis process to monitor their motivational profile and to modify your teaching approaches. It is relatively easy for a teacher to do this, but it is not possible in most self-instructional settings because decisions about learner motivation have to be made when the materials are being written. This means that the "front-end" analysis of motivation is especially important. Some efforts have been made (Astleitner & Keller, 1995; Song and Keller, 2001), particularly in computer-based instruction, to more or less continuously monitor student motivation and to have the computer automatically select motivational tactics to match the learner's motivational state. For example, if a learner indicates at some point in a lesson that his or her confidence level is low, the computer would respond by introducing some tactics designed to improve confidence. Song and Keller's (2001) work on a prototype of such motivationally adaptive instruction in computer-based instruction was successful. However, this is an area that is wide open for active research.

Step 4: Analyze Existing Materials

Overview

The instructional materials you are currently using, or are considering for adoption, will have motivational features that may be relevant to the motivational needs of your audience. But, on the other hand, the current materials may have deficiencies that will be demotivational. These deficiencies can be of two types. First, the materials might have an absence of needed motivational tactics. If the materials are perceived by the students to be boring or irrelevant, then you will need to determine what type of tactics to add and where to add them. Second, they may contain either too many motivational elements or inappropriate activities, such as games or cartoons that are not suitable for your audience. In situations where the students are highly motivated to learn the content or to become prepared to take a test in as little time as possible, they will be annoyed by features such as games or simulations that are included only for motivational purposes but are not critical to learning the content. The purpose of this step is for you to analyze your current instructional material, which could be a unit, a module, an entire course, or whatever segment of instruction you wish to motivationally enhance, to identify their motivational strengths and deficiencies.

By examining the current materials to determine what motivational tactics currently exist in the course and where it does not have needed motivational tactics, you will make a list of the problems to be solved in the design steps of this process (Worksheet 4, Table 8.11). When reviewing the course, you would consider the characteristics of your audience as recorded in the previous worksheets.

Table 8.11. Motivational Design Worksheet 4.

ANALYZE EXISTING MATERIALS

Use this worksheet to record your analysis of an existing course or set of course materials or of a course you are evaluating in consideration for adopting. If you are using a checklist of some type, you may wish to attach the results of that analysis as supporting information, or substitute those results in their existing format in place of this worksheet.

11. Attention Getting and Sustaining Features
   - Positive Features
   - Problematic Areas

12. Relevance Generating Features
   - Positive Features
   - Problematic Areas

13. Confidence Generating Features
   - Positive Features
   - Problematic Areas

14. Satisfaction Generating Features
   - Positive Features
   - Problematic Areas

15. General Comments

Instructions for Worksheet 4 – Analyze Existing Materials

When you review existing course materials to evaluate their motivational properties, there are three questions to consider:

1. Are there motivational tactics in these materials that are *appropriate* for my audience?
2. Are there motivational tactics in these materials that are *inappropriate* for my audience?
3. Are there *deficiencies* in motivational tactics; that is, is there a lack of tactics in areas that were identified in the audience analysis, or areas needed to sustain motivation?

All of these questions depend on the motivational characteristics of the audience. Therefore, it is necessary to refer to the information in Worksheets 2

(Obtain Audience Information) and 3 (Analyze Audience) while reviewing the materials. A tactic that might be perfect for one audience could be unacceptable to a different audience. For example, a group of high achievers in mathematics might enjoy a competitive game in which people work in teams to solve math problems and get rewards based on speed and accuracy. But, in a class of students who are challenged by mathematics, this type of game could add to their feelings of helplessness and increase their fear of failure. This would make them too low on confidence and too high on relevance, which would put them into a dysfunctionally high level of stress.

To conduct this analysis, it is helpful to use a checklist of motivational tactics such as the "Motivational Tactics Checklist" or one of the others included in Chapter 11. Such lists can help you identify the features of the instruction that are motivational in addition to, or instead of, being primarily instructional in nature.

While reviewing the materials, you can record your observations on Worksheet 4 (Table 8.11). For each of the four categories of motivation, list the positive features and problems. Remember that problems can be of two types. The first type consists of deficiencies, which refers to areas in the materials where motivational enhancements are required to meet the needs of the audience. In these instances, describe the type of deficiency that exists. Later, in the design phase, you will list specific tactics that might be used to solve the problem. If you happen to think of specific tactics that might solve the problem, then go ahead and make note of them. You don't want to take the risk of losing a potentially valuable idea! Use this worksheet if you are reviewing an existing course or set of course materials, or for evaluating courses that you are considering purchasing. Consider each of the four categories with its subordinate categories of characteristics and process questions (see ARCS Model publications) in conducting your review.

The second type of problem consists of what we might call motivational excesses. This refers to the presence of motivational tactics that are inappropriate for the audience. It can result from having too many tactics whose primary purpose is motivational when the audience is already highly motivated, or by having inappropriate types of tactics. In your review, make note of these problems and indicate whether a given tactic should be removed or revised.

Notice that there is a final section that includes general comments. You may very well have observations about the overall motivational appeal of these materials that are not confined to one of the four categories. Record those comments in this final section or on a separate page.

CONSIDER THE AUDIENCE

The purpose of this analysis is to determine how motivating this course will be for its intended audience. Consequently, you should consider the results of Worksheets 2, and 3 when conducting this analysis.

Sample Worksheets

The analysis of the current state of the corporate course is quite detailed. Clearly, it is a well-designed course that probably was expensive to design and develop. However, in spite of this, there are numerous problems regarding its motivational appeal. The deficiencies that are identified here will be valuable input into the design steps that occur later! Overall, this is a very good example of this worksheet (Table 8.12).

The elementary school course is instructor-led and does not have the elaborate set of materials that support the corporate computer-based course. In the elementary course, the materials were designed to guide the students in the specific skills and tasks required to be successful and the author of this

Table 8.12. Worksheet 4 Current Materials Analysis Example: Corporate Training Environment.

Corporate Example: Worksheet 4:
Current Materials Analysis

Attention Getting and Sustaining Features

Positive Features
- **Course title:** The course title, *ESE is Easy*, is a simple but impressionable theme repeated throughout.
- **Use of graphics:** Custom-made graphics are used in the introductory module, demonstrating the functions and processes of ESE. In addition, simulation screens support instruction throughout the TBT, providing the learner with a visual representation of content as they proceed through the course.
- **Use of audio:** The course narrator is an experienced professional who maintains learner attention by way of changing his tone, etc.
- **Variations in formatting:** Each module is represented by a designated color, while each type of page has its own format (i.e., introductory, text with graphic, simulation, multiple choice, etc.)

Deficiencies or Problematic Areas
- **Course sequence:** Since ESE will be used during various phases of a project, the course is designed so that the learners will step through each module as if they are using ESE to perform tasks during a project. This is positive from a job application perspective, but it is a somewhat boring, linear approach. Early lessons do not create curiosity about what the results will be.
- **Use of scenarios for curiosity:** There is nothing at the beginning or during the lesson to engage the learner in some curiosity arousing scenarios.

Table 8.12 (continued)

- **Lack of variation:** Even though the production qualities are good, they lack innovative variation to sustain attention.

Relevance Generating Features

Positive Features
- **Introductory scenario:** The course begins with a brief scenario depicting a project manager who is stressed out because of a plethora of work and an inadequate means to complete project management tasks. Once the project manager says, "There has got to be a better way," the narrator jumps in with a pitch about ESE and how it can be used to complete such tasks.
- **Introductory module:** The first module provides the learner with a brief introduction to ESE functions and describes how the tool can be used to complete various tasks during a project's life cycle.
- **Module introductions:** At the beginning of each module, the learner sees the model depicted in the SI-Pro Project Playbook. Each module correlates to a phase in the project.

Deficiencies or Problematic Areas
- **Module lessons:** Although each module begins with a model and narration which relates ESE functions to the SI-Pro Project Playbook, the modules do not maintain this relevance throughout. Once the correlation is made, it is not mentioned again during instruction, and the connection is lost.
- **Job relevant scenarios and cases:** The instruction explains how ESE is used in relation to SI-Pro, but it lacks "real world" scenarios and cases to provide job relevant problem-solving activities.

Confidence Building Features

Positive Features
- **Slow and steady pace:** The narrator presents the material at a slow, but steady, pace. He pronounces words perfectly, so the material is easy to follow.
- **User controls navigation:** Users are given control over how quickly or slowly they want to proceed through the course by the navigation bar located at the bottom of the screen. Users may go back to unclear events, pause to take notes, or do virtually anything required to complete the course with ease.

Deficiencies or Problematic Areas
- **New delivery mode:** For many of the learners, technology-based training is a new vehicle for instruction. These learners, especially those who are also unsure of their computer skills, may feel uncomfortable or uneasy about being forced to complete training via CDROM.

Table 8.12 (continued)

- **Unclear description of expectations:** The introductory module gives a general description of the course objectives; however, the learner is left astray during the remainder of the course.
- **Lack of navigation directions:** The introductory module neglects to inform the learner of how to use the navigation bar. For those first-time users of TBTs, this could be quite distressing.

Satisfaction Producing Features

Positive Features
- **Checkpoint questions:** After each segment of instruction, or approximately every 10–15 events, the learner is presented with a couple of checkpoint questions before moving on to new material. This allows the learner to review the material just presented, in small segments, while it is still "fresh" in their thoughts.

Deficiencies or Problematic Areas
- **Ambiguous criteria for practice exercises:** The real key to learning how to use the ESE tool is by using it in practice exercises. The TBT does have practice exercises, but it does not provide clear criteria for successful completion of them. Once the learners step through each module's exercise, they have no way of checking to see if they truly completed the step correctly.

worksheet does a good job of describing them (Table 8.13). The deficiencies occur, for the most part, in regard to a lack of adequate activities and management strategies to maintain the interest of the students and to help them cope with procrastination which is difficult to avoid when there is so much time between meetings and assignment deadlines.

Table 8.13. Worksheet 4 Current Materials Analysis Example: Elementary School Gifted and Talented Class.

Elementary School Example: Worksheet 4
Current Materials Analysis

NOTE: There are very few materials associated directly with this unit. This is because most of the required skills have been taught previously in other units of work pertaining to learning and inquiry. The primary document for this unit is a welcoming letter that explains the

Table 8.13 (continued)

purpose of the project, the meeting schedule, and an overview of the timeline. The students also receive
- a timeline listing what assignments and meetings will occur each month,
- a document on which to record their topic and primary resources,
- an independent project contract to fill out,
- and a form on which to write their project outline (research sources, materials needed, and steps to complete the project).

The project facilitator may have handed supplemental materials out in previous years, but there is no mention of them in the documentation for this project.

1. Attention Getting and Sustaining Features
   a. Positive Features
   - The project overview and instructions are in the form of a letter to the students, which gives it a little more interest than a typical "technical" document.
   - The students receive a "tailor made" folder for their independent study project. It has interesting tidbits of information on it and places to record information that might be useful.
   - The theme for the year is presented to stimulate interest.
   b. Deficiencies or Problematic Areas
   - The documents are typed in capital letters and have no visual appeal.
   - There is little, apart from mentioning the year's theme, at the beginning to stimulate curiosity.

2. Relevance Generating Features
   a. Positive Features
   - Students are allowed to choose their own topics within the framework of the overall theme of the year.
   b. Deficiencies or Problematic Areas
   - The theme for the previous year was "The World in Crisis." It has the potential for giving students an opportunity to select personally relevant topics, but the theme itself is somewhat abstract and remote from the lives of children of these ages.

The students are not shown or encouraged to think about the relevance of the inquiry skills they are learning. It would be easy to relate this to the current emphasis in organizations on knowledge workers, knowledge acquisition, knowledge management, and digital literacy.

3. Confidence Building Features
   a. Positive Features
   - The unit handouts describe the objectives and all the due dates for various assignments and meetings.

Table 8.13 (continued)

- The unit builds on skills that the students have previously mastered.
- Students are allowed to work with a partner.
- Students get feedback on each assignment that they turn in.
- Students are encouraged to "take risks." Each student is told that if the project does not work out, he or she can "write about your attempts, what went wrong, and other approaches you might have tried."

b. Deficiencies or Problematic Areas
- Students are working "in the dark." They do not have examples of previous students' projects to examine.
- They do not get progress consultation and coaching from the project facilitator while they are working on specific assignments.

4. Satisfaction Producing Features
a. Positive Features
- Students are told how the projects will be graded.

b. Deficiencies or Problematic Areas
- Students are not given any examples or testimonies to illustrate the good feelings they might expect to experience when they finish the project.

5. General Comments (Include comments that pertain to the overall unit or documents.)
None

Summary

When you have finished this worksheet you will have a document which, when combined with the audience analysis, will help you create motivational objectives in the next step that is focused on the specific motivational needs of your audience. This document will greatly simplify the design process because you will know exactly where in the instructional materials to focus your motivational tactics and for what purposes.

Chapter 9 – Identifying Motivational Goals and Tactics

Forethoughts

Scene: Teachers' Lounge, late August

Jane: "Hey, Jim! How are you?"

Jim: "Doin' good. How're you?"

Jane: "Great! I want to ask you a question. I heard from Tom that you are going to make a dramatic change in your 11th grade English course. Something about fun and games?"

Jim, laughing: "Well, that's partly right. The games part. Maybe they will have fun, but my changes are based on educational psychology. And, it is *stories* and games, not fun and games."

Jane: "What do you mean by that?"

Jim: "Games are very popular now as entertainment, as you no doubt know from trying to keep your students from playing games on their handheld devices during class, but did you know that games have also become very popular in education?"

Jane: "I had heard something about that, but I thought it was just a fad."

Jim: "Maybe it is, but I think maybe it is more than that. Games that promote learning are sometimes called 'serious games.' Another thing that has become very popular is story-based learning. Have you heard about that?"

Jane: "Not since I read stories to my kids. Are you going to start reading stories to your English classes," Jane said quizzically?"

Jim: "Nope; that's not what I mean. It means that every unit of work is based on a scenario, or story, like a case study. Only, in this case, the students are given a problem and they have to figure out what knowledge and skills they need to know to be able to work on the problem, learn it, and apply it while working together collaboratively. "

Jane: "Hmmm. I understand your words, but I don't quite get it. Can you give me an example? "

J.M. Keller, *Motivational Design for Learning and Performance*,
DOI 10.1007/978-1-4419-1250-3_9, © Springer Science+Business Media, LLC 2010

Jim: "Sure! Let's say that I want my students to understand the characteristics of Ernest Hemmingway's writing, his contributions to litera- ture, and his influence on 20th century culture in the United States. This means that they have to learn some basic principles of literary criticism, decide which of his works to read, learn something about his life and the literary influences on his writing, learn about the cultural and political environment that influenced him, and also read how he influenced other people. I provide them with a list of potential resources, guidance, and links to some of the relevant materials that will help them get started as they figure out what research they need to do. I also act as a coach or facilitator to assist them. But, basically, they are a self-managed team and they are responsible for preparing a final product that addresses the central ques- tions. "

Jane: "That sounds like it could be exciting. But, how do games fit into that approach?"

Jim: "I am planning to put the story-centered modules into a game- focused setting. For example, I will set it up as an adventure game. It could be organized around a detective motif, an adventurer motif, or something like that. I will build in obstacles, 'wise men,' and other events that can help or hinder them. They will get points or prizes in the form of treasure chests full of relevant information when they achieve one of the milestones. I might even put one of the modules into a *Second Life* environment."

Jane: "Sounds like a whole lot of work to design these modules!"

Jim: "Yep. No doubt I will be working weekends, but I'm excited and I think it will be worth it."

Jane: "Good luck! Let me know how it goes."

Jim: "Sure will."

... to be continued

What do you think about Jim's ideas? Will they provide sufficient and appropriate motivation to these 11th graders? Are they feasible? Or, is he likely to encounter motivational challenges? What might the challenges be, if there are any?

Introduction

Now that you have collected information about the situation and the audience and analyzed the audience and the existing materials, it is time to set your goals for the project and to create the list of motivational tactics that you will use to enhance your instruction. Your goals will be expressed in the form of objectives that describe the things you want to achieve and how you will know if you've achieved it. They should not be confused with affective objectives that describe attitudes and feelings that you want the learners to experience in regard to the goals of the instruction. Those are written in the context of designing the instruction, not when preparing motivational enhancements. Your objectives in this context are project objectives; that is, they describe changes in attitudes toward your instruction that will overcome the motivational barriers that you described in the earlier worksheets. For this reason, it is important to review the earlier worksheets to pinpoint the motivational goals that you wish to achieve. Also, it is important to realize that there are two types of goals that can be specified. The first consists of motivational enhancements designed to overcome specific problems with the existing instruction. For example, if you can predict that students will be powered by a given type of content, then you will write an objective indicating that the students will not find this material to be boring. The second type of goal, or objective, referrers to those things you will do to sustain motivation. For example, let's say that you expect that your instruction will stimulate the students' curiosity and they will find it to be interesting. However, you realize that this initial interest will not persist for a long period of time unless you do some things to reinforce it. In this case, you might write an objective indicating that your goal is to maintain student curiosity throughout the lesson. This objective, like the one in the previous example, will provide a basis for designing appropriate motivational tactics. In addition to writing the objectives, it is helpful to describe how you will know if you have accomplished your objectives. In other words, you should describe the types of assessments, or measures, you will use to confirm your objectives.

After completing this step, it will be time to create your list of motivational tactics. There are two steps in this process. The first is to brainstorm as many ideas as you can think of that are related to the motivational issues in your situation. Again, it is important to be aware of the contents of your previous worksheets as you do this brainstorming. Specific guidance and instructions are provided later in the chapter, but it is worthwhile to mention a few basic principles in this introduction. The first is that no matter how successful some of your tactics are, they will not stay that way forever. One mistake made by designers and instructors is that when they find a tactic that is highly successful, they are elated and they tend to overuse it. Every new tactic has a novelty effect along with any deeper level of motivational connection that it makes. The mere fact that it is new can stimulate a certain amount of interest. But when the newness wears off, the tactic will continue to be motivating only if it has a substantial and meaningful connection with the students' motivational requirements. Even then, they will tire of it eventually because a desire for novelty is one aspect of the human motivation!

Another principle refers to your *cognitive orientation* as you create tactics. During the brainstorming phase it is helpful to be open minded and uncritical. The more tactics you can list, especially if you are working on a complex or lengthy course, the better it is to have a large number of tactics to consider. You can draw upon your own past experience, things you have observed other people do, or resource books with tips for teachers and trainers. Do not reject an idea even if it seems to be excessively complicated or expensive to develop. You might not be able to implement the entire strategy, but you might be able to think of a simpler way to accomplish the same goal.

The final principle to be mentioned here refers to the final selection of motivational tactics. When you reveal your list of tactics and make decisions about which ones to actually include, you must consider a variety of constraints. These are listed in the instructions for Worksheet 7, but briefly, they refer to the amount of time you will have to develop your tactics, their relevance to the course objectives, and the time required to implement them. Always remember that in an instructional environment, the role of the motivational tactics is to stimulate and sustain students' motivation to learn. Therefore, the motivational tactics are subordinate to the instructional tactics.

Given these considerations, let's find out what happened with Jim's curriculum innovations.

Scene: Faculty Lounge, December, holiday faculty luncheon.

Jane: "Hi, Jim! I haven't seen you hanging out in here for a long time."

Jim, a few pounds lighter and a few new wrinkles in his forehead: "That's because I haven't been hanging out here for a long time. How are you, Jane?"

Jane: "Great. You look like you have had some stress. Is everything okay?"

Jim: "Yeah, sure. I have just been working very hard. It's that new curriculum I have been developing."

Jane: "Really! I guess I am not surprised. But, how has it been going? I have been curious about it."

Jim: "It started off with a bang. The students really loved the first module. They threw themselves into it, learned a lot of basic skills on their own, assigned tasks to each other, worked cooperatively, and produced some fine products with creative twists."

Jane: "Wonderful! I wonder if I should try something like that in my Social Studies class. But, if it went so well, why are you feeling stressed?"

Jim: "I said it started off with a bang. The first module, which lasted four weeks, was terrific. Then, the second module which was also four weeks went well, too. There wasn't as much excitement as with the first module, but the students were still highly motivated by this engaging and novel approach to learning. But then, in the third four-week module, they started cooling off."

Jane: "How do you know? What did they say?"

Jim: "They asked me questions such as, 'Mr. Proctor, why can't you just teach us the basic things we need to know. It would be much faster. We are tired of having to do all that work to learn something that could be taught in a short time. Then, you could put us in groups to do the assignment. Also, the game part of it was fun, but it gets kind of lame after doing it twice.'"

Jane: "Interesting. I guess that no matter what you do, the students get tired of doing the same type of thing over and over again?

Jim: "Yes, I think that is true. Also, for most things in school, they just want to follow the quickest path to the goal. They enjoy a novel approach once in a while, but when the novelty wears off, they want efficiency!"

Jane: "Just like adults! Will you use this approach again?"

Jim: "Yes, definitely. I exhausted myself building these modules, but I will use them judiciously – probably not more than once a semester when this approach is the best way to accomplish my learning objectives."

Jane: "No wonder you look tired but also excited. Would you like to have a glass of this eggnog?"

Jim, gratefully: "With pleasure!"

In summary, Jim has learned the hard way, through experience, the things you are learning from your study of motivational design! Now, you are ready to prepare project objectives (Step 5) and your list of motivational tactics (Steps 6 and 7).

Step 5: List Objectives and Assessments

Overview

In this step, you will write your motivational design objectives and assessments. In your objectives, describe the motivational behaviors that you wish to observe in the learners. When writing objectives, the distinction between closing motivational gaps and maintaining motivation is important. In some settings, as indicated by the audience analysis, there will be specific motivational problems that require attention. For example, if your audience is not likely to see the relevance of a given topic of instruction, then you may want to write an objective that addresses this problem.

But, even if there aren't any major motivational problems, it will still be necessary to maintain motivation. That is, you will have to include sufficient motivational tactics to avoid having the instruction become boring, and you will have to use a challenge level that sustains the confidence of your learners. You should write motivational enhancement objectives for all of the major motivational problems that you expect to have. You do not need to write objectives for every area in which you simply have to sustain motivation that is already satisfactory at the beginning. But, if you expect it to become a challenge to sustain motivation, such as maintaining confidence or satisfaction, then it is beneficial to write objectives for these potential problems.

Writing objectives (Worksheet 5, Table 9.1) will help you focus your effort on key motivational tactics during the design process and provide a means for verifying whether you have accomplished your motivational goals. There will also be a long-range benefit for you. After you gain experience in identifying motivational problems, writing objectives, designing motivational solutions, and assessing the results, your own confidence and expertise will grow tremendously.

Table 9.1. Motivational Design Worksheet 5.

LIST OBJECTIVES AND ASSESSMENTS	
1. MOTIVATIONAL DESIGN OBJECTIVES: List objectives that describe any desired changes that you wish to bring about in the motivational profile (attitudes) of the learners. 1. 2. 3. 4. continue as necessary	**2. ASSESSMENTS:** Describe what measurements or observations you will use to determine whether you have accomplished your motivational objectives. 1. 2. 3. 4. continue as necessary

Instructions for Worksheet 5: List Objectives and Assessments

Worksheet 5 has two columns. In the first column, list as many objectives as possible that are appropriate for your project. In the second column, describe the assessment you will use for each objective.

Motivational Objectives

Write all objectives that describe specific changes in the motivational characteristics of the learners that you wish to achieve. Please note that these are your motivational design objectives and they describe the motivational outcomes that you wish to achieve with the learners. For example, if you are teaching an entry-level class in word processing to a group of students who lack confidence in their ability to use computers, one of your motivational objectives might be the following: "After 20 minutes of hands-on exercises during the first hour of class, the students will express a satisfactory or higher level of confidence when given a brief self-report measure by the instructor."

Your motivational objectives should conform to the same principles as learning objectives. They should state the behavior you expect to observe, any conditions that are important to mention, and the standards if it is possible to identify a criterion of acceptable performance. Keep in mind that these are project objectives, not learning objectives. If you are using a systematic process of instructional design, you will write learning objectives that describe knowledge, skill, attitudinal, or psychomotor behaviors that you expect the students to learn. In the present situation, your goal is to specify the ways in which students will reveal that they are motivated to learn, not what they have learned.

Assessments

Describe how you will determine whether you have accomplished your motivational objectives. The assessment might be implied or described above in your objective, but usually it helps to have a fuller description of the kinds of observations you will make, or the specific kinds of measurements you will use, and when you will use them. For example, the sample objective given above stated that, "students will express a satisfactory or higher level of confidence when given a brief self-report measure by the instructor, and that it will be given after the first 20 minutes of the exercise." This example has a far more complete description of the objective than most objectives, but even it could use a little more detail. The description of the assessment for this objective could state that "each student will be given two questions about his or her confidence level to answer on a slip of paper. One question will ask how confident they are about their overall ability to learn word processing, and the second question will ask them to describe anything that still bothers or worries them about using the computer. The teacher will summarize the results while the students are working on the next exercise."

Almost any type of measurement is acceptable if it is used carefully. You can use more subjective measures such as body language that indicates whether the class seems more relaxed and eager to learn, and either spontaneous or elicited verbal comments. You can also use more precise measures such as the amount of time the students stay on task before getting bored and acting distracted. The type of measurement to use depends on several factors including how much time you have, how important it is to be precise, and how to obtain the measurement without disrupting the normal instruction. If your only purpose is to satisfy your own opinion that there has been a satisfactory motivational improvement, then the more subjective measures are probably satisfactory. But, if you are doing a research study or have to prepare a report to convince other people that your motivational strategies have succeeded, then you will need to use measures that are more objective, or that can be demonstrated to have satisfactory levels of reliability and validity.

Examples

As in the previous chapter there are two examples of each worksheet. Both the corporate example (Table 9.2) and the elementary school example (Table 9.3) illustrate ways of composing objectives and assessment.

Table 9.2. Worksheet 5 Motivational Objectives and Assessments Example: Corporate Training Environment.

Corporate Example: Worksheet 5:
Objectives and Assessments

Motivational Design Objectives and Assessments

Overview: Since this is a self-directed course, it is not possible to observe learner motivation while taking the course. Motivational feedback will be collected in two ways: (1) During pilot tests of the lesson, learners will be observed and asked questions indicated in the following sections. (2) When the course is implemented, learners will fill out a post-course questionnaire.

	Motivational Design Objectives	Assessments
Attention	Learners will report that the training was mentally stimulating and kept their attention throughout.	Learners will be asked about the interestingness of each module and the whole course.
Relevance	Learners will report that they appreciate the relevance of this tool to their job and that the instruction provided activities that helped them see exactly how they would apply it in actual situations.	Learners will be asked about each of these relevance issues.

Confidence	Learners will (1) complete the course and practice exercises in a reasonable amount of time; (2) report a satisfactory level of confidence after completing the first module; and (3) continue to report satisfactory levels of confidence during the rest of the course.	Learners in the pilot group will be timed to see if they are able to complete the course in approximately 4 hours. Learners in the pilot group will be asked about confidence while they are working on the material. Learners will fill out a post-course questionnaire.
Satisfaction	Learners will be able to name the unique features of ESE and how it will benefit them in their daily tasks.	Upon completion of the course, learners in the pilot group will be asked to list some features of ESE and how this will assist them in projects. Similar questions will be asked in the post-course questionnaire.

As you read the objectives and assessment, critique them with regard to their appropriateness. The objectives are good, but do the assessments provide measures of exactly what the objectives specify? Consider the assessment for the relevance objective. It is rather vague as is the third assessment for confidence. As previously indicated, these embedded samples have mostly positive features, but there are some aspects of them that illustrate typical problems that you want to try to avoid!

In the elementary school example, the third assessment is appropriate for the objective. But, notice how the first two are strategies for helping the students achieve their associated objectives, not assessments of whether it was achieved. This is a problem that I encounter fairly often. Strategies, such as reviewing material with the student, will be listed later in Worksheets 6 and 7. At this point, the question is, "How will you know if the objective has been achieved?" The fourth assessment is probably on the right track, but it is incomplete.

Table 9.3. Worksheet 5 Motivational Objectives and Assessments Example: Elementary School Environment.

Elementary School Example: Worksheet 5
Objectives and Assessments

MOTIVATIONAL DESIGN OBJECTIVES List objectives that describe any desired changes that you wish to bring about in the motivational profile (attitudes) of the students.	ASSESSMENTS For each objective describe what measurement you will use to determine whether you have accomplished it.
1. Students will set realistic goals for their projects.	1. The resource teacher will review each project, discuss it with the student, and provide feedback to help the student achieve an appropriate goal.
2. Students will sustain their interest throughout the duration of the project.	2. The resource teacher will review progress reports, meet with students, and assess progress.
3. Students will develop an appreciation of the relevance to them of this project.	3. Students will describe ways in which the skills, if not the content, of their project relates to other kinds of inquiry that they will conduct in their lives, and the increasing importance of personal inquiry skills in today's and tomorrow's society.
4. Students will demonstrate their enthusiasm for the project by using varied forms of expression and media to communicate their ideas interestingly.	4. The resource teacher will review the reports.

Summary

Now that you have completed all of the analysis steps and the first design step which consists of writing objectives and assessment, you are ready to consider what tactics will help you accomplish those goals. The next step can be fun because you are encouraged to think of as many ways to accomplish your goals as you possibly can. Afterward, in Step 7, you will analyze your ideas to select the most feasible ones.

Step 6: List Potential Tactics

Overview

There are two steps in selecting tactics. The first, which is Step 6 (Worksheet 6, Table 9.4), is a preliminary selection phase in which you prepare a list of possible motivational tactics, or solutions, that pertain to the specific objectives and to the general situation as described in the worksheets for Steps 1 through 5. Then, in Step 7: Final Tactic Selection (Worksheet 7, Table 9.7), you will apply a set of

Table 9.4. Motivational Design Worksheet 6.

LIST POTENTIAL TACTICS Motivational tactics for consideration:			
	Begin- ning	During	End	Through- out
A				
R				
C				
S				

selection criteria to choose, combine, and organize the tactics that you will actually use.

Step 6 is called preliminary tactic selection because it is primarily a brainstorming phase. You list tactics that pertain to the objectives in Step 5, but also include tactics that will help sustain motivation throughout the course. Usually, there will be many possible tactics, ranging from simple to elaborate, that can be used for any motivational objective. The goal here is to list as many as possible without restricting your creative thought. Even if some of your ideas might not be feasible from a time or cost perspective they can lead to other ideas that may be useful, and sometimes you can find ways later to approximate the "ideal" even if you cannot fully implement the idea. In the next step you will review the possibilities and select the most appropriate ones.

Instructions for Worksheet 6: List Potential Tactics

The worksheet has a separate row for each of the four motivational categories and four columns to help you think about each part of the course. Consider things you can do at the *beginning* of the instruction to stimulate motivation, those things you can do *during* the module or course to sustain motivation, and those things to do at the *end* to bring closure and provide continuing motivation. Also consider things you might wish to do *throughout* the course for motivational maintenance. Such things as examples and case studies that continue throughout the course help sustain interest. They become a continuing "story" and the learner looks forward to the next "episode."

Good sources of ideas are provided by the results of Worksheet 4 (Analyze Existing Materials), the Motivational Tactics Checklist (Chapter 11), other checklists contained in Chapter 11, and professional books that contain ideas for motivating students and making your subject matter interesting. Be sure to keep your motivational objectives in mind, but at the same time, list as many ideas as possible. Even if you don't use all of the ideas in this motivational design project, you might use some of them in the next one. It is always helpful to build a catalog of motivational ideas. You will be surprised at how often you refer back to it.

Sample Worksheets

The corporate sample worksheet pertains to a face-to-face course so it contains many activities that can be implemented directly by the instructor. It also describes a variety of types of materials that can be used to add interest and relevance.

Many of the tactics listed in this worksheet are very good, but it is best to list concrete examples to support generalized ideas. For example, under "Attention," the designer said, "Ask a few open-ended questions that prompt interest." This is a good principle but it is not yet an actual strategy, or tactic. It would be best to include an example of one or two open-ended questions that could be used. The designer might have said, "Ask the class members to list three obstacles or frustrations that they experience with the current data management system, and then list and discuss them." Similarly in the first cell after Relevance, the designer could provide concrete examples of how to "match functions of ESE with actual project management uses," and what some of the ways are "that ESE is going to simplify their daily tasks and make life easier." This additional level of detail provides concrete ideas to include in the final design and the integration of motivational strategies with instruction Table 9.5.

Notice that there are some distinctive differences in the strategies listed in the elementary school sample worksheet compared to the corporate one. Some of the differences are due to the different age groups and the characteristics of a corporate versus elementary school setting, but others are the result of two different types of courses and differences in motivational challenges as identified in the analysis phases. The corporate course is a workshop in which the participants are together all day. In the elementary school setting the resource teacher has only a limited amount of time with the students in any given meeting and their meetings occur only at infrequent intervals. Thus, the elementary school teacher has numerous challenges related to sustaining the interest and effort of the students.

Table 9.5. Worksheet 6 Preliminary Design Example: Corporate Training Environment.

Corporate Example: Worksheet 6:
Preliminary Design

Brainstorming Phase Results

	Beginning	During	End
A	– Improve graphics in introductory module	– Convert the checkpoint questions into a game	– Provide learners will some open-ended questions that require them to think about ESE uses.
	– Ask a few open-ended questions that prompt interest – Show more pictures of plans, reports, etc. created in ESE	– Make the checkpoint questions challenging – Pose questions that can only be answered by proceeding to the next section – Provide some problematic situations regarding SI-Pro, and ask, "What would you do here?"	
R	– Match functions of ESE with actual project management uses – Inform learners of ways that ESE is going to simplify their daily tasks and make life easier – Show more completed	– Ask learners to list examples of how ESE functions can be used in various ways during a project – Provide more case scenarios in which	– Step through a summary of how ESE can be used for project management

	examples of documents created in ESE	learners have to engage in problem solving to determine how best to use the tool	
C	– Clearly define expectations of the learners for the course – State that in order to complete the course, learners will only need very basic computer skills – Stress *ESE* is easy and that they will enjoy the course	– Define module objectives at the beginning of each module – Ensure that checkpoint questions and practice exercises are challenging, but not too difficult – Improve feedback by providing specific exercise results for comparison – Relate the content and exercises back to the specific objectives that the learner is mastering	– Ensure final practice exercises are challenging , but attainable – Provide a summary of objectives the learner accomplished during the course
S	– Show the relationship between the ESE training and the ESE functions	– Provide clear, positive feedback for module practice exercises – Make sure practice exercises are not too simple or too hard	– Provide positive feedback for accomplishment – Review the learner's newly acquired skills

Regarding the strategies in the elementary school example, notice that the resource teacher has several creative ways of dealing with this challenge. She includes numerous concretely described strategies such as, "Select students from time to time to do 3 minute 'commercials' about their project. Help them develop their presentation so that it has an interesting 'grabber' at the beginning, and some kind of twist in it." These types of concretely stated strategies contribute to a strong and effective design document (Table 9.6).

Table 9.6. Worksheet 6 Preliminary Design Example: Elementary School Setting.

Elementary School Example: Worksheet 6:
Preliminary Design

• • •TACTICS• • •	Preliminary Ideas		
	Beginning	**During**	**End**
A	• (Capture Interest) Show visual representations by showing students examples of previous independent projects. • (Variability) Shift interaction between student–teacher to student–student. Students will be permitted to work as partners on projects. • (Inquiry) Give learners the opportunity to select topics, projects, and assignments that appeal to their curiosity. Students will be permitted to choose any subject they are interested in and develop a project in any medium they elect.	• (Capture Interest) Select students from time to time to do 3 minute "commercials" about their project. Help them develop their presentation so that it has an interesting "grabber" at the beginning, and some kind of twist in it. • (Variability). Use "mini newsletters," homemade postcards, and other devices to share information about project topics and progress.	• (Variability) Set up an award ceremony with students helping to create the motif and decorations.

R	• (Goal Focus) Ask students to relate the instruction to their own future goals. Studies show that children in the 10–12 age range who know what they want to be when they grow up and work toward that goal will have a high chance for success. We will discuss relating the project to future goals. • (Motive Matching) Choose a theme for the year that has more personal relevance to the concerns of children of these ages. They wonder what is going to become of them in the future, so a theme that asks them to project themselves into the future would allow them to select topics of current interest and relate them to the future.	• (Choice) Provide meaningful alternative methods for accomplishing a goal. Students have a tendency to think in terms of a written report for an independent study. I would like the students to work together in small groups after they have selected a topic and brainstorm various methods they could use to approach their study and project.	• (Goal Focus) Have students create a list of "award categories to be given in a final meeting. Let students vote to select winners.

| C | • (Learning Requirements) Incorporate clearly stated learning goals into instructional materials.
• (Learning Requirements) Provide self-evaluation tools which are based on clearly stated goals. A student self-evaluation form will be provided.
• (Expectations) Help students set realistic goals. When I meet with students to approve their independent project contracts, I hope to guide them into setting challenging but realistic goals. | • (Difficulty) Organize materials on an increasing level of difficulty. Students will begin researching at the knowledge and comprehension level. Students will perform tasks at various levels of Bloom's taxonomy. The final project will be at one of the higher levels of thinking, syntheses, or evaluation. | • (Self-Confidence) Help students understand that the pursuit of excellence does not mean that anything short of perfection is failure. One of the goals we have in our talented and gifted program is for the students to learn to be "risk takers." I feel an independent project is an excellent place for a student to attempt something "new or different" and not be afraid of failure. I would like to impress upon the students that if they try something for their project and it does not work, that is acceptable. What a pupil could do is write about his attempts, what went wrong, and other approaches he might have tried. |

S	• (Natural Consequences) Have a student who masters a task to help others. I intend to have "independent project sessions" where students can work on their projects and help each other.	• (Scheduling) Provide intermittent reinforcement. I am going to set up periodical meetings with students and working time to interact with the child on his/her study. • (Positive Outcomes) Give verbal praise. Give personal attention to students. Provide informative, helpful feedback. I will make every effort to incorporate these strategies into the independent project course.	• (Natural Consequences) Explain and demonstrate how the newly acquired inquiry skills can be used in many other contexts that will be beneficial in the future. • (Positive Outcomes) Have a set of inexpensive prizes (certificates, school logo items, for a variety of types of outcomes such as most interesting, most scientific. • (Equity). Follow the award ceremony with refreshments and some kind of a small commemoration of achievement for everyone who completed the project.

Transition

After you finish this worksheet, you will move to the next step (Worksheet 7) in which you will select and combine the most feasible ideas. Also, do not consider this worksheet of ideas to be a "closed book." As you continue working through the process, you may continue to have new ideas and to include them in your plan. We have found that once you begin to train your mind to generate ideas for motivational tactics, you will be more spontaneous and productive in thinking of still more possibilities.

Step 7: Select and Design Tactics

Overview

In this step you will choose the motivational strategies to actually incorporate into your instructional materials. All of the previous worksheets can help provide guidance for this step. In addition to the rich variety of potential strategies that you just created, you have information about the instructional environment (Worksheet 1), the audience (Worksheets 2 and 3), the current materials (Worksheet 4), and your motivational objectives (Worksheet 5). The instructions for Step 7 include criteria that will help you to select strategies that best meet the needs of the situation. In many instances, you do not "select" strategies. Instead, you will combine one or more strategies into a single strategy that meets several needs. In other words, as explained below, if you ask students to list challenges they face with their current system just as the corporate designer did in the attention phase of her preliminary design, this strategy can also be used to build relevance. Thus, a single strategy can have multiple motivational effects.

Another issue concerns the time it takes to implement motivational strategies. Instructors sometimes say that they never have enough time to cover all the content so they cannot take time to include motivational strategies. However, trying to "cover all the content" often results in the participants not being able to remember or apply any of it. Thus, it is far more rational and effective to weight the content, spending more time on the most important parts and moving rapidly over the less important, in order to have time for motivational and applied learning activities that result in performance improvement. This can be done if you have applied the motivational analysis process carefully, and have written good, clear objectives together with concrete strategies that are well integrated with the learning objectives. This way, you will be able to create a final set of tactics that do not require too much time and that improve students' motivation to learn.

Worksheet 7 (Table 9.7) does not contain separate categories for attention, relevance, confidence, and satisfaction. This is because you are encouraged to think in terms of the integration of motivational tactics. This will prepare you for Step 8 in which you will integrate motivational tactics into your instructional strategy. At the end of each tactic statement, include in parentheses an A, R, C, S, or a combination of abbreviations that indicate which ARCS components represented in that tactic.

Table 9.7. Motivational Design Worksheet 7.

SELECT AND DESIGN TACTICS
(At the end of each tactic, list the A, R, C, and S components represented by that tactic.)
Beginning:
During:
End:
Throughout:

Instructions for Worksheet 7: Select and Design Tactics

Now is when you consider feasibility and select the most appropriate motivational strategies based on several criteria. You should consider all of the following in making your final selections:

1. Amount of instructional time required. The motivational strategies should not take too much time in proportion to the instructional time.
2. Contribution to the instructional objectives. Motivational strategies, especially games, simulations, and analogies, can become more interesting than the instruction itself.
3. Reasonable amount of development time and cost. Some motivational ideas can be excellent, but simply require too much time or money to create relative to the life span of the course.
4. Compatibility with the learning styles of the audience.
5. Compatibility with the teaching styles of the instructors.
6. Judiciousness of use. Use as many motivational tactics as you believe to be necessary based on all your analyses, but no more. A cardinal principle of motivational design is:

Do not try to motivate learners who are already motivated!

If students are already highly motivated, then concentrate on effective instructional design and on the maintenance of motivation. Excessive "motivational" enhancements will slow them down and irritate them.

There is no quantitative way to apply these principles to the selection of strategies. The basic process is that for each motivational tactic, you consider whether it is acceptable in regard to each of these criteria. Sometimes you have to choose between criteria. A particular tactic might not be the least expensive approach, but if it appears to have a high probability for being appealing and effective, then you might want to use it anyway. When selecting tactics, also consider the information in Worksheets 1–4. Choose tactics that are appropriate for the delivery system and other conditions pertaining to the course, to the size and type of audience, and to the characteristics of the learners.

Synthesis is important in this final design step. Motivational solutions are seldom pure forms of attention, relevance, confidence, or satisfaction in their effects. When determining how to combine tactics into integrated solutions, consider all of the motivational tactics you listed in Worksheet 6 that you will consider for the *beginning* phase of the instruction. Can you combine any of the A-R-C-S tactics into a single solution? For example, you might be able to write an opening dialog or mini-case study that combines attention and relevance. You may even be able to include confidence by using an example of someone who has succeeded in mastering this material. After you have prepared your initial set of motivational tactics, do the same thing for the *throughout, during,* and *end* phases.

Table 9.8. Worksheet 7 Final Design Example: Corporate Training Environment.

Corporate Example: Worksheet 7:
Final Design

Selection and Synthesis Phase

Throughout
- Ask open-ended questions that require the learners to think and/or prompt their interest (A, R).
- Remind learner of how ESE is going to simplify their life by centralizing project management tasks (A, R).
- Make sure checkpoint questions are challenging, but attainable (C, S).
- Relate the content and exercises back to the objectives that the learners are mastering (R, C, S).

Beginning
- Show examples of actual project plans, WBSs, SOWs, etc., created using the ESE tool (C, R).
- Clearly define expectations of the learner with respect to the general course objectives (C).
- State that to successfully complete the course, the learner will only need basic computer knowledge (C).
- Provide clear navigation instructions (C).
- Show the relationship between the ESE training course and ESE functions that can be used during project management (R, S).
- Stress the *ESE is Easy* theme (S).
- Include an opening scenario that is interactive and based on a real problem in the workplace (A, R).

During
- Convert checkpoint questions into a game (A).
- Pose questions that can only be answered by proceeding to the next section of the course (A).
- Define module objectives at the beginning of each module (C, S).
- Improve feedback by providing specific exercise results for comparison (C, S).

End
- Step through a summary of how ESE can be used in various ways during project management (R, S).
- Provide a summary of objectives the learner accomplished during the training course (C, S).
- Provide positive feedback for course completion (S).
- Review a list of the learner's newly acquired skills (S).

Table 9.9. Worksheet 7 Final Design Example: Elementary School Setting.

Elementary Example: Worksheet 7:
Final Design

BEGINNING
- Use examples from everyday life, such as news reporters, authors, and people who want to know more about cars, home construction, or anything else. (A,R)
- Compare independent research to activities such as exploring and other types of adventures. (A)
- Shift interaction from student – teacher to student – student by permitting learners to work as partners on the project. (A,C)
- Ask what they do when they want to know more about something, even something like a new game or toy. (A)
- Show examples of previous projects. (A, C)
- Permit learners to choose any topic they wish (A, R) and develop it in any medium they wish. (C)
- Ask learners to relate the assignment to their future goals. (R)

DURING
- Provide meaningful alternative methods for accomplishing their goals: Let each small group brainstorm various methods they could use to approach their study and project. (R).
- Explain what experience and research has shown that makes it difficult to stay on schedule and finish this kind of independent work. (C)
- Help learners set challenging but realistic goals by reviewing their plans and providing detailed feedback. (C)
- Provide self-evaluation tools that they will use at designated intervals in the project. (C, S)
- Give detailed attention to each student/group at intervals during the project. (S)
- Give meaningful positive feedback every time an individual or group does something good, and give corrective, not critical feedback to help them improve. (S, C)

END
- Have some kind of presentation and special event, such as a "fair" to allow students to demonstrate their work and see what the others have done. Make it fun, not evaluative or competitive. Keep the grading activities separate from the event. (S)
- When doing these presentations, let the groups share any "tips for success" that they have come up with and that might help everyone as they go into the next phase of the project. (S)

Sample Worksheets

The two examples for Worksheet 7 illustrate some of the ways in which these templates can be modified to fit your situation. The corporate example (Table 9.8) includes the "Throughout" category which applies well in the intensive, face-to-face workshop. Also, this group of tactics is placed at the beginning of the list instead of at the end as in the template illustrations. Notice how each strategy has a notation at the end indicating its presumed motivational effects.

The elementary school example (Table 9.9) does not include the "Throughout" category. Due to the infrequent meetings of this group, there are differences in the tactics at each stage. Many of the tactics from the brainstorming phase have been combined and this has resulted in a somewhat short list of final strategies. Each of these strategies has an important function to serve in regard to the interest levels of the students.

Summary

Notice that there are not large numbers of strategies in the two examples. In keeping with one of the key principles of motivational design, only include motivational tactics that are related to the motivational requirements identified in the design process, that are necessary to sustain motivation, and that support the achievement of the learning goals.

These first seven worksheets contain a great deal of detail. They are most useful for three purposes: learning the motivational design process, designing motivational elements in a complete course or large sections of a course, and managing the motivational design process when using a team approach by providing documentation of each person's work. In many projects such as motivationally enhancing a lesson it is not necessary to apply the complete set of worksheets. A simplified approach is described in Chapter 11, but it is important to realize that in order to apply the simplified approach effectively you must be knowledgeable about the complete process including an understanding of the basic motivational concepts described in Chapters 4-7 and the audience analysis process.

You have now completed the primary elements of motivational design. Now it is time to consider your motivational tactics in relation to the whole course. The next step is to integrate motivational tactics into the instructional lesson plan. As you do this, you can expect to modify some of your tactics so they are smoothly combined with the learning activities.

10

Chapter 10 – Integrating Motivational and Instructional Strategies

Forethought

Here are two questions for you to consider

1. How is a lesson plan like a blueprint (Figure 10.1)?
2. What are the benefits of detailed lesson plans, or are they just more annoying documents to produce?

Introduction

Blueprints are an essential part of construction. A contractor would not even consider the possibility of initiating the con-

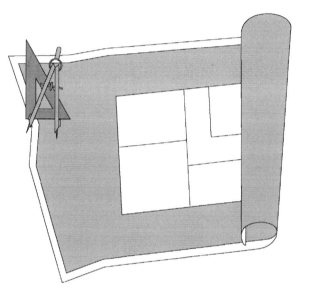

Figure 10.1. Developing the Blue Print.

struction of a building without first having a detailed set of blueprints. The blueprints describe the specific ways in which all of the components, or subsystems such as electrical, mechanical, plumbing, and framing, are designed and will be constructed and interconnected. Similarly, a lesson plan contains descriptions of the objectives, content, instructional tactics, and materials that are required to develop, or shall we say "construct," a lesson. However, unlike the contractor, it is not uncommon for instructors to list a few key ideas and launch into a lesson without having worked out all the details. Depending on the instructor's skill and experience, the lesson might be "okay," but it is unlikely to be as effective as it would be with detailed planning. A good set of lesson plans is especially beneficial when beginning to teach a new course instead of preparing a single lesson.

J.M. Keller, *Motivational Design for Learning and Performance*,
DOI 10.1007/978-1-4419-1250-3_10, © Springer Science+Business Media, LLC 2010

This chapter covers Step 8 of the motivational design process and it builds upon a fairly standard template for a lesson plan but adds sections dealing with motivation to allow you to systematically plan the ways in which you will integrate the tactics from Step 7 into your program of instruction. It also includes a detailed example of a lesson plan for the elementary school project that has been used in previous chapters. In the latter part of this chapter, there are descriptions of the activities to include in development, Step 9, and evaluation, Step 10.

Step 8: Integrate with Instructional Design

Overview

Now is the time to integrate motivational tactics with the primary elements of instruction (Keller, 2000 February) which include the learning objectives, content, and learning activities. The first suggestion is to review the unit of instruction that you are developing and list all of its elements. Then, you can review the motivational tactics that you selected and determine exactly where to locate them in the lesson. This will prepare you to make development decisions and prepare the materials as described in the next step.

If you are just learning to do motivational design you will find this step to be useful, because this is where everything comes together. However, if you have expertise in instructional design and already have some experience in designing the motivational aspects of your lessons, then you might consider this step to be somewhat redundant. Experienced designers will normally be thinking about the exact placement of their motivational tactics as they identify them.

This illustrates one of the differences between a novice and an expert. When you learn a new process or skill, it is normal to go through it step by step a few times until you learn all the elements. Then, as you develop expertise, you integrate your knowledge and skills and do not perform each step in isolation from the others. If you are a novice, you will find this worksheet helpful in preparing your final, integrated, plan. If you are more experienced, then this worksheet might still be useful for the following reasons:

First, it gives you a plan of work for complex instructional plans.

Second, it provides guidance if more than one person is working on the project.

Third, it provides a historical record and plan in case you leave the project and someone else has to begin where you left off.

And, fourth, if you have to work on this course again in the future after having worked on a variety of other projects, or taught other courses, it will save you a tremendous amount of time in re-orienting yourself to the structure and content of the course and the specific motivational enhancements.

Instructions for Worksheet 8 – Detailed Lesson Plan

This section contains a lesson plan template (Table 10.1) that has many features in common with a large variety of lesson plans used in schools and adult training settings. It also has some features that are unique, such as the distinctions between strategies and tactics and the inclusion of motivational planning. As with all the other templates in this book, this one can be modified to be compatible with your terminology and design preferences. The template itself is not what is important; the purpose represented by the template and the kinds of information included in it are the important elements!

Following are instructions for the various fields in Worksheet 8 (Table 10.1):

1. When you insert the course title, include course number, reference number, or any other information used by your organization to catalog the course.

Table 10.1. Motivational Design Worksheet 8.

DETAILED LESSON PLAN

1. Course Title:	4. Lesson Instructional Strategy Overview:
2. Module Title: Module Objective:	
	5. Lesson Motivational Strategy Overview
3. Lesson Title: Lesson Terminal Learning Objective (TLO):	a. Sustaining strategy:
	b. Enhancement strategy:

6. Sequenced Learning Objectives	7. Content Outline	8. Instructional Tactics	9. Motivational Tactics	10. Assessments	11 Materials	12. Time Rqd.

2. If your course has several distinct modules, or units, you can use this block to record the title and overall objective for it.

3. The information in this block should be very specific. It presents the terminal objective and title for the lesson you are developing.

4. Describe the instructional strategy. This refers to the overall instructional approach used in this lesson. It could be a straight-forward "instructivist" approach following the events of instruction (Gagné, Wager, Golas, & Keller, 2005) or some other version of a "content, example, practice" approach. Or, it could be a Socratic Dialog approach, experiential learning process, or any one of the many approaches available (Joyce & Weil, 1972).

5. Here, you will describe your overall motivational strategy. It is based on the audience motivational analysis in Worksheet 3. See Table 10.2 for an example of a motivational strategy description.

6. This column is used to list the learning objectives to be accomplished in the lesson. They should be in sequential order with the enabling objectives listed first and the terminal objective at the end. These provide the outline of your lesson.

7. The content column should contain more than just an outline of topics or key words. It is best to write actual paragraphs and descriptions of what will be included. This is actually the first step in development. After finishing your detailed lesson plan, it should be fairly easy to begin writing the actual content of your lesson.

Table 10.2. Worksheet 8 Detailed Lesson Plan: Elementary School Environment.

Elementary School Example: Worksheet 8:	
Detailed Lesson Plan	
Detailed Lesson Guide for: *Independent Study Project for 5th and 6th Graders*	
1. **Course Title:** English (5th and 6th grade special project)	4. **Overall Instructional Strategy:** The overall approach is coaching and guidance with tutorials, and interactive sessions are key points in the course.
2. **Module Title:** Independent Project Development	
Module Objective: Plan, conduct, and report the results of an independent research project.	5. Lesson Motivational Strategy Overview
	a. Sustaining strategy (for sustaining desired levels of motivation): The overall assignment will be motivating, but it will be necessary to use a variety of approaches to sustain interest and high levels of sharing results to keep them interested and productive.
3. **Lesson Title:** 1. Identifying a research topic and goal.	
Lesson Terminal Learning Objective (TLO): Learners will obtain background information in their areas of interest and define their topic and objective.	**b. Enhancement strategy (for areas of motivation that require improvement):** They will have trouble seeing the relevance of this assignment at some points, and their confidence will waver during the extended time required to complete all parts of the project.
NOTE: This is the first of three lessons pertaining to this independent project. Each lesson covers several class meetings spread at intervals during the year-long project. The second and third lessons are still in development.	Therefore, the overall enhancement strategy is to (1) organize assignments on an increasing level of difficulty from knowledge and comprehension at the beginning to synthesis and evaluation at the end, (2) provide encouragement at points in the process that you know to be challenging or discouraging, (3) provide timely, positive feedback at every interval that an assignment is completed.

Table 10.2 (continued)

Detailed Lesson Design Guide for: Independent Study Project for 5th and 6th Graders, continued.						
6. Sequenced Intermediate Learning Objectives (ILOs) and TLOs	**7. Content Outline**	**8. Instructional Tactics** (Activities, Self-Checks, Tests)	**9. Motivational Tactics (Activities)** Classify as A, R, C, S, or Combo	**10. Assessments**	**11. Materials**	**12. Time Rqd.**
1.1 Identify a general area of interest.	Purpose and approach of the independent research project. Examples of topics from past classes. Things to consider in selecting a topic of interest. Things to consider in selecting a partner or working independently on this project.	Ask a series of questions about how people obtain information about things they are interested in. Explain the project to them. Give examples of topics chosen by learners in previous classes. Then ask how they would go about identifying an area that they want to know more about. Allow them to select a partner if they wish. They can change their decisions at a later time.	Use examples from everyday life, such as news reporters, authors, and people who want to know more about cars, home construction, or anything else. (A,R) Compare independent research to activities such as exploring and other types of adventures. (A) Shift interaction from student–teacher to student–student by permitting learners to work as partners on the project. (A,C)	Review topics for adequate scope and feasibility.	OHP of previous topics.	Class 1: 20 min.
1.2 Gather background information in the area of interest.	Sources of information that are readily available to these learners. Guidelines on how to gather material. How much and what kinds of things they are to gather for this assignment.	Explain the guidelines for gathering information. Explain what kinds of materials they must gather before making their final topic selection.	Ask what they do when they want to know more about something, even something like a new game or toy. (A)	Review reference lists in terms of relevance to topic and adequacy.	OHP: Gathering information. Handout: Gathering information.	Class 1: 30 min.
1.3 Prepare a topic description.	Characteristics and elements of a topic description. Examples from a variety of different topic areas.	Explain what goes into a good topic statement. Present the examples. Have learners practice writing some descriptions. Have some of the individuals or groups share theirs with the rest of the class. Give feedback.	Show examples of previous projects (A, C) Permit learners to choose any topic they wish (A, R) and develop it in any medium they wish. (C) Ask learners to relate the assignment to their future goals. (R)	Review topic description for feasibility and relationship to future goals.	Examples of previous projects. Handout: Requiremen ts for a good goal statement.	Class 2: 20 min.
1.4 Prepare a research plan.	The elements of a good research plan including activities, methods, and deadlines.	Present the elements of a research plan. Ask how this is similar to the gathering information they already did (it's the same except more formal and focused). Ask them to prepare drafts of their research plans, which they will finish as homework.	Provide meaningful alternative methods for accomplishing their goals: Let each small group brainstorm various methods they could use to approach their study and project. (R).	Review research plan in terms of adequacy and feasibility.	Handout: Guidelines for, and example, of, a research plan.	Class 2: 30 min.
1.5 Accept individual responsibility for independent learning decisions and deadlines while working cooperatively with one or more partners.	How to plan for success, including such things as setting and keeping deadlines, anticipating obstacles and overcoming them, and communicating with your partner.	Ask the learners why they sometimes don't finish what they start, or they don't get things done on time. List the answers on the board. Ask them if they can think of things that will make this assignment more difficult to do on time than normal classroom assignments and homework. List the answers on the board. Have learners review their research plans to see if they want to modify deadlines and responsibilities to be more realistic.	Explain what experience and research has shown that makes it difficult to stay on schedule and finish this kind of independent work. (C) Help learners set challenging but realistic goals by reviewing their plans and providing detailed feedback. (C) Provide self-evaluation tools that they will use at designated intervals in the project. (C)		Handouts: Self-evaluation tools.	Class 3: 20 min.
1.6 Use varied forms of expression and media to communicate ideas.	How to prepare both written and oral reports of their topics and research plans.	Present guidelines for how to prepare and present their topic descriptions and research plans to the rest of the class.	Give detailed attention to each student/group at intervals during the project. (S) Give meaningful positive feedback every time an	Provide formative feedback on presentations		Class 3: 30 min (for plan-ning). Class 4:

Table 10.2 (continued)

Detailed Lesson Design Guide for: *Independent Study Project for 5th and 6th Graders, continued.*						
6. Sequenced Intermediate Learning Objectives (ILOs) and TLOs	7. Content Outline	8. Instructional Tactics (Activities, Self-Checks, Tests)	9. Motivational Tactics (Activities) Classify as A, R, C, S, or Combo	10. Assessments	11. Materials	12. Time Rqd.
		Provide examples. Review written reports and presentation outlines before they do their presentations.	individual or group does something good, and give corrective, not critical feedback to help them improve. (S, C) When doing these presentations, let the groups share any "tips for success" that they have come up with and that might help everyone as they go into the next phase of the project. (S)	Review final reports for grading.		50 min (for presen- tations).

8. What kinds of instructional tactics will you use? For each objective and content summary, describe the instructional techniques that will be used. These can include lectures (hopefully short! as in lecturettes), panel discussions, demonstrations, case analyses, video supplements such as "YouTube" clips, practice activities, self-check quizzes. It is better to include short descriptions that include specific detail such as sample instructions and questions than just a one or two word label that identifies the type of activity.

9. This column is where you list the motivational tactics associated with each part of the lesson. It is possible to have a motivational tactic without a corresponding instructional tactic and vice versa. And in still other cases, the two might be intertwined, which is why there is a dotted line between these two columns. For example, the lesson might begin with a motivational tactic such as a thought provoking question that precedes the first episode of instruction. In this case, leave the corresponding part of the instructional strategy column blank. Next, the lesson might contain a case analysis for the purpose of creating a sense of relevance while demonstrating how a given sales technique is conducted. In this case, the description of this activity would include both instructional and motivational components and could be contained in the instructional strategy column with a brief note in the motivational tactic column or written across the two columns.

10. It is important in the learning process for both the student and the instructor to know what is being accomplished. Assessments provide evidence as to what is being learned and can also indicate how the learners feel about the process. Attitudes are important in addition to achievement because they indicate whether the learners will continue to be interested in the topic and will give positive reports of the lesson to others. This assessment column is for you to list formative as well as summative assessments.

Include self-check quizzes, scoreable practice activities, peer review and feedback activities, and tests.

11. It is helpful, especially in classroom or workshop settings, to list the auxiliary materials that will be used in each part of the lesson. If all of the PowerPoint programs, handouts, web links, easel paper, marking pens, tape, and so forth are listed, it helps the instructor visualize how the material will be taught and to prepare a materials packing list.

12. Finally, it is useful to include time estimates for each part of the lesson. The biggest error made in this column is to underestimate how long each part of the lesson will take. People sometimes list estimates such as two minutes for opening comments, 25 minutes for a collaborative learning activity. Both of these are highly unrealistic. Even the shortest introduction will take five minutes, especially when you consider the time it takes for people to get oriented and "tuned in." Collaborative learning activities will seldom take less than 40 minutes and often longer. If you are transitioning from a "whole class" lecture or discussion into a collaborative activity, it takes time for people to reorganize into groups, for you to present the instructions, for people to get "tuned in" to the activity, for a momentum to build in the group, for them to reach a set of conclusions, for you to remind them of what is expected, for them to prepare their debriefing comments, and for each group to present its results. When you break a complex activity down into small component parts and estimate the time requirement for each part, you are more likely to arrive at a more realistic estimate.

You might find that this activity causes you to make further modifications to your list of motivational tactics. That is perfectly acceptable and normal as this whole design process includes frequent reconsideration of previous decisions. As you work though the process your understandings and ideas change as you gain new insights from your changing perspectives. This helps you generate more creative solutions than you could have produced at the beginning.

When finished, the reader should see that all of the items in Columns 6–10 are in chronological order. This will help the designer and instructor visualize the flow of the lesson.

Example of a Detailed Lesson Plan

The example contained in Table 10.2 builds on the elementary school example from previous chapters. It is highly detailed and illustrates how the motivational tactics are integrated with the other parts of the lesson. It also contains numerous examples of motivational tactics that can be adapted and used in other settings as well as this one.

Step 9: Select and Develop Materials

Overview

In the previous worksheets you identified types of motivational tactics to include and where to position them within the lesson. In this step, you will decide whether you can locate existing motivational materials to use or will have to create them. Some of your tactics will probably not require a search for materials because those tactics can be implemented directly, or require only a modification to the existing instructional content. But, if you want to use a game, simulation, or experiential learning activity and do not already have a specific one in mind, then you might want to search for existing material that can be adapted or, at least, can serve as a model for what you want to do.

This worksheet (Worksheet 9, Table 10.3), like many of the others, provides an outline for planning your work and recording the results of your decisions. The actual tactics will be developed and integrated into the lesson. If it would be helpful for documentation and future reference, then you could attach copies of the tactics to the worksheet.

Table 10.3. Motivational Design Worksheet 9.

SELECT AND/OR DEVELOP MATERIALS
Use this worksheet to
1. Identify existing motivational materials and activities, if any, that will meet your needs:
2. List instructional tactics or learning activities that support course objectives and can be modified to incorporate motivational tactics:
3. List the items (materials or tactics) that will have to be modified or created to meet the motivational requirements:
4. Prepare a development schedule (tasks, who, when, how long):
5. Describe each of the resulting motivational tactic products (characteristics, time required, special conditions):

Instructions for Worksheet 9 – Select and Develop Materials

1. After reviewing your motivation tactics, determine which ones might best be implemented with existing materials or modifications of existing materials. Publishers such as Pfeiffer, a division of Jossey-Bass, Inc., the American Society for Training and Development, and publishers that provide activity suggestions and packages of materials for teachers are good sources of ideas. If, for example, you want to include an experiential activity that involves the development of teamwork, there are many such activities in these

materials. You can get good ideas by looking through them and selecting an existing activity to use or adapt to your situation.

2.   There might be teaching or learning activities with motivational properties that are already in the lesson. These often require only minimal modification to achieve the motivational goal you have in mind. Identify these items in this section of the worksheet.
3.   In this section, list the motivational tactics that you will have to create, or the materials that will require substantial modification. These are the items that will normally require the greatest amount of development work.
4.   Prepare a schedule of work that includes a time schedule and list the tasks, who will do them, and any special resources that are required. As with previous worksheets and their tasks, prepare this development schedule only if it is useful in managing your work or the work of other people.
5.   In this last section, you might find it useful to list the specific "products" that will be developed. This can serve as a checklist that will help you monitor your work and the work of others.

Transition

As in all design processes, now that you have completed the blueprint and developed a draft of all your instructional and motivational materials, it is time to determine if and how you will evaluate them.

Step 10: Evaluation and Revision

Overview

In a formal instructional design project, it is part of the process to evaluate the materials in terms of how well the learners like them and how well they perform on achievement tests. Sometimes, a formal evaluation of how well the students like an activity might not be necessary. If you are developing a lesson that you will teach in a classroom, you will have a sense of how well the students like it and can informally discuss it with them. But, in most situations it is preferable to conduct a more formal evaluation, especially if someone else is going to teach the course. Also, if it is some type of independent learning material instead of classroom instruction or if you want concrete evidence of learners' reactions to the material, then a formal evaluation is called for.

Instructions for Worksheet 10 – Evaluation and Revision

This worksheet (Table 10.4) provides an outline for a very simple and efficient evaluation plan. It does not describe various types of research design or statistical methods. Its purpose is to provide support for you to

Table 10.4. Motivational Design Worksheet 10.

EVALUATION AND REVISION
Use this worksheet to summarize the results of your evaluation planning and implementation.
1. List the evaluation questions
2. List the evaluation materials to be used (for example, questionnaire, observation checklist)
3. Describe the evaluation plan (sample, where, when)
4. Summarize results
5. List revisions, if any

record the results of your evaluation planning and evaluation outcomes. For more detailed information about instructional evaluation, you may consult textbooks and articles on this topic.

1. Decide specifically what you want to know, and list your questions here. You might want to ask if they liked a particular activity, if they thought it was a good use of their time, if it was relevant to the content of the lesson, if they thought it was fun, and so forth. Try to cover the different components of motivation as defined in the ARCS model in addition to any other specific things you want to know. By asking their reactions to attention, relevance, confidence, and satisfaction, you will be able to compare.

2. List the data collection methods you will use. Among the things you can do are that you can write a questionnaire and give it to the learners, you can create a checklist and fill it out yourself as you observe their involvement or lack of involvement in a given activity, you can personally interview some of the learners if they trust you enough to give truthful answers, and you can record comments that you happen to overhear.

3. Decide whom you will collect information from and when you will collect it. Normally, everyone is included in the evaluation, but there might be situations in which you want to include only a few people. If you teach several classes of the same subject, you might want to do a more detailed evaluation in one of the classes. If it comes out positive, then you might want to spend less time on evaluation in the other classes. As in the previous worksheet, develop a plan that identifies who will be included in your evaluation, where and when the evaluation will occur, and who will do it.

4. After you obtain the learners' reactions, you can analyze the results and summarize them here. The methods you use to summarize the results will depend on what type of information you collected. It is not likely that you will get involved with statistical analysis unless you are doing a very formal project. Most likely, you will simply read the results, make a list of the points that are mentioned by the

learners, and how many times each point was made. If you use a questionnaire, then you can tally the number of each type of response to each item.

5. Finally, you can draw your conclusions from the results. If there are specific complaints, then you will need to identify which parts need to be revised. If there are suggestions for improvement, then you can summarize those. Try to record specific points that can lead to revisions. A comment such as, "the motivational example in Lesson 3 took too long," is more helpful than, "I didn't like Lesson 3." If there are a lot of very general statements as in the second example, then you might have to go back and collect additional information to find out why the students did not like Lesson 3.

Summary

It can be difficult to do formal evaluation, because it does require time and coordination to make it successful. However, even if your time is limited you can obtain useful feedback by having some people, preferably one or two students from your target audience, review the materials while they are still in draft form. These reviews can provide extremely useful feedback regarding clarity and interest of the materials. Then, when you implement the course, you can get informal feedback from the students if not formal questionnaire comments.

It is normal to have some things work well, and other things not work so well the first time you try them. Just remember that almost any instructor who has an assortment of successful motivational activities has been through a process of trial and revision. A formal evaluation can help you get through the development and improvement cycles more quickly.

This concludes your motivational planning. On the one hand, this process represents a large step forward from the purely intuitive or charismatic approaches that are most typical when dealing with learner motivation. Traditional approaches to motivation incorporate principles of positive reinforcement and frequently rely on one's intuitive talent and creativity (or lack thereof!) to make instruction interesting. The ARCS Model reduces the reliance on intuition by providing a process based on validated principles of human motivation. Yet, on the other hand, it is not totally an algorithmic or mechanistic process. Far from it. The process helps insure that you will have motivating instruction, and it illustrates how there are specific tactics that can be designed and implemented to achieve learner motivation. However, the process will still benefit from your knowledge and experience. The more you work systematically with motivational design, the more you will learn to integrate successful techniques from your own experience and from your observations of others.

Chapter 11 – Tools to Support Motivational Design

Forethought

Is the design process more like an orderly progression from beginning to end, as in the image of the stair steps on the left (Figure 11.1), or a somewhat unpredictable adventure as in the picture of the skier? What kinds of tools can help with this process?

Figure 11.1. Orderly Progression or Unpredictable Adventure?

Processes and the tools that support them can be orderly and predictable or little more than general guidelines. The first type can be classified as *algorithmic* and the second as *heuristic*. Algorithmic processes and tools lead predictably to solutions. These include such things as flowcharts or checklists that explain how to start or stop a piece of machinery, how to fill out an application for social security, how to compute the amount of interest you will pay over the lifetime of a loan, recipes for baking cakes, and instructions for how to replace a flat tire. These tools are like calculators in that they provide answers, or guaranteed solutions to problems if they are applied exactly as intended.

Other tools help you arrive at a solution but do not guarantee that you will achieve it. They are called heuristics and are more in the nature of "rules of thumb." They give you leverage in trying to solve your

J.M. Keller, *Motivational Design for Learning and Performance*, 267
DOI 10.1007/978-1-4419-1250-3_11, © Springer Science+Business Media, LLC 2010

problem, but still require an application of your own problem-solving skills to achieve it. Examples of these are checklists that provide lists of things to consider packing for overseas travel, other kinds of packing lists, symptoms to consider when trying to identify a problem with your health or automobile, or a strategy or set of tactics to use when designing instruction or learning how to troubleshoot an electrical circuit. The directional indicators in the skier illustration (Figure 11.1) are examples of heuristic tools. They give the skier a general sense of what direction to go, but there are too many uncontrollable factors in the skier's environment to be able to guarantee that the skier will arrive at an exact destination.

When attempting to understand human behavior and design solutions or interventions to improve peoples' knowledge, performance, or attitudes, there are far more heuristics available than algorithms. Landa (1974, 1976) conducted intensive studies of the development and use of algorithms in the context of instruction, learning, and performance and he demonstrated how powerful and effective they can be. However, they are limited in their scope of application. They are particularly effective in technical and procedural areas of learning and performance, but not as feasible in problem-solving or knowledge construction areas. The situation in motivational contexts is even more limited where most aspects of motivational design are heuristic. The tools described in this chapter can help you be more consistent in your efforts to analyze learner motivation and to design strategies, but it is still necessary for you to use judgment combined with experience and creativity to create effective motivational strategies. Your ability to produce innovative, creative solutions will grow with experience and effort. This is a learnable skill and it has been demonstrated by many people who have applied themselves to implementing the systematic motivational design process.

Introduction

This chapter contains six tools that support or supplement those that were presented in earlier chapters. Four of them provide heuristic support for specific kinds of motivational design tasks and two are measurement instruments that have been validated and used in many research studies.

- Simplified approach to motivational design
- Motivational Idea Worksheet
- Two motivational measurement instruments
  - The Course Interest Survey
  - The Instructional Materials Motivational Survey
- Motivational Tactics Checklist
- Motivational Delivery Checklist

Motivational Design Matrix: A Simplified Approach

Introduction

The complete ten-step motivational design process is useful for large-scale projects as when motivationally enhancing a whole course or workshop, or when multiple people are working on the project. The ten-step model provides guidance for in-depth analysis of the audience and environment and supports documentation of each step for coordination and future reference. However, many projects do not require this degree of support. When a teacher or instructional developer is designing a single lesson or module, a much simpler approach would be desirable.

Suzuki developed and validated a *simplified approach to motivational design* (Suzuki & Keller, 1996) that was subsequently applied in two distributed learning environments. The first was in the development of motivationally adaptive computer-based instruction (Song & Keller, 2001). The second application was in the development of student support methods for a multinational distance learning course (Visser, 1998).

In Sendai, Japan, a team of 25 teachers in eight subject areas at Sendai Daichi Junior High School had been developing computer application projects for several years as part of a demonstration project sponsored by the Japanese national government. During the final two years of the project (1994–1995) they were asked to incorporate systematic motivational design into their process. Suzuki (as reported in Suzuki & Keller, 1996) developed the simplified approach to motivational design because the full, ten-step model would require too much time for training and implementation. The goal of the simplified approach was to ensure that the teachers would identify key motivational characteristics in the learners, the content area to be taught, and the hardware or software to be used. The teachers then evaluated this information and prescribed tactics based on identified motivational problems. This process helped ensure that teachers avoided the inclusion of excessive numbers of tactics, or tactics derived from their own preferred areas of interest without regard to the characteristics of the students and the situation.

The resulting design process is represented in a matrix (Table 11.1). In the first row, the designer lists salient characteristics of the learners' overall motivation to learn. The second row contains the designer's judgments about how appealing the learning task will be to the learners. The third and fourth rows ask about learners' expected attitudes toward the medium of instruction and the instructional materials. Each of the entries in these rows has a "plus" or "minus" sign to indicate whether it is a positive or negative motivational characteristic. Based on the information in these first three rows, the motivational designers decide how much motivational support is required and what types of tactics to use. They refer to reference

Table 11.1. Report Matrix to Support Simplified Design Process (adapted from Suzuki & Keller, 1996).

Simplified Motivational Design for E-mail and Internet Class

DESIGN FACTORS	ARCS CATEGORIES			
	Attention	Relevance	Confidence	Satisfaction
Learner Characteristics -(Learners' attitudes toward)	-Elective course, High interest (+)	-High commitment (+)	-Low skills in typing and in conversational English (-)	-Newly formed group of students (-), but familiar teacher (+)
Learning Task -(Learners' attitudes toward)	-New, attractive, adventurous (+)	-High public interest to the Internet (+) -Useful in future (+) -Limited access to computers (-)	-Seems difficult (-) -First exposure (-)	-High applicability of acquired skills (+) -Exciting outcome (+)
Medium: -Computer in this lesson (Learners' attitudes toward)	-Interesting new use as a networking tool (+)	-Familiar as a stand-alone learning tool (+)	-Unstable network connection may make students worried (-)	-Immediate feedback (+)
Courseware Characteristics -(E-mail software)			-English usage (-)	-Participatory for every students (+)
Summary	-Minimal tactics required:	-Minimal tactics required:	-Necessary to build confidence:	-Minimal tactics required:
Motivational Tactics For The Lesson	-Emphasize opportunity to communicate worldwide -Demonstrate immediate transmission and response features	-Demonstrate how it extends one's communication capabilities	-Set objectives cumulatively from low to high -Team teaching with an Assistant English Teacher - Use translation software	-Provide reinforcement by receiving messages from "network pals"

lists of potential tactics (Keller & Burkman, 1993; Keller & Suzuki, 1988) and also create their own based on the identified needs.

In this example, the Internet teacher determined that confidence is the only real problem area, and he listed some specific things to deal with it. He also listed some specific tactics for the other categories, but they serve to maintain motivation instead of solving a specific problem. A benefit of his application of this process was that in his initial motivational plan, before he applied this process, this teacher had a much longer list of tactics that he thought would be exciting and motivational. After doing the analysis and applying various selection criteria that are listed in the training materials on motivational design, he realized that his list of tactics would be too time consuming and would actually distract from the students' intrinsic interest in the subject. By using the design process, he was able to simplify the motivational plan and target it to specific needs.

An evaluation of the effectiveness of this motivational design process (Suzuki & Keller, 1996) verified that the teachers were able to use the matrix accurately with only a few entries not being placed appropriately, and more than two-thirds felt that it definitely helped them produce a more effective motivational design. Some teachers had difficulties with the analysis phase, which indicates that this is a critical area to address in training people to use the process.

Application in Motivationally Adaptive Instruction

This simplified design process was modified and has been used in at least two subsequent projects. The first of these was the in the development of *motivationally adaptive computer-based instruction* and the second was in a distance learning course.

One of the challenges that has been mentioned in regard to conducting the formal motivational design process to guide the development of motivational strategies for the beginning of a course is that learner motivation changes over time and it can change in unpredictable ways. In a classroom or other instructor-led setting, an expert instructor can continuously gauge the audience's motivational condition and make adjustments as appropriate. But in self-directed learning environments, this type of continuous adjustment has not been a feature. Once the instruction has been designed and "packaged," everyone receives the same program, with the exception of limited branching and other learner control options. These options can have a positive effect on motivation, but they do not adequately reflect the range of motivational conditions that characterize learners at different points in time.

It would be possible to include a large number of motivational tactics to cover a broad range of motivational conditions, but this would most likely have a negative effect on motivation and performance. The reason is that when students are motivated to learn, they want to work on highly task-relevant activities. They do not want to be distracted with unnecessary motivational activities such as extrinsic games or "ice break-ers." For this reason, it would be beneficial to have computer or multimedia software that can sense a learner's motivation level and respond adaptively.

Song (Song, 1998; Song & Keller, 2001) designed and tested an approach to motivationally adaptive instruction. He built checkpoints into an instructional program on genetics for junior high school students. At predetermined points, students in the primary treatment group received a screen asking several questions about their motivational attitudes. Based on the responses, which were compared to actual performance levels, students would receive motivational tactics designed to improve attention, rele-vance, or confidence. He used a variation of the simplified ARCS model design process to create specifications for tactics to be included in the adaptive treatment. The resulting motivation and performance of this group was compared to a group that received highly efficient instruction with only a minimum of motivational tactics that centered primarily on acceptable screen layout. A second comparison group received the max-imum number of tactics; that is, they received all of the tactics that were in the pool of potential tactics for the treatment group.

The results indicated that both the adaptive and full-featured treat-ments were superior to the minimalist treatment. In most instances, the adaptive treatment was superior to the full-featured one. There were limitations on the types of computer features that could be used in this study (for example there was no sound), but a more sophisticated treatment and also one which was longer than one hour would, based on these results, be expected to show even stronger treatment effects.

This study was a pioneering effort. Earlier papers that discussed or tested adaptive motivational design (Astleitner & Keller, 1995; del Soldato & du Boulay, 1995) were extremely rigorous but more limited in their approach; that is, they tended to focus on a particular aspect of motivation such as persistence or confidence. Song's study is more holistic and provides a good foundation for a series of follow-up studies.

Application in Distance Learning

The second extension of the simplified design process is in distance learning (Visser, 1998) and provides another example of the multicultural nature of this work. Visser, who lived in France, conducted her research with a distance learning course offered by a university in the United Kingdom and was working under the sponsorship of her university in The Netherlands. Furthermore, her study included an adaptation of a motivational strategy developed and validated in an adult education setting in Mozambique (Visser & Keller, 1990).

There is no doubt that there are serious motivational challenges among distance learners especially when they are not able to avail themselves of social networks. This was the case in Visser's sample and would still be true in many parts of the world that rely on paper-based instructional materials that are distributed to distant learners with limited or no Internet support. The attrition rate alone can be viewed as an indication of motivational problems. Student comments often focus on their feelings of isolation, lack of feeling of making steady progress, and great doubts about being able to finish the course given their other responsibilities and time constraints.

Visser (Visser, 1998) used the simplified ARCS model design process to analyze the audience, conditions, and potential solutions in her situation. Her application of this process was contextualized in two ways. First was its restriction to a somewhat formal and traditional distance learning course, which uses textual material supplemented by an occasional audio or video-cassette. Based on her global assessment of the motivational problems in this situation, she concluded that it might be possible to have a positive effect on motivation by focusing on the student support system rather than on the instruction which could not be easily revised.

The second way in which her study was contextualized was its focus on the validation of a particular motivational strategy, although it does allow for the incorporation of multiple tactics. Her approach was to implement a program of "motivational messages" that would be sent to students according to two schedules. The first was a set of fixed points based on predictions of the moments during the course when these messages might have the strongest effect. These messages were the same for everyone. The second schedule consisted of personal messages sent to students when the tutor deemed it appropriate. These messages were in the form of greeting cards, which conveyed messages of encouragement, reminders, empathy, advice, and other appropriate content areas.

Design of the messages was based on the results of her application of the simplified design process. It was similar to the format created by Suzuki, but she modified the row headings to include specific aspects of the situation to consider in the analysis (Table 11.2). It is well known in distance education courses that learners typically are positive and excited at the beginning of a class but become disinterested and discouraged later in the course. Therefore, she made a distinction between her predictions of precourse attitudes (Row 1) and midterm attitudes (Row 2). Her responses to those issues came primarily from her experience in teaching this type of course with similar audiences. The third row (Table 11.2) predicts attitudes toward the course content and the fourth row asks about their attitudes toward the support they receive while taking the course. In the fifth row she summarized the results of the first four rows and used this as a basis for deciding what motivational tactics to use. Her matrix (L. Visser, 1998) provided an effective summary of major issues and decisions even though she went beyond the matrix in the final stages of designing strategies.

Table 11.2. Design Factor Categories from Visser (1998).

Simplified Design for a Distance Learning Course				
Analysis and Design Categories	**A**	**R**	**C**	**S**
1. Precourse attitudes of students toward distance learning				
2. Midterm attitudes toward distance learning				
3. Student reactions to this course content				
4. Characteristics of student support during the course				
5. Summary				
6. Examples of motivational tactics to be used in motivational messages				

To assess the effectiveness of this intervention, she compared retention rates in the experimental section of the course to three other sections that did not receive motivational messages and she did a qualitative review of student responses to various course evaluation and feedback instruments. She did not ask them directly about the effects of the motivational messages to avoid stimulating attitudes that may not have been present spontaneously in the students' minds. Improved retention rates of 70–80%, which are similar to conventional education, and student comments both offered clear support for the motivational messages.

Motivational Idea Worksheet

Introduction

The *Motivational Idea Worksheet* (Table 11.3) is even more simplified than the simplified design matrix. This worksheet can be quite helpful in generating an idea for a single motivational tactic to use in a specific place in a lesson, or simply recording an idea for a motivational tactic that has popped into your mind even if you don't yet know when or where you will use it. Have you ever been listening to a presentation at a conference, observed a colleague using a tactic that you thought was interesting, or read something that gave you an idea? If so, this one-page worksheet is useful for documenting your idea and cataloging it according to its motivational

Table 11.3. Motivational Idea Worksheet.

Motivational Idea	
Author _____	Date _____
This is the Setting Class/Topic: Audience: **Other Helpful Information** 　(For example, experience, attitude, 　gender, etc.):	**This is the Situation (Problem)**
Here is the Idea! Relevance	**Tactic Description**
__ R.1. Relate to Goals: How can I best meet my learner's goals? Do I know their goals? __ R.2. Match Interests: How and when can I link my instruction to the learning styles and personal interests of the learners? __ R.3. Tie to Experiences: How can I tie the instruction to the learner's experiences? **C**onfidence __ C.1. Success Expectations: How can I assist in building a positive expectation for success? __ C.2. Success Opportunities: How will the learning experience support or enhance the students' beliefs in their competence? __ C.3. Personal Responsibility: How will the learners clearly know their success is based on their efforts and abilities instead of luck or instructor bias? **S**atisfaction __ S.1. Intrinsic Satisfaction: How can I encourage and support their intrinsic enjoyment of the learning experience? __ S.2. Rewarding Outcomes: What will provide rewarding consequences to the learner's successes? __ S.3. Fair Treatment: How can I build learner perceptions of fair treatment?	*(continue on other side)* **Result:** (How well did this idea work? Are there any special things to do or watch out for?)

characteristics. I have students in my motivational classes and workshops fill these out as we go through the psychological foundations part of the program. Then, when we get to the design process they already have several ideas to incorporate.

Instructions

In the Setting block (Table 11.3) you can include information about the learning topic or class that this idea applies to. The motivational idea that you are recording or trying to create could apply to a foreign language vocabulary lesson, a Civil War history lesson, a math lesson on triangles, an instructional systems lesson on system theory and cybernetics, or anything else. Also in this block, you can make comments about the intended audience and other pertinent information such as whether your idea is for middle school children with math anxiety, the accelerated learners in your 3rd period German language class, or masters' students in instructional systems who have no background in training design or delivery.

In the Situation, or Problem, block you can briefly describe the situation in which the motivational problem is occurring or will be expected to occur. It could be such things as the introductory part of a lesson on the Pythagorean Theorem in your middle school math class, the orientation lecture when inexperienced masters students are in the same classroom with students who have had work experience related to the topic, creating interest among advanced German language students who will be bored with the standard lesson, or creating a positive learning climate with employees assigned to mandatory training.

The third step is to check the motivational goals that you are hoping to achieve. For example, the primary goals with the German language students might be A.2 (Stimulate an attitude of inquiry) and R.3 (Tie to experiences). Identifying your specific motivational goals helps keep you focused on the purpose of the motivational idea as you compose it. This step constitutes your motivational analysis of the audience and helps you focus your idea for a motivational tactic.

The largest block on the page is where you compose your motivational idea. You can describe it in any way you wish, but you might want to have one or two sentences that give an overview of what it is and then elaborate on it. Also, it is a good idea to record your thoughts about how you will implement it. Will you divide the class into groups? How many? Do you have a YouTube video that you will include? What is the URL? (Keep in mind that YouTube is not totally stable; sometimes a favorite video disappears.)

Finally, if you implement your strategy, you can record the results. New ideas are sometimes totally successful on the first try, but often they aren't, at least not in the way you intended! Your best strategies will probably result from modifications and fine-tuning or your original idea.

ARCS-Based Measures of Motivation

Introduction

There are two measurement tools that can be used in conjunction with the ARCS model. The first, called the *Course Interest Survey* (CIS), was designed to measure students' reactions to instructor-led instruction. The second, called the *Instructional Materials Motivation Survey* (IMMS), was designed to measure reactions to self-directed instructional materials. These are situation-specific self-report measures that can be used to estimate learners' motivational attitudes in the context of virtually any delivery system. The CIS can be used in face-to-face classroom instruction and in both synchronous and asynchronous online courses that are instructor facilitated. The IMMS can be used with print-based self-directed learning, computer-based instruction, or online courses that are primarily self-directed.

Furthermore, they were designed to be in correspondence with the theoretical foundation represented by the motivational concepts and theories comprising the ARCS Model (Keller, 1987a, 1987b). Because this theory incorporates psychological constructs from the empirical literature on human motivation (Keller, 1979, 1983, 1999), many of the items in the CIS and IMMS are similar in intent, but not in wording, to items in established measures of constructs such as need for achievement, locus of control, and self-efficacy, to mention three examples.

As situational instruments, the CIS and IMMS are not intended to measure students' generalized levels of motivation toward school learning; that is, they are not trait- or construct-type measures. The goal with these instruments was to be able to measure how motivated students are with respect to a particular course. The expectation is that these surveys can be used with undergraduate and graduate students, adults in non-collegiate settings, and with secondary students. They can also be used with younger students who have appropriate reading levels. With younger students or ones who are not sufficiently literate in English, some of the items may have to be read aloud and paraphrased to relate them to the classroom experiences of the audience.

Furthermore, both instruments can be adapted to fit specific situations. That is, the "default" wording of items contains phrases such as "this course," or "this lesson." These can be changed to fit the specific situation that is being assessed, such as "this lecture," "this computer-based instruction," or "this workshop." Also, it is possible to change the tense of the items to use them as a pretest. However, the substance of the items cannot be changed because they are based on specific attributes of motivation.

Development Process

A pool of potential items was developed for each instrument by reviewing motivational concepts, strategies, and measurement instruments. These items were reviewed by 10 graduate students who were well versed in the motivational literature. They responded to each item then discussed the items which seemed ambiguous, unrelated to the appropriate higher-order concept (i.e., attention, relevance, confidence, or satisfaction), or otherwise difficult to respond to.

The original item pool was reduced and revised with respect to obvious things that could be done to remove ambiguity, sharpen the key concept in each item, and eliminate "double barreled items by dividing them into two items or improving their focus." Then, the items were subjected to a further ambiguity check by responding in a contrived manner called "faking it." A different group of ten adults who were mostly graduate students but not experts in the area of motivational knowledge were told to respond twice to the instrument they received. The first time they were to "fake good," and the second time to "fake bad." That is, they were to assume they were taking a course which was highly motivating and to answer each item in a way that would indicate their highly positive motivation. Second, they were to assume that the course was totally unmotivating and to answer accordingly. This test revealed a few items that could "go either way," which meant they were poor discriminators. For example, both motivated and unmotivated students could agree with an item such as, "the instructor is very likeable." These items were then revised and retested or deleted.

Course Interest Survey

The CIS has 34 items with approximately equal numbers in each of the four ARCS categories. The items are listed (Table 11.4) in the order that they are normally administered. However, each of the four subscales can be used and scored independently. Also, the format of the survey can be modified to use Likert-type scales and electronic scoring methods. In this section, descriptions of the scoring procedure, reliability estimation, and original validity test are presented.

Scoring

The CIS can be scored for each of the four subscales or the total scale score (Table 11.5). The response scale ranges from 1 to 5 (see Table 11.4). This means that the minimum score on the 34 item survey is 34, and the maximum is 170 with a midpoint of 102. The minimums, maximums, and midpoints for each subscale vary because they do not all have the same number of items.

Table 11.4 The Course Interest Survey Instrument.

Instructions
Course Interest Survey

There are 34 statements in this questionnaire. Please think about each statement in relation to the class you have just taken and indicate how true it is. Give the answer that truly applies to you, and not what you would like to be true, or what you think others want to hear.

Think about each statement by itself and indicate how true it is. Do not be influenced by your answers to other statements.

Record your responses on the answer sheet that is provided and follow any additional instructions that may be provided in regard to the answer sheet that is being used with this survey.

Use the following values to indicate your response to each item.

  1 (or A) = Not true
  2 (or B) = Slightly true
  3 (or C) = Moderately true
  4 (or D) = Mostly true
  5 (or E) = Very true

1. The instructor knows how to make us feel enthusiastic about the subject matter of this course.
2. The things I am learning in this course will be useful to me.
3. I feel confident that I will do well in this course.
4. This class has very little in it that captures my attention.
5. The instructor makes the subject matter of this course seem important.
6. You have to be lucky to get good grades in this course.
7. I have to work too hard to succeed in this course.
8. I do NOT see how the content of this course relates to anything I already know.
9. Whether or not I succeed in this course is up to me.
10. The instructor creates suspense when building up to a point.
11. The subject matter of this course is just too difficult for me.
12. I feel that this course gives me a lot of satisfaction.
13. In this class, I try to set and achieve high standards of excellence.
14. I feel that the grades or other recognition I receive are fair compared to other students.
15. The students in this class seem curious about the subject matter.
16. I enjoy working for this course.
17. It is difficult to predict what grade the instructor will give my assignments.
18. I am pleased with the instructor's evaluations of my work compared to how well I think I have done.
19. I feel satisfied with what I am getting from this course.

Table 11.4 (continued)

20. The content of this course relates to my expectations and goals.
21. The instructor does unusual or surprising things that are interesting.
22. The students actively participate in this class.
23. To accomplish my goals, it is important that I do well in this course.
24. The instructor uses an interesting variety of teaching techniques.
25. I do NOT think I will benefit much from this course.
26. I often daydream while in this class.
27. As I am taking this class, I believe that I can succeed if I try hard enough.
28. The personal benefits of this course are clear to me.
29. My curiosity is often stimulated by the questions asked or the problems given on the subject matter in this class.
30. I find the challenge level in this course to be about right: neither too easy not too hard.
31. I feel rather disappointed with this course.
32. I feel that I get enough recognition of my work in this course by means of grades, comments, or other feedback.
33. The amount of work I have to do is appropriate for this type of course.
34. I get enough feedback to know how well I am doing.

Table 11.5. Scoring Guide for the Course Interest Survey (CIS).

Attention	Relevance	Confidence	Satisfaction
1	2	3	7 (reverse)
4 (reverse)	5	6 (reverse)	12
10	8 (reverse)	9	14
15	13	11 (reverse)	16
21	20	17 (reverse)	18
24	22	27	19
26 (reverse)	23	30	31 (reverse)
29	25 (reverse)	34	32
	28		33

An alternate scoring method is to find the average score for each subscale and the total scale instead of using sums. For each respondent, divide the total score on a given scale by the number of items in that scale. This converts the totals into a score ranging from 1 to 5 and makes it easier to compare performance on each of the subscales.

There are no norms for the survey. As it is a situation-specific measure there is no expectation of a normal distribution of responses.

Scores are determined by summing the responses for each subscale and the total scale. Please note that the items marked reverse (Table 11.5) are stated in a negative manner. The responses have to be reversed before they can be added into the response total. That is, for the reversed items, $5=1, 4=2, 3=3, 2=4$, and $1=5$.

CIS Internal Consistency (Reliability) Estimation

The survey was first administered to a class of 45 university undergraduates, and the internal consistency estimates were satisfactorily high. A pretest version was prepared by rewriting items in the future tense and was administered to an undergraduate class of 65 students. The internal consistency estimates were high, but further revisions were made to improve the instrument. The standard version of the survey was then administered to 200 undergraduates and graduate students in the School of Education at a university in the Southeast. Information was also obtained about the students' course grades and grade point averages. The internal consistency estimates, based on Cronbach's alpha, were satisfactory (Table 11.6).

Table 11.6. CIS Internal Consistency Estimates.

Scale	Reliability Estimate (Cronbach's α)
Attention	0.84
Relevance	0.84
Confidence	0.81
Satisfaction	0.88
Total scale	0.95

CIS Situational Validity

CIS scores from the 200 university undergraduates and graduates used for internal consistency estimation were correlated with their course grades and grade point averages (Table 11.7). All of the correlations with course grade are significant at or beyond the 0.05 level, and none of the correlations with grade point average are significant at the 0.05 level. This supports the validity of the CIS as a situation-specific measure of motivation, and not as a generalized motivation measure, or "construct" measure, for school learning.

Table 11.7. CIS Correlations with Course Grade and GPA.

ARCS Categories	Course Grade	GPA
Attention	0.19	0.01
Relevance	0.43	0.08
Confidence	0.51	0.01
Satisfaction	0.49	0.03
Total Scale	0.47	0.04

Instructional Materials Motivation Scale

The IMMS has 36 items. The Relevance and Confidence subscales both have 9 items, the Satisfaction subscale has 6, and the Attention subscale has 12. The primary reasons for the disproportionate numbers of items in the Attention and Satisfaction subscales are that boredom and lack of stimulation are such ubiquitous characteristics in instructional writing and the satisfaction category does not have as many points of connection to printed material as the others. As with the CIS, the IMMS items are listed (Table 11.8) in the order that they are normally administered, but each of the four subscales can be used and scored independently. Also, the format of the survey can be modified to use Likert-type scales and electronic scoring methods. In the remainder of this section as in the previous one, descriptions of the scoring procedure, reliability estimation, and original validity test are presented.

Scoring

As with the CIS, the IMMS survey can be scored for each of the four subscales or the total scale score (Table 11.9). The response scale ranges from 1 to 5 (see Table 11.8). This means that the minimum score on the 36 item survey is 36, and the maximum is 180 with a midpoint of 108. The minimums, maximums, and midpoints for each subscale vary because they do not all have the same number of items.

An alternate and preferable scoring method is to find the average score for each subscale and the total scale instead of using sums, especially with the unequal sizes of the subscales. For each respondent, divide the total score on a given scale by the number of items in that scale. This converts the totals into a score ranging from 1 to 5 and makes it easier to compare performance on each of the subscales.

One cannot designate a given score as high or low because there are no norms for the survey. Scores obtained at one point in time, as in a

Table 11.8. The Instructional Materials Motivation Survey Instrument.

Instructions
Instructional Materials Motivation Survey

There are 36 statements in this questionnaire. Please think about each statement in relation to the instructional materials you have just studied and indicate how true it is. Give the answer that truly applies to you, and not what you would like to be true, or what you think others want to hear.

Think about each statement by itself and indicate how true it is. Do not be influenced by your answers to other statements.

Record your responses on the answer sheet that is provided and follow any additional instructions that may be provided in regard to the answer sheet that is being used with this survey. Thank you.

Use the following values to indicate your response to each item.

1 (or A) = Not true
2 (or B) = Slightly true
3 (or C) = Moderately true
4 (or D) = Mostly true
5 (or E) = Very true

1. When I first looked at this lesson, I had the impression that it would be easy for me.
2. There was something interesting at the beginning of this lesson that got my attention.
3. This material was more difficult to understand than I would like for it to be.
4. After reading the introductory information, I felt confident that I knew what I was supposed to learn from this lesson.
5. Completing the exercises in this lesson gave me a satisfying feeling of accomplishment.
6. It is clear to me how the content of this material is related to things I already know.
7. Many of the pages had so much information that it was hard to pick out and remember the important points.
8. These materials are eye-catching.
9. There were stories, pictures, or examples that showed me how this material could be important to some people.
10. Completing this lesson successfully was important to me.
11. The quality of the writing helped to hold my attention.
12. This lesson is so abstract that it was hard to keep my attention on it.
13. As I worked on this lesson, I was confident that I could learn the content.

Table 11.8 (continued)

14. I enjoyed this lesson so much that I would like to know more about this topic.
15. The pages of this lesson look dry and unappealing.
16. The content of this material is relevant to my interests.
17. The way the information is arranged on the pages helped keep my attention.
18. There are explanations or examples of how people use the knowledge in this lesson.
19. The exercises in this lesson were too difficult.
20. This lesson has things that stimulated my curiosity.
21. I really enjoyed studying this lesson.
22. The amount of repetition in this lesson caused me to get bored sometimes.
23. The content and style of writing in this lesson convey the impression that its content is worth knowing.
24. I learned some things that were surprising or unexpected.
25. After working on this lesson for awhile, I was confident that I would be able to pass a test on it.
26. This lesson was not relevant to my needs because I already knew most of it.
27. The wording of feedback after the exercises, or of other comments in this lesson, helped me feel rewarded for my effort.
28. The variety of reading passages, exercises, illustrations, etc., helped keep my attention on the lesson.
29. The style of writing is boring.
30. I could relate the content of this lesson to things I have seen, done, or thought about in my own life.
31. There are so many words on each page that it is irritating.
32. It felt good to successfully complete this lesson.
33. The content of this lesson will be useful to me.
34. I could not really understand quite a bit of the material in this lesson.
35. The good organization of the content helped me be confident that I would learn this material.
36. It was a pleasure to work on such a well-designed lesson.

pretest, can be compared with subsequent scores or with the scores obtained by people in a comparison group. Also, as it is a situation-specific measure, there is no expectation of a normal distribution of responses.

Scores are determined by summing the responses for each subscale and the total scale. Please note that the items marked reverse (Table 11.9) are stated in a negative manner. The responses have to be reversed before they can be added into the response total. That is, for these items, $5 = 1$, $4 = 2$, $3 = 3$, $2 = 4$, and $1 = 5$.

Table 11.9. IMMS Scoring Guide.

Attention	Relevance	Confidence	Satisfaction
2	6	1	5
8	9	3 (reverse)	14
11	10	4	21
12 (reverse)	16	7 (reverse)	27
15 (reverse)	18	13	32
17	23	19 (reverse)	36
20	26 (reverse)	25	
22 (reverse)	30	34 (reverse)	
24	33	35	
28			
29 (reverse)			
31 (reverse)			

IMMS Internal Consistency (Reliability) Estimation

The survey was administered to a total of 90 undergraduate students in two undergraduate classes for preservice teachers at a large Southern university. The internal consistency estimates, based on Cronbach's alpha, were satisfactory (Table 11.10).

Table 11.10. IMMSS Reliability Estimates.

Scale	Reliability Estimate (Cronbach α)
Attention	.89
Relevance	.81
Confidence	.90
Satisfaction	.92
Total scale	.96

IMMS Validity Test

Validity was established by preparing two sets of instructional materials covering the concept of behavioral objectives. These materials were part of a unit of work on lesson planning and instructional design in an applied educational psychology course for undergraduate preservice teachers. Both lessons had the same objectives and technical content. The lesson for the control group was prepared according to standard principles of instructional design, but was not enhanced in any way to make it interesting. The experimental lesson was enhanced with strategies to stimulate curiosity, illustrate the practical relevance of the content, build confidence, and provide satisfying outcomes. Students were randomly assigned to the two lessons which they completed during one class period, including testing. Scores on the experimental lesson were significantly higher than for the control lesson.

Status of the CIS and IMMS

The four subscales of these instruments can have high intercorrelations which makes it difficult to apply traditional factor analysis to the instrument and obtain this factor structure (Huang, Huang, Diefes-Dux, & Imbrie, 2005). This is in part because these instruments are designed to measure situation-specific attitudes and not psychological constructs. Situational measure can vary tremendously, especially when respondents have a largely positive attitude toward the given situation. Thus, we used other methods to support the conceptual structure of the ARCS model and the associated measurement instruments. Naime-Diffenbach (1991) manipulated the motivational properties of a set of instructional materials by enhancing their attention and confidence characteristics and stripping all possible motivational aspects of their relevance and satisfaction characteristics. Her study confirmed that when there is actual variation in materials in accordance with these motivational dimensions the differences will be reflected in scores on the measurement instrument.

Small and Gluck (1994) used a magnitude scaling approach to estimate the perceived closeness or distance between different aspects of motivational attributes and their study confirmed the four component taxonomy of the ARCS theory. Recent studies such as Yu's (2008) study of motivation and usability in a self-paced online learning environment provide additional confirmation of the internal consistency and empirical validity of the IMMS.

Both of these instruments have been used in many studies and have even been translated into several other languages. It is beyond the scope of this book to include a summary of this literature, but its existence helps confirm the utility and validity of these instruments.

Motivational Tactics Checklist

Introduction

The *Motivational Tactics Checklist* (Table 11.11) was developed and revised over a period of several years. It focuses primarily but not exclusively on "print" types of material, whether on paper or on computer

Table 11.11. The Motivational Tactics Checklist.

ATTENTION

A1. PERCEPTUAL AROUSAL (CONCRETENESS).
What can I do to capture their interest?

1. Are there references to specific people rather than "mankind," "people," or other such abstractions?
2. Are general principles, ideas, or other abstractions illustrated with concrete examples or visualizations?
3. Are complex concepts or relationships among concepts made more concrete by use of metaphors or analogies?
4. Are items in a series presented in a list format rather than paragraph format?
5. Are step-by-step procedures or relationships among concepts made more concrete by use of flow charts, diagrams, cartoons, or other visual aids?

A2. INQUIRY AROUSAL (CURIOSITY AROUSAL)
How can I stimulate an attitude of inquiry?

1. Are topics introduced or developed problematically (i.e., is a sense of inquiry stimulated by presenting a problem which the new knowledge or skill will help solve)?
2. Is curiosity stimulated by provoking mental conflict (e.g., facts that contradict past experience; paradoxical examples; conflicting principles or facts; unexpected opinions)?
3. Is a sense of mystery evoked by describing unresolved problems which may or may not have a solution?
4. Are visuals used to stimulate curiosity or create mystery?

A3. VARIABILITY
How can I maintain their attention?

Variation in Format

1. Is white space used to separate blocks of information (text and/or illustrations)?
2. Are a variety of typefaces used to highlight titles, quotes, rules, key words, etc.?
3. Are there variations in layout (e.g., variation in spatial location of blocks of information)?
4. Are there variations in types of material (e.g., alternations between blocks of text, figures, tables, pictures)?

Table 11.11 (continued)

Variation in Style and Sequence
5. Is there variation in writing function (e.g., exposition, description, narration, persuasion)?
6. Is there variation in tone (e.g., serious, humorous, exhortation)?
7. Is there variation in the sequence of the elements of the instruction (e.g., is a sequence such as "introduction", "presentation", "example", "exercise" varied by changing the order, adding an extra exercise)?
8. Is there variation between content presentations and active response events (e.g., questions, problems, exercises, puzzles)?

RELEVANCE

R1. GOAL ORIENTATION
How can I relate the instruction to the learners' goals?

Present Worth
1. Is the immediate benefit of the instruction either stated or self-evident?
2. Are comments, anecdotes, or examples included that stress the intrinsic satisfactions of the subject of instruction?
3. Future Value
4. Are there statements describing what the learner will be able to do after finishing these instructional materials?
5. Are some of the examples and exercises clearly related to the knowledge and skills that the students will need in the future?
6. Is the student told how the successful accomplishment of this instruction is related to future goal accomplishment (e.g., is success in this instructional situation important for admission to subsequent courses, selection of a major area of study, or admission to advanced levels of study, salary increase, job retention, or promotion)?
7. Is the learner told how this instruction will improve his or her general life coping skills?
8. Is the learner encouraged to think of this instruction as contributing to the development of an intrinsically interesting area of study and development?

R2. MOTIVE MATCHING
How and when can I link my instruction to the learning styles and personal interests of the learners?

Basic Motive Stimulation
1. Is personal language used to make the learner feel that he or she is being talked to as a person?
2. Are examples (anecdotes, statistics, etc.) provided that illustrate achievement striving and accomplishment?

Table 11.11 (continued)

3. Are statements or examples included that illustrate the feelings associated with achievement?
4. Is the learner encouraged to visualize the process of achieving and succeeding, and the feelings associated with it?
5. Are exercises included that allow for personal goal setting, record keeping, and feedback?
6. Are exercises included that require cooperative work groups?
7. Are puzzles, games, or simulations included that stimulate problem solving, achievement-striving behavior?
8. In the exercises (including puzzles, games, and simulations), are the learners encouraged to compete against each other, themselves (i.e., trying to beat their own record), or against a standard?

Role Models

9. Are there anecdotes about noteworthy people in the area of study, the obstacles they faced, their accomplishments, and the consequences?
10. Are there examples, testimonials, etc., from persons who attained further goals after successfully completing the course of instruction.
11. Are there references to, or quotations from, people who can convincingly describe the benefits of the particular skill/knowledge area?

R3. FAMILIARITY

How can I tie the instruction to the learner's experiences?

Connection to Previous Experience

1. Are there explicit statements about how the instruction builds on the learner's existing skills or knowledge?
2. Are analogies or metaphors used to connect the present material to processes, concepts, skills, or concepts already familiar to the learner?

Options for Individualization

3. Is the learner given choices in the content of assignments (e.g., is the learner allowed to choose examples and topics of personal interest for at least some of the assignments)?
4. Is the learner given choices in the type of assignment (e.g., is the learner allowed to select from a variety of means to accomplish a given end)?

CONFIDENCE

C1. LEARNING REQUIREMENTS

How can I assist in building a positive expectation for success?

Table 11.11 (continued)

1. Are there clear statements, in terms of observable behaviors, of what is expected of the learners as evidence of successful learning? 2. Is there a means for learners to write their own learning goals or objectives?

C2. POSITIVE CONSEQUENCES

How will the learning experience support or enhance the students' beliefs in their competence?

Challenge Level

1. Is the content organized in a clear, easy to follow, sequence?
2. Are the tasks sequenced from simple to difficult within each segment of the materials?
3. Is the overall challenge level (reading level, examples, exercises) appropriate for this audience?

Anxiety Reduction

4. Are the materials free of "trick" or excessively difficult questions or exercises?
5. Are the exercises consistent with the objectives, content, and examples?
6. Are methods for self-evaluation, such as answers to exercises, provided?
7. Is confirmational feedback provided for acceptable responses, and corrective feedback provided for responses that do not meet criteria?

C3. PERSONAL RESPONSIBILITY

How will the learners clearly know their success is based on their efforts and abilities?

1. Are learners given choices in sequencing; i.e., how they can sequence their study of different parts of the material?
2. Are learners allowed to go at their own pace?
3. Are learners given choices among ways of demonstrating their competency (i.e., alternative methods of exercising and testing)?
4. Are learners given opportunities to create their own exercises or methods of demonstrating competency?
5. Are learners given choices over work environment; i.e., working in a room with other people, or away from other people?
6. Are learners given opportunities to record comments on how the materials could be improved or made more interesting?

SATISFACTION

S1. INTRINSIC REINFORCEMENT

How can I encourage and support their intrinsic enjoyment of the learning experience?

Table 11.11 (continued)

Positive Recognition
1. Is the student given opportunities to use a newly acquired skill in a realistic setting as soon as possible? 2. Is there verbal reinforcement of the learner's intrinsic pride in accomplishing a difficult task? 3. Do the materials include positive, enthusiastic comments which reflect positive feelings about goal accomplishment? 4. Are there opportunities for learners who have mastered a task to help others who have not yet done so? 5. Are there acknowledgements of any actions or characteristics that were necessary for success? 6. Are there acknowledgements of any risks or challenges that were met?
Continuing Motivation
7. Is information provided about areas of related interest? 8. Are learners asked, or informed, about how they might continue pursue to their interest in the topic? 9. Are the learners informed about new areas of application?
S2. EXTRINSIC REWARDS
What will provide rewarding consequences to the learner's successes?
1. Are games with scoring systems included to provide an extrinsic reward system for routine, boring tasks such as drill and practice? 2. Are extrinsic rewards used to reinforce intrinsically interesting tasks in an unexpected, non-controlling, manner? 3. Are public congratulations given for good performance? 4. Are students given personal attention while working to accomplish the task, or after successful task accomplishment? 5. Are reinforcements used frequently when learners are trying to master a new skill? 6. Are reinforcements used more intermittently as learners become more competent at a task? 7. Are threats and surveillance avoided as means of obtaining task performance? 8. Are certificates or "symbolic" rewards used to reward success in individual or intergroup competitions, or at the end of a course?
S3. EQUITY
How can I build learner perceptions of fair treatment?
1. Are the content and types of problems in the final exercises and posttests consistent with the knowledge, skills, and practice exercises in the materials? 2. Is the level of difficulty on final exercises and posttests consistent with preceding exercises?

displays. It can be used to guide critiques of existing materials or for ideas when creating new materials. However, this is a catalog of ideas and characteristics, not a set of recommendations for every instructional product. As with all other aspects of motivational design, this list should be used in conjunction with the results of an audience motivational analysis. The instructions provide some guidance about how this is done.

Instructions

When using this checklist in support of the design and development of new materials, it can be reviewed for ideas and display features that are appropriate based on the characteristics of your audience. In this case, you can develop an adaptation of this list to include only those items which you will use to guide design and as an evaluative checklist during developmental tryouts and pilot tests.

When you use this checklist for guidance when reviewing existing products, there are several decisions to be made. As you examine the materials and consider the tactics, you can decide whether the materials are satisfactory, have a deficiency, or have an excess of tactics.

Satisfactory: This means that the given tactic is contained in the materials and it is an appropriate tactic to use with your audience.

Deficiency: A deficiency is when you identify motivational tactics to add to the materials given the characteristics of your audience.

Excess: An excess occurs when the materials contain motivational tactics that are not appropriate for your audience. An example of excess would be the inclusion of a set of cartoons that are considered to be "babyish" for the intended audience or to detract from the seriousness of the content.

As before, you can develop a custom version of this checklist by deleting all the items that do not apply, adding supplemental tactic descriptions, and then using it as a design and evaluation aid.

Motivational Delivery Checklist

Introduction

The *Motivational Delivery Checklist* (Table 11.12) was developed by Bonnie H. Armstrong and me and is included here with the permission of both of us. This checklist is used to assess the motivational characteristics of instructor-led classes. It incorporates features that pertain to presentation style, learner focus, and other elements of good motivational and instructional design. In some cases, a less than satisfactory performance by the instructor could be the result of deficiencies in the material provided to the

Table 11.12. List of Items in the Motivational Delivery Checklist.

Motivational Delivery Checklist

DURING INTRODUCTORY SECTION:
Attention:
  1. Uses a "hook", e.g., poses a problem or paradox of interest to learners.
  2. Relates instruction to element of basic appeal to learners.
Relevance:
  3. If no previous learner analysis is available, uses an icebreaker to find out learner experiences, interests, and goals.
  4. Explains how the objectives relate to learners' jobs and professional roles.
  5. Explains how the objectives related to learners' personal interests, experiences, and goals.
Confidence
  6. Uses an icebreaker when learners don't know each other or come from diverse groups.
  7. If learners are likely to be nervous or uncomfortable, uses small group instead of individual responses in icebreaker or other warm-up activities.
  8. Uses "roadmaps" to help learners see what will occur during the class and what they will be doing.
  9. Explains class rules.
 	
THROUGHOUT CLASS:
Attention
10. Uses vigorous and energetic movements.
11. Uses language and facial expresses which convey enthusiasm.
12. Maintains equal eye contact among learners.
13. Varies tone of voice for inflection and to emphasize main points.
14. Maintains volume of voice loud enough for all to hear and varied enough to create interest.
15. Varies pace of speech.
16. Uses correct pronunciation and enunciates clearly.
Relevance
17. Allows time for learner comments and questions, either throughout the class or at specified periods.
18. Uses examples related to current or future jobs.
19. Uses language and terminology appropriate to learners and their context.
Confidence
20. Uses learners' names.
21. Uses active listening to respond to learner comments and questions.
22. Uses positive body language by looking friendly and using open gestures and postures.
23. Uses friendly facial expression to confirm or modify a learner's response, even if wrong.

Table 11.12 (continued)

24. After asking a question, pauses long enough to allow learners to respond.
25. Maintains eye contact with learner making a comment or asking a question.
26. Makes eye contact with every learner regularly.
27. Emphasizes any correct components of a learner's response or comment..
28. Uses neutral, task-oriented words to correct a learner.
29. Allows the learner who receives correction to ask questions for clarity and responds appropriately to such questions.
30. Provides feedback on performance promptly.

Satisfaction

31. Makes statements giving recognition and credit to learners as appropriate.
32. Makes statements attributing learner success to learner effort.
33. Provides tangible rewards at the end of boring, repetitive, lengthy, or complex sections, e.g., a refreshment break at the end of a lecture.
34. Makes comments, when deserved, acknowledging the effort and achievement of the class.

OCCASIONALLY:

Attention

35. Uses questions to pose problems or paradoxes.
36. Uses questions to elicit learner perspectives or feelings.
37. Incorporates learner experiences, interests, or goals into examples, stories, problems.
38. Uses audiovisual aids when appropriate.

Relevance

39. Incorporates specific learner experiences, interests, or goals into examples.

Confidence

40. Requests feedback and receives it with friendly facial expression and neutral appreciative words.
41. Asks for specifics and clarification if learners appear confused, angry, distressed, or uninterested.
42. Manages feedback by stopping it when necessary.
43. Accepts feedback without explaining or rationalizing.
44. Makes statements showing learners that he/she believes they can succeed and that he/she is there to help them.
45. Makes statements attributing learner success to learner effort.

AT THE END OF INSTRUCTION:

Satisfaction

46. Gives recognition of accomplishment at the end of instruction, e.g., verbal acknowledgement or a certificate of achievement.
47. Expresses appreciation, when earned, of learner effort and accomplishment.

instructor. The investigation into the cause of the problem would occur after the problem was noted on this worksheet. The instructor can also use this checklist in advance of instruction to assess the completeness of the instructional materials, and as an aid to rehearsal.

Instructions

You may use the checklist in any manner that serves your requirements. One approach is to check each item using the following notation:

E = Excellent   O = Omitted (But should be included)
S = Satisfactory   NA = Not Applicable
I = Needs Improvement

Summary

This chapter described several design aids, measurement instruments, and checklists that can assist you in motivational design and research activities. All of these items have been created in the context of application and proven to be useful, but they are only a small sampling of tools that people have developed, many of which I have been told about but have not seen. If you begin to implement the systematic process of motivational design, it is highly likely that you will create tools that benefit you as you do this work.

To me, the most important point to take from this chapter is that it underscores the fact that motivational design can be a systematic process. You can follow the process described in this book and use various tools and methods of documentation to constantly improve your skills with practice!

12

Chapter 12 – Motivational Design Research and Development

Forethoughts

What is one thing that

- a study in the Netherlands on the usability of instruction manuals for seniors (Loorbach, Karreman, & Steehouder, 2007),

- the design of pharmaceutical instruction in Bangkok (Wongwiwatthananukit & Popovich, 2000),

- research in South Korea on cross-cultural differences in online learning (Lim, 2004),

- a training program in North Ireland to promote breast feeding (Stockdale et al., 2008),

- research in Greece on a usability evaluation method (Zaharias & Poylymenakou, 2009),

- a review in Germany of challenges to maintaining persistence in online learning (Deimann & Keller, 2006), and

- action research on undergraduate motivation at Florida State University (Kim & Keller, 2008)

have in common?

Figure 12.1. The Quest for Motivational Solutions!

Introduction

The purpose of this chapter is to illustrate some of the diverse settings (Figure 12.1) in which research and development incorporating the ARCS model is occurring and that were not described in earlier parts of

J.M. Keller, *Motivational Design for Learning and Performance*,   297
DOI 10.1007/978-1-4419-1250-3_12, © Springer Science+Business Media, LLC 2010

this book. Diversity in this context refers to several things including geography, organizations, and school subjects. Researchers and practitioners in virtually every part of the world are incorporating the ARCS model in their research and practices, as illustrated in part by the above list of studies. This illustrates the cross-cultural adaptability of the model and its perceived applicability to many areas of research and practice. The model is also incorporated in every type of organization in which instruction occurs. These include universities, elementary through secondary schools, health care organizations, corporations, military organizations, and government agencies. With regard to subject matter areas, it has been incorporated in mathematics education, second language learning, social studies, midwifery education, pharmaceutical training, nuclear power operations training, sales training, school administrator training, management training, nutrition education, and basically any subject that is taught in formal education settings. And, it has been studied in conjunction with instructional delivery system design including self-directed computer-based instruction, online instruction, distance learning, mobile learning, and, of course, classroom instruction. In these various areas, purposes range from disciplined inquiry into learner motivation and learning to motivational design support for instructional development.

Even though the model has this broad range of applicability, there are several key challenges to be considered with regard to motivational design inquiry. One of them concerns inquiry design. Some of the research consists of traditional experimental or quasi-experimental designs but it also includes correlational studies, qualitative studies, action research, and what might be called evaluation or validation studies whose aim is to confirm whether a given strategy or intervention is effective. The overarching purpose of motivational design research is to understand how to improve people's motivation to learn by means of learning environment design and guidance for learner self-motivation. This implies that motivational design research and development will occur most often in applied settings where there can be multiple obstacles such as

- minimal control over the application environment;
- challenges in isolating and manipulating specific variables;
- unintended influences due to novelty effects;
- challenges in diagnosing the motivational profiles of learners and tracking their changes over time; and
- difficulties in measuring results in ways that render clear inferences and conclusions.

These problems are characteristic of many areas of inquiry and are discussed in books on research design, but there are three issues that are somewhat specific to motivational design research. They relate to problems with diagnosing motivational gaps, designing tactics for different types of delivery systems, and methods of delivering motivational tactics.

With respect to the first issue, "identifying motivational gaps," there are three types to consider. The first is whether there are gaps that impede the participant's desire to learn the given material. The second is whether there are motivational deficiencies in the instructional materials or other aspects of the learning environment such as student support by means of motivational feedback and guidance. Methods for assessing and analyzing these kinds of gaps were presented in detail in Chapter 8. The third type of gap is whether the learner wants to close the gap. A student might be aware that he or she has low confidence or can't perceive any relevance for the instructional content. But, does this imply a desire to close the gap? Maybe not. The learner's attitude might be that he simply doesn't care about the situation. This problem relates back to one of the basic assumptions underlying motivational design mentioned in Chapter 1 which is that you cannot control another person's motivation. If he or she truly does not want to learn, there is little if anything you can do about it. However, you might be able to inspire the student to learn by doing such things as using persuasive techniques, expressing your own enthusiasm for the subject, or challenging the learner to a competition. The point is that knowing that there are specific motivational problems with a student's feelings of curiosity, perceptions of relevance, and expectancies for success does not automatically imply that strategies aimed at changing those attitudes will result in a motivated student. First, the student must be inspired to want to learn the subject and then helpful strategies can be implemented.

Even though there is substantial guidance for audience motivational analysis in Chapter 8, the process is most easily applied in face-to-face settings where learners can be analyzed prior to the beginning of the instructional event and their motivational states can be monitored during the event. But, as will be mentioned in reference to some of the studies and projects described in this chapter, it is very challenging to find ways to assess learner motivation in distributed learning settings, especially with regard to monitoring changes in motivation levels.

The second issue under consideration here has to do with the design of strategies for different delivery systems. Strategies that are both accessible and effective in a face-to-face setting may not be possible in distributed learning systems. An instructor can design motivational tactics to be integrated with the instructional materials and also provide motivational support when appropriate. For example, an instructor in a classroom can engage the students in a motivating simulation and can also recognize when a student has done something noteworthy. The instructor can then provide immediate motivational feedback, or when the student is having difficulties the instructor can offer encouragement. But, the detection of motivational problems followed by meaningful feedback cannot be done in distributed systems in a spontaneous manner, at least not at the present time. It might become more possible with the development of highly sophisticated intelligent tutoring systems, but at present we are limited to more primitive methods. Even so, innovative techniques for embedding motivational tactics in distributed learning settings and for providing motivational support to students have been created and tested. They will be mentioned while describing the various studies and projects in this chapter.

The third issue is related to the previous one but its focus is on problems regarding the delivery of motivational strategies in distributed learning settings. A technique that has been used for years in computer-based instruction is to embed motivational or corrective feedback that is presented automatically following the learner's response in a self-check exercise or test. A typical message following a correct answer is something like "Congratulations! You are doing a great job." This type of feedback can be useful but it is severely limited and does not address numerous motivational challenges regarding learner problems with confidence, perceived relevance, persistence, etc. The studies included in this chapter contain numerous innovative strategies for motivational feedback and guidance including the use of animated pedagogical agents, motivational and volitional e-mail messages, and motivationally adaptive computer programs.

In summary, a key point in this book is that the ARCS model provides a problem-solving approach to motivational design. Strategies, or tactics, are created after identifying what the specific motivational problems or goals are in a given situation. However, there are many challenges in applying this process due to the difficulty of identifying what the motivational problems are and then finding a way to deliver the appropriate motivational tactics to learners at an appropriate time. To be most effective, the tactics must be delivered when the learner is experiencing a motivational challenge related to the specific tactic. If students in an instructional design class are instructed to conduct a job/task analysis which they have never done before and it will be a week before they actually begin working on this assignment, it does little good to tell them to expect to feel somewhat challenged but that they should just keep trying. The time to give them motivational encouragement is when they are working on the task and are experiencing those feelings. Then, they will be receptive to expressions of empathy and suggestions for how to cope with the task.

This chapter describes several areas of motivational design research and application related to these problems, especially in the context of online, computer-based, and other forms of technology-assisted and distributed instruction.

Motivational Messages

A motivational strategy that has general application to many of the instructional delivery settings described in this chapter is called "the clinical use of motivational messages." This concept was formalized by Jan Visser (Visser & Keller, 1990) and it refers to the creation and delivery of motivational messages based on a continuous diagnosis of the audience's motivation. This process was developed while Visser taught a face-to-face course in a setting where there were severe motivational challenges. The class had 15 participants who were government workers and was conducted on-site where they were employed. The motivational challenges were due to the conditions in Mozambique at that time in which there was constant danger from rebellious groups and an extremely low standard of living, lack of tangible incentives for taking the course, the difficulty level of the course, and difficulties in being responsive to the demands of the course while maintaining adequate job performance. Due to these many motivational challenges, Visser developed the concept of motivational messages as a means of providing motivational support on a "just-in-time" basis. He applied the ARCS systematic motivational design process to diagnose specific learner motivation problems that could be categorized as to their motivational challenge (attention, relevance, etc.) and then created tactics designed to alleviate the problems and stimulate motivated effort toward accomplishing the goals. Some messages were in the form of a mini-poster or a letter, but most were produced in the form of a greeting card with an attention getting cover and the appropriate message on the inside. This format is illustrated in an example in Chapter 6 (Figure 6.2) of a group message that was designed with the intention of alleviating anxiety. Another example (Figure 12.2) illustrates an individual message designed to give positive feedback and encouragement to a student who has been struggling to perform well.

Figure 12.2. Example of an Individualized Motivational Message to Boost Confidence.

The content of the messages was determined by weekly analyses of up to five types of data, depending on what was available at a given time. The first was derived from the instructor's familiarity with motivational stress points based on his experience in teaching the class. For example, the topic of the class was the systematic process of instructional design and students frequently found the instructional analysis task to be difficult. They would find it depressing to receive a great deal of critical feedback after their first draft of a product was formatively evaluated and so he prepared a message to help them view this feedback objectively and productively. He also collected weekly, anonymous self-reports in which the students would describe the three greatest motivational challenges and three most positive motivational influences they experienced during the previous week and also describe areas of the course, if any, in most urgent need of attention to improve it. The other three sources of information consisted of spontaneous comments by the students about their progress or lack thereof, comments solicited by the facilitator, and evaluation of the students' progress.

Based on an analysis of these inputs in keeping with the dimensions of the ARCS model, Visser prepared one or more of three types of messages. The first type addressed motivational challenges that the instructor could predict based on past experience in teaching the class (Figure 6.2). Messages in the second category were in response to unexpected events that affected the motivational level of the entire class. And, the third type consisted of messages to individual students whom Visser learnt were having personal motivational challenges. For example, one of his students who was fluent in English (Portuguese is the national language in Mozambique) got danger-ously far behind in her course assignments because the workload at her regular job had increased dramatically and excessively. Visser (1990) sent her a signed note saying, ''A Special Message for You. When you are required to do the impossible, you can't be but frustrated. However, be satisfied with the try you gave it, and with what you know could have been the quality of your work had you been given proper conditions'' (p. 384). The student later reported to him that it brought tears to her eyes.

He prepared the messages and distributed them in between class meetings by leaving them without comment at the students' work stations or handing them off in person. This was because he wanted the messages to appear to be a normal part of the course, and he did not want to call special attention to them. They became known as "little notes" among the students.

By using a variety of measures (Visser, 1990; Visser & Keller, 1990) it was clear that the messages had a positive effect on the attitudes and persistence of the students. The retention rate was higher than normal, as were the students' persistent efforts and achievement.

Critical attributes of the clinical use of motivational messages were that they were based on data indicating the specific types of motivational challenges faced by the students, they dealt explicitly with motivational aspects of the learners' feelings and attitudes, and they were timely. This is in contrast to motivational tactics that are embedded into instructional materials and delivery as an integral part of a course which are not targeted to specific motivational gaps in the participants' attitudes toward learning.

Instructor-Facilitated Learning Environments

Instructor-facilitated environments can be face-to-face, online, or blended. Most of the examples of motivational strategies in the earlier parts of this book, including the two examples of the motivational design worksheets (Chapters 8, 9 and 10), pertained to classroom settings, so this chapter will focus on examples in technology-assisted settings whether in a blended course or online class.

Blended learning settings generally refer to classroom courses augmented by online components. The flexibility of a blended course can result in a more continuous set of learning activities during the week in contrast to the fixed schedule of weekly meetings. More than 100 activities are described by Bonk and Zhang (2008) for use in online and blended courses and teachers can take advantage of online features such as discussion forums, chat rooms, and collaborative group tasks. For example, in the learner motivation course that I teach on campus, I will sometimes have a discussion forum related to one or more of the assigned readings, especially when I want **everyone** in the class to express their thoughts, which typically does not happen in class in which a few students become the predictable active responders. Last semester during the first week of class, I opened two forums. In the first I asked them to describe the concept of motivation as they experienced it; that is, what constitutes "motivation" in their lives. In the second forum I asked them to discuss the role of design in motivation planning; that is, can one design for motivation or is that too mechanical; should one expect motivation to be the result of spontaneous activities? Every student is required to post a response by a certain date but they cannot see each other's responses until I release them on that date. This way, each student must consider the question and formulate a response without "borrowing" from what other students have said. This led to a rich discussion with a high rate of responding. I also have them do collaborative homework assignments and then present the results in class. This worked particularly well with assignments such as the one we did on factors related to intrinsic motivation and extrinsic reinforcement and how they influence each other. Each group had a list of concepts to investigate. Their task was to prepare definitions, negative examples (How to Kill the Joy of Learning), and positive examples (How to Sustain the Joy of Learning). During class time, each group was responsible for teaching and facilitating a discussion of their concepts.

These strategies are easy to implement, manageable with respect to time demands on the instructor, and productive, especially when the instructor participates in the discussions. However, this is due, at least in part, to the relatively small size of the class which seldom exceeds 20 participants. In large classes the situation is different in kind, not just size. In these classes it might not be feasible to use all of the same learning strategies that could be used in the smaller class, but the problem of student support becomes more salient. In extremely large classes it might not be feasible to the instructor to know every student or to be aware of specific motivational problems being faced by one or more students, but the online part of the course can help with this.

One way to provide student motivational support could be by means of e-mails using the motivational message (Visser & Keller, 1990) method. This approach was tested in two different blended studies (Keller, Deimann, & Liu, 2005; Kim & Keller, 2008) within an undergraduate archeology class. In these studies, messages were prepared to provide motivational support at times in the course when, based on past experience, predictable motivational problems were expected to occur based on observations of the course instructor and her teaching assistant. In this study volitional messages were also included to encourage beneficial self-regulatory behaviors. The messages were created and distributed by the researchers not the instructor, and diagnostic question-naires were sent to the students each week to identify their motivational attitudes and amount of effort as measured by time spent studying. Also, in these classes, in contrast to the one taught by Visser, the instructors had a general knowledge of the motivational challenges faced by the students, but had no regular interactions with the students outside of class and did not have personal knowledge of events in the students' lives that might adversely affect their studies. Also, the instructors were not able to personally distribute messages outside of class. The messages were distributed via e-mail which might be considered to be somewhat impersonal compared to the paper messages that were delivered personally in the Visser study. However, con-sidering the widespread use of this medium, it was assumed that students might view such messages as a type of personal attention (Woods, 2002).

In the first study (Keller, Deimann, & Liu, 2005), a set of motivational messages based on characteristic motivational problems as identified by the instructor and her graduate teaching assistant was prepared. One group, the bundled group, received the entire set of messages, called "study tips," at the beginning of a 4-week test period so that the students could have the benefit of all messages at once. A second group, the distributed group, received the study tips at intervals following a model of motivation and volition (Keller, 2008b) in which one progresses from motivational tactics to commitment tactics to volitional support (self-regulation) tactics. The control group received placebo messages, which were also sent to the other groups, to control for the novelty effects that might result from general knowledge that an experiment was underway. The results indicated that there was a positive influence on con-fidence and achievement, but not the other components of motivation. These results offered limited support for the potential benefits of attempting to support student motivation by means of e-mail-based motivational messages.

In the second study (Kim & Keller, 2008) which occurred during the 4 weeks subsequent to the first study, *personalized motivational messages* were developed. An effort was made to make the messages more personal based on diagnostic questionnaires, sending the messages individually to students with their names in the salutation and customizing the motivational message content for the individual students.

After the second major test in the class, students were asked, among other things, whether they were satisfied with the results of their test. Prior to taking the test they had received e-mails with study tips in attachments and a final e-mail asking if they had opened the attachments and which of the study tips were useful to them. Based on these inputs, messages were personalized by varying the introductions and including their names in the salutation. For example, the three examples of messages in Table 12.1 were sent to students who said they were dissatisfied with their test results. The messages varied depending on whether the student did not open the attachments, did open them but did not check any of the tactics as being useful, or opened them and also checked some strategies as being useful. The body of the message following the introduction contained additional motivational

Table 12.1. Samples of Individualized Motivational Messages.

Example 1: Student did not open study tips attachment
Dear Frank ,
Congratulations!
In the previous logbook you said that you were not completely satisfied with your grade on Test 2, and I also noticed that you want to earn higher grades than you have earned so far. I have some suggestions, in the form of Study Tips and messages such as this one that might help you raise your grades on the two remaining tests.
Recently, a group of students in the class received these Study Tips in attachments. The overall class average on the second test was the same as the first one, but the grades for a small group of students who said they used these tips went up by two/thirds of a grade (for example, from a C to a B-). Thus, the evidence tells us that these Tips can be very helpful.
If you would like to take advantage of this opportunity, here is what to do.
Example 2: Student opened study tips attachment but did not use any tactics
Dear Francis,
In the previous logbook you said that you were not completely satisfied with your grade on Test 2, and I also noticed that you want to earn higher grades than you have earned so far. I have some suggestions in the form of Study Tips and messages, such as this one, that might help you raise your grades on the two remaining tests.

Table 12.1 (continued)

A few weeks ago, you received some Study Tips in an attachment which you said you opened but did not check any of the strategies as being useful. However, some of students in the class who opened them did use some of the strategies and said they were useful. The grades went up for eighty-two percent of these students and their average improvement was two/thirds of a grade (for example, from a C to a B-). Some went up more, some less, but the evidence tells us that these Tips can be very helpful. In contrast, the overall class average on the second test was the same as the first one.

If you would like to take advantage of this opportunity, here is what to do.

Example 3: Student opened study tips attachment and used some tactics
Dear Fay,

Congratulations on the big increase in your test grade. However, in the previous logbook you said that you were not completely satisfied with your grade on Test 2, and I also noticed that you want to earn higher grades than you have earned so far. I have some suggestions in the form of Study Tips and messages, such as this one, that might help you raise your grades on the two remaining tests.

A few weeks ago, you received some Study Tips in an attachment which you said you opened and checked some of the strategies as being useful. You might be interested to know that almost every student who opened the strategies and said they were useful had a grade increase, even though the total number was small. The average improvement was two/thirds of a grade (for example, from a B to an A-). Some, including yours, went up more, some less, but the evidence tells us that these Tips can be very helpful. In contrast, the overall class average on the second test was the same as the first one. **This time, I encourage you to try again and to use the strategies even more systematically, and maybe you will continue to see an increase!**

If you would like to take advantage of this opportunity, here is what to do.

---

features but this part was the same in each case and is not reproduced here. A sample of the complete message is contained in Kim and Keller (2008).

The results of this study indicated that the students who received these personalized messages had an overall higher level of confidence following the treatment and the gap between their test grades and the comparison group had closed. A key lesson learned from the two preceding studies was that it is critical to create a desire within the student to receive the motivational tactics in order for them to be useful. The researchers thought they had identified critical motivational problems in the audience analysis phase of planning. However, the information about problems came from the instructor and teaching assistant. This information was true for some students but not others. And even when it was true, it did not mean that all of those students wanted assistance with motivational and volitional problems. The motivational tactics were most effective when the students said they wanted to see them.

Online Instructor-Facilitated Learning Environments

Online instructor-facilitated courses can be synchronous which means that everyone attends a virtual meeting at the same time, asynchronous which means that people log on and work independently, or a combination of the two as when the primary pattern is asynchronous but students meet virtually in small groups for an assignment. And, of course, there can be still other variations on these conditions. The key criterion is that the instructor is actively involved in the course. This can be by means of leading virtual meetings, participating in discussion forums, providing mediated presentations, and by providing guidance and feedback. In general, the same principles and strategies that apply in the online portion of a blended course also apply here, but there is quite a lot of published material that is aimed primarily at online courses.

Johnson and Aragon (2002) proposed an instructional strategy framework for online learning environments that contains seven principles based on three areas of psychology: behavioral learning theory, cognitive learning theory, and social learning theory. They contend that in order for powerful online learning to occur, online learning environments need to contain a combination of these principles: (1) address individual differences, (2) motivate the student, (3) avoid information overload, (4) create a real-life context, (5) encourage social interaction, (6) provide hands-on activities, and (7) encourage student reflection. Their framework is based on well-established concepts and principles from instructional psychology and instructional design, but they do not provide independent empirical support for their model. However, they do provide concrete examples of activities that have proven successful in their own teaching settings. For example, they illustrate their second principle, "motivate the student," by briefly describing the ARCS model and then describing three techniques they have used.

The first strategy they mention for motivation is to incorporate games into the online environment and the example they use is based on the popular television show called "Who Wants to Be a Millionaire." Their second example of a motivational strategy is related to situations where a course contains a great deal of streaming audio or "talking head" video. They make it more interesting by including several people in a simulated broadcast environment with multiple disk jockeys (DJs) and "guests" who call in. Their third strategy suggestion is to incorporate multimedia whenever possible. They refer to contemporary audiences that expect to have a variety of media with relatively frequent changes of pace just as they would see in popular television shows. The authors mention that it can be helpful to have a variety of graphic images, photographs, and video clips including entertaining clips that illustrate specific concepts and procedures from the class.

A limitation of their framework is that they do not provide guidance for when to use given strategies representing these principles. For example, their recommendation for using a variety of multimedia whenever possible illustrates one of the three subcategories of Attention in the ARCS model (see Chapter 4); specifically the third one dealing with variability to sustain curiosity. The strategy needs to be modified based on the characteristics of a given audience. Some audiences would be annoyed by short, frequently changing modes of presentation. Some academic topics require a more sustained presentation such as an illustration of a complex procedure. In other words, all seven of their categories should be augmented by a process of audience analysis to determine when and how to apply each principle.

Thus, it is important to examine learner characteristics in conjunction with selecting or creating motivational strategies. Lim and Kim (2003) attempted to identify demographic and motivational characteristics of learners in relation to learning and motivational outcomes in an online setting. Their demographic variables included gender, work experience, marital status, distance education experience, and age. A significant improvement in learning occurred for the students in each subcategory of these demographics with the exception of those who had no previous distance education experience. However, there were only 7 students who had no prior distance education experience compared to the 70 who did have. There were no differences in final outcome within these categories except for gender. The women outperformed the men, but marital status, being under or over 30 years of age, or being employed full-time, part-time, or unemployed did not make any difference. In this study there were twice as many women as men (54 versus 23) and the authors do not have an explanation for the gender difference. It would be interesting to investigate this in further studies.

The authors constructed an application score for motivation based on students' responses to reasons for taking the course. These included such things as opportunity to use what they learned, relevance of learning content to their work, personal interest, and personal motivation to apply what they learned. The authors found that all motivation variables except course interest were related to learning but only two, reinforcement and self-efficacy, were related to their learning application scores.

This study offers some interesting points in support of learner characteristics that may affect their online learning attitudes and performance. However, it will need to be augmented by numerous other studies before any firm conclusions can be drawn.

With respect to guidance for online course development and motivational tactics, there are books containing guidance that could be used to supplement the systematic motivational design procedure that is part of the ARCS model. Bonk and Zhang (2008) describe more than 100 strategies that can be used in online learning and they provide a set of indices for each one. They rate the strategies in terms of risk, time, cost, learner-centeredness, and overall duration. These are subjective ratings which assist an instructor in matching strategy constrains with instructional goals and learning activity characteristics. The strategies in their book fall into four categories which constitute an acronym (R2D2) representing the four parts of their model: Read (auditory and verbal learners); Reflect (reflective and observational learners); Display (visual learners), and Do (tactile and kinesthetic learners). In contrast, Ko and Rossen (2001) provide a practical guide to the overall process of planning for online learning, creating an online course and syllabus, developing the online learning environment, designing learning activities, and preparing students for the online learning experience. Several of the sections can be viewed from a motivational perspective. For example, the online learning activities and building the online learning environment provide concrete strategies and design considerations to be considered in the context of a systematic motivational design process. Also, the section on preparing learners provides a context for incorporating motivational tactics.

In summary, it is interesting to note that virtually all of the guidance that is being offered in the literature with respect to learner characteristics, learning environments, and learning activities with regard to various e-learning (that is, electronic-based learning) environments has more features in common regardless of whether one is engaged in classroom instruction, blended instruction or online instruction than unique features that differentiate them. In recognition of this, Specter and Merrill (2008) proposed in a special edition of *Distance Learning* that the "e" in "e-learning" be replaced by "e3" which stands for effective, efficient, and engaging learning. That is, they propose that in the digital age the same basic principles will apply to all delivery systems. There will be differences with respect to specific strategies or tactics that are effective in a given environment and how these strategies have to be configured for various delivery systems, but the basic principles will apply more or less universally. In that edition of the journal, reference was made to Merrill's first principles of learning (Merrill, 2002) which specified that instruction is likely to be effective when

- it is centered around meaningful problems and tasks;
- learning goals and tasks are explicitly linked to knowledge and skills already mastered;
- new knowledge and skills are demonstrated in their natural context;
- students have opportunities to work on a variety of related problems and tasks of increasing complexity with feedback from a variety of sources; and when

- students can regulate their own performance and integrate new knowledge and skills into other activities.

Merrill derived these principles from the vast literature on instructional psychology and instructional systems design. He found that these general principles subsume the many concrete and specific principles and findings in the literature.

Similarly, I included an article (Keller, 2008a) entitled, "First Principles of Motivation to Learn and e3-Learning." The first four of these principles were originally derived from the comprehensive synthesis of the literature on human motivation and learning which formed the basis for the ARCS model. A fifth principle was added which relates to volition, or self-regulation. These principles are the following:

1. Motivation to learn is promoted when a learner's curiosity is aroused due to a perceived gap in current knowledge.
2. Motivation to learn is promoted when the knowledge to be learned is perceived to be meaningfully related to one's goals.
3. Motivation to learn is promoted when learners believe they can succeed in mastering the learning task.
4. Motivation to learn is promoted when learners anticipate and experience satisfying outcomes to a learning task.
5. Motivation to learn is promoted and maintained when learners employ volitional (self-regulatory) strategies to protect their intentions.

Together, these two lists of principles provide a basis for analyzing learner characteristics, learner needs, and instructional characteristics. Both sets of these principles have been validated in many empirical studies as documented by Merrill (2002) and Keller (2008a) and other associated publications.

Self-Directed Learning Environments

Self-directed learning environments present challenges that are different from instructor-facilitated settings. A cardinal difference between the two settings is that the instructional materials are prepared in advance of the instructional event and are then delivered as self-paced print materials, as computer-based instruction, or an online program via the web. This means that motivational strategies as well as instructional strategies have to be included in the materials at the time they are developed based on predictions about learner attitudes, abilities, and entry-level knowledge and skills. As one means of trying to add individualization, efforts have been made since the early days of programmed instruction to design adaptive instructional programs that are responsive to individual differences in student performance. A simple form of this is to direct the student along a remedial path after making a mistake. More complex versions attempted to offer alternate paths based on learning styles and entry-level knowledge. For the most part, these efforts were not highly successful because it was more cost-effective to develop programs that accommodated a variety of learning styles and to specify the required entry-level knowledge before beginning the program.

Anticipating the motivational attitudes of learners and designing tactics in advance is also quite challenging. It isn't too difficult to identify motivational tactics to include at the beginning of a lesson that will help capture the learners attention and to use instructional strategies such as case studies that help build relevance, but there can be significant differences in the entry-level motivational profiles of learners and their motivational attitudes can change as they progress through the program. Even so, many self-instructional programs can be greatly improved by giving systematic attention to the motivational characteristics of the lesson based on an application of the ARCS design process.

There have been attempts to incorporate adaptive features into the motivational features of self-instructional programs. Several of them are reviewed in this section. They include the development of motivationally adaptive computer-based instruction, incorporation of animated pedagogical agents to supplement instructional support with motivational support, and the development of reusable motivational objects.

Motivationally Adaptive Computer-Based Instruction

There can be a range of motivational conditions that characterize learners at different points in time while working through a computer-based program. One way to deal with this problem would be to include a large number of motivational tactics to cover a broad range of motivational conditions to ensure that the program is responsive to many types of motivational problems that might arise. However, this would most likely have a negative effect on motivation and performance because when students are motivated to learn, they want to work on highly task-relevant activities and they do not want to be distracted with unnecessary motivational activities. For example, students who already feel highly confident about their ability to learn the content will be annoyed by receiving motivational messages aimed at improving their confidence. For these reasons, it would be desirable to have computer-based programs that can identify learners' motivational levels and respond adaptively with the appropriate strategies.

There has been a persistent, though not voluminous, series of studies of motivationally adaptive computer-based instruction (Astleitner & Keller, 1995; del Soldato & du Boulay, 1995; Rezabek, 1994). Rezabek discussed the use of intrinsic motivational strategies for the development of a motivationally adaptive instructional system. He created a model that integrated Csikszentmihalyi's flow theory (Csikszentmihalyi, 1990) with the ARCS model and then proposed sets of tactics that could be used to maintain an optimal flow experience during an instructional event by incorporating them into an adaptive instructional system. However, he did not develop or test a prototype of his model or explain exactly what types of adaptivity would be included in his adaptive instructional system.

The phrase "adaptive instruction" is frequently used without specifying what is meant by it apart from most general interpretation as offering feedback or alternative pathways based on learner behaviors. Jonassen (1985) introduced a taxonomy for adaptive lesson design which provided a basis for a six-level model of motivational adaptivity proposed by Astleitner & Keller (1995):

1. At the first level the instructional system reacts to the learner's actual performance. Fixed motivational feedback is given based on right or wrong completion of a task.
2. The second level expands on the first by encouraging or the development of a performance. That is, the computer gives feedback as a reaction to several past performances, such as summary feedback at the end of a module or unit.
3. The third level introduces differentiated feedback based on different kinds of performances. Motivational feedback is presented, or branching options are offered, based on, for example, whether a difficult or easy task was completed successfully.
4. The fourth level introduces adaptability options based on individual difference measures that are taken prior to the beginning of instruction. The lesson contains several tracks based on measured differences in learner motivation and learners are automatically directed into a path based on their profiles. For example, students who score low in self-efficacy would be entered into a track containing tactics designed to improve this aspect of confidence. The high self-efficacy track would not contain these additional features. This is not a highly individualized form of adaptation, but it can accommodate some important differences in individual motivational dynamics.
5. The fifth level contains a variety of types of adaptive options ranging from simple management functions (e.g., control over pacing and sequencing) to more complex control over the motivational characteristics of the instructional events. Keller and Keller (1991) outlined important types of learner control in relation to motivation.
6. At this highest level of adaptability, the computer would be able to react to motivational states of learners. In this case, the computer models the motivational states of the learner based on actual and past learner performances or self-reported indicators and then implements appropriate motivational tactics during the teaching–learning interaction.

Astleitner and Keller (1995) tested the highest level of this model with a simulation of performance under several different motivational conditions based on an adaptation of Atkinson and Birch's (1970) theory of the dynamics of action. In this model, four different sets of conditions were created based on such things as performance, difficulty level, outcome expectancies, and outcome certainty (the belief that achieving a given outcome can be replicated). The results of implementing a simulation based on this model illustrate that there are differences in percentages of time spent on a task and different patterns of action tendencies based on the motivational characteristics of each condition. This model and simulation were highly theoretical but provide a basis for more pragmatic adaptations of the approach.

Del Soldato and du Boulay (1995) introduced a motivational adaptive model that was more concrete and operational than that of Astleitner and Keller (1995). They used the framework of an intelligent tutoring system and specified that the system must detect the student's motivational state and then conduct motivational planning to introduce strategies to counteract negative motivational states. They suggested four sources of information for motivational diagnosis. The first consists of questionnaires administered during the pre-instructional period. As in the ARCS audience analysis process this provides information to guide the inclusion of appropriate motivational strategies at the beginning of instruction. But this pre-instructional information is static and must be supplemented on an ongoing basis in order to have an adaptive program. The second kind of information consists of data collection during the lesson. For example, a student can click on standardized sets of prompts such as,"OK," "too difficult," "too easy," or "please give me a hint." A third type of data is based on student requests for help. A very different level of confidence is indicated by a student who requested help before attempting to solve a problem compared to a student who requests help only after making several attempts. Their fourth type of data consists of learners' self-evaluations of their motivational states during the instruction. For example, a student could move a slider on a scrollbar to indicate his level of confidence at any given point in time. In the planning function within their intelligent tutor, the computer would assess the influence, the overall structure of the lesson, and determine what motivational tactics to introduce.

Their model demonstrated several features that can be incorporated into a motivationally adaptive environment. They focused primarily on the requirements of developing an effective intelligent tutoring system to support the motivational aspects of adaptive instruction, and their work was limited in that it did not fully incorporate motivational theory or multiple dimensions of motivational characteristics of learners. They focused on confidence in relation to effort and the relative amount of independence demonstrated by the learner while working through the tutorial.

Song (Song & Keller, 2001) expanded upon the preceding studies by developing an approach that was adaptive at the sixth level of the taxonomy of Astleitner and Keller (1995). Song prepared three versions of a lesson on genetics for 10th grade students. The lessons differed with respect to their levels of motivational enhancements. The first was motivationally unenhanced and contained minimal motivational tactics. It was not possible to remove all features that might influence motivation without damaging the quality of the lesson. For example, including an explanation at the beginning of the lesson of what the objectives are and how the learner will be assessed has positive motivational benefits but it is also a feature of a well-designed lesson. However, there were very few features that could be considered to affect motivation independently of their necessity for instructional effectiveness. This motivationally unenhanced version of the lesson was used with one of the control groups. Song also developed a pool of 24 motivational tactics that could be used in the lesson and included all of them in a second control group called the motivationally saturated group. In the third group, the motivationally enhanced group, he incorporated a motivationally adaptive process that allowed the instructional program to be modified for each learner based on the motivational state of the learner.

At predetermined points, students in the motivationally adaptive group received a screen asking several questions about their motivational attitudes and they responded to a short practice quiz which allowed them to check their understanding. Based on their responses to the motivational questions, students would receive motivational tactics designed to improve attention, relevance, or confidence. For example, if a student said the lesson was becoming boring, the computer would add tactics to enhance the curiosity arousal features of the lesson. The computer would also compare the students motivational attitudes to their performance on the progress quiz and this would influence the motivational tactic that was introduced. For example, if a student said that he or she felt confident and the student had also performed well on the quiz the computer would give them a congratulatory message but would not add any motivational tactics designed to improve confidence. However, if a boy, for example, said he was not confident in his ability to learn the content but he had gotten the progress quiz questions correct, the computer would introduce a tactic designed to reinforce his achievement and encourage positive feelings of expectancy for success.

The results indicated that both the adaptive and full-featured treatments were superior to the minimalist treatment and in most instances the adaptive treatment was superior to the full-featured one. There were limitations on the types of computer features that could be used in this study (for example, there was no sound), but a more sophisticated treatment and also one which was longer than 1 hour could be expected, based on these results, to show even stronger treatment effects.

These early studies were promising in their results in two ways. They demonstrated that it is feasible to consider the development of motivationally adaptive lessons and they also demonstrated there can be positive results from these techniques. However, all of the studies were prototypical in nature and require further development before they can become fully operational. They also provide a foundation for another area of development in self-directed learning which is the incorporation of animated pedagogical agents to facilitate motivation as well as instruction.

Pedagogical Agents (Agent-Facilitated Computer-Based Instruction)

There is an already large and growing body of research which demonstrates that animated pedagogical agents can be beneficial in support of learning and attitude development in a computer-based learning environment. These pedagogical agents are animated life-like characters that support learning in a computer-based learning environment (Johnson, Rickel, & Lester, 2000) by assisting with direct instruction, being available to answer questions, serve as coaches to provide guidance and problem-solving situations, and to give feedback to learners based on their performance. Generally speaking, learners readily accept these avatars as meaningful social agents (Baylor, 2007). Research shows that people seem to assume that their computers with the embedded agents have the same characteristics as human beings (Reeves & Nass, 1996). Through a series of experiments, Reeves and Nass (1996) concluded that "individual interactions with computers, television, and new media are fundamentally social and natural, just like interaction in real life" (p. 5). Furthermore, consistent with Johnson's definition of pedagogical agents (Johnson, Rickel, & Lester, 2000) and Picard's concept of "affective computing" (Picard, 1997), it is reasonable to assume that an affective pedagogical agent can be used to provide learners with affective support providing that the agent can sense and recognize a learner's affective state and respond appropriately to a learner's emotional status in real time. One of the benefits of these agents is that they can express emotions by means of facial expressions and verbal comments as they provide feedback and guidance to students.

In a study designed to alleviate math anxiety and improve performance among a group of high school dropouts who were studying for their high school equivalency certificate, Shen (2009) incorporated two agents. The primary agent, Dr. Hendricks, served as a tutor by actively explaining the concept of the Pythagorean Theorem, how to apply it, and the steps in solving problems with it. Dr. Hendricks also provided motivational support to the students by means of cognitive and emotional motivational messages. The cognitive messages were designed to instill confidence, illustrate the relevance of the material being learned, and stimulate curiosity by means of questions and other specific tactics. Dr. Hendricks also provided emotional support by means of messages designed to help reduce student anxiety and promote positive feelings regarding the learning experience. From time to time, especially when students were working on certain problems, Dr. Hendricks would ask them if they were feeling anxious. If they clicked on the "Yes" response, he asked them if they would like to talk to a buddy. If they again said "yes," a screen opened with the other agent. This agent, Kate, had been introduced as a peer and she invited the students to express their concerns by typing them into a text window on the screen. This was consistent with one of the tactics called venting in a model of emotional support called COPE (Carver, Scheier, & Weintraub, 1989).

Shen found significant results with respect to reductions in math anxiety and improvements in performance for the emotional support portion of the treatment but not for the cognitive motivational message component. The emotional support component was personal in that it gave the students an opportunity to express themselves and also provided a connection with their long-established feelings of anxiety toward learning mathematics. The cognitive messages were based on a general appraisal of attitudes in the audience and may have been regarded as too abstract by this particular audience. The overall design and results from the study provide strong support for the actual and potential benefits of agents with regard to affecting learner attitudes and performance. Further research is needed to refine the cognitive motivational support component, to learn more about the possibilities for emotional support, and to test a generalizability of these results with a variety of types of audiences.

Reusable Motivational Objects

Reviews of the literature on computer-based instruction and technology-rich learning environments have consistently shown benefits in terms of better achievement and more positive attitudes, especially in K-12 education (Kulik, 1994; Sivin-Kachala, 1998). But, the development of these programs requires far more time during the design phase, which might be one of the reasons for the superior results from this type of instruction, than instructor-led courses which can be much more spontaneous. And, this increased design and development time translates into higher costs (Robinson & Anderson, 2002). In an effort to reduce costs and shorten the development time of computer-based instruction, the concept of reusable learning objects (RLO), which are based on the techniques of object-oriented program (Friesen, 2003; Masie, 2002), was developed. RLOs consist of an objective, content, practice, and assessment but there can be variations in the structure. They include "tags," or metadata, that allow them to be stored in repositories and easily retrieved. The expectation is that any number of lessons can be constructed by assembling RLOs that are appropriate for the overall topic of the lesson and characteristics of the learners. To be maximally efficient and reusable, RLOs should be decontextualized as much as possible. For example, if an RLO designed to teach the concept of "holy" includes an image of the Christian cross, it would not be effective with an audience of people of the Jewish, Muslim, or Hindu faith. In environments where the same elements of instruction are used in many different lessons, as when a company that develops self-instructional lessons on computer applications or a military organization that teaches basic concepts of electronic circuitry in many different content areas, it is much easier to decontextualize RLOs. But, even in these environments there are limitations on the effectiveness of RLOs and lessons constructed entirely from RLOs because of the severe limitations including contextual examples. Also, there has been no provision for incorporating motivational tactics into the learning objects or into programs of instruction that are constructed from learning objects.

In this regard, Oh (2006) introduced the concept of reusable motivational objects (RMO) and he developed and tested a prototype of this concept in his dissertation (Oh, 2006). He specified that the RMOs could be fixed or flexible. The ones that are fixed specify an exact strategy to use in a given context which makes them similar to RLOs. But, it was assumed that most RMOs cannot be decontextualized to the same degree as RLOs because key elements of most motivational tactics are related to building connections with the learners' attitudes and environments. For each type of RMO, he listed five types of metadata:

1. Related topic. It is necessary with fixed RMOs to specify the topic, such as the Pythagorean Theorem, to which they apply.
2. Title. This is a unique title that applies to one and only one RMO.
3. Sequence. This indicates whether the RMO should appear in the introductory part of the lesson, in the middle of the lesson, or toward the end.
4. Motivational category. Each RMO should be classified as to the major ARCS category and subcategory that describes its motivational goal. For example, "Attention – Inquiry – Arousal."
5. Target audience. This could specify grade level, such as 6th – 8th graders, or professional specialization, such as realtors or engineers.

The purpose of Oh's initial study of RMOs was to determine their feasibility, effect on instructional design performance, and efficiency. Graduate students in math education who were subject matter experts and had training in lesson planning were provided with stimulus materials that enabled them to build lessons incorporating both RLOs and RMOs. They were compared to groups that had RLOs only and RLOs plus RMOs and a motivational design job aid (MDA). Performance was an efficiency score based on the ratio of time spent on task to a product's score as determined by evaluators using a checklist. In other words, a combination of high-quality output and short development time would produce the highest efficiency scores. High-quality output combined with long development time or low-quality output combined with quick development time would result in lower efficiency scores. Attitudes toward the RMOs and MDA were measured with the Instructional Material Motivation Survey (see Chapter 11).

Oh (2006) found that the RMO significantly affected motivational design performance but the MDA did not add to the effect. There were no differences in attitudes toward the design process, but this may have been due in part to the fact that the performance time was relatively short and participants did not have experience with instructional design methods other than the one used in their assigned groups. However, based on their positive effect on the quality of the finished products, it can be concluded that the concept of RMO is feasible with regard to developing meaningful motivational objects, they can be used effectively even by teachers with minimal instructional design skills, and they provide a means of representing the motivational first principles in this type of learning environment.

Motivational Design of Job Aids and Manuals

The ARCS model can be used to guide the development of motivational features in job aids and other materials such as manuals. Job aids are commonly used in settings as diverse as consumer banks, airplanes, telephone books, restaurant bathrooms, and board games. They provide clear, often illustrated, summaries of principles, procedures, or decision rules. For example, The "employees must wash hands" signs in the restrooms of business establishments, the illustrated guidelines for constructing "assemble-it-yourself" furniture, the emergency evacuation cards in the seat pockets of airplanes, the step-by-step guidance for relighting the pilot light on your water heater, and the payment calculators available in booklets or online that tell you your monthly payment after you input the loan amount, interest rate, and number of months or years of the loan are all examples of job aids. Imagine, as Paul Elliott (1999) points out, how difficult and cumbersome life would be if you had to memorize each of these processes or remember how to calculate answers from formulas!

Job aids can make life simpler and safer and can even eliminate or reduce the time required for training (Elliott, 1999). For example, Knebel et al. (2000) tested the use of print-based job aids by health care providers in developing countries where electronic performance support systems would not be readily available. They found that these job aids which are inexpensive to produce often reduced or even replaced the need for off-site training. They also found that the job aids helped reduce non-compliance due to such things as forgetfulness, time constraints, and some organizational barriers. But in spite of their potential and actual benefits, job aids are frequently underutilized or not used at all (Tilaro & Rossett, 1993). One reason why people choose to use them or not use them may be related to the combination of their internal desires to succeed and the characteristics of the job aids themselves (Tilaro & Rossett, 1993). On the one hand, if people are motivated to perform well, they are more likely to use job aids and any other performance support tools that are available. On the other hand, if they are not so highly motivated, a motivationally enhanced job aid might result in higher levels of utilization.

Table 12.2. Job Aid for Motivational Design of Job Aids (Based on Tilaro & Rossett, 1993).

ATTENTION

Subcategory	Process Questions (Challenges)	Strategies/Tactics
A1. Perceptual Arousal	*Original Version:* What can I do to capture their interest? *Job Aid Version:* • What can I do to capture the workers' interest?	*Original Version:* Create curiosity and wonderment by using novel approaches, injecting personal and/or emotional material. *Job Aid Version:* • Replace words with pictures. • Use humor where possible. • Maximize visibility.
A2. Inquiry Arousal	*Original Version:* How can I stimulate an attitude of inquiry? *Job Aid Version:* • How can I stimulate interest in using this job aid (JA)?	*Original Version:* Increase curiosity by asking questions, creating paradoxes, generating inquiry, and nurturing thinking challenges. *Job Aid Version:* • Create small, compact, and simple JAs. • Make sure the JA is accessible and convenient to use. • Follow good design principles. • Balance aesthetics, usability, visibility, and other variables.
A3. Variability	*Original Version:* How can I maintain their attention? *Job Aid Version* • How can I maintain the workers' attention?	*Original Version:* Sustain interest by variations in presentation style, concrete analogies, human interest examples, and unexpected events. *Job Aid Version:* • Put critical information first and "chunk" data. • Use color coding, highlighting, boldfacing, outlining, or bulleted items.

RELEVANCE

Subcategory	Process Questions (Challenges)	Strategies/Tactics
R1. Goal Orienta-tion	*Original Version:* How can I best meet my learner's needs? (Do I know their needs?)	*Original Version:* Provide statements or examples of the utility of the instruction, and either present goals or have learners define them.

Table 12.2 (continued)

		Job Aid Version: • How can I meet worker needs? Do I know their needs?	Job Aid Version: • Conduct needs assessments, i.e., perform thorough work, worker, and workplace analyses. • Determine the goal of the JA based on where, when, how, and why it will be used.
R2. Motive Matching		*Original Version:* How and when can I link my instruction to the learning styles and personal interests of the learners?	*Original Version:* Make instruction responsive to learner motives and values by providing personal achievement opportunities, cooperative activities, leadership responsibilities, and positive role models.
		Job Aid Version: • How can I link the JA to the way employees prefer to work or to their personal interests?	*Job Aid Version:* • Look at the JA from the worker's point of view. • Build JAs based on ones that employees have created for themselves. • Make employees partners in the developmental process.
			• Look for "buy-in" factors from end users and management.
R3. Familiarity		*Original Version:* How can I tie the instruction to the learners' experiences?	*Original Version:* Make the materials and concepts familiar by providing concrete examples and analogies related to the learners' work or background.
		Job Aid Version • How can I tie the JA to the workers' experiences?	*Job Aid Version:* • Use subject matter experts (SMEs). • Modify already-existing JAs. • Pilot test rough drafts of the JA.

CONFIDENCE

SubCategory	Process Questions (Challenges)	Strategies/Tactics
C1. Learning Require- ments	*Original Version:* How can I assist in building a positive expectation for success?	*Original Version:* Establish trust and positive expectations by explaining the requirements for success and the evaluative criteria.

Table 12.2 (continued)

	Job Aid Version:	*Job Aid Version:*
	• How can I build positive expectations for success when using this JA?	• Anticipate potential problems, such as "change anxiety," and develop strategies to combat them. • Train workers to use the job aid. • Let workers know what is expected of them.
C2. Success Opportuni- ties	*Original Version:* How will the learning experience support or enhance the learners' beliefs in their competence? *Job Aid Version:* • How will using the JA support or enhance the workers' belief in their competence?	*Original Version:* Increase belief in competence by providing many, varied, and challenging experiences that increase learning success. *Job Aid Version:* • Provide situations for workers to experience success with the JA. • Review old JAs regularly. • Keep a list of who has received the JA for future updates.
C3. Personal Control	*Original Version:* How will the learners clearly know their success is based on their efforts and abilities? *Job Aid Version* • How will workers know their success is based on their efforts and abilities?	*Original Version:* Use techniques that offer personal control (whenever possible) and provide feedback that attributes success to personal effort. *Job Aid Version:* • Create JAs that enable employees to self-monitor. • Get sign-off from SMEs and management during all phases of development.
		• Find an "owner" to maintain the JA.

SATISFACTION

Sub- Category	Process Questions (Challenges)	Strategies/Tactics
S1. Intrinsic Reinforce- ment	*Original Version:* How can I encourage and support their intrinsic enjoyment of the learning experience?	*Original Version:* Provide feedback and other information that reinforces positive feelings for personal effort and accomplishment.

Table 12.2 (continued)

	Original/Job Aid Version	
	Job Aid Version: • How can use of the JA be encouraged and supported?	*Job Aid Version:* • Seek input from end users for improving the JA. • Provide feedback to show the benefits of using the JA. • Show management the connection between the JA, improved performance, and bottom-line results.
S2. Extrinsic Rewards	*Original Version:* What will provide rewarding consequences to the learners' successes? *Job Aid Version:* • What will provide positive consequences for successes with JAs?	*Original Version:* Use verbal praise, real or symbolic rewards, and incentives, or let learners present the results of their efforts ("show and tell") to reward success. *Job Aid Version:* • Link organizational incentives and rewards to improved performance. • Have recognition programs for good ideas. • Encourage supervisors to coach and applaud.
S3. Equity	*Original Version:* What can I do to build learner perceptions of fair treatment? *Job Aid Version* • How can workers be convinced of fair treatment?	*Original Version:* Make performance requirements consistent with stated expectations, and use consistent measurement standards for all learners' tasks and accomplishments. *Job Aid Version:* • Standardize rating scales for evaluation-type JAs. • Distribute JAs to all workers who might need them.

Tilaro and Rossett (1993) applied the ARCS model to the design of job aids by examining the motivational properties of several job aids and creating a table of tactics by modifying the original ARCS tables of process questions and major supporting strategies (Tables 3.3, 3.4, and 3.5) to contain tactics that are more directly tied to job aid design. A direct comparison of the two versions is presented in Table 12.2.

Tilaro and Rossett (1993) point out that not all four of the ARCS categories need to be applied to every job aid. For example, the primary motivational goal of some job aids is limited to capturing attention by using\ large colorful type and reinforcing relevance by reminding the audience of the importance of the given procedure. In contrast, the emergency procedures job aid in airline seat pockets must accomplish both of these goals and also help the passengers feel confident that they can do the right things in an emergency. These motivational goals are, of course, subordinate to the primary goal of a job aid which is to guide and instruct. They present a four-step process for building job aids (planning, building, installing, and maintaining) and their article contains numerous helpful examples.

Summary

This chapter has described issues, strategies, and models pertaining to motivational design in the context of technology-assisted instruction, both instructor-led and self-directed types of delivery systems. It has also described some recent and current areas of research and development on motivational design. Within all of these areas of work on adaptive instruction, motivational objects, job aids, and other innovative uses of technology there are many interesting research questions that can be investigated.

References

Adams, J. S. (1965). Inequity in social exchange. In L. Berkowitz (Ed.), *Advances in experimental social psychology* (Vol. 2). New York: Academic Press.

Allport, G. (1937). *Personality: A psychological interpretation*. New York: Holt, Rinehart, & Winston.

Allport, G. (1943). The ego in contemporary psychology. *Psychological Review, 50,* 451–478.

Alschuler, A. S. (1973). *Developing achievement motivation in adolescents.* Englewood Cliffs, NJ: Educational Technology Publications.

Alschuler, A. S., Tabor, D., & McIntyre, J. (1971). *Teaching achievement motivation: Theory and practice in psychological education.* Middletown, CT: Education Ventures, Inc.

Arnstine, D. (1966). Curiosity. *Teachers College Record, 67,* 595–602.

Aronson, E. (1992). The Return of the Repressed: Dissonance Theory Makes a Comeback. *Psychological Inquiry, 3*(4), 303.

Ashton, P., & Webb, R. (1986). *Making a difference: Teachers' sense of efficacy and student achievement.* New York: Longman.

Astleitner, H., & Keller, J. M. (1995). A model for motivationally adaptive computer-assisted instruction. *Journal of Research on Computing in Education, 27*(3), 270–280.

Bandura, A. (1969). *Principles of Behavior Modification.* New York: Holt, Rinehart and Winston, Inc.

Bandura, A. (1977). Self-efficacy: Toward a unifying theory of behavioral change. *Psychological Review, 84,* 191–215.

Bandura, A. (1982). Self-efficacy mechanism in human agency. *American Psychologist, 37*(2), 122–147.

Bandura, A. (1986). *Social foundations of thought and action: A social cognitive theory.* Englewood Cliffs, NJ: Prentice Hall.

Bandura, A. (1997). *Self-Efficacy. The Exercise of Control.* New York: Freeman.

Banks, W. P., & Krajicek, D. (1991). Perception. *Annual Review of Psychology, 42,* 305–331.

Baylor, A. (2007). Pedagogical agents as social interface. *Educational Technology, January-February,* 11–14.

Beck, R. C. (1990). *Motivation: Theories and principles* (3rd ed.). Englewood Cliffs, NJ: Prentice-Hall.

Berlyne, D. E. (1950). Novelty and curiosity as determinants of exploratory behaviour. *British Journal of Psychology, 41,* 68–80.

Berlyne, D. E. (1954a). An experimental study of human curiosity. *British Journal of Psychology, 45*(4), 256–265.

Berlyne, D. E. (1954b). A theory of human curiosity. *British Journal of Psychology, 45*(3), 180–191.

Berlyne, D. E. (1963). Complexity and incongruity variables as determinants of exploratory choice and evaluative ratings. *Canadian Journal of Psychology, 17,* 274, 290.

Berlyne, D. E. (1965). Motivational problems raised by exploratory and epistemic behavior. In S. Koch (Ed.), *Psychology: A study of a science* (Vol. 5). New York: McGraw-Hill.

Bialer, I. (1961). Conceptualization of success and failure in mentally retarded and normal children. *Journal of Personality, 29,* 303–320.

Bloom, B. S. (Ed.). (1956). *Taxonomy of educational objectives, the classification of educational goals – handbook I: Cognitive domain.* New York: David McKay.

Boekaerts, M. (2001). Motivation, Learning, and Instruction. In N. J. Smelser & P. B. Baltes (Eds.), *The international encyclopedia of the social and behavioral science* (pp. 10112–10117). Oxford: Elsevier.

Bonk, C. J., & Zhang, K. (2008). *Empowering online learning: 100+ Activities for reading, reflecting, displaying, & doing.* San Francisco: Jossey-Bass.

Brehm, J., & Cohen, A. (1962). *Explorations in cognitive dissonance.* New York: Wiley.

Briggs, L. J. (1984). Whatever happened to motivation and the affective domain? *Educational Technology, 24*(5), 33–44.

Brophy, J. E. (1981). Teacher Praise: A Functional Analysis. *Review of Educational Research, 51,* 5–32.

Brophy, J. E. (1983). Conceptualizing student motivation. *Educational Psychologist, 18*(3), 200–215.

Brown, M. B., Aoshima, M., Bolen, L. M., Chia, R., & Kohyama, T. (2007). Cross-cultural learning approaches in students from the USA, Japan and Taiwan. *School Psychology International, 28*(5), 592–604.

Caron, A. J. (1963). Curiosity, achievement, and avoidant motivation as determinants of epistemic behavior. *Journal of Abnormal and Social Psychology, 67*(6), 535–549.

Carstensen, L. L., & Fredrickson, B. L. (1998). Influence of HIV status and age on cognitive representations of others. *Health Psychology, 17,* 494–503.

Cartwright, D., & Harary, F. (1956). Structural balance: A generalization of Heider's theory. *Psychological Review, 63*(5), 277–293.

Carver, C. S., Scheier, M. F., & Weintraub, J. (1989). Assessing coping strategies: a theoretical based approach. *Journal of Personality and Social Psychology, 56,* 267–295.

Cattell, R. B. (1950). *Personality: A systematic, theoretical and factual study.* New York: McGraw-Hill.

Cattell, R. B. (1957). *Personality and motivation structure and measurement.* New York: World Book.

Cattell, R. B., & Cattell, H. E. P. (1995). Personality structure and the new fifth edition of the 16PF. *Educational and Psychological Measurement, 55*(6), 926–937.

Chen, H., Wigand, R. T., & Nilan, M. S. (1999). Optimal experience of Web activities. *Computers in Human Behavior, 15*(5), 585–608.

Condry, J. (1977). Enemies of exploration: Self-initiated versus other-initiated learning. *Journal of Personality and Social Psychology, 35*, 459–477.

Corno, L. (1989). Self-regulated learning: A volitional analysis. In B. J. Zimmermann & D. H. Schunk (Eds.), *Self-regulated learning and academic achievement. Theory, research and practice* (pp. 111–141). New York: Springer.

Corno, L. (2001). Volitional Aspects of Self-Regulated Learning. In B. J. Zimmerman & D. H. Schunk (Eds.), *Self-regulated learning and academic achievement. Theoretical perspectives (Second Edition)* (pp. 191–226). Mahwah, NJ: Erlbaum.

Corno, L., & Randi, J. (1999). A Design Theory for Classroom Instruction in Self-Regulated Learning? In C. M. Reigeluth (Ed.), *Instructional-design theories and models* (Vol. 2, pp. 293–318). Mahwah, NY: Erlbaum.

Craik, K. (1943). *The nature of explanation*. Cambridge, UK: Cambridge University Press.

Crandall, V. C., Katkovsky, W., & Crandall, V. J. (1965). Children's beliefs in their own control of reinforcement in intellectual-academic situations. *Child Development, 36*, 91–109.

Cronbach, L. J., & Snow, R. E. (1976). *Aptitudes and instructional methods*. New York: Irvington.

Croyle, R., & Cooper, J. (1983). Dissonance arousal: Physiological evidence. *Journal of Personality and Social Psychology, 45*, 782–791.

Csikszentmihalyi, M. (1975). *Beyond boredom and anxiety*. San Francisco: Jossey-Bass.

Csikszentmihalyi, M. (1990). *Flow: The psychology of optimal experience*. New York: Harper & Row.

Day, H. I. (1968a). A curious approach to creativity. *The Canadian Psychologist, 9*(4), 485–497.

Day, H. I. (1968b). Role of specific curiosity in school achievement. *Journal of Educational Psychology, 59*(1), 37–43.

Day, H. I., & Langevin, R. (1969). Curiosity and intelligence: Two necessary conditions for a high level of creativity. *The Journal of Special Education, 3*(3), 263–268.

de Charms, R. (1968). *Personal causation*. New York: Academic Press.

deCharms, R. (1968). *Personal causation*. New York: Academic Press.

deCharms, R. (1976). *Enhancing motivation change in the classroom*. New York: Irvington.

Deci, E. L. (1971). The effects of externally mediated rewards on intrinsic motivation. *Journal of Personality and Social Psychology, 18*, 105–115.

Deci, E. L. (1972). Intrinsic motivation, extrinsic reinforcement, and inequity. *Journal of Personality and Social Psychology, 22,* 113–120.

Deci, E. L. (1975). *Intrinsic motivation.* New York: Plenum Press.

Deci, E. L., & Porac, J. (1978). Cognitive evaluation theory and the study of human motivation. In M. R. Lepper & D. Green (Eds.), *The hidden costs of reward.* Hillsdale, NJ: Lawrence Erlbaum Associates.

Deci, E. L., & Ryan, R. (1985). *Intrinsic motivation and self-determination in human behavior.* New York: Plenum.

Deci, E. L., & Ryan, R., M. (2000). The "what" and "why" of goal pursuits: Human needs and the self-determination of behavior. *Psychological Inquiry, 11*(4), 227–268.

Declerck, C. H., Boone, C., & DeBrabander, B. (2006). On feeling in control: A biological theory for individual differences in control perception. *Brain and Cognition, 62,* 143.

Deimann, M., & Keller, J. M. (2006). Volitional aspects of multimedia learning. *Journal of Educational Multimedia and Hypermedia, 15*(2), 137–158.

del Soldato, T., & du Boulay, B. (1995). Implementation of motivational tactics in tutoring systems. *Journal of Artificial Intelligence, 6*(4), 337–338.

Dewey, J. (1913). *Interest and effort in education.* Boston: Houghton Mifflin Co.

Dick, W., & Carey, L. (1996). *The systematic design of instruction* (4 ed.). New York: Harper Collins.

Dollinger, S. J. (2000). Locus of control and incidental learning: An application to college student success. *College Student Journal, 34*(4), 537–541.

DuCette, J., & Wolk, S. (1973). Cognitive and motivational correlates of generalized expectancies for control. *Journal of Personality and Social Psychology, 26,* 420–426.

DuCette, J., Wolk, S., & Friedman, S. (1972). Locus of control and creativity in black and white children. *Journal of Social Psychology, 88,* 297–298.

Duffy, T. M., Lowyck, J., & Jonassen, D. H. (Eds.). (1993). *Designing environments for constructivist learning.* New York: Springer-Verlag.

Dweck, C. S. (1975). The role of expectations and attributions in the alleviation of learned helplessness. *Journal of Personality and Social Psychology, 31,* 647–695.

Dweck, C. S. (1986). Motivational processes affecting learning. *American Psychologist, 41*(10), 1040–1048.

Dweck, C. S. (2006). *Mindset.* New York: Random House.

Eccles, J. S., & Wigfield, A. (2002). Motivational Beliefs, Values, and Goals. *Annual Review of Psychology, 53,* 109–132.

Elliot, A. J., & Devine, P. G. (1994). On the motivational nature of cognitive dissonance: Dissonance as psychological discomfort. *Journal of Personality and Social Psychology, 67*(3), 382–394.

Elliot, A. J., & Dweck, C. S. (2005a). Competence and motivation: Competence as the core of achievement motivation. In A. J. Elliot & C. S. Dweck (Eds.), *Handbook of competence and achievement motivation* (pp. 3–12). New York: The Guilford Press.

Elliot, A. J., & Dweck, C. S. (Eds.). (2005b). *Handbook of competence and motivation*. New York: The Builford Press.

Elliott, P. H. (1999). Job aids. In H. D. S. E. J. Keeps (Ed.), *Handbook of human performance technology: Improving individual and organizational performance worldwide* (2 ed., pp. 430–441). San Francisco: Jossey-Bass Pfeiffer.

Engelhard, G., & Monsaas, J. A. (1988). Grade level, gender, and school related curiosity in urban elementary schools. *Journal of Educational Research, 82*(1), 22–26.

Englehard, G. (1985). The discovery of educational goals and outcomes: A view of the latent curriculum of schooling. (Doctoral dissertation, University of Chicago, 1985). *Dissertation Abstracts International, 46*, 2176-A.

Ericsson, K. A. (2006). The influence of experience and deliberate practice on the development of superior expert performance. In K. A. Ericsson, N. Charness, P. Feltovich & R. R. Hoffman (Eds.), *Cambridge handbook of expertise and expert performance* (pp. 39–68). Cambridge, UK: Cambridge University Press.

Farmer, T. M. (1989). *A Refinement of the ARCS motivational design procedure using a formative evaluation methodology*. Bloomington: Indiana University.

Festinger, L. (1957). *A theory of cognitive dissonance*. Evanston, IL: Row, Peterson.

Festinger, L., & Carlsmith, J. M. (1959). Cognitive consequences of forced compliance. *Journal of Abnormal and Social Psychology*(58), 203–210.

Filcheck, H. A., McNeil, C. B., Greco, L. A., & Bernard, R. S. (2004). Using a whole-class token economy and coaching of teacher skills in a preschool classroom to manage disruptive behavior. *Psychology in the Schools, 41*(3), 351–361.

Flanagan, J. (1967). Functional education for the seventies. *Phi Delta Kappan, September*, 27–33.

Fleming, M., & Levie, W. H. (1978). *Instructional message design: Principles from the behavioral sciences*. Englewood Cliffs, NJ: Educational Technology Publications.

Flesch, R. (1948). A new readability yardstick. *Journal of Applied Psychology, 32*, 221–233.

Flesch, R., & Lass, A. H. (1949). *A new guide to better writing*. New York: Harper and Row.

Fredrickson, B. L., & Carstensen, L. L. (1990). Choosing social partners: How old age and anticipated endings make people more selective. *Psychology and Aging, 5*, 335–347.

Friesen, N. (2003). Three objections to learning objects. In R. McGreal (Ed.), *Online education using learning objects*. London, UK: Taylor & Francis Books Ltd.

Fromm, E. (1955). *The Sane Society*. Greenwich, CN: Fawcett.

Gagné, R. M. (1965). *The conditions of learning*. New York: Holt, Rinehart and Winston, Inc.

Gagné, R. M., Wager, W. W., Golas, K. C., & Keller, J. M. (2005). *Principles of Instructional Design* (5th ed.). Belmont, CA: Wadsworth/Thomson Learning, Inc. .

Gallup, H. F. (1974). Problems in the implementation of a course in personalized instruction. In J. G. Sherman (Ed.), *PSI: Personalized system of instruction*. Philippines: W. A. Benjamin, Inc.

Gardner, R., Sainato, D. M., Cooper, J. O., Heron, T. E., Heward, W. L., Eshleman, J. W., et al. (Eds.). (1994). *Behavior analysis in education: Focus on measurably superior instruction*. Pacific Grove, CA: Brooks/Cole Publishing Company.

Garner, R., Gillingham, M. G., & White, C. S. (1989). Effects of "seductive details" on macroprocessing and microprocessing in adults and children. *Cognition and Instruction, 6*(1), 41–57.

Geirland, J. (1996). Go with the flow: An interview with Mihaly Csikszentmihalyi [Electronic Version]. *Wired (Online)*, 4. Retrieved 09212008 from http://www.wired.com/wired/archive/4.09/czik.html

Geiwitz, J. P. (1966). Structure of boredom. *Journal of Personality and Social Psychology, 3*(5), 592–600.

Gibson, S., & Dembo, M. H. (1984). Teacher efficacy: A construct validation. *Journal of Educational Psychology, 76*, 569–582.

Goleman, D. (1995). *Emotional intelligence*. New York: Bantam Books.

Gollwitzer, P. M. (1993). Goal Achievement: The Role of Intentions. *European Review of Social Psychology, 4*, 141–185.

Gollwitzer, P. M., & Brandstätter, V. (1997). Implementation intentions and effective goal pursuit. *Journal of Personality and Social Psychology, 73*(1), 186–199.

Goodlad, J. I. (1984). *A place called school: Prospects for the future*. Chicago: Aldine publishing.

Greene, B. A., & DeBacker, T. K. (2004). Gender and orientations toward the future: Links to motivation. *Educational Psychology Review, Asked*(2), 91–120.

Greenwald, A. G., & Ronis, D. L. (1978). Twenty years of cognitive dissonance: Case study of the evolution of a theory. *Psychological Review, 85*(1), 53–57.

Harlow, H. F. (1953). *Motivation as a factor in the acquisition of new responses*. Lincoln: University of Nebraska Press.

Harp, S. F., & Mayer, R. E. (1997). The role of interest in learning from scientific text and illustrations: On the distinction between emotional interest and cognitive interest. *Journal of Educational Psychology, 89*(1), 92–102.

Harp, S. F., & Mayer, R. E. (1998). How seductive details do their damage: A theory of cognitive interest in science learning. *Journal of Educational Psychology, 90*(3), 414–434.

Harrow, A. (1972). *A taxonomy of the psychomotor domain. A guide for developing behavioral objectives.* New York: David McKay.

Hawking, S. (2005). Public lectures: Does God play dice? [Electronic Version]. Retrieved September 27, 2008 from http://www.hawking.org.uk/lectures/lindex.html.

Healy, S. D. (1979). *The roots of boredom.* New Brunswick: Rutgers The State University of New Jersey.

Hebb, D. O. (1955). Drives and the conceptual nervous system. *Psychological Review, 62,* 243–253.

Hebb, D. O. (1958). The motivating effects of exteroceptive stimulation. *American Psychologist, 13,* 109–113.

Heider, R. (1946). Attitudes and cognitive organization. *The Journal of Psychology, 21,* 107–112.

Heider, R. (1958). *The psychology of interpersonal relations.* New York: Wiley.

Hidi, S., & Baird, W. (1986). Interestingness—A neglected variable in discourse processing. *Cognitive Science, 10*(2), 179.

Hidi, S., Baird, W., & Hildyard, A. (1982). That's important but is it interesting? Two factors in text processing. *Discourse Processing,* 63–75.

Hilgard, E. R. (1949). Human motives and the concept of self. *American Psychologist, 4,* 374–382.

Hoffman, R. (2007). Pandora's Box [Electronic Version]. *Encyclopedia Mythica,* http://www.pantheon.org/areas/folklore/folktales/articles/pandora.html. Retrieved July 21, 2007.

Holden, K. B., & Rotter, J. B. (1962). A nonverbal measure of extinction in skill and chance situations. *Journal of Experimental Psychology, 63*(519–520).

Hsieh, T. T., Shybut, J., & Lotsof, E. J. (1969). Internal versus external control and ethnic group membership. *Journal of Consulting and Clinical Psychology, 33,* 122–124.

Hu, Y. (2008). *Motivation, usability and their interrelationships in a self-paced online learning environment* Unpublished doctoral dissertation, Virginia Polytechnic Institute and State University, Blacksburn, VA.

Huang, W. D., Huang, W.-Y., Diefes-Dux, H., & Imbrie, P. K. (2005). A preliminary validation of Attention, Relevance, Confidence and Satisfaction model-based Instructional Material Motivational Survey in a computer-based tutorial setting. *British Journal of Educational Technology, 37*(2), 243–259.

Hull, C. L. (1943). *Principles of behavior.* New York: Appleton-Century-Crofts.

Hummon, N. P., & Doreian, P. (2003). Some dynamics of social balance processes: bringing Heider back into balance theory. *Social Networks, 25*(1), 17–49.

Humphreys, M. S., & Revelle, W. (1984). Personality, motivation, and performance: A theory of the relationship between individual differences and information processing. *Psychological Review, 91*(2), 153–184.

Hunt, D. E., & Sullivan, E. V. (1974). *Between Psychology and Education*. Hinsdale, IL: Dryden.

Huseman, R. C., Matfield, J. D., & Miles, E. W. (1987). A new perspective on equity theory: The equity sensitivity construct. *Academy of Management Review, 12*(2), 232–234.

Ifamuyiwa, S. A., & Akinsola, M. K. (2008). Improving senior secondary school students' attitude towards mathematics through self and cooperative-instructional strategies. *International Journal of Mathematical Education in Science and Technology, 39*(5), 569.

James, W. (1890). *The principles of psychology* (Vol. 2). New York: Henry Holt.

Jenson, W. R., Sloane, H. N., & Young, K. R. (1988). *Applied behavior analysis in education: A structured teaching approach*. Englewood Cliffs, NJ: Prentice Hall.

Jessor, R., Graves, T. D., Hanson, R. C., & Jessor, S. L. (1968). *Society, personality, and deviant behavior*. New York: Holt, Rinehart & Winston.

Johnson-Laird, P. N. (1983). *Mental models: Toward a cognitive science of language, inference and consciousness*. Cambridge: Harvard University Press.

Johnson-Laird, P. N. (2005). Mental models in thought. In K. Holyoak & R. J. Sternberg (Eds.), *The Cambridge handbook of thinking and reasoning* (pp. 179–212). Cambridge, UK: Cambridge University Press.

Johnson, S. D., & Aragon, S. R. (2002). An instructional strategy framework for online learning environments. In T. M. Egan & S. A. Lynham (Eds.), *Proceedings of the academy for human resource development* (pp. 1022–1029). Bowling Green, OH: AHRD.

Johnson, W. L., Rickel, J. W., & Lester, J. C. (2000). Animated pedagogical agents: face-to-face interaction in interactive learning environments. *International Journal of Artificial Intelligence in Education, 11*, 47–78.

Jonassen, D. H. (1985). A taxonomy of interactive adaptive lesson designs. *Educational Technology, 25*(6), 7–17.

Jones, E. E., Kanhouse, D. E., Kelley, H. H., Nisbett, R. E., Valins, S., & Weiner, B. (1971). *Attribution: Perceiving the causes of behavior*. Morristown, NJ: General Learning Press.

Joyce, B., & Weil, M. (1972). *Models of teaching*. Englewood Cliffs, NJ: Prentice-Hall, Inc.

Jussim, L., & Eccles, J. (1992). Teacher expectancies II: Construction and reflection of student achievement. *Journal of Personality and Social Psychology, 63*, 947-961.

Kabat-Zinn, J. (1990). *Full catastrophe living: Using the wisdom of your body and mind to face stress, pain, and illness.* New York: Dell Publishing.

Kagan, J. (1972). Motives and development. *Journal of Personality and Social Psychology, 22*(1), 51-66.

Kaplan, S., & Kaplan, R. (1978). *Humanscape: Environments for people.* North Scituate, MA: Duxbury Press.

Kazdin, A. E. (1982). The token economy: A decade later. *Journal of Applied Behavior Analysis, 15*(3), 431-445.

Kazdin, A. E., & Bootzin, R. R. (1972). The token economy: An evaluative review. *Journal of Applied Behavior Analysis, 5*(3), 343-372.

Keller, F. S. (1968). Goodbye teacher. *Applied Behavior Analysis, 1*, 78-79.

Keller, J. M. (1979). Motivation and instructional design: A theoretical perspective. *Journal of Instructional Development, 2*(4), 26-34.

Keller, J. M. (1983a). Investigation of the effectiveness of a learned helplessness alleviation strategy for low aptitude learners. In G. Zeeuw, W. Hofstee, & J. Yastenhouw (Eds.), *Funderend Onderzoek van het Onderwijs en Onderwijsleerprocessen* (pp. 191-202). Lisse, The Netherlands: Swets & Zeitlinger B.V.

Keller, J. M. (1983b). Motivational design of instruction. In C. M. Reigeluth (Ed.), *Instructional design theories and models: An overview of their current status.* Hillsdale, NJ: Lawrence Erlbaum Associates.

Keller, J. M. (1984). The use of the ARCS model of motivation in teacher training. In K. S. A. J. Trott (Ed.), *Aspects of educational technology volume XVII: Staff development and career updating.* London: Kogan Page.

Keller, J. M. (1987a). Development and use of the ARCS model of motivational design. *Journal of Instructional Development, 10*(3), 2-10.

Keller, J. M. (1987b). Strategies for stimulating the motivation to learn. *Performance and Instruction, 26*(8), 1-7.

Keller, J. M. (1987c). The systematic process of motivational design. *Performance and Instruction, 26*(9), 1-8.

Keller, J. M. (1988). Motivational design. In R. McAleese & U. C. (Eds.), *Encyclopaedia of educational media communications and technology* (2nd ed., pp. 406-409). Westport, CT: Greenwood Press.

Keller, J. M. (1994). Motivation in instructional design. In T. Husen & T. N. Postlethwaite (Eds.), *International encyclopaedia of education* (2nd ed.). Oxford: Pergamon Press.

Keller, J. M. (1999). Motivation in cyber learning environments. *Educational Technology International, 1*(1), 7-30.

Keller, J. M. (2000 February). *How to integrate learner motivation planning into lesson planning: The ARCS model approach.* Paper presented at the VII Seminario, Santiago, Cuba.

Keller, J. M. (2008a). First principles of motivation to learn and e3-learning. *Distance Education, 29*(2), 175–185.

Keller, J. M. (2008b). An integrative theory of motivation, volition, and performance. *Technology, Instruction, Cognition, and Learning, 6*(2), 79–104.

Keller, J. M., & Burkman, E. (1993). Motivation principles. In M. Fleming & W. H. Levie (Eds.), *Instructional message design: Principles from the behavioral and cognitive sciences*. Englewood Cliffs, NJ: Educational Technology Press.

Keller, J. M., Deimann, M., & Liu, Z. (2005). Effects of integrated motivational and volitional tactics on study habits, attitudes, and performance. In *Proceedings of the Annual Meeting of the Association for Educational Communications and Technology*. Orlando, Florida.

Keller, J. M., & Kopp, T. W. (1987). An Application of the ARCS Model of Motivational Design. In C. M. Reigeluth (Ed.), *Instructional theories in action* (pp. 289–320). Hillsdale, NJ: Erlbaum.

Keller, J. M., & Suzuki, K. (1988). Application of the ARCS model to courseware design. In D. H. Jonassen (Ed.), *Instructional designs for microcomputer courseware design* (pp. 401–434). New York: Lawrence Erlbaum, Publisher.

Kim, C. M., & Keller, J. M. (2008). Effects of motivational and volitional email messages (MVEM) with personal messages on undergraduate students' motivation, study habits and achievement. *British Journal of Educational Technology, 39*(1), 36–51.

Knebel, E., Lundahl, S., E., R. A., Abdallah, H., Ashton, J., & Wilson, N. (2000). *Use of manual job aids by health care providers: What do we know?* (No. USAID Contract No. HRN-C-00-96-90013). Bethesda, Maryland: Center for Human Services.

Ko, S., & Rossen, S. (2001). *Teaching Online: A Practical Guide*. New York: Houghton Mifflin Company.

Koberg, D., & Bagnall, J. (1976). *The all new universal traveler*. Los Altos, CA: William Kaufman, Inc.

Koffka, K. (1935). *Principles of gestalt psychology*. New York: Harcourt, Brace and World.

Kopp, T. (1982). Designing the boredom out of instruction. *NSPI Journal, May*, 23–27, 29.

Krathwohl, D. R., Bloom, B. S., & Masia, B. B. (1964). *Taxonomy of educational objectives, handbook II: Affective domain*. New York: David McKay.

Krishna, D. (1971). "The self-fulfilling prophecy" and the nature of society. *American Sociological Review, 36*, 1104–1107.

Kuhl, J. (1984). Volitional aspects of achievement motivation and learned helplessness: Toward a comprehensive theory of action control. In B. A. Maher & W. B. Maher (Eds.), *Progress in experimental personality research* (pp. 101–171). Orlando: Academic Press.

Kuhl, J. (1985). Volitional mediators of cognitive-behavior-consistency; self-regulatory processes and action versus state orientation. In J. Kuhl & J. Beckmann (Eds.), *Action control. From cognition to behavior* (pp. 101–128). Berlin: Springer.

Kuhl, J. (1987). Action control: The maintenance of motivational states. In F. Halisch & J. Kuhl (Eds.), *Motivation, intention and volition* (pp. 279–291). Berlin: Springer.

Kuhn, T. S. (1970). *The structure of scientific revolutions* (2nd ed.). Chicago: University of Chicago Press.

Kulik, J., Kulik, C.-L. C., & Cohen, P. A. (1979). A meta-analysis of outcome studies of Keller's personalized system of instruction. *American Psychologist, 34,* 307–318.

Kulik, J. A. (1994). Meta-analytic studies of findings on computer-based instruction. In E. L. Baker & J. H. F. O'Neil (Eds.), *Technology assessment in education and training.* Hillsdale, NJ: Lawrence Erlbaum.

Landa, L. N. (1974). *Algorithmization in learning and instruction* (V. Bennett, Trans.). Englewood Cliffs, NJ: Educational Technology Publications.

Landa, L. N. (1976). *Instructional regulation and control: Cybernetics, algorithmization and heuristics in education* (S. Desch, Trans.). Englewood Cliffs, NJ: Educational Technology Publications.

Lang, F. R., & Carstensen, L. L. (2002). Time counts: Time perspective, goals, and social relationships. *Psychology and Aging, 17*(1), 125–139.

Lenehan, M. C., Dunn, R., Ingham, J., Signer, B., & Murray, J. B. (1994). Effects of learning-style intervention on college students' achievement, anxiety, anger, and curiosity. *Journal of College Student Development, 35,* 461–466.

Lepper, M. R., Green, D., & Nisbett, R. E. (1973). Undermining children's intrinsic interest with extrinsic rewards: A test of the overjustification hypothesis. *Journal of Personality and Social Psychology 28,* 129–137.

Lepper, M. R., & Greene, D. (1975). Turning play into work: Effects of adult surveillance and extrinsic rewards on children's intrinsic motivation. *Journal of Personality and Social Psychology, 31,* 479–486.

Lepper, M. R., & Greene, D. (1978). *The hidden costs of reward: New perspectives on the psychology of human motivation.* Hillsdale, NJ: Lawrence Erlbaum Associates.

Lewin, K. (1935). *A dynamic theory of personality.* New York: McGraw-Hill.

Lewin, K. (1938). *The conceptual representation and the measurement of psychological forces.* Durham, NC: Duke University Press.

Lim, D. H. (2004). Cross cultural differences in online learning motivation. *Educational Media International, 41*(2), 163–175.

Lim, D. H., & Kim, H. (2003). Motivation and Learner Characteristics affecting Online Learning and Learning Application. *Journal of Educational Technology Systems, 31*(4), 423–439.

Livingston, J. S. (1969). Pygmalion in management. *Harvard Business Review, 47*(July – August), 81–89.

Loorbach, N., Karreman, J., & Steehouder, M. (2007). Adding motivational elements to an instruction manual for seniors: Effects on usability and motivation. *Technical communication, 54*(3), 343–358.

Lowenstein, G. (1994). The psychology of curiosity: A review and interpretation. *Psychological Bulletin, 116*(75–98).

Main, R. G. (1993). Integrating Motivation into the Instructional Design Process. *Educational Technology, 33*(12), 37–41.

Malone, T. (1981). Toward a Theory of Intrinsically Motivating Instruction. *Cognitive Science, 4*, 333–369.

Manojlovich, M. (2005). Promoting nurses' self-efficacy: A leadership strategy to improve practice. *Journal of Nursing Administration, 35*(5), 271–278.

Markle, S. M. (1969). *Good frames and bad: A grammar of frame writing* (2nd ed.). New York: Wiley.

Martin, B. L., & Briggs, L. J. (1986). *The affective and cognitive domains: Integration for instruction and research.* Englewood Cliffs, NJ: Educational Technology Publications.

Masie, E. (2002). *Making sense of learning specifications & standards: A decision maker's guide to their adoption.* Saratoga Springs, NY: The MASIE Center.

Maslow, A. H. (1954). *Motivation and personality.* New York: Harper & Row.

Maw, W. H., & Magoon, A. J. (1971). The curiosity dimension of fifth-grade children: A factorial discriminant analysis. *Child Development, 42*, 2023–2031.

Maw, W. H., & Maw, E. W. (1961). Information recognition by children with high and low curiosity. *Educational Research Bulletin, 40*(8), 197–201, 223.

Maw, W. H., & Maw, E. W. (1964). *An exploratory study into the measurement of curiosity in elementary school children* (No. Project No. 801 (SAE 8519)): United States Office of Education, Department of Health, Education, and Welfare.

Maw, W. H., & Maw, E. W. (1966). Self appraisal of curiosity. *Journal of Educational Research, 61*, 462–466.

Maw, W. H., & Maw, E. W. (1970a). Nature of creativity in high- and low-curiosity boys. *Developmental Psychology, 2*(3), 325–329.

Maw, W. H., & Maw, E. W. (1970b). Self concepts of high- and low-curiosity boys. *Child Development, 41*, 123–129.

Maw, W. H., & Maw, E. W. (1977). Nature and assessment of human curiosity. In P. McReynolds (Ed.), *Advances in psychological assessment* (Vol. 4). San Francisco: Jossey-Bass.

McClelland, D. C. (1965). Toward a theory of motive acquisition. *American Psychologist, 20*, 321–333.

Mcclelland, D. C. (1976). *The achieving society.* New York: Irvington Publishers.

McCrae, R. R., & Costa, P. T. (1987). Validation of the five-factor model of personality across instruments and observers. *Journal of Personality and Social Psychology, 52*, 81–90.

McCrae, R. R., & John, O. P. (1992). An Introduction to the five-factor model and its applications. *Journal of Personality, 60*(2), 175–215.

McDougall, W. (1908). *An introduction to social psychology.* London: Methuen.

McDougall, W. (1970). The nature of instincts and their place in the constitution of the human mind. In W. A. Russel (Ed.), *Milestones in motivation*. New York: Appleton-Century-Crofts.

McMullin, D., & Steffen, J. (1982). Intrinsic motivation and performance standards. *Social Behavior and Personality, 10*, 47–56.

McQuillan, J., & Conde, G. (1996). The conditions of flow in reading: two studies of optimal experience. *Reading Psychology, 17*(2), 109–135.

Means, T. B., Jonassen, D. H., & Dwyer, R. M. (1997). Enhancing relevance: Embedded ARCS strategies vs. purpose. *Educational Technology Research and Development, 45*(1), 5–18.

Medsker, K. L., & Holdsworth, K. M. (Eds.). (2001). *Models and strategies for training design*. Silver Spring, MD: International Society for Performance Improvement.

Mehrabian, A., & O''Reilly, E. (1980). Analysis of personality measures in terms of basic dimensions of temperament. *Journal of Personality and Social Psychology, 38*(3), 492–503.

Merrill, M. D. (2002). First principles of instruction. *Educational Technology Research and Development, 50*(3), 43–59.

Merton, R. K. (1936). The unanticipated consequences of purposive social action. *American Sociological Review, 1*(6), 894–904.

Merton, T. K. (1948). The self-fulfilling prophecy. *Antioch Review, 8*(2), 193–210.

Messick, S. (1979). Potential uses of noncognitive measurement in education. *Journal of Educational Psychology, 71*, 281–292.

Milgram, S. (1965). Some conditions of obedience and disobedience to authority. *Human Relations, 18*, 57–76.

Muller, P. A., Stage, F. K., & Kinzie, J. (2001). Science achievement growth trajectories: Understanding factors related to gender and racial-ethnic differences in precollege science achievement. *American Educational Research Journal, 38*(4), 981–1012.

Murray, H. A. (1938). *Explorations in personality*. Oxford: Oxford University Press.

Naime-Diffenbach, B. (1991). *Validation of attention and confidence as independent components of the ARCS motivational model*. Unpublished doctoral dissertation, Florida State University, Tallahassee, FL.

Nicholls, J. (1984). Conceptions of ability and achievement motivation. In R. Ames & C. Ames (Eds.), *Research on motivation in education* (Vol. 1). Orlando, FL: Academic Press.

Nichols, J. (1984). Achievement motivation: Conceptions of ability, subjective experience, task choice, and performance. *Psychological Review, 91*, 328–346.

Nichols, J. D., & Miller, R. B. (1994). Cooperative learning and student motivation. *Contemporary Educational Psychology, 19*, 167–178.

Norman, W. T. (1963). Toward an adequate taxonomy of personality attributes: Replicated factor structure in peer nomination personality ratings. *Journal of Abnormal and Social Psychology, 66*, 574–583.

O'Leary, K. D., & Drabman, R. (1971). Token reinforcement program in the classroom: A review. *Psychological Bulletin, 75*, 379–398.

Oh, S. Y. (2006). *The effects of reusable motivational objects in designing reusable learning object-based instruction* Tallahassee, FL: The Florida State University.

Okey, J. R., & Santiago, R. S. (1991). Integrating instructional and motivational design. *Performance Improvement Quarterly, 4*(2), 11–21.

Paradowski, W. (1967). Effect of curiosity on incidental learning. *Journal of Educational Psychology, 58*(1), 50–55.

Paris, S. G., & Oka, E. R. (1986). Children's reading strategies, metacognition, and motivation. *Developmental Review, 6*(1), 25–56.

Parsons, O. A., Schneider, J. M., & Hansen, A. S. (1970). Internal-external locus of control and national stereotypes in Denmark and the United States. *Journal of Consulting and Clinical Psychology, 35*, 30–37.

Paunonen, S. V., & Ashton, M. C. (2001). Big Five factors and facets and the prediction of behavior. *Journal of Personality and Social Psychology, 81*, 524–539.

Pavlov, I. P. (1906). The scientific investigation of psychical faculties or processes in the higher animals. *Science, 24*, 613–619.

Pavlov, I. P. (1927). *Conditioned reflexes* (G. V. Anrep, Trans.). London: Oxford University Press.

Penney, R. K., & McCann, B. (1964). The children's reactive curiosity scale. *Psychological Reports, 15*, 323–334.

Peters, R. A. (1978). Effects of anxiety, curiosity, and perceived-instructor threat on student verbal behavior in the college classroom. *Journal of Educational Psychology, 70*(3), 388–395.

Phares, E. J. (1976). *Locus of control in personality.* Morristown, NJ: General Learning Press.

Piaget, J. (1952). *The origins of intelligence in children.* New York: International Universities Press.

Picard, R. W. (1997). *Affective Computing.* Cambridge, MA: MIT Press.

Pintrich, P. R., & De Groot, E. V. (1990). Motivational and self-regulated learning components of classroom academic performance. *Journal of Educational Psychology, 82*(1), 33–40.

Pintrich, P. R., & Schunk, D. H. (2002). *Motivation in Education. Theory, Research, and Applications* (2 ed.). Upper Saddle River, NJ: Merrill Prentice Hall.

Premack, D. (1962). Reversibility of the reinforcement relation. *Science, 136*, 255–257.

Pressey, S. L. (1926). A simple apparatus which gives tests and scores – and teaches. *School and Society, 23*(586), 373–376.

Raynor, J. O. (1969). Future orientation and motivation of immediate activity: An elaboration of the theory of achievement motivation. *Psychological Review, 76*(6), 606–610.

Raynor, J. O. (1974). Relationships between achievement-related motives, future orientation, and academic performance. In J. W. Atkinson & J. O. Raynor (Eds.), *Motivation and achievement*. Washington, DC: V. H. Winston.

Reeves, B., & Nass, C. (1996). *The media equation: How people treat computers, television, and new media like real people and places.* Cambridge: Cambridge University Press.

Reigeluth, C. M. (Ed.). (1983). *Instructional design theories and models: An overview of their current status*. Hillsdale, NJ: Lawrence Erlbaum Associates.

Reigeluth, C. M. (Ed.). (1999). *Instructional design theories and models: An overview of their current status*. Hillsdale, NJ: Lawrence Erlbaum Associates.

Renninger, K. A., Hidi, S., & Krapp, A. (1992). *The role of interest in learning and development*. Hillsdale, NJ: Erlbaum.

Rezabek, R. H. (1994). *Utilizing intrinsic motivation in the design of instruction*. Paper presented at the Washington, DC: Association for Educational Communications and Technology.

Robertson, I. T., & Sadri, G. (1993). Managerial self-efficacy and managerial performance. *British Journal of Management, 4*, 37–46.

Robinson, R., & Anderson, M. (2002). *The ever-changing courseware landscape: Migration strategies and lessons learned*. Paper presented at the Distance Learning 2002, Texas.

Rogers, C. R. (1954). *Client centered therapy*. Boston: Houghton Mifflin.

Rosenthal, R., & Jacobson, L. (1968). *Pygmalion in the classroom*. New York: Holt, Rinehart & Winston.

Rotter, J. B. (1954). *Social learning theory and clinical psychology*. New York: Prentice-Hall.

Rotter, J. B. (1966). Generalized expectancies for internal versus external control of reinforcement. *Psychological Monographs, 80*(1, Whole No. 609).

Rotter, J. B. (1972). An introduction to social learning theory. In J. B. Rotter, J. E. Chance & E. J. Phares (Eds.), *Applications of a social learning theory of personality*. New York: Holt, Rinehart, & Winston.

Rotter, J. B., Liverant, S., & Crowne, D. P. (1961). The growth and extinction of expectancies in chance controlled and skilled tasks. *Journal of Abnormal and Social Psychology, 52*, 161–177.

Ryan, R., M., & Deci, E. L. (2000). Intrinsic and extrinsic motivations: classic definitions and new directions. *Contemporary Educational Psychology, 25*, 54–67.

Saloman, G. (1984). Television is "easy" and print is "tough": The differential investment of mental effort in learning as a function of perceptions and attributions. *Journal of Educational Psychology, 76*(4), 647–658.

Saxe, R. M., & Stollak, G. E. (1971). Curiosity and the parent-child relationship. *Child Development, 42*, 373–384.

Schachter, S. (1964). The interaction of cognitive and physiological determinants of emotional state. In L. Berkowitz (Ed.), *Advances in experimental social psychology* (Vol. 1). New York: Academic Press.

Schaefer, E. S., & Bell, R. Q. (1958). Development of a parental attitude research instrument. *Child Development, 29*, 339–361.

Schank, R. C. (1979). Interestingness: Controlling inferences. *Artificial Intelligence, 12*(3), 273–297.

Schrank, W. (1968). The labeling effect of ability grouping. *Journal of Educational Research, 62*, 51–52.

Schrank, W. (1970). A further study of the labeling effect of ability grouping. *Journal of Educational Research, 63*, 358–360.

Schunk, D. H. (1981). Modeling and attributional effects on children's achievement: A self-efficacy analysis. *Journal of Educational Psychology, 73*(1), 93–105.

Schunk, D. H. (1985). Self-efficacy and classroom learning. *Psychology in the Schools, 22*(2), 208–223.

Schunk, D. H. (1996). Goal and self-evaluative influences during children's cognitive skill learning. *American Educational Research Journal, 33*, 359–382.

Seligman, M. E. (1975). *Helplessness*. San Francisco: Freeman.

Seligman, M. E. (1991). *Learned optimism: How to change your mind and yourself*. New York: A. A. Knopf.

Selye. (1973). The evolution of the stress concept. *American Scientist, 61*, 692–699.

Shellnut, B., Knowlton, A., & Savage, T. (1999). Applying the ARCS model to the design and development of computer-based modules for manufacturing engineering courses. *Educational Technology Research and Development, 47*(2), 100–110.

Shen, E. (2009). *The effects of agent emotional support and cognitive motivational messages on math anxiety, learning, and motivation*. Tallahassee, FL: Florida State University.

Shernoff, D. J., Csikszentmihalyi, M., Schneider, B., & Shernoff, E. S. (2003). Student engagement in high school classrooms from the perspective of flow theory. *School Psychology Quarterly, 18*(2), 158–176.

Simpson, E. (1972). *The classification of educational objectives in the psychomotor domain: The psychomotor domain* (Vol. 3). Washington, DC: Gryphon House.

Sins, P. H. M., Joolingen, W. R. v., Savelsbergh, E. R., & Hout-Wolters, B. v. (2008). Motivation and performance within a collaborative computer-based modeling task: Relations between students' achievement goal orientation, self-efficacy, cognitive processing, and achievement. *Contemporary Educational Psychology, 33*, 58–77.

Sins, P. H. M., Savelsbergh, E. R., & Joolingen, W. R. v. (2005). The difficult process of scientific modeling: an analysis of novices' reasoning during computer-based modeling. *International Journal of Science Education, 27*(14), 1695–1721.

Sivin-Kachala, J. (1998). *Report on the effectiveness of technology in schools (1990–1997)*: Software Publisher's Association.

Skinner, B. F. (1954). The science of learning and the art of teaching. *Harvard Educational Review, 24*, 86–97.

Skinner, B. F. (1968). *The Technology of Teaching*. New York: Appleton-Century-Crofts.

Sloane, H. N., & Jackson, D. A. (1974). *A Guide to Motivating Learners*. Englewood Cliffs, NJ: Educational Technology Publications.

Small, R. V., & Gluck, M. (1994). The relationship of motivational conditions to effective instructional attributes: A magnitude scaling approach. *Educational Technology, 34*(8), 33–40.

Smock, C. D., & Holt, B. G. (1962). Children's reactions to novelty: An experimental study of "curiosity motivation". *Child Development, 33*, 631–642.

Song, S. H. (1998). *The effects of motivationally adaptive computer-assisted instruction developed through the arcs model*. Unpublished doctoral dissertation, Tallahassee, FL: Florida State University.

Song, S. H., & Keller, J. M. (2001). Effectiveness of motivationally adaptive computer-assisted instruction on the dynamic aspects of motivation. *Educational Technology Research and Development, 49*(2), 5–22.

Spector, J. M., & Merrill, M. D. (2008). Editorial: Effective, efficient, and engaging (e3) learning in the digital era. *Distance Education, 29*(2), 123–126.

Spence Laschinger, H. K., & Shamian, J. (1994). Staff nurses' and nurse managers' perception of job-related empowerment and managerial self-efficacy. *Journal of Nursing Administration, 24*(10), 38–47.

Sperber, D., & Wilson, D. (1986). *Relevance: Communication and Cognition*. Cambridge, MA: Harvard University Press.

Steers, R. M., & Porter, L. W. (1983). *Motivation and work behavior*. New York: McGraw-Hill.

Stockdale, J., Sinclair, M., Kernohan, W. G., Keller, J. M., Dunwoody, L., Cunningham, J. B., et al. (2008). Feasibility study to test Designer

Breastfeeding™: a randomised controlled trial. *Evidence Based Midwifery, 6*(3), 76–82.

Suzuki, K., & Keller, J. M. (1996). *Creation and cultural validation of an ARCS motivational design matrix.* Paper presented at the annual meeting of the Japanese Association for Educational Technology, Kanazawa, Japan.

Sweller, J. (1988). Cognitive load during problem solving: Effects on learning. *Cognitive Science, 12,* 257–285.

Sweller, J. (1994). Cognitive Load Theory, Learning Difficulty, and Instructional Design. *Learning and Instruction, 4,* 295–312.

Tennyson, R. D. (1992). An educational learning theory for instructional design. *Educational Technology, 32*(1), 36–41.

Thomas, W. I., & Thomas, D. S. (1928). *The child in America.* New York: Knopf.

Tilaro, A., & Rossett, A. (1993). Creating motivating job aids. *Performance and Instruction, 32*(9), 13–20.

Tolman, E. C. (1932). *Purposive behavior in animals and men.* New York: Appleton-Century.

Tolman, E. C. (1949). *Purposive behavior in animals and men.* Berkeley: University of California Press.

Torrance, E. P. (1963). The creative personality and the ideal pupil. *Teachers College Record, 3,* 220–226.

Torrance, E. P. (1965). *Rewarding creative behavior: Experiments in classroom creative behavior.* Englewood Cliffs, NJ: Prentice-Hall.

Torrance, E. P. (1969). Curiosity of gifted children and performance on timed and untimed test of creativity. *The Gifted Child Quarterly, 13,* 3.

Tosti, D. T. (1978). Formative feedback. *NSPI Journal*(October), 19–21.

Truchlicka, M., McLaughlin, T. F., & Swain, J. C. (1998). Effects of token reinforcement and response cost on the accuracy of spelling performance with middle-school special education students with behavior disorders. *Behavioral Interventions, 13*(1), 1–10.

Tschannen-Moran, M., Woolfolk Hoy, A., & Hoy, W. (1998). Teacher efficacy: Its meaning and measure. *Review of Educational Research, 68,* 202–248.

Turner, M. L., & Engle, R. W. (1989). Is working memory capacity task dependent? *Journal of Memory and Language*(49), 127–154.

Van Calster, K., Lens, W., & Nuttin, J. R. (1987). Affective attitude toward the personal future: Impact on motivation in high school boys. *American Journal of Psychology, 100*(1), 1–13.

Van Merriënboer, J. J. G., Kirschner, P. A., & Kester, L. (2003). Taking the load off a learner's mind: Instructional design for complex learning. *Educational Psychologist, 38*(1), 5–13.

Venn, J. (1888). *Logic of Chance* (3 ed.). London: Macmillan.

Vidler, D. C. (1974). Convergent and divergent thinking, test anxiety, and curiosity. *The Journal of Experimental Education, 43*(2), 79–85.

Vidler, D. C. (1977). Curiosity. In S. Ball (Ed.), *Motivation in education*. New York: Academic Press.

Viney, L. L., & Caputi, P. (2005). Using the origin and pawn, positive affect, CASPM, and cognitive anxiety content analysis scales in counseling research. *Measurement and Evaluation in Counseling and Development, 38*, 115–126.

Visser, J. (1990). *Enhancing learner motivation in an instructor-facilitated learning context*. Unpublished Dissertation. Tallahassee, FL: Florida State University.

Visser, J., & Keller, J. M. (1990). The clinical use of motivational messages: an inquiry into the validity of the ARCS model of motivational design. *Instructional Science, 19*, 467–500.

Visser, L. (1998). *The development of motivational communication in distance education support*. Unpublished doctoral dissertation, Educational Technology Department. The Netherlands: The University of Twente.

Vodanovich, S. J. (2003). Psychometric measures of boredom: A review of the literature. *The Journal of Psychology, 137*(6), 569–595.

Vroom, V. H. (1964). *Work and motivation*. New York: John Wiley and Sons.

Weil, M., & Joyce, B. (1978). *Information processing models of teaching*. Englewood Cliffs, NJ: Prentice Hall, Inc.

Weiner, B. (1992). *Human motivation*. Newbury Park: Sage Publications.

Weiner, B. (Ed.). (1974). *Achievement motivation and attribution theory*. Morristown, NJ: General Learning Press.

Weinstein, R., Madison, S., & Kuklinski, M. (1995). Raising expectations in schooling: Obstacles and opportunities for change. *American Educational Research Journal, 32*, 121–159.

Westbrook, L. (2006). Mental models: a theoretical overview and preliminary study *Journal of Information Science, 32*(6), 563–579.

Westbrook, M. T., & Viney, L. L. (1980). Scales measuring people's perception of themselves as Origins and Pawns. *Journal of Personality Assessment, 44*(2), 167–174.

Wheelwright, P. (1951). *Aristotle* (2 ed.). New York: The Odyssey Press.

Wheelwright, P. (1962). *Metaphor and Reality* (2 ed.). Bloomington, IN: Indiana University Press.

Wheelwright, P. (1966). *The presocratics*. New York: The Odyssey Press.

White, R. W. (1959). Motivation reconsidered: The concept of competence. *Psychological Review, 66*(5), 297–333.

Wicklund, R. A., & Brehm, J. W. (1976). *Perspectives on cognitive dissonance*. Hillsdale, NJ: Erlbaum.

Wilensky, R. (1983). Story grammars versus story points. *The Behavioral and Brain Sciences, 6*(579–623).

Wlodkowski, R. J. (1984). *Motivation and teaching: A practical guide*. Washington, DC: National Education Association.

Wlodkowski, R. J. (1999). *Enhancing adult motivation to learn, Revised edition*. San Francisco: Jossey-Bass Publishers.

Wohlwill, J. F. (1987). Introduction. In D. Gorlitz & J. F. Wohlwill (Eds.), *Curiosity, imagination and play: On the development of sponta-neous cognitive and motivational processes* (pp. 1–21). Hillsdale, NJ: Lawrence Erlbaum Associates.

Wolk, S., & DuCette, J. (1974). Intentional performance and incidental learning as a function of personality and task dimensions. *Journal of Personality and Social Psychology, 29,* 90–101.

Wongwiwatthananukit, S., & Popovich, N. G. (2000). Applying the arcs model of motivational design to pharmaceutical education. *American Journal of Pharmaceutical Education, 64,* 188–196.

Wood, R., & Bandura, A. (1989). Social cognitive theory of organizational management. *Academy of Management Review, 14*(3), 361–384.

Woods, R. H. (2002). How much communications is enough in online courses?: Exploring the relationship between frequency of instructor-initiated personal email and learners' perceptions of and participation in online learning. *International Journal of Instructional Media, 29*(4), 377–394.

Woodworth, R. S. (1918). *Dynamic psychology.* New York: Columbia University Press.

Woolfolk, A., & Hoy, W. (1990). Prospective teachers' sense of efficacy and beliefs about control. *Journal of Educational Psychology, 82,* 81–91.

Yeigh, T. (2007). Information-processing and perceptions of control: How attribution style affects task-relevant processing. *Australian Journal of Educational and Developmental Psychology, 7,* 120–138.

Yerkes, R. M., & Dodson, J. D. (1908). The relation of stimulus to rapidity of habit formation. *Journal of Comparative Neurological Psychology, 18,* 459–482.

Zaharias, P., & Poylymenakou, A. (2009). Developing a usability evaluation method for e-learning applications: Beyond functional usability. *International Journal of Human-Computer Interaction, 25*(1), 75–98.

Zimmerman, B. J. (1989). A social cognitive view of self-regulated academic learning. *Journal of Educational Psychology, 81,* 329–339.

Zimmerman, B. J., & Schunk, D. H. (Eds.). (2001). Self-regulated learning and academic achievement. *Theoretical perspectives* (2nd ed.). Mahwah, NJ: Erlbaum.

Zuckerman, M. (1971). Dimensions of sensation seeking. *Journal of Consulting and Clinical Psychology, 36,* 45–52.

Zuckerman, M. (1978). The search for high sensation. *Psychology Today, February,* 38–46, 96–97.

Zuckerman, M. (1979). *Sensation seeking: Beyond the optimal level of arousal.* Hillsdale, NJ: Erlbaum.

Index

Made in the USA
Lexington, KY
01 May 2012